TEHRAN   YALTA

POTSDAM

THE SOVIET PROTOCOLS

Edited and With an Analytical

Introduction

by

ROBERT BEITZELL

ACADEMIC INTERNATIONAL

1970

THE RUSSIAN SERIES / Volume 17

TEHRAN, YALTA AND POTSDAM: THE SOVIET PROTOCOLS

Reprinted from the 1969 edition.
Library of Congress Catalog Card Number: 76-111540
SBN 87569-013-0

Copyright © 1970 Academic International

ACADEMIC INTERNATIONAL/orbis academicus
Box 666, Hattiesburg, Mississippi 39401

CONTENTS

The Potsdam Conference (July 17-August 2, 1945)

Appendices (Materials deleted from the 1969 edition)

AN ANALYTICAL INTRODUCTION

On June 17, 1961, the State Department published a book of documents on the Tehran Conference.[1] The Soviet Foreign Ministry immediately charged that the American record falsified history and during July and August released its minutes of the Conference.[2] The Soviet editors further stated that they intended to bring out materials on the other wartime meetings of the Big Three. Nothing more, however, was heard from the Soviet Foreign Ministry for the next four years. Then, between June 1965 and September 1966, it published the minutes of the Plenary Sessions at Yalta and Potsdam. In their Introduction to this second series the editors made no mention of the falsification of history. Instead they said they were releasing the material to "celebrate the twentieth anniversary of the Soviet peoples' victory in the Great Patriotic War" and praised "the anti-Hitler coalition led by the U.S.S.R., the United States and Britain...." [3] This book contains the official Soviet translation into English of both sets of documents. It is clear from the content, circumstances of release, and accompanying editorial comment that they represent two types of source material.

1961 was a very cold year in Soviet-American relations. April was the month of the Bay of Pigs. In June at the Vienna Summit Conference, Nikita Khrushchev threatened John Kennedy with a unilateral Soviet Peace Treaty with East Germany. On August 13 Walter Ulbricht ordered the erection of the Berlin Wall. Western protests over this were met by a Soviet announcement that it was resuming atmospheric atomic testing. In October the Soviet Union exploded a fifty megaton hydrogen bomb. The Soviet documents on the Tehran Conference reflect this deepening of the Cold War. In their Introduction the editors state that the most important assistance rendered the Soviet Union by her wartime Allies — the opening of the Second Front — came "when the war, as a result of the heroic efforts and historic victories of the Soviet Army, was already drawing to a close...[and] did much more to further certain political interests of the United States and Britain than to speed up the defeat of Nazi Germany." [4] It is admitted that the wartime conferences were of "great importance in creating a foundation for the friendly Soviet-Anglo-American relations after the war" but, and the Soviet editors quote Khrushchev, "soon after the...war ended, the influence of reactionary and militaristic groups began to be increasingly evident in the policy of the United States..., Britain and France." [5] This led the Western powers "to enforce their will on other countries by economic and political pressure, threats and military provocation...." [6] The editors are equally outspoken as to why they are publishing the Tehran minutes. It is to "refute the inventions about the Soviet stand which are contained...in the collection of 'documents' published by the State Department." [7] According to the Soviet Foreign Ministry, its documents will "help to restore the truth of history." [8]

Although no agreed record of the Tehran Conference exists, since each delegation kept its own minutes, a careful comparison of the American and Soviet texts reveals numerous deletions and a few additions to the proceedings by the Soviet editors. Some of the deletions are petty. Roosevelt, in a naive effort to flatter Stalin, praised Tito and the Communist resistance movement in Yugoslavia on several occasions at Tehran.[9] There is no mention of Tito and the Partisans in the Soviet text. Other deletions are of a diplomatic character. The editors do not include Stalin's harsh criticism of DeGaulle.[10] All in all, over fifty items appearing in the American text are absent from the Soviet. Four of these deletions are of such importance as to seriously distort the record of the proceedings at Tehran.

The first is the omission of Stalin's pledge to bring Russia into the war against Japan after Germany's collapse.[11] This was regarded by the American and British delegations as one of the most significant events of the Conference. The second major omission involves Stalin's attitude toward Germany. The American minutes have Stalin calling for the radical dismemberment of Germany and the summary execution of 50,000 to 100,000 German officers.[12] According to the Soviet editors, it was Stalin rather than Churchill who blocked Big Three agreement on Germany's partition by having the question referred to the European Advisory Commission in London.[13] The third deletion is Roosevelt's private pledge, made on December 1, 1943, not to oppose Russian reoccupation of Latvia, Lithuania and Estonia, and half of prewar Poland.[14] The fourth deletion involves Turkey. Churchill wanted to force her into the war and mentioned that a change in the regime at the Bosporus and Dardanelles might be used as a threat. Stalin was interested.[15] None of these items appear in the Soviet transcript.

Soviet additions are far less numerous than the deletions. Two, however, have a distinctly Cold War flavor. During the first Plenary Session on November 28, 1943, the Russian editors have Stalin remark, unchallenged by either Roosevelt or Churchill, that "the [Murmansk] convoys arrived without losses, without having met the enemy."[16] The statement is untrue, unlikely, and if made would certainly have provoked a spirited rebuttal. The second such addition occurs during the last Plenary Session, December 1, 1943. The Soviet editors have Churchill saying he was "very well aware of the Russian position at the start of the war, and considering [British] weakness...and the fact that France went back on the guarantees she gave in Munich, I understand that the Soviet Government could not at the time risk its life in that struggle."[17] No such remark appears in the American text nor was Churchill a likely apologist for the Molotov-Ribbentrop Pact.

If, however, the papers reveal a great deal about the policies and anxieties of the Soviet Foreign Ministry in 1961, they also record, and record honestly, the central issue debated by the Big Three at Tehran — the cross channel versus the Mediterranean assault on Hitler's Fortress Europe. By the fall of 1943 the long argument between British and American strategies in the European war was supposedly over and the Americans had won. During the Washington Conference of May 12 to 25, 1943, and again at the Quebec Conference of August 14 to 23, 1943, Churchill and the British Chiefs of Staff accepted what the Prime Minister called "a lawyers' bargain" on Europe. The Americans agreed to the invasion of Italy in September 1943, provided that the British agreed to a gradual closing down of the Mediterranean theatre and accepted the cross channel attack on France in May 1944. It tells a great deal about American opposition to what they regarded as British Mediterranean diversions that George Marshall, the principal American spokesman on the Combined Chiefs of Staff, argued against an Italian campaign even after learning of the Italian Government's offer to surrender.

By October 1943, the keeping of the first half of this bargain convinced Churchill that the second half was unsound. In September, Anglo-American forces launched three attacks in the Mediterranean. These were Operation Baytown, the invasion of Italy across the Straits of Messina; Operation Avalanche, the invasion of Italy at Salerno; and Operation Accolade, the capture of Italian occupied islands in the Aegean. Hitler's decision as usual was to hold everywhere. German paratroopers and aircraft were rushed to the Aegean, and Accolade failed. By Operation Axis, the Germans occupied Italy and General Mark Clark found himself engaged in a touch-and-go build-up race at

Salerno. Failure in the Aegean and what the Allied commanders regarded as a dangerous situation at Salerno did not, in Churchill's opinion, augur well for a cross channel attack against long prepared positions only eight months away.

If the military situation was unsatisfactory, Churchill could and did find solace in diplomacy. By the fall of 1943, Italy had surrendered and switched sides. The British had also received peace feelers from Rumania and Hungary. Churchill asked for a meeting with Roosevelt and the American Chiefs of Staff to consider these new opportunities and difficulties, but he had little hope of persuading Washington to drop or postpone Overlord, the cross channel assault. It was at just this point, October 1943, that Soviet Foreign Minister Vyacheslav Molotov, during the Moscow Foreign Ministers' Conference, asked for an Anglo-American and Soviet agreement to force Turkey into the war before the year ended.

Since the Russians from the time of the German attack in 1941 had done nothing but call for the invasion of France, Churchill was astounded. He asked his Foreign Secretary Anthony Eden to tell Stalin that Turkish intervention would delay the channel operation. Stalin was undisturbed and Churchill began talking about extending his right hand to the Russians along the Danube. Where before Churchill had opposed Soviet participation in Anglo-American strategic talks, he now informed Washington that Russia's presence was necessary. He did not directly oppose Overlord; but he and the British Chiefs of Staff did propose operations in Turkey, Greece, Yugoslavia, and Rumania which Roosevelt and the American Chiefs of Staff feared would eat up resources for Overlord. The British and Russians signed in Moscow on November 1 an agreement to bring Turkey into the war by Christmas, 1943. Within a short time the Americans signed a similar agreement, but with a restrictive clause that nothing should be done in the Mediterranean which might jeopardize Overlord. Washington feared history was repeating itself. In 1942 the British had agreed in principle to the invasion of France in 1943, and then induced the Americans into Mediterranean operations that resulted in the cancellation of the attack. Eden rightly judged that the whole thing was a mares nest. Nevertheless, Churchill more than anyone else was responsible for bringing the Big Three together at Tehran. He hoped Stalin would support a Mediterranean attack.

Eden proved to be correct. At Tehran, as both the American and Soviet documents show, Stalin had little interest in Turkish intervention and insisted on Overlord in May. For two days Churchill used every argument he could for an expanded Mediterranean campaign. It was a hopeless task and on his sixty-ninth birthday,

Tuesday, November 30, 1943, Churchill gave way. The hoped for Soviet support had not materialized and George Marshall found in Stalin a firm supporter. The sole effect of Churchill's arguments was to generate increasing animosity in Stalin, while Roosevelt played the role of a not-very-neutral arbitor. The Soviet minutes accurately record this debate. They also include a transcript of a private talk held on November 30, 1943, between Stalin and Churchill not contained in the American materials during which Churchill pledged his support for Overlord. [18] It was one of the most decisive events of the Second World War.

The second series of Soviet documents, those treating the Plenary Sessions at the Yalta and Potsdam Conferences, also contain deletions, but, and this is particularly true of the Potsdam minutes, the deletions are far fewer and much less significant than those made in the Tehran records. Moreover, the tone of the editorial comment is far less ascerbic. There is the familiar Soviet disclaimer of any responsibility for postwar tensions. As the editors put it, the wartime meetings "created the possibilities for the further development of friendly relations between the three Great Powers after the victory over the common enemy...and...it was not the Soviet Union's fault that these possibilities were deliberately ignored by certain circles in the United States and Britain...." [19] No longer, however, is the Anglo-American contribution to victory belittled. The conferences themselves are declared to have "played a prominent part not only in the common struggle...[but] also in working out the principles of the postwar settlement." [20]

The few discrepancies that do exist between the American and the Soviet texts for the most part follow familiar lines. At Yalta as at Tehran, Stalin continued to press for German dismemberment and this is downplayed in the Russian version. [21] During the Potsdam Conference, Stalin remarked that his annexation of Koenigsberg was payment of a "blood debt" owed by Germany to the Soviet Union. [22] This, too, is deleted. Another non-topic was Soviet pressure for a change at the Bosporus and Dardanelles. Stalin raised the question at Yalta and again at Potsdam where he asked for a Russian military base in the area. [23] Stalin's opinions about the French also remained unchanged. He argued against, although he did not block, the Yalta decision to give France an occupation zone in Germany and membership in the Berlin Control Commission. [24] This does not appear in the Soviet text. Also deleted from the Soviet versions of the Yalta talks was an exchange between Stalin and Churchill during which the Soviet Premier noted that he had no questions to ask about British activities in Greece, the implication being that in reciprocity the British should not ask questions about Soviet activities in Poland. [25] One minor but illuminating difference mars the almost complete Soviet transcript of the Potsdam discussions. The American and British representatives tried in 1945 to find out about the fate of some oil equipment they owned in Rumania, and which had disappeared during the Soviet occupation.[26] The Soviet Union — in 1966 — does not loot. But just as the badly cut-up Soviet transcript of the proceedings at Tehran mirrors the central issues discussed by the Big Three, so does the almost complete record of the proceedings at Yalta and Potsdam.

There were several reasons for the change in Soviet policy between 1961 and 1966 that is reflected in the two sets of documents. The most important were Mao Tse-Tung's challenge to Soviet leadership of the Communist bloc and the sobering experience of the 1962 Cuban missile crisis. Neither event ended the Cold War. They did, however, influence Khrushchev and other leaders of Soviet policy to shift away from a position of aggressive coexistence toward the United States and into an attitude of hesitant *detente*. After seven years of debate, the Soviet Union and the United States in 1963 signed a partial nuclear test ban treaty. This was quickly followed by the "hot line" agreement and a United Nations resolution sponsored by both powers which banned nuclear weapons from outer space. Even the Berlin issue was allowed to cool although the Wall remained to cut off the flood of refugees from East Germany and so to give stability to that unhappy land. American and Soviet interests still conflicted but not with the directness and the intensity of 1961-62. The *detente* has also proved hardy: it survived Khrushchev's fall in 1964; the American decision in 1965 to bomb North Vietnam; the Arab-Israeli War of June 1967; and most recently, the Soviet invasion of Czechoslovakia on August 20, 1968. The last three events put a heavy strain on the new relationship between Washington and Moscow but both powers avoided the confrontation politics of the early 1960's. In their general accuracy and in their freedom from editorial polemics, the Soviet documents on Yalta and Potsdam reflect this *detente*.

Included as appendices at the end of the present volume are the editorial introductions to the minutes of the Tehran Conference and the Yalta and Potsdam Conferences which prefaced the publication of these documents in *International Affairs*. Added also as appendices are the Soviet records of conversations between Stalin and Roosevelt on November 28 and 29, 1943, between Stalin and Churchill on November 30, 1943, and between Roosevelt, Stalin and Churchill on November 30, 1943. These meetings took place during the Tehran Conference and were printed in *International Affairs*. The Soviet Foreign Ministry in 1969 reissued their materials on the wartime conferences but deleted both the original introductions and these conversations.[27] In addition it should be noted that the Tehran Declarations appearing on pages 45-47 are from the new Soviet publication and were not in the *International Affairs* series. The last appendix is the Soviet introduction to the 1969 edition. Scholars interested in a line-by-line comparison of the American and Soviet texts will find this in an excellent study by Alexander Fischer. [28] Subject to certain restrictions, the original minutes of the American delegation can be seen at the Historical Office, Bureau of Public Affairs, Department of State. The American publications also include documents dealing with the arrangements for the meetings, background materials, and the minutes of lower level discussions which have not yet been released by the Soviet Union.

Robert Beitzell

Orono, Maine

NOTES TO THE ANALYTICAL INTRODUCTION

1. U.S. Department of State, *Foreign Relations of the United States, Diplomatic Papers. The Conferences at Cairo and Tehran, 1943.* (Washington, D.C.: Government Printing Office, 1961). Cited hereafter as *U.S. Tehran Papers.*

2. Appendix I. Introduction, *Tehran Conference of the Three Great Powers.*

3. Appendix VI. Introduction, *The Crimea and Potsdam Conferences of the Leaders of the Three Great Powers.*

4. Appendix I.

5. *Ibid.*

6. *Ibid.*

7. *Ibid.*

8. *Ibid.*

9. *U.S. Tehran Papers,* p. 529.

10. *Ibid.,* p. 484.

11. *Ibid.,* p. 489.

12. *Ibid.,* p. 554.

13. Appendix I.

14. *U.S. Tehran Papers,* pp. 594-596.

15. *Ibid.*, p. 566.

16. Post p. 6.

17. Post p. 41.

18. Appendix IV. *Transcript of a Talk Between Stalin and Churchill, November 30, 1943.*

19. Appendix VI.

20. *Ibid.*

21. For Stalin's views on dismemberment as recorded by Charles E. Bohlen, Assistant to the Secretary of State, see U.S. Department of State, *Foreign Relations of the United States, Diplomatic Papers. The Conferences at Malta and Yalta, 1945.* (Washington, D.C.: Government Printing Office, 1955) p. 615. Cited hereafter as *U.S. Yalta Papers.*

22. U.S. Department of State. *Foreign Relations of the United States, Diplomatic Papers. The Conference of Berlin (The Potsdam Conference), 1945.* (2 vols.; Washington, D.C.: Government Printing Office, 1960), II, 305. Cited hereafter as *U.S. Potsdam Papers.*

23. *U.S. Yalta Papers,* pp. 903-904 and *U.S. Potsdam Papers,* II, 257-258, 1427-1428.

24. *U.S. Yalta Papers,* pp. 628-630.

25. *Ibid.,* pp. 781-782.

26. *U.S. Potsdam Papers,* II, 136-137.

27. Soviet Ministry of Foreign Affairs. *The Tehran, Yalta & Potsdam Conferences, Documents.* (Moscow: Progress Publishers, 1969).

28. Alexander Fischer (Hrsg.). *Teheran - Jalta - Potsdam, Die sowjetischen Protokolle von den Kriegskonferenzen der "Grossen Drei."* (Koeln: *Verlag Wissenschaft* und Politik, 1968)

THE TEHRAN CONFERENCE

(November 28 to December 1, 1943)

The First Sitting of the Conference
of the Heads of Government of the U.S.S.R.,
the United States and Great Britain

Tehran, November 28, 1943

Opened: 16.00; Closed: 19.30

Roosevelt: As the youngest head of Government present here I should like to take the liberty of speaking first. I should like to assure the members of the new family—the members of the present conference gathered around this table—that we are gathered here for one purpose, for the purpose of winning the war as soon as possible.

I should also like to say a few words about the conduct of the conference. We do not intend to make public anything that will be said here, but we shall address each other as friends, openly and candidly. I think that this conference will be a success, and that our three nations, which united in the course of the present war, will strengthen their ties and will create the prerequisites for the close co-operation of future generations. Our staffs can discuss military matters, and our delegations, although we do not have any fixed agenda, can discuss other problems as well, such, for example, as problems of the post-war settlement. If, however, you do not wish to discuss such problems, they can be left aside.

Before beginning our work I should like to know if Mr. Churchill wishes to say a few general words on the importance of this meeting, and what this meeting means to humanity.

Churchill: This is the greatest concentration of world forces that ever existed in the history of mankind. We hold

1

the solution of the problem of reducing the length of the war, the winning of victory, the future of mankind. I pray that we may be worthy of this remarkable opportunity granted to us by God, the opportunity of serving mankind.

Roosevelt: Would Marshal Stalin like to say anything?

Stalin: In greeting this conference of the representatives of the three Governments I should like to make a few remarks. I think we are being pampered by history. She has given us possession of very big forces and very great opportunities. I hope that we shall do everything at this conference to make due use, within the framework of our co-operation, of the power and authority that our peoples have vested in us. Let us now begin our work.

Roosevelt: May I start with a general review of the war and the requirements of the war at the present time. Of course, I shall speak of this from the standpoint of the U.S.A. We, like the British Empire and the Soviet Union, hope for an early victory. I should like to start with a review of that part of the war which concerns the United States rather than the Soviet Union and Great Britain. I mean the war in the Pacific Ocean, where the United States bears the brunt of the war, receiving help from the Australian and New Zealand forces. . . .

Taking up the more important question, which is of greater interest to the Soviet Union—the operation across the Channel—I should like to say that we have been drawing up our plans for the last year and a half, but because of the shortage of tonnage we were unable to decide on a date for this operation. We want not only to cross the Channel, but to pursue the enemy into the heart of the territory. The English Channel is that unpleasant strip of water that excludes the possibility of starting the expedition across the Channel before May 1, that is why the plan drawn up at Quebec was based on the premise that the expedition across the Channel would be made on approximately May 1, 1944. All landing operations involve special craft. If we undertake large-scale landing operations in the Mediterranean, the expedition across the Channel will have to be postponed for two or three months. That is why we should like to have the advice of our Soviet colleagues on the matter, and also advice on how best to use the forces now in the Mediterranean area, considering that there are few ships there too. But we do not want to defer the date of the invasion across the Channel beyond May or June. At the same time there are many places where Anglo-American forces could be used. They could be used in Italy, in the Adriatic area, in the Aegean area, and finally, to help Turkey if she enters the war. All this we must decide here. We should very much like to help the Soviet Union and to draw off a part of the German forces from the Soviet front. We should like to have the advice of our Soviet friends on how we could best ease their position.

Would Mr. Churchill like to add anything?

Churchill: May I speak and express my opinion after Marshal Stalin has expressed his. At the same time I should like to say that I agree in principle with what has been said by President Roosevelt.

Stalin: As for the first part of Mr. President's speech concerning the war in the Pacific Area, we can say the following: We Russians welcome the successes that have been and are being scored by the Anglo-American forces in the Pacific.

As for the second part of Mr. President's speech about the war in Europe, I also have several remarks to make.

First of all, a few words in the form of a report about the way we have been and are conducting operations since the July offensive of the Germans. If I am going into too great detail I could shorten my statement.

Churchill: We are prepared to hear everything you wish to say.

Stalin: I must say, in passing, that we ourselves have been lately preparing for an offensive. The Germans were ahead of us, but since we had been preparing for an offensive and had massed a great force, after we beat back the German offensive, it was relatively easy for us to go over to the offensive. I must say that although the opinion about us is that we plan everything beforehand, we did not expect the successes we scored in August and September. Contrary to our expectations the Germans proved to be weaker than we expected. At present, according to our intelligence, the Germans have 210 divisions on our front, and another six divisions on the way there. In addition, there are 50 non-German divisions, including the Finns. Thus, altogether the Germans have 260 divisions on our front, including up to 10 Hungarian, up to 20 Finnish, and up to 16 or 18 Rumanian.

3

Roosevelt: What is the numerical strength of a German division?

Stalin: The German division consists roughly of from 8,000 to 9,000 men, excluding auxiliary forces. With the auxiliary forces the division numbers from 12,000 to 13,000 men. Last year, there were 240 divisions on our front, 179 of them German. This year, there are 260 divisions on our front, 210 of them German, with six German divisions on their way to the front. From 300 to 330 divisions are operating on the Russian side. Thus, we have more divisions than the Germans together with their satellites. This surplus of forces is being used for offensive operations. Otherwise there would have been no offensive. But as time goes on the difference between the number of Russian and German divisions becomes smaller. Another great difficulty is that the Germans are barbarously destroying everything as they retreat. This makes ammunition supply more difficult. That is the reason why our offensive has slowed down. In the last three weeks the Germans launched offensive operations in the Ukraine, south and west of Kiev. They have recaptured Zhitomir, an important railway junction. This has been announced. It looks as if one of these days they will take Korosten, also an important railway junction. In that area the Germans have five new tank divisions and three old tank divisions, altogether 8 tank divisions, and also 22 or 23 infantry and motorised divisions. Their goal is to recapture Kiev. Thus, we are faced with some difficulties in the future.

That is the report part about our operations in the summer.

Now a few words about the place where operations of the Anglo-American forces in Europe would be desirable in order to ease the situation on our front. I may be mistaken, but we Russians thought that the Italian theatre was important only to the extent of ensuring free navigation of Allied shipping in the Mediterranean Sea. Only in that sense is the Italian theatre of operations important. That is what we thought, and that is what we continue to think. As for the idea of launching an offensive from Italy directly against Germany, we Russians think that the Italian theatre is not suitable for such purposes. Consequently, the fact is that the Italian theatre is important for free navigation in the Mediterranean, but it is of no significance in the sense of further operations against Germany, because the Alps block the way and hinder any advance towards Germany. We Russians believe that the best result would be yielded by a blow at the enemy in Northern or North-Western France. Even operations in Southern France would be better than operations in Italy. It would be a good thing if Turkey were prepared to open the way for the Allies. After all, it would be nearer from the Balkans to the heart of Germany. There, the way is not blocked either by the Alps or the Channel. But Germany's weakest spot is France. Of course, this is a difficult operation, and the Germans in France will defend themselves desperately; nevertheless that is the best solution. Those are all the remarks I have.

Churchill: We have long since agreed with the United States to attack Germany via Northern or North-Western France, and extensive preparations for this are under way. It would be necessary to give many facts and figures to show why we were unable to carry out these operations in 1943. But we have decided to attack Germany in 1944. The place for the attack against Germany was selected in 1943. We are now faced with the task of creating the conditions for the possibility of transferring an army into France across the Channel in the late spring of 1944. The forces that we shall be able to accumulate for that purpose in May or June will consist of 16 British and 19 American divisions. But these divisions are stronger numerically than the German divisions of which Marshal Stalin spoke. These forces would be followed by the main force, and it is planned that the whole of Operation Overlord[1] will involve the transfer of about a million men across the Channel in May, June and July. Together with the armies in the Mediterranean and the Indian Ocean it is all we Britons can give, considering our 46-million population and the numerical strength of our air force. Remanning of the above-mentioned divisions depends on the United States. But the date I mentioned is still far off. It will arrive in six months' time. In the talks between the President and myself we asked each other how best to use our forces in the Mediterranean in order to help the Russians, without any detriment to Overlord, so that this operation could be carried out in time or, possibly, with some delay. We have already sent seven battle-wise divisions from the Mediterranean area, and also a part of the landing

---

[1] Overlord—the code name for the forced crossing of the Channel.

craft for Overlord. Taking this into account, and the bad weather in Italy besides, I must say that we are somewhat disappointed at not yet having taken Rome. Our first task is to take Rome, and we expect to wage the decisive battle in January and to win it. General Alexander, the Commander of the 15th Army Group who is under the orders of General Eisenhower, believes that it is quite possible to win the battle for Rome. In addition, it may be possible to capture and destroy more than 11 or 12 enemy divisions. We are not planning to move on into Lombardy or to cross the Alps into Germany. We merely plan to move on somewhat north of Rome up to the Pisa-Rimini line, after which we could make the landing in Southern France and across the Channel.

The next important question is to convince Turkey to enter the war. This would make possible the opening of communications through the Dardanelles and the Bosporus, and we could send supplies to Russia across the Black Sea. Besides, we could use the Turkish airfields to fight the enemy. It would take only a small force to occupy Rhodes and other islands. We could then establish direct contact with the Russians and send them supplies continuously. We have been able up to now to send only four convoys to Russia's northern ports, because of a shortage of escorts but if a way is opened across the Black Sea we could regularly send supplies to southern Russian ports.

Stalin: It should be said that these convoys arrived without losses, without having met the enemy on the way.

Churchill: How can we make Turkey enter the war? What will she have to do? Will she have to attack Bulgaria and declare war on Germany? Will she have to start offensive operations or should she refrain from advancing into Thrace? What would be the Russian attitude to the Bulgarians who still remember that Russia liberated them from the Turks? What effect would that have on the Rumanians, who are already looking for ways out of the war? How would that affect Hungary? Would not the result of this be great political changes among many countries? All these are questions on which our Russian friends, naturally, have their own views.

Are our operations in the eastern part of the Mediterranean, which could cause some delay in the operation across the Channel, of any interest to the Soviet Government?

We do not as yet have any definite decision on this question, and we have come here to settle it.

Roosevelt: There is another possibility. It might be expedient to make a landing in the northern part of the Adriatic when the Soviet armies approach Odessa.

Churchill: If we take Rome and block Germany from the south, we would then commence operations in Western or Southern France, and also extend assistance to the guerrilla armies. These operations are not yet worked out in detail. A commission could be set up to study the question and draw up a document in full detail.

Stalin: I have a few questions: I understand that there are 35 divisions for invasion operations in the north of France.

Churchill: Yes, that is correct.

Stalin: Before the operations to invade the north of France it is planned to carry out the operation in the Italian theatre to take Rome, after which it is planned to go on the defensive in Italy.

Churchill: Yes. We are already withdrawing seven divisions from Italy.

Stalin: I also understand that three other operations are planned, one of which will consist of a landing in the Adriatic area.

Churchill: The carrying out of these operations may be useful to the Russians. After the seven divisions are dispatched from the Mediterranean area, we shall have up to 35 divisions for the invasion of Northern France. In addition, we shall have 20 or 23 divisions in Northern Italy.

I should like to add that the greatest problem is the transfer of the necessary forces. As I have already pointed out, Operation Overlord will be started by 35 divisions. From then on the number of troops will be increased by divisions transferred from the U.S.A.; their number will go up to 50 or 60. I want to add that in the next six months the British and American air force now in Britain will be doubled and trebled. In addition, work is being continuously carried on to accumulate forces in Britain.

Stalin: Another question. Did I understand correctly that apart from the operations to take Rome it is planned to carry out another operation in the Adriatic, and also an operation in Southern France?

Churchill: The plan is to carry out an attack in Southern France at the moment Operation Overlord is launched.

7

Troops that can be released from Italy will be used for this. But this operation has not yet been worked out in detail.

Stalin: Another question: if Turkey enters the war, what is to be done in that case?

Churchill: I can say that it would take no more than two or three divisions to take the islands along the west coast of Turkey so as to allow the supply ships to go to Turkey, and also to open the route to the Black Sea. But the first thing we shall do is send the Turks 20 air squadrons and several air defence regiments, which can be done without detriment to other operations.

Stalin: In my opinion, it would be better to make Operation Overlord the basis of all operations in 1944. If a landing were made in Southern France at the same time as that operation, both groups of forces could join in France. That is why it would be well to have two operations: Operation Overlord and the landing in Southern France as a supporting operation. At the same time the operation in the Rome area would be a diversionary operation. In carrying out the landing in France from the North and the South, there could be a build up of forces when these forces are joined. France is Germany's weak spot. As for Turkey, I doubt that Turkey will enter the war. She will not join the war no matter what pressure we exert. That is my opinion.

Churchill: We understood that the Soviet Government is highly interested in making Turkey enter the war. Of course, we may fail to make Turkey enter the war, but we must try to do everything in this respect.

Stalin: Yes, we must try to get Turkey to enter the war.

Churchill: I agree with Marshal Stalin's considerations concerning the undesirability of dispersing the forces, but if we have 25 divisions in the Mediterranean area, three or four divisions and 20 air squadrons may well be set aside for Turkey, particularly since they are at present being used to protect Egypt, and they could be moved from there to the north.

Stalin: That is a big force, these 20 air squadrons. Of course, it would be a good thing if Turkey entered the war.

Churchill: I'm afraid that in this six-month period, during which we could take Rome and prepare for big operations in Europe, our army will remain inactive and will not exert pressure on the enemy. I fear that in that case Parliament

8

would reproach me for not giving any assistance to the Russians.

Stalin: I think that Overlord is a big operation. It would be considerably facilitated and would be sure to have an effect if it were supported from the south of France. I personally would go to this extreme. I would go on the defensive in Italy, abandoning the capture of Rome, and would start an operation in Southern France, drawing off German forces from Northern France. In about two or three months I would start the operation in the north of France. This plan would ensure the success of Operation Overlord; the two armies could meet, and that would result in a build up of forces.

Churchill: I could adduce even more arguments but I wish to say only that we would be weaker if we did not take Rome. Besides, in order to carry out an air offensive against Germany it is necessary to reach the Pisa-Rimini line. I should like the military specialists to discuss this question. The struggle for Rome is already on, and we expect to take Rome in January. Refusal to take Rome would mean our defeat, and I could not explain this to the House.

Roosevelt: We could carry out Overlord on time if there were no operations in the Mediterranean. If there are operations in the Mediterranean this will defer the date of Operation Overlord. I should not like to delay Overlord.

Stalin: From the experience of our operations we know that success is gained where the blow is dealt from two sides, and that operations undertaken from one side do not yield enough effect. That is why we try to strike at the enemy from two sides to make him shuttle his forces from one side to another. I think that in this case too it would be well to carry out the operation from the south and the north of France.

Churchill: I personally quite agree with this, but I think that we might undertake diversionary acts in Yugoslavia, and also make Turkey join the war, regardless of the invasion of Southern or Northern France. I personally regard the idleness of our army in the Mediterranean as a highly negative fact. That is why we cannot guarantee that the date of May 1 will be met precisely. It would be a big mistake to fix that date. I cannot sacrifice the operations in the Mediterranean just to keep the date of May 1. Of course we must come to a definite agreement on the matter. This question could be discussed by our military specialists.

Stalin: All right. We did not expect a discussion of purely military matters, that is why we did not invite representatives of the General Staff to come along, but I think that Marshal Voroshilov and I can arrange something.

Churchill: What are we to do with the question of Turkey? Should we also refer it to the military specialists?

Stalin: It is both a political and a military question. Turkey is an ally of Great Britain and has friendly relations with the U.S.S.R. and the United States. Turkey should no longer play between us and Germany.

Churchill: I may possibly have six or seven questions concerning Turkey. But I should first like to consider them.

Stalin: Very well.

Roosevelt: Of course, I favour making Turkey enter the war, but if I were in the place of the Turkish President, I would ask a price that could be paid only by inflicting damage on Operation Overlord.

Stalin: There should be an effort to make Turkey fight. She has many idle divisions.

Churchill: We all have feelings of friendship for each other, but we naturally have differences. We need time and patience.

Stalin: That's right.

Roosevelt: And so, the military experts are meeting tomorrow morning, and at four o'clock there is a session of the conference.

Conference of Military Representatives

November 29, 1943, at 10.30

Admiral Leahy suggests that General Brooke should report on the Mediterranean theatre of military operations.

Gen. Brooke says that the cardinal task facing the Anglo-Americans is to exert pressure on the enemy wherever possible. At the same time it is desirable to stem the tide of German divisions that could be directed by the Germans to Northern France where their increase would be undesirable. Operation Overlord will divert a great number of German divisions. But this operation cannot take place before

May 1, as the most suitable date for the landing. That is why there will be a break of five or six months before the start of this operation, during which something must be done to draw off the German divisions. Brooke says that the British have big forces in the Mediterranean, which they wish to use in the best possible way.

Addressing General Marshall, Brooke says that if he says anything that does not accord with the opinion of the Americans, he, Brooke, asks that he be interrupted.

Gen. Marshall asks Brooke to continue his review.

Brooke says that the Anglo-American plans provide for active operations on all fronts, including those in the Mediterranean. At present there are 23 German divisions in Central and Northern Italy. The Anglo-Americans have enough forces to move the front up into Northern Italy. But in view of the terrain, the Anglo-American forces are unable to exert enough direct pressure on the German troops, and that is why it will be necessary to carry out a flanking operation from the sea. It is expected that this operation will involve 11 or 12 divisions which the German Command will be forced to reman. As a result of these operations, the present number of German divisions will be kept in Italy; besides, these divisions will be considerably weakened.

On the question of Turkey Brooke says that if the purely political considerations are left aside, Turkey's entry into the war would be highly desirable from the purely military standpoint, and would yield great advantages. First, it would open the sea lanes through the Dardanelles. This would be of great significance in the sense of a possible withdrawal from the war by Rumania and Bulgaria. In addition, contact could be established with the Russians across the Black Sea and supplies sent to Russia that way. Finally, the establishment of Allied air bases in Turkey would make possible raids on key German objectives, in particular the oil fields in Rumania, etc. The shorter route for cargoes across the Black Sea instead of the roundabout way via Persia would release tonnage that could be used elsewhere. To open the way to the Black Sea it would be enough to take several islands along the Turkish coast, beginning from the island of Rhodes. That will not be a difficult operation and will not entail the use of big forces. Brooke says that in the Mediterranean the British have special landing barges which could be used for the operations he described. Operation Overlord would need to be postponed only for the period required for the use of these craft in the Mediterranean. At the same time these operations would hold up the German troops which could otherwise be used by the Germans during Operation Overlord. Brooke says that it is highly important to ensure airfields in Italy in order to start raids on industry in Southern Germany. These air operations, together with raids carried out from Britain, would be highly important for the conduct of the war in 1944. If the proposal made yesterday were accepted, to go on the defensive in Italy before the operation there is completed, it would be necessary to maintain large forces there in order to hold back the German troops. In consequence, only a limited force could be released for operations in Southern France. Brooke says that he is in full agreement with the strategy proposed by Marshal Stalin to deal the enemy a blow in two places. But this is easier done when the operations are developed on land, than when a sea landing is concerned. In that case two such operations are not always able to support each other because it is not easy to manage the alternation of reserves between the two groupings. If we were to land six or eight divisions in the south of France at present, the Germans could easily cope with them. That is why it is necessary that the two operations should be undertaken closer in time to each other. But this will require a great number of landing facilities. Brooke says that the Allies had planned to carry out a small landing in the Mediterranean during Operation Overlord in order to draw off a part of the German forces from Overlord. But the difficulties lie in the timely reinforcement of such an auxiliary landing. The fact is that only three or four divisions could be landed right away, later to be brought up to the strength of 35. It is necessary that the Germans should not be able to increase their forces while the Allied force is still insignificant. Brooke says that that is all concerning land operations, and invites Air Force Marshal Portal to make a review of air operations.

Marshal Voroshilov says that it would be better to hear the American report on land operations, and then go on to air operations.

Marshall says that he wants to shed light on the military situation as it appears from the American standpoint. At present the Americans have to fight on two theatres of military operations, namely, in the Atlantic and Pacific oceans. The main problem is that American operations extend over two such great oceans. In contrast to ordinary conditions the Americans do not have a shortage either of troops or supplies. Marshall says that apart from the divisions already in action, there are more than 50 divisions in the U.S.A. which the Americans would like to use as soon as possible. But the problem lies in tonnage and in landing craft. Marshall says that the Americans can still say that they have achieved considerable successes and are now prepared to intensify their pressure on the enemy. It is the desire of the Americans to put into action all their available forces as soon as possible. When mention is made of landing craft it concerns above all ships for the transfer of tanks and motorised units. That is just the kind of vessels lacking for the successful realisation of the operations in the Mediterranean of which General Brooke spoke. Marshall repeats that the Americans do not have any shortage either of troops or supplies. Marshall points out that the Americans are deeply interested in reducing transportation time and the stay of ships in ports. Marshall says that the advantage of Operation Overlord is that it involves the shortest distance to be overcome at the initial moment. Subsequently, it is planned to transfer troops to France directly from the United States. About 60 American divisions are to be transferred to France. Marshall says that no definite decisions have yet been taken in respect of the Mediterranean, because the idea was to discuss this question at Tehran. The question now is what is to be done in the next three, and depending on that, the next six months. Marshall says that it is highly dangerous to undertake an operation in Southern France two months before Operation Overlord, but it is very true, at the same time, that an operation in Southern France would promote the success of Operation Overlord. Marshall thinks that the landing in Southern France should be carried out two or three weeks before Operation Overlord. It must be borne in mind that a serious obstacle to these operations will be the German destruction of all ports. For a long time the armies will have to be supplied across the open coast. American combat engineers have extensive experience in restoring ports, but Marshall nevertheless believes that there will be some delay. He says that during the landing at Salerno only 108 tons a day of supplies could be got through in the first

18 days. Altogether 189,000 men were transferred across the open coast. It must also be borne in mind that this requires strong fighter cover from the air. Marshall says that at Salerno the Anglo-American planes had only from 15 to 20 minutes of action. In Operation Overlord the planes may have up to 30 minutes. Marshall points out once again that the problem facing the Americans is not a shortage of troops or supplies, but a shortage of landing craft. Marshall says that he would like Marshal Voroshilov to understand that in the Pacific the Americans are now carrying out five landing operations accompanied by heavy air battles. Four other landing operations are to be undertaken in the course of January. Marshall says that that is all he wished to say.

Leahy suggests that Air Force Marshal Portal should add to the reports of Brooke and Marshall.

Marshal Portal declares that he will speak only of air operations. Up to now the main raids on Germany were carried out from Britain. Now such raids are being started also from the Mediterranean area. At present, the Anglo-Americans are dropping from 15,000 to 30,000 tons of bombs on Germany a month, and their main purpose is to destroy the enemy's industry, communications and air force. In addition, considerable numbers of German fighter planes are being destroyed from the air. There is a heavy struggle ahead but it can be safely said that the Anglo-American plan of destroying the German Air Force will be crowned with success. That the plan is being successfully implemented is evident from the deployment of the enemy's forces. At present, there are from 1,650 to 1,700 fighters in Western and Southern Germany, while there are only 750 German fighters on all the other fronts. How sensitive the Germans are to the raids is evident from the fact that only one raid by the Anglo-American air force on Southern Germany, undertaken from the Mediterranean, forced the Germans to transfer 300 fighter planes from Central Germany. Portal says that he understands that Soviet aircraft is almost entirely engaged in land battles, but it would be well for the Soviet command to have the possibility of setting aside a part of the air force for bombing Eastern Germany. This would have a great effect on the situation on all the other fronts. Portal says that that is all he wished to say.

Leahy says that it would be well to hear the opinion of Marshal Voroshilov.

Voroshilov says that as he understood from General Marshall's report, the Americans have from 50 to 60 divisions which they want to use in France, and the only delay is in transport and landing facilities. Voroshilov asks what is being done to solve the problem of transport and landing facilities.

Voroshilov says that he understood from General Marshall's report that the Americans regard Operation Overlord as the principal operation, and asks, whether General Brooke, as the chief of the British General Staff, also regards this operation as the principal one, and whether or not he considers that this operation could be replaced by another operation in the Mediterranean area or elsewhere.

Marshall says that he would like to reply to Marshal Voroshilov's question about the preparations for Operation Overlord. Everything is now being done to carry out Operation Overlord, but the whole question turns on transport and landing facilities. Marshall adds that while there was only one American division in Britain in August, at present there are already nine American divisions and more divisions are coming up.

Voroshilov refers to the reports made by Generals Dean and Ismey at the Moscow Conference, which said that there was large-scale construction of landing facilities in Britain and the United States, and that preparations were under way for the construction of temporary floating ports, and asks whether it can now be said that this construction will eventually ensure the necessary quantity of landing craft by the time Operation Overlord is to start.

Marshall replies that General Brooke can say more about the ports. As far as it concerns the United States, everything is being done to have all the necessary preparations completed by the start of Operation Overlord. In particular, landing barges, each to carry up to 40 tanks, are being readied.

Brooke says that he would first like to answer Marshal Voroshilov's first question as to the view taken of Operation Overlord by the British. Brooke says that the British attach great importance to this operation and regard it as an essential part of this war. But for the success of this operation there must be definite prerequisites, which would prevent the Germans from using the good roads of Northern France to bring up reserves. Brooke says that the British believe such prerequisites will exist in 1944. All British forces were reorganised for the forthcoming operations. Special divisions are being trained for the purpose. At present, four divisions have already been transferred from Italy and Africa. A part of the landing ships has also been transferred from the Mediterranean. The British are doing everything to realise these operations, which must be carried out in the course of 1944. But the difficulties of the Anglo-Americans lie in landing ships. In order to be ready for May 1, the bulk of the landing ships should be transferred from the Mediterranean now. But that would result in a suspension of operations in Italy. At the same time the British would like to keep the maximum number of German divisions in continuous action. That is required not only to draw off German forces from the Russian front, but also for the success of Operation Overlord. As for the construction of temporary floating ports, Brooke says that experiments in that respect are now under way. Some of these experiments were not as successful as expected, but at any rate there is success in this matter. Brooke says that the success or failure of the forthcoming operation will depend by and large on the availability of these ports.

Voroshilov says that he wants to ask General Brooke once again whether the British regard Operation Overlord as the principal one.

Brooke says that he had expected this question. He, Brooke, must say that he would not like to see the failure of the operation either in Northern or in Southern France. But in certain circumstances these operations are doomed to failure.

Voroshilov says that Marshal Stalin and the Soviet General Staff regard the operations in the Mediterranean as of secondary significance. Marshal Stalin believes, however, that an operation in Southern France, carried out two or three months before the operation in Northern France, could be of decisive significance for the success of Overlord. The experience of the war, and the successes of the Anglo-American troops in North Africa and the landing operations in Italy, the operations of the Anglo-American air force against Germany, the organisational trim of the forces of the United States and the United Kingdom, the powerful equipment of the United States, the naval strength of the Allies and especially their superiority in the Mediterranean, show that given the will, Overlord can be a success. Will is the only thing required.

Voroshilov says that the military must plan operations in such a way that auxiliary operations, far from hindering the principal operation, should promote it in every way. Voroshilov then goes on to say that Marshal Stalin's proposal is to have the cross-Channel operation supported by the action of Allied forces in the south of France. With that aim in view he allows the possibility of going on the defensive in Italy, and of making a landing in Southern France with the forces released, so as to strike at the enemy from two sides. If the operation in Southern France cannot be carried out two or three months before Operation Overlord, Marshal Stalin does not insist on it at all. This landing can be carried out either simultaneously, or even somewhat later than Operation Overlord. But it must take place.

As for the operations of the Soviet Air Force, it is well known that it is engaged in combat operations together with the land forces. At present, there are on the Soviet-German front 210 German divisions alone, there being 260 enemy divisions altogether, as Marshal Stalin reported. The intensity of the combat operations has drawn our air force to the front and rear of the enemy, and we have no possibility of using any air force for raids on Eastern Germany, but, of course, as soon as this becomes possible, our Supreme Command will take a relevant decision.

Voroshilov says that we regard the operation across the Channel as not an easy one. We realise that this operation is more difficult than the forced crossing of rivers. Still, on the basis of our experience of the forced crossing of big rivers, such as the Dnieper, the Desna, and the Sozh, whose right bank is mountainous and in addition was well fortified by the Germans, we can say that the operation across the Channel, if it is carried out in earnest, will be a success. On the right bank of the above-mentioned rivers the Germans built strong modern reinforced-concrete fortifications, armed them with powerful artillery, and were able to bring our low left bank under fire to a great depth, preventing our troops from approaching the river; still after concentrated artillery, mine-thrower fire, after powerful strikes by the air force, our troops succeeded in crossing these rivers, and the enemy was routed.

I am sure, says Voroshilov, that if well prepared, and,

above all, if well supported by a strong air force, Operation Overlord will be crowned with full success. Needless to say, the Allied air force must secure full domination of the air before the land forces go into action.

Brooke says that the Anglo-Americans also regard the operations in the Mediterranean as operations of secondary importance. But since there are large forces in the Mediterranean area, these operations can and must be carried out in order to help the principal operation. These operations are closely bound up with the entire conduct of the war, and, in particular, with the success of the operation in Northern France.

Brooke says that in connection with Marshal Voroshilov's remarks about the difficulty of the operation across the Channel he would like to say that the British watched the Red Army's forcing of rivers with great interest and admiration. The British think that the Russians have achieved great successes in landing operations. But the cross-Channel operation requires special facilities and needs to be worked out in detail. For several years now the Anglo-Americans have been studying all the necessary details connected with this operation. There are considerable difficulties also in the fact that there are beaches on the shore of France, and big sand banks. That is why in many places ships find it hard to approach the shore itself. All this requires preparations.

Voroshilov says that in August or September the British held exercises in the Channel area. He, Voroshilov, would like to know how the British assess the results of these exercises.

Brooke replies that the purpose of these exercises was to bring about an air battle with the Germans. In addition, these exercises did a great deal for the training of the troops. It was not, of course, a landing exercise. Such exercises are carried out by the British on the coast of Britain.

Voroshilov asks how the Germans reacted to these manoeuvres.

Brooke replies that the Germans failed to react to these manoeuvres to the degree expected by the British.

Marshall says that he must raise an objection to Marshal Voroshilov's statements on a cross-Channel landing. He, Marshall, was trained in land operations, he also had knowledge of the forced crossing of rivers, but when he came up against landing operations across the ocean, he had to start all over again. For if a defeat of troops landed in a forced crossing of a river is only a setback, a defeat in a landing across the ocean is a disaster.

Voroshilov says that he does not agree with this. In such a serious operation as Overlord the main thing is organisation, planning and well thought-out tactics. If the tactics accord with the set task, even a setback for the advance force will be only a setback, and not a disaster. The air force must win domination of the air and must crush the enemy's artillery, and after the intensive artillery preparation only the advance force is to be sent out. After this force consolidates its positions and appears to have succeeded, the main force is to be landed.

Marshall says that another thing that must be borne in mind here is that artillery support from the sea is more complicated than from the opposite bank of a river.

Voroshilov agrees with this and asks what is the expected ratio between the German and the Anglo-American air force by the start of the invasion.

Portal replies that it will be five or six to one.

Voroshilov says that agreement should be reached on the decision to be adopted at this conference.

Brooke says that he considers that not all the questions have yet been discussed at this conference, and therefore proposes that the conference be adjourned until tomorrow.

It is agreed to adjourn the session until November 30.

The talk continued for three hours.

The Second Sitting of the Conference of the Heads of Government of the U.S.S.R., the United States and Great Britain

Tehran, November 29, 1943

Opened: 16.00; Closed: 19.40

Roosevelt: I do not know what went on at the conference of the military this morning. I suggest therefore that Marshal Voroshilov, General Brooke and General Marshall should report to us on their work.

Stalin: I agree, but it appears that the military have not yet finished.

19

Churchill: I think it would still be useful to hear the military.

Brooke: Our conference today was not finished. We started out by examining possible military operations and their interrelation. We examined Operation Overlord and all the ensuing consequences. We concentrated on the period intervening from the present to the date of Operation Overlord; we took into account the fact that if we do not carry out active operations in the Mediterranean in this period before Operation Overlord, we shall be giving the Germans the possibility of transferring their troops to the Soviet-German front, or transferring them to the West with the aim of counteracting Overlord. We examined the possibility of continuing our operations in Italy, where we are holding German divisions, and where we have concentrated large forces. We then turned our attention to the East and examined the desirability of Turkey's entry into the war, and the possible consequences this may have in terms of helping us to conduct the war and open the Dardanelles so as to supply the Soviet Union, and also of opening a way to the Balkans. We examined the possible operations in Southern France in combination with Operation Overlord. The Chief of Staff of the British Air Force reviewed the operations of the Anglo-American Air Force against Germany, and showed the effect of these operations on the over-all course of the war. General Marshall gave figures on the concentration of the American forces in Britain, and spoke of the preparations of the British troops for going over from the defensive to the offensive. The question of Overlord was also studied. Marshal Voroshilov asked several questions which we tried to answer. Marshal Voroshilov set forth the view expressed by Marshal Stalin at the conference yesterday in respect of the operations to be carried out next year. That is about all we had time to examine at our sitting this morning.

Would General Marshall like to add anything to my report?

Marshall: There remains little for me to add to what has been said by General Brooke. His report was sufficiently detailed. The problem facing the Americans is not man power but tonnage, special landing facilities and also the availability of air bases sufficiently close to the area of operations. When I say landing facilities, I mean special landing craft capable of carrying up to 40 tanks or vehicles. It is precisely the number of these vessels that is limited. The transfer of American troops, equipment and ammunition to Britain is proceeding according to plan. One million tons of various equipment has already been transported to Britain. But landing facilities remain the limiting factor. We have a plan for the manufacture of landing facilities, which was expanded both in the United States and in Britain. The accelerated production of landing facilities will result in an increase of their number for invasion across the Channel and for operations in the Mediterranean. In short, preparations for Overlord are proceeding according to plan, insofar as materiel and personnel are concerned. The problem is mainly transport and the distribution of landing facilities. As General Brooke has explained, several divisions have already been transferred from Italy.

Voroshilov: The reports of Generals Brooke and Marshall correspond to the talk we had this morning. My questions were intended to specify the technical preparations for Operation Overlord and they were answered in the manner now set forth by General Marshall. We made no effort to specify the dates for Operation Overlord and all the details connected with the operation considering that these questions could be dealt with at our next meeting if it is held.

Stalin: If possible I should like to know who will be appointed to command Operation Overlord.

Roosevelt: This matter has not yet been decided.

Stalin: In that case nothing will come of Operation Overlord. Who bears the moral and military responsibility for the preparation and execution of Operation Overlord? If that is unknown, then Operation Overlord is just so much talk.

Roosevelt: The British General Morgan is responsible for preparing Operation Overlord.

Stalin: Who is responsible for carrying out Operation Overlord?

Roosevelt: We know the men who will take part in carrying out Operation Overlord, with the exception of the commander-in-chief of the operation.

Stalin: It may happen that General Morgan will consider the operation prepared, but after the appointment of the commander responsible for the execution of the operation it may turn out that the commander will consider the operation unprepared. There must be some one who is responsible both for preparing and executing the operation.

Churchill: General Morgan was given the assignment of preliminary preparations.

Stalin: Who gave General Morgan this assignment?

Churchill: Several months ago the assignment was given to General Morgan by the Joint Anglo-American Staff with the consent of the President and with my consent. General Morgan was assigned to carry out preparations for Overlord together with the American and British staffs, but the commander-in-chief has not yet been appointed. The British Government has expressed its readiness to place its forces under the command of an American commander-in-chief in Operation Overlord, because the United States is responsible for the concentration and remanning of forces and has a greater number of forces. On the other hand, the British Government proposed the appointment of a British commander-in-chief of operations in the Mediterranean, where the British have a greater number of forces. The question of appointing a commander-in-chief cannot be solved at such a broad sitting as today's. This question should be decided by the three heads of Government among themselves, in private. As the President has just told me—and I confirm this—the decision on the appointment of a commander-in-chief will depend on the talks we are now having.

Stalin: I should like to be understood that the Russians do not claim participation in the appointment of the commander-in-chief, but the Russians would like to know who is going to be the commander. The Russians would like him to be appointed sooner, and would like to see him responsible for the preparations as well as for the carrying out of Operation Overlord.

Churchill: We fully agree with what Marshal Stalin has said and I think the President will agree with me if I say that we shall appoint a commander-in-chief in a fortnight, and shall communicate his name. One of the tasks of the conference is to appoint a commander-in-chief.

Stalin: I have no questions in connection with the reports of Brooke and Marshall.

Churchill: I am somewhat worried by the number and complexity of the problems facing us. This conference is unique. Millions of people look to this conference and place their hopes on it, and I very much wish that we should not part until we have reached agreement on political and military questions we have been trusted to solve. Today, I want to indicate several points requiring study in a subcommittee. The British Staff and I have long been studying the situation in the Mediterranean, where we have quite a big army. We want this army to be in action there in the course of the whole year and to be independent of factors that would force it to be idle. In this connection we ask our Russian allies to examine the whole problem and the various alternatives we shall propose to them as to the best use of our available forces in the Mediterranean area.

There are three questions which require detailed study.

The first of these is, of course, the assistance that can be given to Operation Overlord with the use of the forces in the Mediterranean area. What I mean is the scale of the operations which are to be carried out in Southern France from Northern Italy. The President and I spoke of this yesterday. I do not think the matter has been studied sufficiently to allow a final decision. I should welcome a study of this question by our staffs from the standpoint of its urgency. In this connection Marshal Stalin correctly stressed the importance of a flanking movement in Southern France. The date is important. If operations with smaller forces are started at one point and with bigger forces at another, the first operation will be a failure. Our staffs should discuss the operations on a broader plane. I should like to have enough landing facilities in the Mediterranean to transfer two divisions. If these two divisions are available we could undertake an operation to help the advance of the Anglo-American troops along the Italian Peninsula in order to destroy the enemy forces there. There is another possibility of using these forces. They would be sufficient for the capture of the island of Rhodes in the event Turkey entered the war. The third possibility of using these forces is that, minus their losses, they could be used in Southern France in six months to support Operation Overlord. None of these possibilities is excluded. But the matter of the date is important. The use of these two divisions, no matter for which of the three operations I have indicated they might be used in the Mediterranean, cannot be carried out without deferring Operation Overlord, or without diverting a part of the landing facilities from the area of the Indian

Ocean. There is our dilemma. In order to decide which way to choose we should like to hear the view of Marshal Stalin concerning the over-all strategic situation, because we are delighted and inspired by the military experience of our Russian allies. I should like to propose that the study of the question I have raised be continued by our military committee tomorrow.

The next problem I want to speak of is political rather than military, because the military forces we intend to set aside for its solution are insignificant. I have in mind the Balkans. In the Balkans there are 21 German divisions apart from garrison troops. Of this number, i.e., of the 21 divisions, 54,000 German troops are concentrated in the Aegean islands. In addition, there are not less than 12 Bulgarian divisions in the Balkans. Altogether, there are 42 enemy divisions in the Balkans. If Turkey should enter the war the Bulgarians would be forced to withdraw their troops to the front in Thrace against Turkey. This will result in an increased danger to the German divisions in the Balkans. I give these figures to show the enormous importance of this factor in the Balkans, where we do not intend to send our regular divisions and where we intend to limit ourselves to raids by combined detachments. In the Balkans we have neither interests nor ambitions. All we want to do is to tie down the 21 German divisions in the Balkans and to destroy them, if possible. I propose, therefore, that a meeting should be held today of the two Foreign Ministers and a representative appointed by the President to discuss the political aspect of this question. We want to work concertedly with our Russian allies. If there are any difficulties, they can be cleared up between ourselves. The military questions could be discussed later.

I pass now to the next question, the question of Turkey. We British are Turkey's allies, and we have assumed the responsibility of trying to convince or make Turkey enter the war before Christmas. If the President should like to join us or to assume the leadership, that will be acceptable to us, but we shall need the full help of Marshal Stalin in implementing the decision adopted at the Moscow Conference. On behalf of the British Government I can say that it is prepared to warn Turkey that if Turkey does not accept the proposal of entering the war this may have the most serious political consequences for Turkey and have an

24

effect on her rights in respect of the Bosporus and the Dardanelles. This morning, the military committee composed of our generals discussed the military aspect of the Turkish problem, but the problem of Turkey is a political rather than a military problem. We intend to set aside not more than two or three divisions for operations in the area of Turkey if she enters the war, apart from the air force that we shall also make available.

I have raised several questions which are mainly political, for example, the question of what the Soviet Government thinks about Bulgaria, whether it is inclined, in the event that Turkey declares war on Germany and Bulgaria attacks Turkey, to tell the Bulgarians that it will regard Bulgaria as its enemy. This will have a great effect on Bulgaria. There are other political problems as well. I propose that the two Foreign Ministers and a representative appointed by the President should study this question and advise us on how to make Turkey enter the war and what the results of this will be. I think these results will be enormous with decisive possibilities. If Turkey declares war on Germany it will be a great blow for the German people. If we manage to make good use of this fact it should neutralise Bulgaria. As for the other countries in the Balkans, Rumania is already looking for a country to which she can capitulate. Hungary is also in confusion. It is time for us to reap the harvest. Now we must pay the price for this harvest, if we consider it expedient. I propose that these questions should be discussed by our three representatives, who, as a result of their discussion, may tell us what can be done to lighten Russia's burden, and to ensure the success of Operation Overlord.

Stalin: As for the two divisions which Mr. Churchill proposes to set aside for help to Turkey and the partisans, we have no disagreements on this question. We regard the assignment of two divisions and help to the partisans as important. But if we are prevailed upon here to discuss military questions, we regard Operation Overlord as the main and decisive question.

I should like the military committee to have a definite task. I propose that the committee be given a definite directive within whose framework it could work. Of course, the Russians are in need of help. I should like to state that if the question is one of aid to us, we do expect aid from those who carry out the operations planned, and we expect real aid.

What should our directives to the military committee be? They should stipulate that the date of Operation Overlord should not be postponed, and that May should be the time limit for carrying out this operation. Our second directive should stipulate, in conformity with the desires of the Russians, support of Operation Overlord by a landing in the south of France. If it is impossible to land a force in Southern France two or three months before the start of Operation Overlord, it would be worth while doing this simultaneously with Operation Overlord. If transport difficulties do not allow a landing in Southern France simultaneously with Operation Overlord, the operation in Southern France could be undertaken some time after the start of Operation Overlord. I think that a landing in Southern France would be an auxiliary operation in respect of Overlord. This operation would ensure the success of Operation Overlord. Meanwhile, the operation to take Rome would be of a diverting nature. The third directive would instruct the committee to hurry the appointment of the commander-in-chief for Operation Overlord. It would be best to settle these matters during our stay here, and I see no reason why this cannot be done. We believe that until a commander-in-chief is appointed Operation Overlord cannot be expected to be a success. The appointment of a commander-in-chief is the task of the British and the Americans, but the Russians would like to know who is going to be the commander-in-chief. Those are the three directives to the military committee. If the committee works within the framework of these directives its work can be successful and can be finished earlier. I ask the conference to take account of the considerations I have put forward.

Roosevelt: I listened with interest to everything that was said, beginning from Operation Overlord and ending with the question of Turkey. I attach great importance to dates. If there is agreement on Operation Overlord, there is need to come to agreement on the date of this operation.

Operation Overlord can be carried out in the first week of May or it may be postponed somewhat. The postponement of Overlord would result from our carrying out one or two operations in the Mediterranean, which would require landing facilities and planes. If an expedition is carried out in the eastern part of the Mediterranean and fails it will be necessary to transfer additional materiel and troops to that area. In that case Overlord will not be carried out in time.

Stalin: Against Yugoslavia the Germans have eight divisions, of which five are in Greece. In Bulgaria, there are three or four German divisions, and nine in Italy.

Churchill: Our figures differ from these.

Stalin: Your figures are wrong. In France, the Germans have 25 divisions.

Roosevelt: Our staffs must work out plans in order to tie down the German divisions in the Balkans. These plans must be worked out in such a way that the operations we undertake for that purpose should not prejudice Overlord.

Stalin: That is right.

Churchill: Speaking of measures with respect to the Balkans, I did not mean the use of large forces for these purposes.

Stalin: If possible it would be good to carry out Operation Overlord in May, say the 10th, 15th, or 20th of May.

Churchill: I cannot undertake such an obligation.

Stalin: If Overlord is carried out in August, as Churchill said yesterday, nothing will come of the operation because of the unfavourable weather in that period. April and May are the best months for Overlord.

Churchill: I do not think that we differ in our views, as it may seem. I am prepared to do everything that is within the power of the British Government to carry out Operation Overlord at the earliest possible date. But I do not think that the many possibilities available in the Mediterranean should be coldly rejected as being of no importance, just because their use will hold up Operation Overlord for two or three months.

Stalin: The operations in the Mediterranean of which Churchill speaks are merely diversional. I do not deny the importance of these diversions.

Churchill: In our opinion the numerous British troops must not be idle for six months. They should carry on operations against the enemy, and with the help of our American allies we hope to destroy the German divisions in Italy. We cannot remain passive in Italy, for that will spoil our whole campaign there. We must extend assistance to our Russian friends.

Stalin: According to Churchill it would appear that the Russians want the British to be idle.

Churchill: If the vessels are withdrawn from the Mediterranean, this will considerably reduce the scale of operations in that area. Marshal Stalin will recall that at the Moscow Conference conditions were specified under which Operation Overlord can be a success. These conditions stipulate that by the time of the invasion there should be not more than 12 German mobile divisions in France, and that in the course of 60 days the Germans should be unable to transfer more than 15 divisions to reinforce their troops in France. There is no mistake here, for these conditions are the basis of Overlord. We must tie down as many German divisions as possible in Italy, the Balkans, and in the area of Turkey, if she enters the war. German divisions transferred from France are fighting us at the front in Italy. If we are passive on the front in Italy, the Germans will be able to transfer their divisions back to France to the prejudice of Overlord. That is why we must tie up the enemy by action and keep our front in Italy in an active state so as to pin down a sufficient number of German divisions there.

As for Turkey, I agree to insist on her entry into the war. If she refuses to do this, nothing can be done about it. If she does agree we must make use of the Turkish air bases in Anatolia and take Rhodes. One assault division will be enough for this operation. Subsequently, the garrison in the island will be able to defend it. Having received Rhodes and the Turkish bases we shall be able to expel the German garrisons from the other islands of the Aegean Sea and open up the Dardanelles. That is not an operation that will require a great force. It is a limited operation. If Turkey enters the war and we take Rhodes we shall have secured superiority in this area and the time will come when all the islands in the Aegean Sea will be ours. If Turkey does not enter the war we shall not grieve over the matter and I shall not ask for troops to take Rhodes and the islands of the Aegean Sea. But in that case Germany will not grieve either, for she will continue to dominate the area. If Turkey enters the war, our troops stationed in Egypt for the purposes of defence, and our air force there also defending Egypt, could be advanced to the fore. After the taking of the Aegean Islands these forces could be used in areas north of Egypt. I suggest a thorough discussion of this question. It will be a great misfortune for us, if Turkey does not join the war, from the standpoint of Germany's continued domination of that area. I want the troops and planes now idle in Egypt to be used as soon as possible if Turkey enters the war. Everything depends on the landing facilities. The difficulty lies in the transportation of troops across the sea. I am always prepared to discuss all details with our Allies. But everything depends on the availability of landing facilities. If these landing facilities are left in the Mediterranean or in the Indian Ocean to the prejudice of Overlord, then the success of Overlord and the success of the operation in Southern France cannot be guaranteed. The operations in Southern France will require a great quantity of landing facilities. I ask this to be taken into consideration.

Finally, I consider acceptable and, on behalf of the British Government, agree to the working out of directives for the military committee. I suggest that we work out our own directives to the committee together with the Americans. I think that our views coincide more or less.

Stalin: How long do we intend to stay at Tehran?

Churchill: I am prepared to stop eating until these directives are worked out.

Stalin: What I mean is when shall we end our conference?

Roosevelt: I am prepared to stay at Tehran as long as Marshal Stalin remains at Tehran.

Churchill: If it is necessary I am prepared to stay in Tehran for good.

Stalin: I should like to know how many French divisions there are at present.

Roosevelt: The plan is to arm 11 French divisions. But of this number only five are ready now, and another four divisions are to be equipped shortly.

Stalin: Are these French divisions in action or are they idle?

Roosevelt: One division is fighting in Italy, one or two divisions are in Corsica and Sardinia.

Stalin: How does the command intend to use these French divisions?

Marshall: The plan is to merge the French Corps with the Fifth Army operating on the left flank in Italy. One division is now being transferred to the front in Italy where it will be tested in action. After this a decision will be taken on the most expedient use of the French divisions. The time required to equip another four French divisions depends on the time it will take to train the personnel of these divisions.

Stalin: Are these divisions of the French type?

Marshall: These divisions are of the American type and consist of 15,000 men each. Most of the soldiers are not Frenchmen. In the armoured divisions, three-quarters of the personnel are French and the rest are Africans.

Roosevelt: I should like to say a few words. I think that if we three give instructions to our military committee it will be able to discuss these questions.

Stalin: There is no need for any military committee. We can solve all the questions here at the conference. We must decide on the date, the commander-in-chief and the need of an auxiliary operation in Southern France. We Russians are limited in time of stay at Tehran. We could stay on until December 1, but we have to leave on the 2nd. The President will recall that we agreed on three or four days.

Roosevelt: I think that my proposal will simplify the work of the staff. The military committee must take Operation Overlord as a basis. The committee must table its proposals on the auxiliary operations in the Mediterranean. It must also bear in mind that these operations may hold up Overlord.

Stalin: The Russians would like to know the date on which Overlord is to start in order to prepare their blow at the Germans.

Roosevelt: The date of Operation Overlord was determined at Quebec. Only the most serious changes in the situation can justify any changes in the date determined for this operation.

Churchill: I have just heard the directive which the President proposed to give the committee. I should like to have the opportunity of considering the President's proposals. I have no objections to this in principle, but I should like to have time to examine the President's proposals. I am very pleased to spend December 1 at Tehran, and to leave on December 2. It is not clear to me whether or not the President proposes the establishment of a military committee, for Marshal Stalin suggests that we do without a committee. Personally, I want such a committee.

As for determining the date of Operation Overlord, if it is decided to have an examination of strategic questions in the military committee. . . .

Stalin: We are not demanding any examination.

Roosevelt: We are all aware that the contradictions between us and the British are small. I object to the postponement of Operation Overlord, while Churchill lays emphasis on the importance of operations in the Mediterranean. The military committee could clear up these questions.

Stalin: We can solve these problems ourselves, because we have more rights than the military committee. If I may permit myself an incautious question, I should like to know whether the British believe in Operation Overlord or simply speak of it to reassure the Russians.

Churchill: Given the conditions which were indicated at the Moscow Conference, I am quite sure that we shall have to transfer all our available forces against the Germans when Operation Overlord is launched.

Roosevelt: We are very hungry now, and I propose that we adjourn to attend the dinner given for us today by Marshal Stalin. I propose that our military committee should continue its conference tomorrow morning.

Stalin: There is no need for the meeting of a military committee. That is superfluous. Only we ourselves can speed up our work.

Churchill: Would it be better for the President and myself to co-ordinate our views and then report to you our common standpoint?

Stalin: This would accelerate our work.

Churchill: And what about the committee consisting of Hopkins and the two Ministers of Foreign Affairs?

Stalin: This committee is not required either. But if Mr. Churchill insists, we do not object to its formation.

Roosevelt: Tomorrow, Hopkins, Molotov and Eden could have talk with each other at luncheon.

Stalin: What are we going to do tomorrow? Will the proposals of Churchill and Roosevelt be ready?

Roosevelt: The proposals will be ready, and I suggest that Churchill, Marshal Stalin and I have luncheon at one-thirty and discuss all questions.

Churchill: That will be our programme for tomorrow.

Stalin: I agree.

The Third Sitting of the Conference
of the Heads of Government of the U.S.S.R.,
the United States and Great Britain

Tehran, November 30, 1943

Opened: 16.30; Closed: 17.20

Roosevelt: The decision of the British and American staffs was communicated to Marshal Stalin and has satisfied him. It would be desirable for General Brooke to announce this decision to the conference if Marshal Stalin has no objections.

Stalin: I agree.

Churchill: General Brooke will make this announcement on behalf of both the Americans and the British.

Brooke: The chiefs of the Joint Staffs have advised the President and the Prime Minister to inform Marshal Stalin that Operation Overlord will be started in May. This operation will be supported by an operation against Southern France, with the scale of this operation depending on the number of landing craft available at the time.

Churchill: Needless to say the Joint British and American Staffs will be in close contact with Marshal Stalin in order to permit the co-ordination of operations by all the allies, so that a blow is dealt at the enemy simultaneously from both sides.

Stalin: I am aware of the importance of the decisions adopted by the staffs of our allies, and the difficulties in implementing these decisions. There may be a danger not at the start of Overlord but when the operation is unfolded, when the Germans try to transfer a part of their troops from the Eastern Front to the Western to hamper Overlord. In order to prevent the Germans from manoeuvring their reserves and transferring any sizable forces from the Eastern Front to the West, the Russians undertake to organise a big offensive against the Germans in several places by May, in order to pin down the German divisions on the Eastern Front and to prevent the Germans from creating any difficulties for Overlord. I informed President Roosevelt and Prime Minister Churchill of this today, but I wish to repeat my statement before the conference.

Roosevelt: I am highly satisfied with Marshal Stalin's

statement that steps will be taken to co-ordinate the blows at the enemy. I hope that our nations have now realised the need of joint action, and that the forthcoming operations of our three countries will show that we have learned to act together.

The United States has not yet appointed a commander-in-chief for Operation Overlord, but I am sure that a commander-in-chief will be appointed in the next three or four days, as soon as we return to Cairo.

I have only one proposal to make, namely, that our staffs should without delay start elaborating the proposals adopted here. That is why I suppose they could return to Cairo tomorrow, if Marshal Stalin has no objections to this.

Stalin: I agree with this.

Churchill: I want to say that today we adopted a serious decision. Now the President and I and our staffs must work out this question in detail and decide where we are to find the necessary landing craft. We have ahead of us five months, and I think that we shall be able to obtain the required number of landing craft. I have already given an assignment to study this matter and a detailed report will be submitted as soon as our staffs return home. For Operation Overlord to succeed we must have a considerable superiority of forces, and I hope that our staffs will be able to assure this. By June, we shall already be in bitter action against the enemy. I believe that we have finished discussing military matters. We could now discuss political questions. For this we could use December 1 and 2, and could leave on December 3. We have scored a great success and it would be well if we left after solving all questions, and announced to the public that we have reached complete agreement. I hope that the President can stay until December 3, as I can, if Marshal Stalin agrees to stay.

Stalin: I agree.

Roosevelt: I am very happy to hear that Marshal Stalin has agreed to stay for another day. I also wanted to say about the communiqué: our staffs could give us a draft of this communiqué.

Stalin: In the part relating to military matters?

Churchill: Of course. The communiqué must be brief and mystifying.

Stalin: But without any mysticism.

Churchill: I am sure that the enemy will shortly learn

33

of our preparations because he will be able to discover them by the great accumulation of trains, by the activity of our ports, etc.

Stalin: A big operation cannot be hidden in a sack.

Churchill: Our staffs will have to think how to camouflage these preparations and to mislead the enemy.

Stalin: In such cases we mislead the enemy by building dummies of tanks, planes, and mock airfields. Then we set the dummies of the tanks and planes in motion with the aid of tractors. Intelligence reports on these movements to the enemy, and the Germans believe that the blow is being prepared in that very place. Meanwhile, there is absolute quiet where the offensive is really being staged. All transportation takes place at night. We set up in several places from 5,000 to 8,000 dummies of tanks, up to 2,000 dummies of planes, and a great number of dummy airfields. In addition, we mislead the enemy with the aid of the radio. In areas where no offensive is planned, radio stations exchange messages. These stations are monitored by the enemy, and he receives the impression that a great force is deployed there. Enemy planes often bomb these places night and day although they are absolutely empty.

Churchill: Sometimes truth has to be safeguarded with the aid of untruth. In any case, steps will be taken to mislead the enemy.

The Fourth Sitting of the Conference of the Heads of Government of the U.S.S.R., the United States and Great Britain

Tehran, December 1, 1943

I. SITTING DURING LUNCHEON

Opened: 13.00; Closed: 15.00

Hopkins: The question of inviting Turkey to enter the war is connected with the question of how much support Turkey can get from Great Britain and the United States. In addition, it is necessary to co-ordinate Turkey's entry into the war with the over-all strategy.

Roosevelt: In other words, Inönü is going to ask us whether we shall support Turkey. I think this question must be further worked out.

Stalin: Churchill said that the British Government was making available 20 or 30 squadrons and 2 or 3 divisions for aid to Turkey.

Churchill: We gave no consent in respect of two or three divisions. In Egypt, we have 17 squadrons which are not used at present by the Anglo-American command. These squadrons, in the event of Turkey's entry into the war, would serve for the purpose of her defence. In addition, Britain agreed to make available to Turkey three anti-aircraft defence regiments. That is all the British promised Turkey. The British did not promise Turkey any troops. The Turks have 50 divisions. The Turks are good fighters, but they have no modern weapons. As for the two or three divisions mentioned by Marshal Stalin the British Government has set these divisions aside for the capture of the Aegean Islands in the event Turkey enters the war, and not for aid to Turkey.

Roosevelt: (addressing Churchill): Isn't it a fact that the operation against Rhodes will require a great quantity of landing facilities.

Churchill: This operation will require no more facilities than are available in the Mediterranean.

Roosevelt: My difficulty is that the American Staff has not yet studied how many landing craft will be required by the operations in Italy, the preparations of Overlord in Britain, and for the Indian Ocean. That is why I must be careful in respect of promises to Turkey. I'm afraid these promises may hamper the fulfilment of our agreement of yesterday.

Stalin: Apart from entering the war, Turkey will also make her territory available to the allied air force.

Churchill: Of course.

Stalin: I think that we have finished with this question.

Churchill: We have not offered anything we are unable to give. We offered the Turks three new squadrons of fighters to bring the total number of squadrons, including those in Egypt, up to 20. Perhaps, the Americans could add anything to this number? We promised the Turks some anti-aircraft defence units, but we did not promise them any troops, for we haven't any. As for landing facilities, these will be needed in March, but I believe we shall be able to find them in the period between the taking of Rome and the start of Operation Overlord.

Roosevelt: I want to consult with the military. I hope Churchill is right, but my advisers say that there may be difficulties in the use of landing craft between the taking of Rome and the start of Overlord. They believe that it is absolutely necessary to have the landing craft for Operation Overlord by April 1.

Churchill: I do not see any difficulties. We have not made any proposals to Turkey, and I don't know if Inönü will accept them. He will be in Cairo and will acquaint himself with the situation. I can give the Turks 20 squadrons. I won't give the Turks any troops. Besides, I don't think they need troops. But the point is that I don't know whether or not Inönü is coming to Cairo.

Stalin: He might fall ill?

Churchill: Easily. If Inönü does not agree to go to Cairo to meet the President and myself, I am prepared to go on a cruiser to see him in Adana. Inönü will go there, and I shall paint for him the unpleasant picture that will face the Turks if they refuse to enter the war, and the pleasant picture in the opposite case. I shall then inform you of the results of my talks with Inönü.

Hopkins: The question of supporting Turkey in the war was not discussed by the American military, and I doubt the expediency of inviting Inönü to Cairo before the military have studied this matter.

Stalin: Consequently, Hopkins proposes not to invite Inönü.

Hopkins: I am not proposing not to invite Inönü, but I stress that it would be useful to receive information beforehand on the aid we could give the Turks.

Churchill: I agree with Hopkins. We must agree on the possible aid to the Turks.

Stalin: Can't this be done without the military?

Churchill: Together with the military we must study the question of landing facilities. We may be able to get more than we hope by taking them from the Indian or Pacific oceans or building them. If that is impossible we should abandon the idea. However, in any case, it has been decided that Overlord must not suffer.

Roosevelt: I think that it would be useful if I outlined the situation in the Pacific in connection with the possible withdrawal of landing facilities from there, as Churchill suggests. I must point out, first, that the distance from the Pacific to the Mediterranean is enormous. Second, in the Pacific we are moving northwards so as to cut Japanese communications, and we need landing facilities in that area.

Hopkins: Is it true that Churchill and Eden have not spoken to the Turks about the taking of the Aegean Islands?

Eden: No, I have not spoken of this. I only asked the Turks to make available air bases and did not touch upon the question of landing facilities.

Roosevelt: If I see the Turkish President I shall make the offer to take Crete and the Dodecanese Islands because they are rather close to Turkey.

Churchill: I want the Turks to give us air bases in the area of Smyrna, which the British helped the Turks to build. When we get these air bases we shall expel the German air force from the Islands. For this purpose we are prepared to pay with one of our planes for every destroyed German plane. The task of expelling the German garrisons from the Islands will be feasible if we ensure air superiority in that area. There is no need to storm the island of Rhodes where there are 8,000 Italians and 5,000 Germans. They can be starved out. If we get bases in Turkey our ships with air support will be able to cut German communications and the goal will be reached.

Stalin: That is correct. It seems that the 20 squadrons now in Cairo are idle. If they go into action nothing will be left of the German air force. But a certain number of bombers should be added to the fighter squadrons.

Roosevelt: I agree with Churchill's proposal to make available for Turkey's defence 20 squadrons with a certain number of bombers.

Churchill: We are offering Turkey limited air cover and anti-aircraft defence. It is winter now, and an invasion of Turkey is improbable. We intend to continue supplying Turkey with arms. Turkey is receiving mainly American weapons. At the present time we are offering Turkey the invaluable opportunity of accepting the Soviet Government's invitation to take part in a peace conference.

Stalin: What kind of weapons is Turkey short of?

Churchill: The Turks have rifles, pretty good artillery, but they have no anti-tank artillery, no air force, no tanks.

We organised military schools in Turkey, but attendance is low. The Turks have no experience in handling radio equipment. But the Turks are good fighters.

Stalin: It is quite possible that if the Turks give airfields to the allies, Bulgaria will not attack Turkey, and the Germans will be expecting Turkey's attack. Turkey will not attack the Germans, but will simply be in a state of war with them. But this will give the allies airfields and ports in Turkey. If events took such a turn, that would not be bad either.

Eden: I told the Turks that they could make air bases available to the allies without fighting, for Germany would not attack Turkey.

Roosevelt: In this respect Portugal could serve as an example for Turkey.

Eden: Numan would not agree with my standpoint. He said Germany would react, and that Turkey prefers to enter the war of her own free will, instead of being dragged in.

Churchill: That is true. But I must say the following. When you ask Turkey to stretch her neutrality by giving us air bases, the Turks reply that they prefer a war in earnest; when you tell the Turks about entering the war in earnest, they reply that they have not got the arms. If the Turks give a negative reply to our proposal we must let them know our serious considerations. We must tell them that in that case they will not participate in the peace conference. As for Britain, we shall tell them on our part that we are not interested in Turkish affairs. In addition, we shall stop supplying Turkey with arms.

Eden: I should like to specify the demands we are to present to Turkey in Cairo. I understand that we must demand of the Turks entry into the war against Germany.

Stalin: Precisely, against Germany. . . .

II. ROUND-TABLE SITTING

Opened: 16.00; Closed: 19.40

Roosevelt: At this sitting I should like us to discuss the questions of Poland and Germany.

Stalin: And also the question of a communiqué.

Roosevelt: The Communiqué is already being prepared.

Molotov: Can we receive an answer now concerning the transfer to us of a part of the Italian merchant fleet and navy?

Roosevelt: The answer to this question is very simple. We have received a great number of Italian ships. They should, I think, remain in the temporary use of the United Nations and should be used in the best way. After the war they should be distributed among the United Nations.

Molotov: If these ships cannot be conveyed into our ownership we ask that they be given to us for temporary use. We shall use them in the interests of the allies and all the United Nations.

Stalin: If Turkey does not enter the war, the Italian ships transferred to us cannot be sailed into the Black Sea, and we should then like to have them in the North Sea. We are aware that Great Britain and the United States are in need of ships, but we are not asking for many.

Churchill: I am for it.

Roosevelt: I am also for it.

Churchill: I should like to see these ships in the Black Sea.

Stalin: We also prefer to have them in the Black Sea.

Churchill: It may be well to send the Italian ships handed over to the Soviet Union into the Black Sea with the British ships to help the Soviet Navy.

Stalin: All right, please.

Churchill: We must settle the matter of transferring the ships with the Italians, because they are helping us with their fleet. Some Italian ships are fighting, others are patrolling. The submarines are being used for supply. Of course, it is desirable to put the Italian fleet to the best possible use instead of having it against us. That is why I request two months in which to settle with the Italians the question of transferring the Italian ships to the Soviet Union. This is a delicate matter and it is necessary to go about it like a cat with a mouse.

Stalin: Can we then receive these ships by the end of January of next year?

Roosevelt: I agree.

Churchill: I agree.

Stalin: Our crews will man these ships.

Churchill: We should like to help the Russian Navy in the Black Sea with our own ships. In addition, we should be happy to help in repairing the Soviet naval bases in the Black Sea, for instance, Sevastopol. We should also be happy if the Soviet Government considers it useful to send four or five submarines into the Black Sea to sink the Rumanians and Germans there. I must say that we have neither claims nor interests in the Black Sea.

Stalin: Very well, we shall be grateful for any assistance extended to us.

Churchill: There is one point we could make use of in the event Turkey joins the war. If Turkey is afraid to enter the war but will agree to stretch her neutrality, Turkey may permit several submarines to pass through the Bosporus and the Dardanelles into the Black Sea with supply ships for them. American submarines are sinking many Japanese ships in the Pacific Ocean; our submarines sank a great number of German and Italian ships in the Mediterranean; now our submarines could help in the Black Sea.

Stalin: Have we finished with this question?

Churchill: Yes.

Roosevelt: I should like to discuss Poland. I wish to express the hope that the Soviet Government will be able to start talks and restore its relations with the Polish Government.

Stalin: The agents of the Polish Government, who are in Poland, are connected with the Germans. They are killing partisans. You cannot imagine what they are doing there.

Churchill: That is a big issue. We declared war on Germany because Germany attacked Poland. I was surprised when Chamberlain failed to fight for the Czechs in Munich, but suddenly in April 1939 gave Poland a guarantee. I was surprised when he rejected more favourable opportunities and returned to the policy of war. But at the same time I was also pleased with this fact. For the sake of Poland and in pursuance of our promise we declared war on Germany, although we were not prepared, with the exception of our naval forces, and played a big part in inducing France to enter the war. France has collapsed. But we turned out to be active fighters thanks to our insular position. We attach great importance to the reason for which we entered the war. I understand the historical difference between ours and the Russian standpoint on Poland. But at home we pay a great deal of attention to Poland, for it was the attack on Poland that prompted us to undertake the present effort. I was also very well aware of the Russian position at the start of the war, and considering our weakness at the beginning of the war, and the fact that France went back on the guarantees she gave in Munich, I understand that the Soviet Government could not at the time risk its life in that struggle. But now the situation is different, and I hope that if we are asked why we entered the war we shall reply that it happened because we gave Poland a guarantee. I want to return to my example of the three matches, one of which represents Germany, another Poland, and the third, the Soviet Union. All these three matches must be moved to the West in order to settle one of the main problems facing the allies: to ensure the Soviet Union's Western borders.

Stalin: Yesterday there was no mention of negotiations with the Polish Government. Yesterday it was said that the Polish Government must be directed to do this, and that. I must say that Russia, no less than the other Powers, is interested in good relations with Poland, because Poland is Russia's neighbour. We stand for the restoration and strengthening of Poland. But we draw a line between Poland and the emigre Polish Government in London. We broke off relations with that Government not out of any whim on our part, but because the Polish Government joined Hitler in slandering the Soviet Union. All that was published in the press. What are the guarantees that the emigre Polish Government in London will not do the same thing again? We should like to have a guarantee that the agents of the Polish Government will not kill partisans, that the emigre Polish Government will really call for struggle against the Germans, instead of engaging in machinations. We shall maintain good relations with any Government that calls for active struggle against the Germans. But I am not at all sure that the present emigre Government in London is such as it should be. If it sides with the partisans and if we are given a guarantee that its agents will not have ties with the Germans in Poland, we shall be prepared to start talks with it.

Churchill mentioned three matches. I should like to ask him what it means.

Churchill: It would be a good thing now at the round table to hear the views of the Russians on Poland's borders. I think Eden or I could then make them known to the Poles.

We believe that Poland unquestionably should be satisfied at the expense of Germany. We are prepared to tell the Poles that this is a good plan, and that they cannot expect a better one. After this we could raise the question of restoring relations. But I should like to emphasise that we want a strong independent Poland, friendly to Russia.

Stalin: The question is that the Ukrainian lands should go to the Ukraine, and the Byelorussian, to Byelorussia, i.e., the 1939 border established by the Soviet Constitution should exist between us and Poland. The Soviet Government stands for this border and considers that this is correct.

What other questions are there for discussion?

Roosevelt: The question of Germany.

Stalin: What are the proposals on this matter?

Roosevelt: The partition of Germany.

Churchill: I am for partitioning Germany. But I should like to consider the question of partitioning Prussia. I am for separating Bavaria and the other provinces from Germany.

Roosevelt: In order to stimulate our discussion on this question, I want to set forth a plan for partitioning Germany into five states, which I personally drew up two months ago.

Churchill: I should like to stress that the root of evil in Germany is Prussia.

Roosevelt: I should like us to have a picture of the whole before we speak of the separate components. In my opinion, Prussia must be weakened as far as possible, and reduced in size. Prussia should constitute the first independent part of Germany. The second part of Germany should include Hannover and the north-western regions of Germany. The third part—Saxony and the Leipzig area. The fourth part —Hessen Province, Darmstadt, Kassel and the areas to the south of the Rhine, and also the old towns of Westphalia. The fifth part—Bavaria, Baden, Württemberg. Each of these five parts would be an independent state. In addition, the regions of the Kiel Canal and Hamburg should be separated from Germany. These regions would be administered by the United Nations, or the four Powers. The Ruhr and the Saar must be placed either under the control of the United Nations or under the trusteeship of the whole of Europe. That is my proposal. I must add that it is merely exploratory.

Churchill: You have said a mouthful. I think there are two questions: one—destructive, the other—constructive. I have two ideas: the first is to isolate Prussia from the rest of Germany; the second is to separate Germany's southern provinces—Bavaria, Baden, Württemberg, the Palatinate, from the Saar to Saxony inclusive. I would keep Prussia in strict conditions. I think it would be easy to sever the southern provinces from Prussia and include them in a Danubian federation. The people who live in the Danube basin are not the cause of war. At any rate, I would give the Prussians harsher treatment than the other Germans. The southern Germans will not start a new war.

Stalin: I do not like the plan for new associations of states. If it is decided to partition Germany no new associations need be set up. Whether it is five or six states, and two regions into which Roosevelt proposes to divide Germany, this plan of Roosevelt's to weaken Germany can be examined. Like us, Churchill will soon have to deal with great masses of Germans. Churchill will then see that it is not only the Prussians who are fighting in the German Army but also Germans from the other provinces of Germany. Only the Austrians, when surrendering, shout "I'm Austrian", and our soldiers accept them. As for the Germans from Germany's other provinces they fight with equal doggedness. Regardless of how we approach the partitioning of Germany there is no need to set up some new association of Danubian states lacking vitality. Hungary and Austria must exist separately. Austria existed as a separate state until it was seized.

Roosevelt: I agree with Marshal Stalin, in particular, that there is no difference between Germans from the various German provinces. Fifty years ago there was a difference but now all German soldiers are alike. It is true that this does not apply to the Prussian officers.

Churchill: I should not like to be understood as not favouring the partition of Germany. But I wanted to say that if Germany is broken up into several parts without these parts being combined then, as Marshal Stalin said, the time will come when the Germans will unite.

Stalin: There are no steps that could exclude the possibility of Germany's unification.

Churchill: Does Marshal Stalin prefer a divided Europe?

Stalin: Europe has nothing to do with it. I don't know

that there is need to set up four, five or six independent German states. This question must be discussed.

Roosevelt: Should a special committee be set up to study the question of Germany, or should it be referred to the London Commission?

Stalin: This question could be referred to the London Commission, in which there are representatives of our three states.

Churchill: I should now like to return to the Polish question, which appears to me to be more urgent because the Poles can make a great deal of noise. I should like to read out my following proposals on the Polish question. I am not asking you to agree with it in the form in which I have drawn it up, because I have not yet taken a final decision myself.

My proposal says:

"It was agreed in principle that the hearth of the Polish state and people must be situated between the so-called Curzon Line and the line of the Oder River, including Eastern Prussia and the Oppeln Province as part of Poland. But the final drawing of the boundary line requires thorough study and possible resettlement in some points."

Stalin: The Russians have no ice-free ports on the Baltic. That is why the Russians would need the ice-free ports of Königsberg and Memel and the corresponding part of the territory of Eastern Prussia, particularly since these are age-old Slav lands. If the British agree to the transfer of the said territory to us, we shall agree to the formula proposed by Churchill.

Churchill: This is a very interesting proposal which I will make a point of studying.

COMMUNIQUÉ ON THE CONFERENCE OF THE HEADS OF GOVERNMENT OF THE ALLIED COUNTRIES— THE U.S.S.R., THE UNITED STATES AND GREAT BRITAIN— HELD IN TEHRAN

The Conference of the Heads of Government of the three Allied Powers was held in Tehran from November 28 to December 1. J. V. Stalin, Chairman of the Council of People's Commissars of the U.S.S.R., F. D. Roosevelt, President of the United States of America and W. Churchill, Prime Minister of Great Britain, took part in its work.

The Conference adopted the Declaration on the joint action in the war against Germany and the post-war co-operation of the three Powers and also the Declaration Regarding Iran. The texts are published below.

DECLARATION OF THE THREE POWERS

We—the President of the United States, the Prime Minister of Great Britain, and the Premier of the Soviet Union, have met these four days past, in this, the capital of our Ally, Iran, and have shaped and confirmed our common policy.

We express our determination that our nations shall work together in war and in the peace that will follow.

As to war—our military staffs have joined in our round table discussions, and we have concerted our plans for the destruction of the German forces. We have reached complete agreement as to the scope and timing of the operations to be undertaken from the east, west and south.

The common understanding which we have here reached guarantees that victory will be ours.

And as to peace—we are sure that our concord will win an enduring peace. We recognise fully the supreme responsibility resting upon us and all the United Nations to make a peace which will command the good will of the overwhelming mass of the peoples of the world and banish the scourge and terror of war for many generations.

With our diplomatic advisers we have surveyed the problems of the future. We shall seek the co-operation and active participation of all nations, large and small, whose peoples in heart and mind are dedicated, as are our own peoples, to the elimination of tyranny and slavery, oppression and intolerance. We will welcome them, as they may choose to come, into a world family of democratic nations.

No power on earth can prevent our destroying the German armies by land, their U-Boats by sea, and their war plants from the air.

Our attack will be relentless and increasing.

Emerging from these cordial conferences we look with confidence to the day when all peoples of the world may live free lives, untouched by tyranny, and according to their varying desires and their own consciences.

We came here with hope and determination. We leave here, friends in fact, in spirit and in purpose.

Signed in Tehran
on December 1, 1943

ROOSEVELT, STALIN, CHURCHILL

DECLARATION REGARDING IRAN

The President of the United States of America, the Premier of the Union of Soviet Socialist Republics, and the Prime Minister of the United Kingdom, having consulted with each other and with the Prime Minister of Iran, desire to declare the mutual agreement of their three Governments regarding their relations with Iran.

The Governments of the United States of America, the Union of Soviet Socialist Republics and the United Kingdom recognise the assistance which Iran has given in the prosecution of the war against the common enemy, particularly by facilitating transportation of supplies from overseas to the Soviet Union.

The three Governments realise that the war has caused special economic difficulties for Iran and they are agreed that they will continue to make available to the Government of Iran such economic assistance as may be possible, having regard to the heavy demands made upon them by their world-wide military operations and to the world-wide shortage of transport, raw materials and supplies for civilian consumption.

With respect to the post-war period, the Governments of the United States of America, the Union of Soviet Socialist Republics and the United Kingdom are in accord with the Government of Iran that any economic problem confronting Iran at the close of hostilities should receive full consideration along with those of the other members of the United Nations by conferences or international agencies held or created to deal with international economic matters.

The Governments of the United States of America, the Union of Soviet Socialist Republics and the United Kingdom are at one with the Government of Iran in their desire for the maintenance of the independence, sovereignty and territorial integrity of Iran. They count upon the participation of Iran together with all other peace-loving nations in the establishment of international peace, security and prosperity after the war in accordance with the principles of the Atlantic Charter, to which all four Governments have subscribed.

December 1, 1943

CHURCHILL, STALIN, ROOSEVELT

THE CRIMEA CONFERENCE

(February 4-11, 1945)

First Sitting at Livadia Palace

February 4, 1945

Stalin asked Roosevelt to open the sitting.

Roosevelt said that neither law nor history envisaged that he should open conferences. It was pure chance that he had opened the Conference at Tehran. He, Roosevelt, considered it a great honour to open the present Conference. He would like to start by expressing his gratitude for the hospitality accorded him.

The leaders of the three Powers, said Roosevelt, already understood each other well and their mutual understanding was growing. They all wanted an early end of the war and stable peace. That was why the participants in the Conference were able to start their unofficial talks. He, Roosevelt, believed the talks should be frank. Experience showed that frankness in talks made for an early achievement of good decisions. The participants in the Conference would have the maps of Europe, Asia and Africa before them. The day's sitting, however, was to be devoted to the situation on the Eastern front, where the troops of the Red Army had been advancing with such success. He, Roosevelt, asked someone to report on the situation at the Soviet-German front.

Stalin replied that he could offer a report by Army General Antonov, Deputy Chief of the General Staff of the Red Army.

Antonov: "1. On January 12-15, the Soviet forces went over to the offensive on a 700-kilometre front between the Niemen River and the Carpathians.

"General Chernyakhovsky's troops were advancing on Königsberg.

"Marshal Rokossovsky's troops were advancing along the northern bank of the Vistula, cutting off East Prussia from Germany's central areas.

"Marshal Zhukov's troops were advancing south of the Vistula towards Poznań.

"Marshal Konev's troops were advancing on Czestochowa and Breslau.

"General Petrov's troops were advancing on Nowy Targ in the area of the Carpathians.

"The main blow was struck by the forces under Rokossovsky, Zhukov and Konev on a 300-kilometre front between Ostroleka and Kraków.

"2. Because of the unfavourable weather conditions, the operation had been planned for the end of January, when an improvement in the weather had been expected.

"Since the operation had been regarded and prepared as one with decisive aims, the intention had been to conduct it in more favourable conditions.

"However, in view of the alarming situation that had developed on the Western front, in connection with the German offensive in the Ardennes, the High Command of the Soviet forces ordered the offensive to be started not later than mid-January, without waiting for the weather to improve.

"3. When the Soviet forces reached the Narew and the Vistula, the enemy grouping was most solid in the central sector of the front, because a strike from that sector would take our troops to Germany's vital centres along the shortest route.

"In order to create the most advantageous conditions for the offensive, the Soviet High Command decided to thin out this central grouping of the enemy.

"With that end in view, it conducted a supporting operation against East Prussia and continued the offensive in Hungary in the direction of Budapest.

"Both these directions were highly sensitive for the Germans, and they quickly reacted to our offensive by moving some forces from the central sector of the front to the flanks; thus, of the 24 tank divisions on our front, which constituted the Germans' main striking force, 11 tank divisions were moved to the Budapest direction, and 6 tank divisions, to East Prussia (3 tank divisions were in Kurland), thus leaving only 4 tank divisions in the central sector of the front.

"The objective set by the High Command has been attained.

"4. The balance of forces in the direction of the main attack:

"On the front between Ostroleka and Kraków, that is, the direction of our main attack, the enemy had up to 80 divisions; we created a grouping with a view to obtaining the following superiority over the enemy:

"Infantry—more than double (up to 180 divisions).

"Artillery, tanks and aviation—overwhelming.

"In the break-through sectors, the artillery density created was 220-230 pieces (from 76 mm and greater) per kilometre of front.

"5. The offensive was started in highly unfavourable weather conditions (low clouds and fog), which absolutely ruled out air force operations and limited artillery observation to a hundred metres.

"Thanks to the good preliminary reconnaissance and powerful artillery offensive, the enemy's fire system was suppressed and his fortifications destroyed. This enabled our troops to advance 10-15 kilometres on the first day of the offensive, that is, to break through the whole tactical depth of the enemy's defences.

"6. Results of the offensive:

"(a) By February 1, that is, in 18 days of the offensive, the Soviet forces had advanced up to 500 kilometres in the direction of the main attack, averaging 25-30 kilometres a day.

"(b) The Soviet forces have reached the Oder in the sector from Küstrin (north of Frankfort) and to the south, and occupied the Silesian industrial area.

"(c) The main routes linking the enemy's East Prussian grouping with the central areas of Germany have been cut.

"Thus, in addition to the Kurland grouping (26 divisions), the enemy's grouping in East Prussia has been isolated (up to 27 divisions); a number of isolated groupings of Germans (in the area of Lódž, Thorn, Poznań, Schneidemühl, etc., a total of up to 15 divisions) have been encircled and are being destroyed.

"(d) Permanent-type defence positions of the Germans in East Prussia—in the Königsberg and Letzen directions—have been broken through.

"(e) Forty-five German divisions have been routed, with the enemy suffering the following losses:

about 100,000 prisoners
about 300,000 dead

a total of up to 400,000 men

"7. The enemy's probable operations:

"(a) The Germans will defend Berlin, for which purpose they will try to hold back the advance of the Soviet forces on the Oder line, organising defence there with the help of retreating troops and reserves transferred from Germany, Western Europe and Italy.

"The enemy will try to use his Kurland grouping for the defence of Pomerania, transporting it by sea beyond the Vistula.

"(b) The Germans will cover the Vienna direction as solidly as possible, reinforcing it up with troops operating in Italy.

"8. Movement of enemy troops:

"(a) The following have already made their appearance on our front:

9 divisions from the central areas of Germany
6 divisions from the West European front
1 division from Italy
_____
16 divisions

"(b) On the way:
4 tank divisions
1 motorised division
_____
5 divisions

"(c) Up to 30-35 divisions more will probably be moved (from the West European front, Norway and Italy, and reserves in Germany).

"Thus, an additional 35-40 divisions may appear on our front.

"9. Our wishes:

"(a) Speed up the offensive by the Allied forces on the Western front, for which the situation now is very favourable, namely:

"(1) Defeat of the Germans on the Eastern front;

"(2) Defeat of the German grouping which had attacked in the Ardennes;

"(3) Weakening of the German forces in the West in view of the transfer of their reserves to the East.

"It is desirable that an offensive should be started in the first half of February.

"(b) Prevent the enemy from transferring his forces to the East from the Western front, Norway and Italy, by air strikes against his communications; in particular, paralyse the Berlin and Leipzig junctions.

"(c) Prevent the enemy from withdrawing his forces from Italy."

[*The written text of Antonov's report was handed to Roosevelt and Churchill.*]

Stalin asked whether there were any questions.

Roosevelt said he would like to know what the Soviet Government intended to do with the German locomotives, rolling stock and railways. He asked whether the Soviet Government intended to widen the gauge of the German railways.

Antonov replied that since the locomotives and the rolling stock abandoned by the Germans were of little use, the gauge of the German railways would have to be altered in several key directions.

Roosevelt stated that, in his opinion, it would be well for the Allied staffs to jointly discuss this question as the Allied forces were rapidly approaching each other.

Antonov said the Soviet command was altering the gauge on a minimum number of directions needed to ensure the supply of the Soviet forces.

Stalin said the bulk of the railways remained unaltered. The Soviet command had been changing the gauge of the railways none too eagerly.

Churchill declared that he had several questions to ask. He believed there were a number of questions which it would be expedient for the three staffs to discuss. For example, the question of time. It should be determined how much time the Germans would need to transfer eight divisions from Italy to the Soviet front. What should be done to prevent such a transfer? Should not a part of the Allied forces be transferred through the Ljubljana corridor to join up with the Red Army? It would also be necessary to determine the time that would take, and whether it might not be too late to do it.

He, Churchill, had indicated only one of the questions which could be discussed by the staffs. He proposed that General Marshall should make a report on the operations at the Western front whose conduct would be of assistance to the Soviet armies.

Roosevelt agreed with the Prime Minister. He said the Allies had been fighting at a great distance from each other. Germany had shrunk, and that was why closer contact between the staffs of the three countries was of special importance.

Stalin said that was right.

General Marshall declared that the consequences of the German offensive in the Ardennes had been eliminated. In the previous few weeks, General Eisenhower had regrouped his divisions. At the same time, General Eisenhower had continued to exercise pressure on the enemy in the area of the German counter-offensive. As a result of the operations he had conducted, General Eisenhower had discovered that the Germans had rather big forces in the Ardennes. That was why General Eisenhower had begun to concentrate his forces in the north.

In the southern sector of the front, i.e., to the north of Switzerland, the objective of the planned operation was to throw back the Germans into the area of Mühlhausen and Colmar. The objective of the operations being conducted to the north of Strasbourg was to liquidate the bridgehead on the left bank of the Rhine. At the time, the 25th Army group and the U.S. 9th Army, which were under the command of Montgomery, were preparing for an offensive in the northern sector. The U.S. 9th Army would attack in the northeastern direction.

The Allied command hoped to start the first of these operations on February 8. The second operation was to start in a week or possibly somewhat earlier. The Allies expected the Germans to retreat to Düsseldorf, after which the Allied troops would move on to Berlin. As many forces were to be moved into this offensive as allowed by the supply facilities. Paratroops would be used. The crossing of the Rhine in the north was expected to be possible in early March. In the north, there were three suitable places for forcing the Rhine.

For a certain time, the operations on the Western front had developed slowly because of the lack of tonnage. Then, following the opening of Antwerp, things were livening up, and the Allies were able to bring in from 70,000 to 80,000 tons of dry cargo a day, and 12,000 tons of liquid fuel. The Germans were trying to hamper the Allied supply and continued to bombard Antwerp with flying bombs. Information received that day showed that 60 flying bombs and 6 rockets had fallen in the Antwerp area in the previous 24 hours.

Stalin said bombs and rockets rarely hit the target.

Marshall remarked that there was always the possibility of bombs hitting vessels in the port.

He stated that the Allied air force had always been active when the weather permitted. Great destruction had been inflicted by fighters and light and heavy bombers. Information received that day indicated that troop trains on their way to the Soviet-German front had been attacked from the air. Great destruction had been done on the railways north of Strasbourg. Heavy bombers had attacked mainly plants producing fuel to deprive Germany of the possibility of supplying her tanks with fuel. Fuel production in Germany had fallen by 60 per cent. The air force had also been raiding communication lines. Tank works had been heavily raided.

As for the situation in Italy and to the south of Switzerland, he, Marshall, had the following to report. To the south of Switzerland, Germany had one or two divisions, and in Italy, 27 divisions. In Italy, the Allies had a force equal to that of the Germans. In addition, the Allies had an air force in Italy which was destroying the Germans' rolling stock, railways and bridges.

The Germans, Marshall declared, would probably soon resume their submarine offensive because they had produced an improved submarine. The Germans had at the time about 30 submarines at their disposal. Despite the small number of submarines, they could present a serious threat to Allied shipping because the devices developed by the Allies were unable to detect submarines of the improved type. That was why the operations of heavy bombers were directed against the shipyards where submarines were being built. The bomber operations had not detracted from the air force strikes against Germany's industry, in particular, plants making fuel.

Churchill said he would like to hear Field-Marshal Brooke and Admiral Cunningham. The speed of the Soviet advance was at the time highly important, because Danzig was one of the places where many submarines were concentrated.

Stalin asked where else submarines were concentrated.

Churchill replied that it was at Kiel and Hamburg.

Brooke stated that, in his opinion, the Allied plans and operations on the Western front had been given a full exposition.

Churchill said that before the participants in the Conference passed on to other, non-military, questions, he would like to mention one matter relating to the forcing of rivers. The Allies had a special centre for the study of forced river crossings. The officer in command of that centre was then in Yalta. Churchill said they would be grateful if the officer could contact the Soviet military for the purpose of obtaining information on the forcing of rivers. The Russians were known to have great experience, especially in the forcing of ice-bound rivers.

Stalin said he had a number of questions to ask. He would like to know the length of the front on which the break-through was to be made.

Marshall replied that the break-through was to be made on a front between 50 and 60 miles long.

Stalin asked whether the Germans had any fortifications on the front where the break-through was being planned.

Marshall replied that the Germans had built heavy-type fortifications in that sector of the front.

Stalin asked whether the Allies would have the reserves to exploit the success.

Marshall replied in the affirmative.

Stalin said he had asked the question because the Soviet command was aware of the great importance of reserves. That had become especially clear during the winter campaign. He would like to ask how many tank divisions the Allies had concentrated in the sector of the planned break-through. During the winter break-through, the Soviet command had concentrated about 9,000 tanks in the central sector of the front.

Marshall replied that he did not know that, but there would be one tank division for three infantry divisions, i.e., about 10-12 tank divisions for 35 divisions.

Stalin asked how many tanks there were in an Allied division.

Marshall replied: 300 tanks.

Churchill noted that on the entire West European theatre the Allies had 10,000 tanks.

Stalin said that was a great deal. On the front of the main attack the Soviet command had concentrated between 8,000 and 9,000 planes. He asked how many planes the Allies had.

Portal replied that the Allies had nearly as many planes, including 4,000 bombers, each of which was capable of carrying a bomb-load of from 3 to 5 tons.

Stalin asked what superiority the Allies had in infantry. On the front of the main attack the Soviet command had a superiority in infantry of 100 divisions to the Germans' 80.

Churchill declared that the Allies had never had any great superiority in infantry, but the Allies had at times had very great superiority in the air.

Stalin said the Soviet command had great superiority in artillery. He asked whether the Allies were interested to learn how Soviet artillery operated. Stalin said that the Soviet people, being the Allies' comrades-in-arms, could exchange experience with them. A year before, the Soviet command had established a special break-through artillery force. It had produced good results. An artillery division had from 300 to 400 guns. For example, on a front of 35-40 kilometres Marshal Konev had had six artillery break-through divisions supplemented with corps artillery. As a result, there had been almost 230 guns per kilometre of the break-through. After an artillery barrage, many Germans had been killed, others had been stunned and could not come to for a long time. That had opened the gates for the Red Army. From then on the advance had not been difficult.

He, Stalin, was sorry to have taken up time in relating the above. Stalin said he had expressed the wishes in respect of how the Allied armies could help the Soviet forces. He would like to know what wishes the Allies had in respect of the Soviet forces.

Churchill stated that he would like to take the opportunity to express his profound admiration for the might the Red Army had demonstrated in its offensive.

Stalin said that was not a wish.

Churchill declared that the Allies were aware of the difficulty of their task and did not minimise it. But the Allies were confident they would cope with their task. All the Allied commanders were confident of that. Although the attack was to be made against the Germans' strongest point, the Allies were sure that it would be a success and would be of benefit to the operations of the Soviet forces. As for any wishes, the Allies wanted the offensive of the Soviet armies to continue just as successfully.

Roosevelt declared that he was in agreement with Churchill.

Stalin said the Red Army's offensive, for which Churchill had expressed his gratitude, was in fulfilment of a comradely duty. According to the decisions adopted at the Tehran Conference, the Soviet Government had been under no obligation to launch a winter offensive.

The President had asked him whether he, Stalin, could receive a representative of General Eisenhower. He, Stalin, had naturally given his consent. Churchill had sent him a message, asking him whether he, Stalin, was planning to start an offensive in January. He, Stalin, had realised that neither Churchill nor Roosevelt were asking him outright for an offensive; he had appreciated this tact on the part of the Allies, but he had seen that such an offensive had been necessary for the Allies. The Soviet command had started its offensive even before the planned date. The Soviet Government had considered that to be its duty, the duty of an ally, although it was under no formal obligation on this score. He, Stalin, would like the leaders of the Allied Powers to take into account that Soviet leaders did not merely fulfil their obligations but were also prepared to fulfil their moral duty as far as possible.

As for the wishes, he asked about them because Tedder had expressed the wish that the Soviet forces should not stop their offensive until the end of March. He, Stalin, understood this to be possibly the wish not only of Tedder, but also of other Allied military leaders. Stalin said that the Soviet forces would continue their offensive, if the weather permitted and the roads were passable.

Roosevelt stated that he was in complete agreement with the opinion of Marshal Stalin. At the conference in Tehran it had been impossible to draw up a common plan of operations. He, Roosevelt, took it that each Ally was morally bound to advance with the utmost possible speed. At the time of the Tehran Conference there had been a great distance between the Allied forces moving from the East and the West. But the time had come when it was necessary to co-ordinate more thoroughly the operations of the Allied forces.

Churchill declared that he welcomed the words of Marshal Stalin. He, Churchill, believed he could say the following on behalf of the President and himself. The reason why the Allies had not concluded at Tehran any agreement with the Soviet Union on future operations, was their confidence in the Soviet people and its military.

Roosevelt replied that the Tehran Conference had been held before his re-election. It had been still unknown whether or not the American people would be on his side. That was why it had been hard to draw up any common military plan.

Churchill said the question raised by Tedder in his talk with Marshal Stalin could subsequently be discussed by the Allied staffs. Churchill said that the three leaders could, of course, be criticised for failing to co-ordinate the Allied offensives. If the weather hampered the operations of the Soviet forces, perhaps the Allies would then attack on their front. But that question must be decided by the staffs.

Stalin said there was lack of co-ordination. The Soviet forces had stopped their offensive in the autumn. Just then the Allies started their offensive. At the time, it was the other way round. In future, that should be avoided. Stalin asked whether it was expedient for the Allied military to discuss plans for summer operations.

Churchill said that might possibly have to be done. The Allied military could deal with the military questions while the leaders dealt with the political ones.

Stalin replied that that was right.

Cunningham said that he would like to supplement General Marshall's report. The threat of a fresh outbreak of submarine warfare on the part of the Germans was potential rather than actual. The Germans had achieved great success in improving their submarines. But that was not so important. What was important was that the Germans were already building new-type submarines. The submarines would be fitted out with the latest technical devices, and would have a great speed under water. The naval forces would, therefore, find it very hard to fight them. The German submarines were being built at Bremen, Hamburg and Danzig. If he, Cunningham, could express one wish, it was that, as a representative of the naval department, he would like to ask the Soviet forces to take Danzig as soon as possible, because 30 per cent of submarine construction was concentrated there.

Roosevelt asked whether Danzig was within the range of Soviet artillery.

Stalin replied that Danzig was not yet within the range of Soviet artillery. The Soviet command hoped soon to approach Danzig to within the range of artillery fire.

Churchill said the military could meet the next morning.

Stalin said he was in agreement with that. He proposed that the meeting be set for 12 o'clock.

Churchill declared that at the meeting the military should discuss not only the situation on the Eastern and Western fronts, but also on the Italian front, and also the question how best to use the available forces. He, Churchill, also proposed that a meeting be fixed for the next day to discuss political questions, namely, the future of Germany, if she had any.

Stalin replied that Germany would have a future.

Second Sitting at Livadia Palace

February 5, 1945

Roosevelt stated that the sitting would be devoted to political affairs. Questions pertaining to Germany ought to be selected. The questions of a world character—such as those of Dakar and Indochina—could be postponed. One of the questions that had already come up before the Allied Governments was that of occupation zones. It was a matter not of permanent but of temporary occupation. The question was becoming more and more urgent.

Stalin said that he would like the sitting to discuss the following questions. First, the proposals to dismember Germany.[1] There had been an exchange of opinion on the point at Tehran, and then between him, Stalin, and Churchill, in Moscow in October 1944. No decisions had been adopted either in Tehran or Moscow. Some opinion should be arrived at on the question at the Conference.

There was also another question relating to Germany: should Germany be allowed any central government, or should the Allies confine themselves to the establishment of an administration in Germany or, if it was decided, after all, to dismember Germany, should several governments be established there, depending on the number of parts into which Germany would be split up? These points had to be cleared up.

---

[1] Proposals on the dismemberment of Germany were first submitted at meetings of the heads of the Three Powers by the United States and Britain at the Tehran Conference.—*Ed.*

The third question related to unconditional surrender. They all stood on the basis of the unconditional surrender of Germany. But he, Stalin, would like to know whether or not the Allies would leave the Hitler Government in power if it surrendered unconditionally. The one excluded the other. But if that was so, as much should be said. The Allies had the experience of the surrender of Italy, but there they had had the concrete demands which constituted the content of the unconditional surrender. Weren't the three Allies going to determine the concrete content of the unconditional surrender of Germany? That question too should be cleared up.

Finally, there was the question of reparations, Germany's compensation for losses, and the question of the amount of the indemnity.

He, Stalin, raised all those questions in addition to the questions put forward by the President.

Roosevelt declared that, as he saw it, the questions raised by Marshal Stalin referred to a permanent state of affairs. However, they flowed from the question of occupation zones in Germany. The zones might prove to be the first step in the dismemberment of Germany.

Stalin declared that if the Allies intended to dismember Germany they should say so. There had been two exchanges of opinion between the Allies on the dismemberment of Germany after her military defeat. The first time at Tehran, when the President had proposed that Germany should be divided into five parts. At Tehran the Prime Minister too had stood for a dismemberment of Germany, although he had hesitated. But that had been only an exchange of opinion.

The second time the question of Germany's dismemberment had been discussed between him, Stalin, and the Prime Minister in Moscow the previous October. Under discussion had been the British plan for the division of Germany into two states: Prussia with her provinces and Bavaria, with the Ruhr and Westphalia being placed under international control. But no decision had been taken in Moscow, nor had it been possible to take one, because the President had not been present in Moscow.

Churchill declared that he agreed in principle to the dismemberment of Germany, but the method of demarcating the frontiers of the separate parts of Germany was too complicated for the question to be settled there in a matter of five or six days. It would take a very thorough study of the historical, ethnic and economic factors, and weeks of discussions of the question in a subcommittee or committee which would be set up for a detailed elaboration of the proposals and submission of recommendations in respect of the mode of action. The talks the heads of the three Governments had had on the question at Tehran, and the subsequent unofficial talks he, Churchill, had had with Marshal Stalin in Moscow, had been a most general approach to the question, without any precise plan.

He, Churchill, would be unable to give an immediate answer to the question as to how to divide Germany. He could merely hint at what he thought would be the most expedient way of doing it. But he, Churchill, would have to reserve the right to modify his opinion when he received the recommendations of commissions studying the matter. He, Churchill, had in mind the strength of Prussia, the tap-root of all evil. It was quite understandable that if Prussia were separated from Germany, her capability for starting a new war would be greatly restricted. He personally believed that the establishment of another big German state in the south, with a capital at Vienna, would provide a dividing line between Prussia and the rest of Germany. The population of Germany would be equally divided between those two states.

There were other questions which had to be examined. First of all, they agreed that Germany should lose a part of the territory most of which had already been captured by the Russian forces, and which should be given to the Poles. There were also questions relating to the Rhine valley, the frontier between France and Germany, and the question of possession of the industrial areas of the Ruhr and the Saar, which had a war potential (in the sense of a possible manufacture of weapons there). Were the areas to be handed over to countries, such as France, or were they to be left under a German administration, or was control over them to be set up by a world organisation in the form of a condominium over a long but specified period? All that required examination. He, Churchill, had to say he was unable to express any definite ideas on the question on behalf of his Government. The British Government must co-ordinate its plans with those of the Allies.

5*

Finally, there was the question of whether Prussia was to be subjected to an internal fragmentation after she was isolated from the rest of Germany. Talks on the matter had been held at Tehran. It appeared that one question could be decided very swiftly, namely, the establishment of an apparatus to examine all the questions. Such an apparatus would have to submit reports to the Governments before the Governments took any final decisions.

He, Churchill, would like to say that the Allies were rather well prepared to accept an immediate surrender of Germany. All the details of such a surrender had been worked out and were known to the three Governments. There remained the question of reaching official agreement on the zones of occupation and on the control machinery in Germany. Assuming that Germany would surrender within a month, or six weeks, or six months, the Allies would only have to occupy Germany by zones.

Stalin said that was not clear. Some group, like Badoglio in Italy, might say it had overthrown the Government. Would the Allies be prepared to deal with such a government?

Eden said the group would be presented with the terms of surrender which had been agreed upon by the European Advisory Commission.

Churchill stated that he would like to project the possible course of events. Germany was no longer able to wage the war. He proposed to assume that Hitler or Himmler made a proposal of surrender. It was clear that the Allies would tell them that they would not negotiate with them because they were war criminals. If they were the only men in Germany, the Allies would continue the war. It was more probable that Hitler would try to hide or would be killed as a result of a coup in Germany, and another government would be set up there which would propose surrender. In that case, the Allies must immediately consult with each other on whether or not they could talk with those men in Germany. If they decided that they could, those men should be told the terms of surrender. Should the Allies decide that that group of men was unfit to negotiate with, they would continue the war and occupy the whole country. If those new men made their appearance and signed an unconditional surrender on the terms dictated to them, there would be no need to tell them of their future. Unconditional surrender would give the Allies the opportunity to present additional demands to the Germans on the dismemberment of Germany.

Stalin declared that the demand for dismemberment was not an additional, but a highly essential one.

Churchill said it was, of course, an important demand. But he, Churchill, did not believe it must be presented to the Germans at the first stage. The Allies should come to a precise agreement on this point.

Stalin said that that was why he had raised the question.

Churchill said that although the Allies could study the question of dismemberment, he did not think it would be possible to reach a precise agreement on it just then. The matter required study. In his, Churchill's, opinion, that kind of question was more suitable for examination at a peace conference.

Roosevelt declared that it seemed to him Marshal Stalin had not received an answer to his question of whether or not they were going to dismember Germany. He, Roosevelt, believed that the question should be decided in principle, and the details could be left for the future.

Stalin remarked that that was right.

Roosevelt continued that the Prime Minister had said that at the time it was impossible to determine the frontiers of the separate parts of Germany and that the whole question required study. That was right. But the most important thing was still to decide at the Conference the main question whether or not the Allies agreed to dismember Germany. Roosevelt believed it would be well to present the Germans with the terms of surrender and, in addition, to tell them that Germany was to be dismembered. At Tehran, Roosevelt had spoken in favour of a decentralised administration in Germany. During his stay in Germany 40 years before, decentralised administration had still been a fact: Bavaria or Hessen had had a Bavarian or Hessen Government. They had been real Governments. The word "Reich" had not yet existed. But over the previous 20 years, the decentralised administration had been gradually abolished. The whole of the administration had been concentrated at Berlin. It was utopian to talk of plans for a decentralised Germany. That was why, under the conditions, Roosevelt saw no other way out except dismemberment. How many parts were there to be? Six, seven or less? He would not venture to say anything definite on the score. The question had to be studied. But there, in the Crimea, agreement should be reached on whether the Allies were going to tell the Germans that Germany was to be dismembered.

Churchill stated that, in his opinion, there was no need to inform the Germans of the future policy to be conducted in respect of their country. The Germans should be told they would have to await further Allied demands after they surrendered. These further demands would be made on the Germans by mutual agreement between the Allies. As for dismemberment, he, Churchill, believed that such a decision could not be adopted in a matter of a few days. The Allies were dealing with an 80-million people and it would certainly take more than 30 minutes to settle the question of their future. A commission might take a month to work out the question in detail.

Roosevelt said that the Premier introduced the time factor into the question. If the question of dismemberment were to be publicly debated, there would be hundreds of plans. That was why he, Roosevelt, proposed that within the next 24 hours the three Ministers of Foreign Affairs should draw up a plan of procedure to study the dismemberment of Germany and then a detailed plan for the dismemberment of Germany could be drawn up within 30 days.

Churchill declared that the British Government was prepared to accept the principle of Germany's dismemberment and to set up a commission to study the procedure of dismemberment.

Stalin said he had raised the question to clarify what the Allies wanted. Events would develop towards Germany's disaster. Germany was losing the war, and her defeat would be hastened as a result of an early Allied offensive. In addition to a military catastrophe, Germany might suffer an internal catastrophe, because she would have neither coal nor grain. Germany had already lost the Dabrowa coal basin, and the Ruhr would soon be under Allied gun fire. With events developing as rapidly as that, he, Stalin, would not like the Allies to be caught unawares. He had raised the question so that the Allies should be prepared for the events. He fully understood Churchill's considerations that it was hard to draw up a plan for the dismemberment of Germany at the time. That was correct. Nor did he propose that a concrete plan should be drawn up immediately. But the matter should be settled in principle and recorded in the terms of the unconditional surrender.

Churchill declared that an unconditional surrender precluded any armistice agreement. Unconditional surrender was the terms on which military operations were to be terminated. Those who signed the terms of an unconditional surrender submitted to the will of the victors.

Stalin said that terms of surrender were nonetheless signed.

Churchill replied in the affirmative and called attention to Article 12 of the terms of Germany's unconditional surrender worked out by the European Advisory Commission.

Roosevelt noted that the article said nothing at all about Germany's dismemberment.

Stalin said that that was right.

Churchill asked whether the terms of the armistice were to be published.

Stalin replied that the terms would not be made public for the time being, they existed for the Allies and would be presented to the German Government when the time came. The Allies would decide when they were to be made public. The Allies were doing the same thing with Italy, whose terms of surrender would be made public when they deemed it necessary.

Roosevelt asked whether the Germans would be given a government or an administration by the Allies. If Germany was dismembered, each of her parts would have an administration subordinate to the corresponding Allied command.

Churchill said that he did not know that. He, Churchill, found it hard to go beyond the statement made that the British Government was prepared to accept the principle of Germany's dismemberment and the establishment of a commission to work out a plan of dismemberment.

Roosevelt asked whether Churchill was prepared to supplement Article 12 with words about the dismemberment of Germany.

Churchill replied that he was prepared to have the three Ministers of Foreign Affairs examine Article 12 for the purpose of determining the possibility of including the words "dismemberment of Germany" or some other formulation in the Article.

[*A decision was taken to instruct the Ministers of Foreign Affairs to examine the question.*]

Churchill said the question of a government in Germany could be discussed.

Stalin stated that he preferred to discuss the question of reparations.

Roosevelt agreed and said there were two sides to the reparations question. First, the small countries, like Denmark, Norway and Holland, would also want to receive reparations from Germany. Secondly, the question arose of making use of German manpower. He, Roosevelt, wanted to ask what quantity of German manpower the Soviet Union would like to have. As for the United States of America, it needed neither German machinery nor German manpower.

Stalin replied that the Soviet Government had a plan for material reparations. As for the use of German manpower, the Soviet Government was not yet prepared to discuss that question.

Churchill asked whether he could have some information about the Soviet reparations plan.

Stalin said he would let Maisky speak on the question.

Maisky stated that the material reparations plan was based on several key principles.

The first principle was that the reparations were to be received from Germany not in money, as had been the case after the previous world war, but in kind.

The second principle was that Germany was to make its payments in kind in two forms, namely, (a) lump withdrawals from Germany's national wealth, both on the territory of Germany proper and outside, at the end of the war (factories, machine tools, ships, rolling stock, investments in foreign enterprises, etc.), and (b) annual goods deliveries after the end of the war.

The third principle was in short that by way of reparations payments Germany was to be economically disarmed, as otherwise security in Europe could not be ensured. Concretely this meant the removal of 80 per cent of the equipment from Germany's heavy industry (steel, engineering, metalworking, electrical engineering, chemistry, etc.). Aircraft factories and plants producing synthetic fuel were to be removed 100 per cent. All specialised military enterprises (arms factories, munitions plants, etc.) which had existed before the war or had been built during the war, were equally to be removed 100 per cent. The Soviet Government believed that the 20 per cent of Germany's pre-war heavy industry which was to remain, would be quite sufficient to cover the country's actual economic requirements.

The fourth principle was that the reparations period was set at 10 years, with removals from national wealth to be made within two years after the end of the war.

The fifth principle was that for the purpose of precise fulfilment by Germany of her reparations obligations, and also in the interests of security in Europe, strict Anglo-Soviet-American control must be established over the German economy. The forms of control were to be worked out later. But in any case, provision was to be made that the industrial, transport and other enterprises remaining in Germany which constituted the greatest danger from the standpoint of a possible revival of Germany's war potential were to be internationalised, with the U.S.S.R., the U.S.A. and Great Britain participating in their administration. Control over the German economy was to be maintained after the expiry of the period of the reparations payments, i.e., after the first 10 years following the end of the war.

The sixth principle was that in view of the unprecedented immensity of the damage caused by the German aggression, it would be impossible to make it good fully even with the strictest exaction of reparations from Germany. The Soviet Government had tried to make a rough estimate of the scale of the damage—the figures obtained were quite astronomical. That was why the Soviet Government had arrived at the conclusion that if the Allies were to be realistic, only that type of damage should be subject to indemnification which could be characterised as direct material loss (destruction of or damage to houses, plants, railways, research institutions; confiscation of cattle, grain, private property of citizens, etc.). But since Soviet preliminary estimates, under the head of direct material losses alone, had yielded a total amount of damage in excess of the amount of possible reparations by way of direct removal and annual post-war deliveries, it would apparently be necessary to establish a certain *priority* in the receipt of compensation by countries which had the right to it. That priority was to be based on two indicators: (a) the size of the country's contribution to the victory over the enemy, and (b) the amount of direct material losses suffered by that country. Countries having the highest indicators under both heads were to receive reparations first, and the rest, later.

The seventh principle was that the U.S.S.R. considered it fair to receive at least $10,000 million in compensation for its direct material losses, through removals and annual deliveries. That was, of course, only a very insignificant portion of the total amount of direct material losses suffered by the Soviet Union, but in the circumstances the Soviet Government was ready to be satisfied with that figure.

Finally, the eighth principle was that a special Reparations Commission, consisting of representatives of the U.S.S.R., the U.S.A. and Great Britain should be set up, with headquarters in Moscow, to work out a detailed Allied reparations plan on the basis of the principles set forth above.

Such, in brief outline, was the material reparations plan which the Soviet Government placed before the Conference for discussion and approval.

Churchill said he well remembered the end of the previous war. Although he, Churchill, had not directly participated in framing the peace terms, he had access to all the conferences. The reparations had proved to be highly disappointing. Only £1,000 million had been with great effort got out of Germany. But even that amount would not have been obtained but for U.S. and British investments in Germany. Britain had taken from Germany a few old ocean liners, and with the money Germany got from Britain, she built herself a new fleet. He, Churchill, hoped that Britain would not face similar difficulties again.

Churchill had no doubt at all that Russia's sacrifices were greater than those of any other country. He had always believed that the removal of plants from Germany would be a correct step. But he was also quite sure it would be impossible to receive from a defeated and destroyed Germany the quantity of values which would compensate for the losses sustained by Russia alone. He doubted that £250 million a year could be extracted from Germany. At the end of the previous war, the British had also dreamed of astronomical figures—but what had been the result?

Great Britain had suffered very heavily in the current war. A great part of her houses had been destroyed or damaged. Britain had sold all her investments abroad. Britain had to export goods to import foodstuffs; she had to buy abroad half of the food she needed. Fighting for the common cause, Britain had run into heavy debt, apart from

Lend-Lease. Britain's total debt was £3,000 million. No other country among the victors would find herself in such a difficult economic and financial position at the end of the war as Great Britain. If he, Churchill, saw the possibility of maintaining the British economy through the exaction of reparations from Germany, he would resolutely take that way. But he was doubtful of success.

Other countries had also suffered great destruction. Holland was flooded. Norway had suffered heavily. True, their population was not big.

Moreover, what was going to happen to Germany? Churchill saw the spectre of a starving Germany with her 80 million population. Who was going to feed her? Who was going to pay for that? Wouldn't the Allies eventually have to cover a part of the reparations from their own pocket?

Stalin remarked that all those questions would certainly come up sooner or later.

Churchill said if one wanted to ride a horse one had to feed it with oats and hay.

Stalin replied that the horse should not charge at one.

Churchill admitted his metaphor was not very happy, and said that if one put a car in place of the horse one would still have to fill it up with petrol to use it.

Stalin replied that there was no analogy there. The Germans were men and not machines.

Churchill agreed with that too. Returning to the reparations, Churchill spoke in favour of setting up a Reparations Commission which would deliberate in secret.

Roosevelt declared that he, too, well remembered the previous war, and recalled that the United States had lost a great deal of money. It had loaned Germany more than $10,000 million, but it would not repeat its old mistakes. The United States had no intention of using German manpower. The United States did not want any German machine tools. At the end of the previous war, there had been many German assets and German property in the United States. All that had been returned to the Germans.

He, Roosevelt, believed that things would be different after the current war. A special law might have to be issued under which all German property in the United States would remain in American hands. Roosevelt agreed with Churchill that some thought should be given to Germany's future. But despite the generosity of the United States, which was helping other countries, the United States was unable to guarantee the future of Germany. The United States did not want German living standards to be higher than those in the U.S.S.R. The United States wanted to help the Soviet Union to obtain everything necessary from Germany. The Americans wanted to help the British to increase their exports and find new market outlets to replace Germany.

Roosevelt believed that the time was ripe to set up a Reparations Commission to study the needs of the U.S.S.R. and the other European countries. He agreed to have the Commission work in Moscow. Roosevelt very much hoped that everything destroyed in the Soviet Union could be made good. But he was also sure that it would be impossible to cover everything by reparations. Germany should be left with enough industry to keep the Germans from dying of starvation.

Churchill declared that he had no objections to the Reparations Commission being in Moscow.

Maisky said that he would like to reply briefly to Churchill and Roosevelt. In his remarks he intended to deal with three main points.

First, the question on which Churchill had dwelt specifically—the failure of reparations after the previous war. Indeed, that experience had proved to be extremely unsatisfactory. But why? The reason had not been that the total amount of reparations levied on Germany had been excessive. Actually, the amount had been very modest: $30,000 million spread over a period of 58 years. Was that a great deal? According to the state of her national wealth and national income, Germany could have very easily paid such a sum. The trouble had been, however, that the Allies had wanted Germany to pay reparations chiefly in money, and not in kind. Germany had had to find ways of obtaining the necessary amount of foreign exchange. That, for various reasons, had turned out to be a very difficult task. There would have been no complications at all if the Allies had been prepared to receive reparations in kind. But the Allies had not wanted that. As a result there had arisen an insoluble transfer problem, i.e., the conversion of German marks into pounds, dollars and francs, and that problem had killed the reparations after the previous war.

There was another factor which had greatly contributed to the failure of reparations after 1914-1918; it had been the policy of the United States, Britain and France. They had invested large amounts of capital in Germany, thereby encouraging the Germans not to fulfil their reparations obligations. Eventually, Germany has repaid, in the form of reparations, only about one-fourth of the amount the British, Americans and French had loaned Germany in the first years after the 1914-1918 war.

That was the root cause of the failure of the previous reparations. To avoid the difficulties of transfer, it was proposed that all reparations should be paid in kind. It was also hoped that the United States and Britain would not again finance Germany after the end of the war. [*Roosevelt and Churchill indicated by gestures and exclamations that they intended to do nothing of the sort.*] In the circumstances, there was no reason to draw pessimistic conclusions for the new reparations from the unfortunate experience of the old.

Secondly, Churchill had indicated that the reparations figure claimed by the U.S.S.R. would be excessive for Germany. That was hardly fair. In effect, what did the figure of $10,000 million represent? It constituted only 10 per cent of the Federal budget of the United States for 1944/45. [*Stettinius:* "Absolutely correct".] It was also equal to one and a quarter of the U.S. Federal peacetime budget (for example, in the period between 1936 and 1938). As to Britain, the same figure of $10,000 million was equal to no more than Great Britain's war spending over a period of six months, or two and a half times her national peacetime budget (1936-1938).

In that case, was it right to say that the Soviet Union's claims were excessive? It was not. Rather, they were much too modest. But that modesty sprang from the Soviet Government's desire to have no illusions and keep both feet on the ground.

Thirdly, Roosevelt and Churchill had stressed the need to prevent a famine in Germany. The Soviet Government had no intention at all of stripping and starving Germany. On the contrary, in working out its reparations plan, the Soviet Government had always had in mind the creation of conditions in which the German people in the post-war years could exist on the basis of the average European living standard, and the Soviet reparations plan ensured such a possibility. Germany had every chance of building her post-war economy on the basis of an expanding agriculture and light industries. There were all the conditions for it. The Soviet reparations plan provided no special restrictions in respect of the two branches of the German economy just named.

Furthermore, it should be borne in mind that post-war Germany would be entirely free from arms expenditure, because she would be completely disarmed. This would yield a great saving: after all, pre-war Germany had spent, in various forms, up to $6,000 million a year on armaments. [*Churchill* exclaims: "Yes, that is a very important consideration!"] That was why the Soviet Government was convinced that even if the Soviet reparations plan was implemented in full the German people would be ensured a decent life.

Both Churchill and Roosevelt could see from the above that the Soviet reparations plan was thoroughly conceived and based on quite sober and realistic calculations.

Churchill stated that in his opinion all these questions should be examined in commission.

Stalin asked where.

Churchill said a secret commission should be set up, and nothing of its deliberations should be made public.

Stalin replied that nothing would be published about the work of the commission. But the question was where Churchill wanted to set up such a commission. Was it at the Conference?

Churchill replied that there was no need for that at the time. The Conference should merely adopt a decision on the establishment of a Reparations Commission, which would subsequently examine the claims and the assets at Germany's disposal, and also establish the priority in their allocation. It would be desirable to fix the priority with an eye not only to a nation's contribution to the cause of victory, but also the suffering it had gone through. The U.S.S.R. headed the list, whatever the criterion. Any contradictions that might arise in the Commission should be settled by the Governments. As for the Russian reparations plan, it would take time to examine it. It could not be accepted at once.

Roosevelt said that the Reparations Commission should consist of representatives of the three Powers.

Churchill supported Roosevelt's proposal.

Stalin stated that the setting up of a Reparations Commission in Moscow, something all those present had accepted, was a very good thing. But that was not enough. Even the best of commissions could not do much unless it had the proper guide lines for its work. The guide lines should be laid down there, at the Conference.

He, Stalin, believed that the main principle underlying the allocation of reparations should be the following: the states which had borne the main burden of the war and organised the victory over the enemy should be the first to receive reparations. Those states were the U.S.S.R., the United States and Great Britain. Compensation must be received not only by the Russians, but also by the Americans and the British, and to the greatest possible extent. If the United States, as Roosevelt said, was not interested in obtaining machinery or manpower from Germany, other more suitable forms of reparations could be found, for example, raw materials, etc. At any rate, it should be firmly established that those who had made the greatest contribution to the enemy's defeat had a prior right to reparations. Stalin asked whether Roosevelt and Churchill agreed with that.

Roosevelt declared that he agreed.

Churchill did not object either.

Stalin then said that in estimating the assets available in Germany for the payment of reparations, it was not the obtaining situation that should be taken as a starting point but the resources Germany would have after the end of the war, when all her population returned home, and the factories started operating. Germany would then have more assets than she had at the time, and the states of which he had spoken could expect to have very considerable compensation for their damage. The three Ministers of Foreign Affairs would do well to discuss all that and then report to the Conference.

Churchill agreed that the Conference should indicate the main points of the directives for the Commission.

Stalin replied that he considered that to be correct.

Churchill said half in jest that if he seemed to be recalcitrant in discussing the question of reparations it was only because at home he had a Parliament and a Cabinet. If they refused to accept what Churchill had accepted at the Crimea Conference they might drive him out.

Stalin replied, in the same vein, that that was not so easy: victors were not driven out.

Churchill remarked that the three Ministers of Foreign Affairs could discuss the question of reparations the next day and later report to the Conference. He, Churchill, liked the principle: to each according to his needs, and from Germany according to her abilities. That principle should be made the basis of the reparations plan.

Stalin replied that he preferred another principle: to each according to his deserts.

Third Sitting at Livadia Palace

February 6, 1945

[. . .] *Roosevelt* declared that a discussion of the question of an international security organisation could be started that day. Roosevelt believed it was their task to ensure peace for at least 50 years. In view of the fact that neither he, Roosevelt, nor Marshal Stalin, nor Churchill, had been present at Dumbarton Oaks, it would be a good idea for Stettinius to report on the question.

Stettinius said that an agreement had been reached at Dumbarton Oaks to leave certain questions for further examination and future solution. Of those questions the principal one was that of the voting procedure to be applied in the Security Council. At Dumbarton Oaks, the three delegations had had a thorough discussion of that question. Since then it had been subjected to continued and intensive study on the part of each of the three Governments.

On December 5, 1944, the President had sent Marshal Stalin and Prime Minister Churchill a proposal to have the question decided by setting forth Section C of Chapter VI of the proposals, adopted at Dumbarton Oaks, in the following manner:

"C. Voting.

"1. Each member of the Security Council shall have one vote.

"2. Decisions of the Security Council on procedural matters shall be made by an affirmative vote of seven members.

"3. Decisions of the Security Council on all other matters shall be made by an affirmative vote of seven members including the concurring votes of the permanent members: provided that in decisions under Section A of Chapter VIII and under the second phrase of the first paragraph of Section C, Chapter VIII, a party to a dispute shall abstain from voting."

The text which he, Stettinius, had just read out, contained minor drafting amendments made in accordance with the Soviet and British remarks on the initial text proposed by the President.

The American proposal was in complete accord with the special responsibility of the Great Powers for the maintenance of universal peace. In effect, the American proposal demanded unqualified unanimity of the permanent members of the Council on all key issues relating to the maintenance of peace, including economic and military enforcement measures.

At the same time, the American proposal recognised the desirability of a direct declaration on the part of the permanent members that the pacific settlement of any dispute that might arise was a matter of general concern, a matter on which the sovereign states which were not permanent members had the right to set forth their views without any limitations whatsoever. Unless such freedom of discussion was ensured in the Council, the establishment of a world organisation, which they all wanted, might be seriously hampered or even made altogether impossible. Without the right of free and full discussion of such matters in the Council, an international security organisation, even if established, would differ greatly from what had been originally intended.

The document which the American delegation had presented to the two other delegations set forth the text of the provisions which he, Stettinius, had read out and a special list of decisions of the Council which, according to the American proposal, would demand unqualified unanimity, and a separate list of matters (in the sphere of disputes and their pacific settlement) on which a party to the dispute must abstain from voting.

From the standpoint of the Government of the United States, there were two important elements in the question of voting procedure.

The first was that for the maintenance of universal peace, which he, Stettinius, had mentioned, unanimity of the permanent members was needed.

The second was that for the people of the United States it was of exceptional importance that fair treatment for all the members of the Organisation be provided for.

The task was to reconcile those two main elements. The proposals made by the President to Marshal Stalin and Prime Minister Churchill on December 5, 1944, provided a reasonable and just solution and combined the two elements satisfactorily.

Roosevelt declared that in his opinion it would be well to have Stettinius list the types of decisions which were to be adopted in the Security Council on the unanimity principle.

Stettinius said that, according to the formula proposed by the President, the following decisions would require an affirmative vote of seven members of the Security Council, including the votes of all the permanent members:

(I) Recommendations to the General Assembly on:

1. Admission of new members;
2. Suspension of a member;
3. Expulsion of a member;
4. Election of the Secretary-General.

(II) Restoration of the rights and privileges of a suspended member.

(III) Elimination of a threat to the peace and suppression of breaches of the peace, including the following questions:

1. Is the peace endangered as a result of non-settlement of a dispute between the parties by means of their own choice or in accordance with the recommendations of the Security Council?
2. Is there a threat to the peace or breach of the peace from any other action on the part of one or another country?
3. What are the measures to be taken by the Council for the maintenance or restoration of the peace and how are these measures to be implemented?
4. Should not the implementation of enforcement measures be entrusted to a regional body?

(IV) Approval of special agreement or agreements on the provision of armed forces and facilities.

(V) Formulation of plans for a general system of arms regulation and presentation of such plans to the member states.

(VI) Decision on the question whether the nature and activity of a regional body or regional measures for the maintenance of peace and security are compatible with the aims and purposes of the world organisation.

An affirmative vote of seven members of the Security Council, including the votes of all the permanent members, provided, however, that a member of the Council abstained from voting on any decision relating to a dispute to which he was a party, should be required for the following decisions relating to the pacific settlement of a dispute:

(I) Is the dispute or situation brought to the notice of the Council of such a nature that its continuance may endanger the peace?

(II) Should the Council call upon the sides to settle or adjust the dispute or situation by means of their own choice?

(III) Should the Council give recommendations to the sides in respect of the methods and procedures of settlement?

(IV) Should the legal aspects of the matter before the Council be referred to the International Court of Justice for an advisory opinion?

(V) In the event there is a regional body for the pacific settlement of local disputes, should the body be requested to deal with the disputes?

Roosevelt believed the question could be discussed and settled. Big and small nations had one and the same purpose, namely, the preservation of peace, and procedural issues should not hamper the attainment of that aim.

Stalin asked what was new in the proposals set forth by Stettinius as compared with what the President had communicated in his message of December 5.

Roosevelt replied that those proposals were similar, with only minor drafting amendments.

Stalin asked what drafting amendments had been made.

Stettinius set forth these drafting amendments.

Molotov declared that the Soviet delegation also attached great importance to the questions raised and would like to study Stettinius's proposal. That was why he proposed that the discussion of the question be postponed until the next day's sitting.

Churchill remarked that he agreed with that. There should be no undue haste in the study of such an important matter. Its discussion could be postponed until the next day. He had not been quite satisfied with the initial proposals worked out at Dumbarton Oaks, because he had not been quite sure that those proposals had taken full account of the real position of the three Great Powers. After studying the President's new proposals, Churchill's doubts had disappeared, at any rate, as far as the British Commonwealth of Nations and the British Empire were concerned. That also applied to the independent dominions of the British Crown.

Churchill recognised that the question of whether the peace would be built on sound foundations depended on the friendship and co-operation of the three Great Powers; however, the Allies would be putting themselves in a false position and would be unfair to their intentions, if they did not provide for the possibility of the small states freely expressing their claims. Otherwise it would appear that the three chief Powers claimed to rule the world. As it was what they actually wanted was to serve the world and safeguard it from the horrors that had hit most of the nations in the current war. That was why the three Great Powers should show a readiness to submit to the interest of the common cause.

He, Churchill, was naturally thinking primarily of the effect the new situation would have on the future of the British Commonwealth of Nations. He would like to give a concrete example, an example which was a difficult one for Britain—Hong Kong. If the President's proposal was adopted, and China requested the return of Hong Kong, Great Britain would have the right to express her point of view and defend it; however, Great Britain would not be able to take part in voting on the five questions set out at the end of the American document. For her part, China would have the right fully to express her view on the question of Hong Kong, and the Security Council would have to decide on the issue, without the British Government taking part in the voting.

Stalin asked whether Egypt was to be a member of the Assembly.

Churchill replied that Egypt would be a member of the Assembly but not of the Council.

Stalin declared that he would like to take another example, that of the Suez Canal, which was situated on the territory of Egypt.

Churchill asked that his example be examined first. Assuming that the British Government could not agree to the examination of one of the questions dealt with in Paragraph 3, because it considered that the question infringed the sovereignty of the British Empire. In that case, the British Government would be assured of success, because, in accordance with Paragraph 3, every permanent member would have the right to veto the actions of the Security Council. On the other hand, it would be unfair for China not to have the possibility of expressing her view on the substance of the case.

The same applied to Egypt. In the event Egypt raised a question against the British pertaining to the Suez Canal, he, Churchill, would allow the discussion of the question without any apprehension, because British interests were ensured by Paragraph 3, which provided for the right of veto. He also believed that if Argentina made a claim against the United States, the United States would submit to the established procedure of examination, but the United States would have the right to object and veto any decision by the Security Council. It could apply the Monroe Doctrine.

Roosevelt said that in the Tehran Declaration the three Powers had announced their readiness to accept responsibility for the establishment of a peace that would receive the approval of the peoples of the world.

Churchill stated that for the reasons which he had set forth the British Government did not object to the adoption of the U.S. proposals. Churchill believed it would be undesirable to create the impression that the three Powers wanted to dominate the world, without letting the other countries express their opinion.

Stalin declared that he would first of all ask that the Soviet delegation be handed the document which Stettinius had read out, because it was hard to study the proposals it contained by ear. To him, Stalin, it seemed that the said document was a commentary on the President's proposals.

Referring to the interpretation of the American proposals made at the sitting, Stalin said it seemed to him the Dumbarton Oaks decisions had aimed to ensure various countries not only the right to voice their opinion. That right was not worth much. No one denied it. The matter was much more serious. If any nation raised a question of great importance to it, it would do so not only to have the opportunity to set out its view, but to obtain a decision on it. None of those present would dispute the right of nations to speak in the Assembly. But that was not the heart of the matter. Churchill apparently believed that if China raised the question of Hong Kong, her only desire would be to speak out. That was not so. China would demand a decision. In much the same way, if Egypt raised the question of a return of the Suez Canal she would not be content with voicing her opinion on the matter. Egypt would demand a solution of the question. That was why the question was not just of ensuring the possibility of voicing one's opinions, but of much more important things.

Churchill expressed the apprehension that there might be an impression that the three Great Powers wanted to dominate the world. But who was contemplating such domination? Was it the United States? No, it was not thinking of that. [*The President laughed and made an eloquent gesture.*] Was it Britain? No, once again. [*Churchill laughed and made an eloquent gesture.*] Thus, two Great Powers were beyond suspicion. That left the third—the U.S.S.R. So it was the U.S.S.R. that was striving for world domination? [*General laughter.*] Or could it be China that was striving for world domination? [*General laughter.*] It was clear that the talk of striving for world domination was pointless. His friend Churchill could not name a single Power that wanted to dominate the world.

Churchill interposed that he himself did not, of course, believe in the striving for world domination on the part of any of the three Allies. But the position of those Allies was so powerful that others might think so, unless the appropriate preventive measures were taken.

Stalin, continuing his speech, declared that so far two Great Powers had adopted the charter of an international security organisation, which, in the opinion of Churchill, would protect them from being charged with a desire to rule the world. The third Power had not yet given its consent to the charter. However, he would study the proposals formulated by Stettinius, and would possibly see the point more clearly. He believed, however, that the Allies were faced with much more serious problems than the right of nations to express their opinion or the question of the three chief Powers striving for world domination.

Churchill said there was no reason to fear anything undesirable even in the event of the American proposals being adopted. Indeed, so long as they were all alive, there was nothing to fear. They would not allow any dangerous divergences between them. They would not permit another aggression against anyone of their countries. But 10 years or possibly less might pass, and they would be gone. There would be a new generation which had not gone through what they had, and which would possibly view many questions in a different light. What would happen then? They seemed to be setting themselves the task of ensuring peace for at least another 50 years. Or was that the impression he, Stalin, had got because of his naïveté?

The unity of the three Powers was the most important requisite for the preservation of a lasting peace. If such unity was preserved, there was no need to fear the German danger. Thought should, therefore, be given to how best to ensure a united front between the three Powers, to which France and China should be added. That was why the question of the future charter of an international security organisation acquired such importance. It was necessary to create as many obstacles as possible to any divergence between the three chief Powers in future. A charter should be framed that would make it as difficult as possible for conflicts to arise between them. That was the main task.

On the more concrete question of the voting in the Security Council, Stalin asked the conference to excuse him for not having had the time to study the Dumbarton Oaks documents in every detail. He had been very busy with some other matters and hoped to have the indulgence of the British and American delegations.

Roosevelt and *Churchill* indicated by gestures and exclamations that they were well aware of what Stalin had been doing.

Stalin, continuing, said that, as far as he understood, all conflicts which might be brought up for examination by the Security Council fell into two categories. The first included disputes whose settlement demanded the application of economic, political, military or other kinds of sanctions. The second category included disputes which might be settled by peaceful means, without the application of sanctions. Stalin asked whether his understanding was correct.

Roosevelt and *Churchill* replied that it was correct.

Stalin then declared that, as far as he had understood it, there was to be freedom of discussion in the examination of conflicts of the first category, but the unanimity of the permanent members of the Council was required in the adoption of a decision. In that case, all the permanent members of the Council should take part in the voting, i.e., the Power which was a party to a dispute would not be asked to leave. As for conflicts of the second category which were to be settled by peaceful means, another procedure was proposed in that case: the Power which was a party to a dispute (including permanent members of the Council) should not take part in the voting. Stalin asked whether his understanding of the provision was correct.

Roosevelt and *Churchill* again confirmed that Stalin had a fully correct understanding of the provision.

Stalin, concluding, said the Soviet Union was being accused of putting too much emphasis on the question of the voting in the Security Council. The Soviet Union was being reproached for making too much ado on the point. Indeed, the Soviet Union did pay great attention to the voting procedure, because the Soviet Union was most of all interested in the decisions to be adopted by the Security Council. After all, the decisions would be adopted by a vote. Discussions could go on for a hundred years, without deciding anything. But it was the decisions that mattered for the Soviet Union. And not only for it.

He, Stalin, asked those present to return for a moment to the examples given at the sitting. If China demanded the return of Hong Kong or Egypt the return of the Suez Canal, the question would be up for a vote in the Assembly and in the Security Council. Stalin could assure his friend Churchill that China and Egypt would not be alone in that. They would have their friends in an international organisation. That had a direct bearing on the question of voting.

Churchill stated that if the said countries demanded the satisfaction of their claims, Great Britain would say "no". The authority of an international organisation could not be used against the three great Powers.

Stalin asked whether that was in fact the case.

Eden replied that countries might talk and argue but no decision could be adopted without the consent of the three chief Powers.

Stalin asked once again whether that was actually the case.

Churchill and *Roosevelt* replied in the affirmative.

Stettinius declared that no economic sanctions could be applied by the Security Council without the unanimity of the permanent members.

Molotov asked whether the same applied to recommendations.

Churchill replied that that applied only to those recommendations which were mentioned in the five points formulated at the end of the American document. The international security organisation did not exclude diplomatic relations between the great and the small countries. Diplomatic procedures would continue to exist. It would be wrong to exaggerate the power or to abuse it or to raise questions that could divide the three chief Powers.

Stalin said there was another danger. His colleagues surely remembered that during the Russo-Finnish war the British and the French had roused the League of Nations against the Russians, isolated the Soviet Union and expelled it from the League of Nations, by mobilising everyone against the U.S.S.R. A repetition of such things in future must be precluded.

Eden declared that that could not happen if the American proposals were adopted.

Churchill confirmed that in the said case that kind of danger would be ruled out.

Molotov said that was the first time the Soviet side heard of that.

Roosevelt declared that there could be no recurrence of a case similar to the one mentioned by Marshal Stalin, because the expulsion of a member required the consent of all the permanent members.

Stalin pointed out that even if the adoption of the American proposals made it impossible to expel a member, there still remained the possibility of mobilising public opinion against any one member.

Churchill said he could allow a case when a broad campaign was started against a member, but then diplomacy would be operating at the same time. Churchill did not think that the President would want to come out against Britain or support any action against her. He was confident that Roosevelt would want to stop such attacks. Churchill was also confident that Marshal Stalin would not want to come out against Britain, without having a talk with Britain beforehand. He, Churchill, was confident that a way to settle disputes could always be found. At any rate, he could vouch for himself.

Stalin declared that he, too, could vouch for himself; [*half in jest*] perhaps Maisky over there would start attacking Britain?

Roosevelt noted that the unity of the Great Powers was one of their aims. He, Roosevelt, believed that the American proposals promoted the attainment of that aim. If any contradictions should unfortunately arise between the Great Powers, they would be known to all the world, despite any voting procedure. At any rate, it was impossible to eliminate the discussion of contradictions in the Assembly. The American Government believed that by allowing freedom of discussion in the Council, the Great Powers would demonstrate to the world the confidence they had in each other.

Stalin replied that that was correct and proposed that the discussion of the question be continued the next day.

Churchill asked whether they could pass on to the Polish question.

Stalin and *Roosevelt* agreed with Churchill's proposal.

Roosevelt stated that the United States was far away from Poland, and he, Roosevelt, would ask the other two participants in the Conference to set forth their considerations. There were five or six million persons of Polish origin in the United States. His, Roosevelt's, position, like that of the majority of the Poles resident in the United States, coincided with the position he had set forth in Tehran. He, Roosevelt, stood for the Curzon line. That, in essence, was accepted by most Poles, but the Poles, like the Chinese, were always worried about "losing face".

Stalin asked which Poles were meant, the real ones or the émigrés? The real Poles lived in Poland.

Roosevelt replied that all Poles wanted to get something to "save face". His position as President would be eased if the Soviet Government allowed the Poles the possibility of "saving face". It would be well to examine the question of concessions to the Poles on the southern sector of the Curzon line. He, Roosevelt, did not insist on his proposal, but wanted the Soviet Government to take it into consideration.

The establishment of a permanent government in Poland was the most essential part of the Polish question. Roosevelt believed that public opinion in the United States was opposed to America's recognition of the Lublin Government, because the people of the United States had the impression that the Lublin Government represented only a small part of the Polish people. As far as he was aware, the American people would like to see in Poland a government of national unity, including representatives of all Polish parties: the Workers' or Communist Party, the Peasant Party, the Socialist Party, the National Democratic Party and the others. He, Roosevelt, was not personally acquainted with any member of the Lublin Government or any member of the Polish Government in London. He personally knew only Mikolajczyk. During his visit to Washington, Mikolajczyk gave Roosevelt the impression of being a decent man.

He, Roosevelt, believed it was important to set up a government in Poland that would represent the mass of the people in the country and enjoy their support. It might be only a provisional government. There were many methods of forming such a government and it did not matter which one was chosen. He, Roosevelt, had a proposal to establish a Presidential Council, consisting of a small number of outstanding Poles. That Presidential Council would be entrusted with the task of forming a provisional government of Poland. That was the only proposal he had brought with him from the United States three thousand miles away. Roosevelt added, he hoped, of course, that Poland would have the most friendly relations with the Soviet Union.

Stalin said Poland would have friendly relations not only with the Soviet Union but with all the Allies.

Roosevelt said he would like to hear the opinion of Marshal Stalin and Churchill concerning his proposal. Solution of the Polish question would be of great help to the Allied cause.

Churchill said he was authorised to express the British Government's positive attitude to the President's proposal. He had always spoken publicly in Parliament and elsewhere about the British Government's intention to recognise the Curzon line as it was interpreted by the Soviet Government, i.e., with Lvov remaining in the Soviet Union. He, Churchill, and Eden had been much criticised for that, both in Parliament and in the Conservative Party, but he had always believed that after the tragedy Russia had gone through in defending herself against the German aggression, and after the efforts Russia had exerted in the liberation of Poland, the Russian claims to Lvov and the Curzon line were not based on might but on right. Churchill still continued to hold that view.

But Churchill was much more interested in the question of Polish sovereignty and the freedom and independence of Poland than the specification of her frontiers. He wanted the Poles to have a homeland, where they could live as they thought best. He had heard Marshal Stalin announce the same aim several times with the greatest firmness. Since he, Churchill, had always had trust in Marshal Stalin's statements on the sovereignty and independence of Poland, he did not think the question of frontiers was very important.

Great Britain had no material interest in Poland. She had entered the war to defend Poland from the German aggression.[1] Great Britain was concerned with Poland because it was a matter of honour for her. Great Britain could never be satisfied with a solution which did not ensure Poland a position in which she could be master of her own house. But he, Churchill, made one reservation: the freedom of Poland should not mean allowing any hostile intentions or intrigues against the Soviet Union on her part. Churchill said Great Britain would not ask to have Poland free if she had any hostile intentions in respect of the Soviet Union.

Churchill hoped that the participants in the Conference would not leave without taking practical measures on the Polish question. There were now two Polish Governments in respect of which the Allies had differing opinions. He, Churchill, had not had any direct contact with the members of the Polish Government in London. Despite the fact that

---

[1] Here Churchill obviously erred against the truth. When Hitler Germany attacked Poland on September 1, 1939, Britain, formally declaring war on Germany, did nothing to implement her guarantees given Poland earlier. Churchill himself wrote in his memoirs:

"Astonishment was world-wide when Hitler's crashing onslaught upon Poland and the declarations of war upon Germany by Britain and France were followed only by a prolonged and oppressive pause.... We contented ourselves with dropping pamphlets to rouse the Germans to a higher morality. This strange phase of the war on land and in the air astounded everyone. France and Britain remained impassive while Poland was in a few weeks destroyed or subjugated by the whole might of the German war machine. Hitler had no reason to complain of this." (W. Churchill, *The Second World War. The Gathering Storm*, Boston, 1948, pp. 422-423.)—*Ed.*

the British Government recognised the Polish Government in London, it did not deem it necessary to meet with members of that Government. But Mikolajczyk, Romer and Grabski were intelligent and honest men, and the British Government had friendly relations with them.

He, Churchill, asked whether it was possible there to set up a Polish Government like that the President had spoken about, until the time the Polish people could freely elect a government which would be recognised by the Soviet Union, Great Britain, the United States and the other United Nations recognising the Polish Government in London. Churchill believed the establishment of the body of which the President had spoken would pave the way for the elaboration by the Polish people of their constitution and the election of their administration. If that could be done, a great step would be made towards peace and welfare in Central Europe. Churchill supported the President's proposal. But, of course, Churchill added, the Red Army's communication lines had to be ensured in all circumstances.

Stalin said that as Churchill had just stated, for the British Government the question of Poland was one of honour. Stalin understood that. For his part, however, he had to say that for the Russians the question of Poland was not only one of honour but of security as well. It was a question of honour because in the past the Russians had greatly sinned against Poland. The Soviet Government was trying to atone for those sins. It was a question of security because the most important strategic problems of the Soviet state were connected with Poland.

The point was not only that Poland was a neighbouring country. That, of course, was important, but the essence of the problem lay much deeper. Throughout history, Poland had always been a corridor for an enemy attacking Russia. Suffice it to recall only the previous 30 years: in that period, the Germans twice went across Poland to attack Russia. Why had the enemies crossed Poland so easily until then? Chiefly because Poland has been weak. The Polish corridor could not be closed mechanically only by Russian forces on the outside. It could be reliably locked only from the inside, by Poland's own forces. For that Poland must be strong. That was why the Soviet Union had a stake in creating a powerful, free and independent Poland. The question of Poland was a question of life and death for the Soviet state.

Hence the sharp turn from the policy of tsarism the Soviet Union had made in respect of Poland. The tsarist Government was known to have tried to assimilate Poland. The Soviet Government had absolutely changed that inhuman policy and had taken the road of friendship with Poland and of safeguarding her independence. That was where the reasons lay for the Russian desire to have a strong, independent and free Poland.

Then about some of the specific questions which had been dealt with during the discussion and on which there were differences.

First of all, about the Curzon Line. He, Stalin, felt bound to remark that the Curzon Line had not been invented by the Russians. It had been produced by Curzon, Clemenceau, and the Americans who had taken part in the Paris Conference of 1919. The Russians had not been present at that conference. The Curzon Line had been adopted on the basis of ethnic data, contrary to the will of the Russians. Lenin had not accepted that Line. He had not wanted to give Poland Belostok and Belostok Region, which in accordance with the Curzon Line had had to be handed over to Poland.

The Soviet Government had already deviated from Lenin's position. Stalin asked whether the Allies wanted the Soviet leaders to be less Russian than Curzon and Clemenceau. In that case they would disgrace them. What would the Ukrainians say if they accepted the Allies' proposals? They might say that Stalin and Molotov had turned out to be less reliable defenders of the Russians and the Ukrainians than Curzon and Clemenceau. In what light would Stalin appear then on his return to Moscow? No, it was better to let the war against the Germans go on a little longer, but the Soviet Union had to be in a position to compensate Poland in the west at Germany's expense.

During Mikolajczyk's visit to Moscow he had asked Stalin which frontier for Poland in the west the Soviet Government would recognise. Mikolajczyk had been very pleased to hear that the Soviet Union recognised the line along the Neisse River as Poland's western frontier. By way of explanation it should be said that there were two Neisse rivers: one of them ran nearer east, by Breslau, and the other farther west. Stalin believed that Poland's western frontier should run along the Western Neisse, and he asked Roosevelt and Churchill to support him in that.

Another question on which Stalin would like to say a few words was that of the establishment of a Polish Government. Churchill proposed the establishment of a Polish Government there, at the Conference. Stalin hoped that was a slip of the tongue on Churchill's part: how could a Polish Government be set up without the participation of the Poles? Many people called him, Stalin, a dictator, and did not believe he was a democrat, but he had enough democratic feeling to refrain from setting up a Polish Government without the Poles. A Polish Government could be set up only with the participation and consent of the Poles.

A suitable moment for that had been Churchill's visit to Moscow the previous autumn, when he had brought Mikolajczyk, Grabski and Romer along with him. At that time representatives of the Lublin Government had also been invited to Moscow. A meeting had been arranged between the London and the Lublin Poles. There had even been indications of some points of agreement. Churchill should recall that. Afterwards Mikolajczyk had gone to London with the aim of returning to Moscow soon to take the last steps in organising a Polish Government. Instead, however, Mikolajczyk had been dropped from the Polish Government in London for insisting on an agreement with the Lublin Government. The Polish Government in London, headed by Arcyszewski and led by Razkewicz, was opposed to any agreement with the Lublin Government. What was more, it took a hostile attitude to such an agreement. The London Poles called the Lublin Government an assemblage of criminals and bandits. Naturally, the former Lublin Government and later the Warsaw Government paid them in kind, and called the London Poles traitors and turncoats. How were they to be united in the circumstances? He, Stalin, did not know.

The leading members of the Warsaw Government—Bierut, Osóbka-Morawski and Rola-Zymierski—did not even want to hear of any unity with the Polish Government in London. Stalin had asked the Warsaw Poles what concessions they could make. He had got the following answer: the Warsaw Poles could stand in their midst such persons from among the London Poles as Grabski and Zeligowski, but they would not hear of Mikolajczyk being Prime Minister. Stalin was prepared to make every effort to unite the Poles, but only if it had any chance of success. What was to be done? Perhaps the Warsaw Poles should be invited to the Conference? Or perhaps they should be invited to Moscow to talk things over?

In conclusion, Stalin would like to deal with yet another question—a very important one—on which he would be speaking as a military man. What would he, as a military man, want of the Government of a country liberated by the Red Army? He wanted only one thing: that the Government ensured law and order in the Red Army's rear, and that it prevented civil war breaking out behind its front lines. After all, the military did not care much about the kind of government; what was important was that they should not be shot at from behind. There was the Warsaw Government in Poland. In Poland, there were also agents of the London Government who were connected with underground circles styling themselves "forces of internal resistance". As a military man, Stalin compared the activity of the two groups and inevitably arrived at the following conclusion: the Warsaw Government was doing a fair job of ensuring law and order in the Red Army's rear, whereas there was nothing but harm from the "forces of internal resistance". Those "forces" had already managed to kill 212 Red Army men. They were attacking Red Army depots to seize arms. They violated orders on the registration of radio transmitters on the territory liberated by the Red Army. The "forces of internal resistance" were violating all the laws of war. They complained that the Red Army was arresting them. Stalin stated flatly that if those "forces" continued their attacks on Soviet soldiers, they would be shot.

In the final analysis, from the purely military standpoint, the Warsaw Government turned out to be useful, and the London Government and its agents in Poland—harmful. Of course, military men would always support a government which ensured law and order in their rear, without which the Red Army could not continue its successes. Law and order in the rear was one of the conditions of Soviet successes. That was understood not only by the military, but by the non-military as well. That was how matters stood.

Roosevelt proposed that the discussion of the Polish question be postponed until the next day.

Churchill said that the Soviet Government and the British Government had different sources of information. The British Government did not believe that the Lublin Government represented even a third of the Polish people. That was the opinion of the British Government. Of course, there might be a mistake in that. Clearly, one could not believe every story told by people returning from Poland. The British Government wanted an agreement because it was afraid that clashes between the Polish underground army and the Lublin Government might lead to bloodshed and numerous arrests. The British Government recognised that attacks on the Red Army in the rear were inadmissible. But the British Government did not believe the Lublin Government had any ground to consider itself as resting on a broad basis, insofar, at least, as could be judged from the information at the British Government's disposal, which, of course, might not be quite faultless.

Roosevelt pointed out that the Polish question had been giving the world a headache over a period of five centuries.

Churchill stated that an effort should be made to stop the Polish question from giving mankind a headache.

Stalin replied that that must certainly be done.

Fourth Sitting at Livadia Palace

February 7, 1945

Roosevelt said that Marshal Stalin's statement on the Polish question had been heard the day before. He, Roosevelt, was most interested in the question of a Polish Government. He was not so much concerned with this or that Polish frontier. He was not interested in the legitimacy or permanency of a Polish Government, for it was known that Poland had not had any Government at all over a period of several years. He believed, however, that the United States, the Soviet Union and the United Kingdom could help the Poles to set up a Provisional Government until they had the opportunity of staging a free election in the country. There was need to do something new in this sphere, something that would look like a breath of fresh air in this dismal question [. . .].

Stalin said that about an hour and a half before he had received a message from Roosevelt setting forth the following propositions: summon two men from the Lublin Government in Poland and two representatives of the social forces of the other camp (out of a list of five named in the President's letter) and in the presence of these four Poles settle the question of a new Polish Government. In the event of the successs of such a step, the new Government should stage free elections in Poland.

Besides, Roosevelt's message expressed the wish to include representatives of certain other circles in the Polish Government. The message named Mikolajczyk and Grabski. He would like to know where the persons who were named in Roosevelt's message were to be found and who, according to his information, were in Poland. If these men were found it could be ascertained how soon they would arrive. If Wincenty Witos or Sapieha were to come, their arrival would facilitate matters. But he had no knowledge of their addresses and feared the participants in the Conference would be unable to await the arrival of the Poles in the Crimea. The Soviet delegation had worked out a project meeting Roosevelt's proposals. The project had not yet been printed. That is why he proposed that in the meanwhile they should deal with some other matter, say, the question of Dumbarton Oaks.

Roosevelt and *Churchill* agreed.

[*The Soviet delegation then expressed its satisfaction with Stettinius's report and Churchill's explanations on the question of setting up an international security organisation. The Soviet delegation expressed the view that the unity of the three Powers in ensuring post-war security could be attained and that the proposals worked out at Dumbarton Oaks, and the additional proposals made by Roosevelt, could serve as a basis for future co-operation between big and small Powers in matters of international security.*

Considering these proposals acceptable, the Soviet delegation then returned to a question which had been raised at Dumbarton Oaks but had not been resolved there, namely, the question of the participation of Soviet Republics as foundation members of the international security organisation. The Soviet delegation raised the question not in the form in which it had been raised at Dumbarton Oaks, but proposed that three, or at least two, of the Soviet Republics should be among the sponsors of the international organisation (the reference was to the Ukraine, Byelorussia and Lithuania). The Soviet delegation believed that these three Soviet Republics or two, at any rate, ought to be recognised as foundation members.]

Roosevelt declared that he was happy to hear of the Soviet Government's acceptance of his proposals. Consequently, great progress had been reached.

The next question to be solved pertained to which of the countries from among the participants in the war against Germany were to be invited to attend the conference instituting the international organisation. Everyone in the United States wanted the conference to be held as soon as possible. Its convocation at the end of March was said to be desirable. It was physically possible for the representatives of the United Nations to meet within a month. He, Roosevelt, personally believed that the sooner the decision to convoke the conference was adopted, the sooner there could be a start in the examination of the questions raised by the Soviet side, which were of great interest. After the establishment of the organisation the question of its initial members could be tackled.

There was now one important practical point: was an invitation to attend the conference to be issued, alongside the countries fighting against Germany, also to the "associated countries", such as Paraguay, Peru, Uruguay, Chile, Egypt, Iceland, which had broken off relations with Germany but had not declared war on her?

The question of the Ukraine, Byelorussia and Lithuania was a highly interesting one. The participants might take different views of it, for their countries had different state structures and traditions. The British Empire, for instance, consisted of dominions: Canada, Australia, etc. The U.S.S.R. had many Republics. The United States, on the contrary, was a homogeneous country, without any colonies. It had one language. The constitution of the United States provided for only one minister of foreign affairs. That was why the question raised by the Soviet side required study. It was closely bound up with this other question: were the big Powers to have more than one vote in the international organisation? If one country were to be given more than one vote that would be a violation of the rule that each member of the organisation was to have one vote only.

Roosevelt proposed that the Foreign Ministers should be entrusted with the study of the question of the organisation's initial members and also of the time and place of the conference.

Churchill declared that he wanted to express his deep gratitude to the Soviet Government for the great stride it had taken to meet the common views worked out at Dumbarton Oaks. Churchill was sure that the agreement of the three Great Powers on this crucial question would make all thinking men happy.

The question of the number of members of the Assembly had been raised by the Russian Ally in a new form. Everyone would feel that in that respect a great stride had been made towards agreement. Churchill agreed that the United States and the British Empire were in different positions. There were self-governing dominions in the British Empire which had, for a quarter of a century, played a notable part in the international security organisation, which had collapsed on the eve of the current war. All the dominions had worked for the cause of peace and democratic progress. All the dominions had, without hesitation, entered the war against Germany, although they had been aware of Britain's weakness. Britain had had no means of forcing the dominions to follow her or right to urge them to do so, but all the dominions had entered the war of their own accord.

He, Churchill, had heard the Soviet Government's proposal with a feeling of profound sympathy. His heart was touched and turned to great Russia, which was bleeding but smiting the tyrant on her path. Churchill felt that such a great nation as Russia, with her 180-million population, might have reasons to look askance at the British Commonwealth of Nations if she had only one vote, despite the fact that the population of Russia greatly exceeded the white population of the British Empire.

Churchill would be very happy to have the President give the Soviet delegation an answer that could not be considered negative. Churchill himself was unable to exceed his powers. He would like to have time to exchange opinion on the Soviet proposal with the Foreign Minister and the war cabinet in London. Churchill, therefore, begged to be excused for being unable to give an answer to the Soviet delegation's proposal on behalf of the British Government right away.

Roosevelt repeated his proposal to have the Foreign Ministers discuss the question of the Soviet Republics and also of the time and place of the conference, and the countries to be invited to attend. The decision at Dumbarton Oaks had been to convoke the conference as soon as possible. An early convocation of the conference was also important for Roosevelt from the standpoint of domestic politics.

Churchill declared that he would be glad to have the three Foreign Ministers examine the three points proposed by the President. As for the conference, Churchill doubted that it could be called in March. In March, fighting on all the fronts would be at its height. More forces than ever before would be taking part in the battles. The domestic problems in the various countries were highly complicated. Britain, in particular, suffered from a shortage of housing and had to maintain supplies for the fronts. Besides, Britain had a Parliament which was very active and demanded a great deal of time and attention of the ministers, notably the Foreign Minister. A quarter of February was over. Churchill, therefore, asked himself this question: would the state of Europe and the world allow the convocation of a conference in March? And if the conference were called in March would the delegations of the various countries really be headed by their leaders? Wasn't it better to postpone the convocation of the Assembly for some time?

Roosevelt explained that it was not a matter of convoking the Assembly but of a conference to institute the international security organisation. The first Assembly would probably be called within three to six months.

Churchill declared that some of the countries to be represented at the conference would still be under the German yoke at the time of its convocation. There was no saying to what extent their delegations would really be representative of their peoples. Other countries at the time would be starving and suffering from the aftermath of war. In that connection, Churchill named Holland and France. Alongside those unfortunate countries at the conference there would be nations which had in no way suffered from the war and had not taken part in it. Churchill believed that in the circumstances the conference could easily become chaotic. Some peoples would be suffering the tortures of agony, while others would be calmly discussing the problems of the future. For all those reasons, Churchill anticipated difficulties in the convocation of the conference, at any rate, insofar as Great Britain was concerned.

Roosevelt said that it had been decided at Dumbarton Oaks to set up the international organisation as soon as possible. Roosevelt, like the Prime Minister, had domestic political difficulties. However, he would find it easier to secure a two-thirds majority in the Senate if the Plan for establishing the international security organisation went through during the war.

Churchill declared that Great Britain's constitution had an effect on her attitude. A Parliamentary election was likely to be held in Britain soon, and if the Government remained in power it would have to lead the new Parliament. That had to be taken into account. Of course, Great Britain would do everything she could to satisfy Roosevelt's desire. However, Churchill still considered it necessary to make a frank statement about the practical difficulties which, he anticipated, would arise in the realisation of the President's intention. Personally, Churchill would regret deferring the settlement of the question of the organisation's initial members until the convocation of the United Nations conference.

Roosevelt said that he wanted to reiterate his earlier proposal, namely, that the Foreign Ministers should look into the question of the membership, time and place of the conference and then report to the heads of the three Governments on their results.

Stalin expressed agreement with that.

Churchill did not object to the three Foreign Ministers' discussing the question referred to, but emphasised that the question was not at all a technical one. Churchill was not sure that such an examination would be a success but in view of the President's request was prepared to accept his proposal.

Stalin declared that the three Foreign Ministers would meet and then report to the Heads of Government on the results of their work [. . .].

The Soviet delegation then tabled the following proposals on the Polish question:

"1. To accept that Poland's border in the East should run along the Curzon Line with deviations at some points of 5 to 6 kilometres in favour of Poland.

"2. To accept that Poland's western border should run from the town of Stettin (for the Poles) southward along the Oder River, and then on along the Neisse River (Western).

"3. To recognise as desirable to enlarge the Provisional Polish Government through the inclusion of some democratic leaders from among the émigré Polish circles.

"4. To consider desirable that the Allied Governments should recognise the enlarged Provisional Polish Government.

"5. To recognise as desirable that the Provisional Polish Government, enlarged in the manner specified in Paragraph 3, should, within the shortest possible period, call on the population of Poland to take part in a general election to set up permanent organs of state administration in Poland.

"6. To authorise V. M. Molotov, Mr. Harriman and Mr. Kerr to discuss the question of, enlarging the Provisional Polish Government together with representatives of the Provisional Polish Government and to submit their proposals for the consideration of the three Governments."

Roosevelt declared that the Soviet proposals constituted a certain progress. He wanted to have the opportunity of studying them with Stettinius. All he could say at the moment was that he did not like the expression "émigré Polish circles" used in the Soviet proposals. As Roosevelt had said the day before he was not acquainted with any of the exiles, with the exception of Mikolajczyk. Furthermore, he believed that it was not at all necessary to invite specifically persons from abroad to take part in the Polish Government. Suitable men could be found inside Poland herself.

Stalin noted that was, of course, true.

Churchill said he shared Roosevelt's doubts on the word "émigrés". The fact was that the word had first been used during the French Revolution to designate persons expelled from France by the French people. The Poles who were abroad had not been expelled by the Polish people but by Hitler. Churchill proposed that the word "émigrés" should be substituted by the words "Poles abroad".

Stalin agreed to Churchill's proposal.

Churchill, continuing, said that the second paragraph of the proposals spoke of the Neisse River. On the question of the displacement of Poland's border to the west, the British Government wanted to make this reservation: Poland must have the right to take a territory which she wanted and which she was able to administer. It would hardly be the proper thing to have the Polish goose so stuffed with German viands that it died of indigestion. In addition, there were circles in Britain who were apprehensive of the idea of expelling a great number of Germans. Churchill himself was not at all afraid of such a prospect. The results of the resettlement of Greeks and Turks after the previous world war had been quite satisfactory.

Stalin said there was almost no German population in the parts of Germany occupied by the Red Army.

Churchill remarked that that naturally made things easier. Moreover, 6 or 7 million Germans had already been killed, and at least 1 or 1.5 million more would probably be killed before the end of the war.

Stalin replied that Churchill's figures were on the whole correct.

Churchill declared that he was not at all proposing to stop destroying the Germans.

Churchill proposed that the words "and from Poland herself" should be inserted in Paragraph 3 of the Soviet draft.

Stalin replied that that was acceptable.

Churchill said that the Soviet proposals should be studied and then discussed at the following sitting. He considered the proposals a step forward.

Fifth Sitting at Livadia Palace

February 8, 1945

Roosevelt declared that he believed the Foreign Ministers had done a good job of what they had been entrusted to do, and invited Eden to report on their results.

Eden said that the Foreign Ministers had examined the question of the date of the conference, the membership of the international organisation, the granting of the rights of foundation members to two or three Soviet Republics, and also the question of the countries to be invited to attend the inaugural conference. It had been decided to recommend the calling of the conference in the United States on April 25, 1945. A tentative decision had been adopted to invite to the conference members of the United Nations, that is, the countries signing the declaration of the United Nations by a specified day of February 1945. The conference was to draw up a list of the initial members of the international organisation. The delegates of Great Britain and the United States would support the U.S.S.R. in having two Soviet Republics among the initial members of the organisation. The examination of all the details of the invitation had been entrusted to a special sub-committee.

Stalin declared that he had a list of states which had declared war on Germany. Did that mean that all of them were to be included among the members of the Assembly? Ten of these countries had no diplomatic relations with the Soviet Union.

Roosevelt replied that there were several countries which were eager to establish relations with the Soviet Union but had not yet done so. There were others which were not establishing relations with the U.S.S.R., because of the strong influence there of the Catholic Church. But it should be borne in mind that states which had not established relations with the Soviet Union had attended the conferences at Bretton Woods and Atlantic City with it.

Stalin said that it would be hard to build security with states which had no relations with the Soviet Union.

Roosevelt declared that the best way of making these countries establish relations with the U.S.S.R. was to invite them to attend the conference.

Roosevelt then referred to a question which, he said, had a history of its own. Three years previously, Sumner Welles, the then acting Secretary of State, had advised some South American Republics not to declare war on Germany, but merely to break off relations with her. The Republics had followed the American advice. They had subsequently helped the United States a great deal (for instance, by supplying raw materials). They had a good reputation. A month earlier, Roosevelt had sent a letter to six presidents of South American Republics saying that if they wanted to be invited to the conference they had to declare war on Germany. Ecuador had already done so, but had not yet had time to sign the U.N. Declaration. Paraguay was to declare war on Germany in 10 days, and Peru and Venezuela were to follow suit shortly. It would be embarrassing for the American Government to fail to invite these countries to the conference after they had taken the American Government's advice, although, to be quite honest, the advice had been a mistake.

Stalin asked how things stood with Argentina.

Roosevelt replied that Argentina was not on the list submitted by the U.S. delegation.

Stalin said that Argentina had, after all, also broken off relations with Germany.

Roosevelt declared that Argentina was not recognised as one of the United Nations.

Stalin replied that he wanted to call attention to the fact that if invitations to attend the conference were issued not only to countries which had declared war but also to those which had "associated themselves", the countries which had actually fought against Germany would resent sitting next to those who had wavered and cheated during the war.

Churchill said he believed the countries of that category should declare war on Germany before they got an invitation to attend the conference. He agreed that some of these countries had played a rather sad part, biding their time to see who would win. However, it should not be forgotten that if another group of Powers were to declare war on her the impression on Germany would be unnerving. The other enemy countries would find the whole world fighting against them, and that could have a strong impact on them.

Roosevelt declared that he wanted to add Iceland to the list of those to be invited.

Churchill remarked that His Majesty's Government felt a special responsibility in respect of Egypt, because Egypt had twice expressed the desire to declare war on Germany and Italy. However, the British Government had advised Egypt not to do that, as Egypt's continued neutrality had helped to prevent aerial bombardments of Cairo. Moreover, the British found Egypt's neutrality advantageous from various other angles. When the enemy had been within 30 miles of Alexandria, the Egyptian Army had helped the Allies by guarding the bridges and communication lines. Egypt had been of greater use as a neutral than if she had declared war on Germany and Italy. Of course, if Egypt wanted to declare war at that time the British Government would not object. Iceland had also played a useful role in the period before the United States had entered the war. Iceland had allowed American troops into the country, thereby violating her neutrality. Iceland had ensured Allied communication lines. Churchill thought both those countries had grounds to participate in the conference if they were to declare war. The Allies ought to give them that opportunity. Churchill wanted to know whether there was the intention to admit to the conference all Powers declaring war by March 1.

Stalin gave a positive reply to Churchill's question.

Churchill said that Eire would not be among the invited either, because she had a German and Japanese missions. Upon the other hand, he, Churchill, had to speak in favour of inviting Turkey, although the proposal might not meet with universal approval. Turkey had concluded an alliance with Britain before the outbreak of war, at a very dangerous time. When the war started, the Turks believed that their army was not adequately armed for a modern type of war. Nevertheless, Turkey's position was friendly and useful in many respects. The Turks had even offered aid to the British, although the British did not take up their offer. Churchill was asking himself: ought not the Turks to be given a chance to repent on their deathbed?

Stalin replied that Turkey ought to be invited if she declared war on Germany before the end of February.

Roosevelt and *Churchill* voiced their agreement with that.

Roosevelt said that Denmark had been occupied by the Germans in 24 hours, the King had been taken prisoner, and Parliament had been dissolved. Denmark was at the moment under German control. Only one man claiming to represent Denmark had not recognised the new Danish Government. He was the Danish Envoy in Washington. He had been unable to declare war on Germany but he had repudiated the acts of the German-sponsored government. What was to be done with Denmark? There was no doubt that had the Danes been free, they would have sided with the Allies.

Churchill asked whether the Danes had recognised the independence of Iceland.

Stalin replied in the negative.

Churchill did not believe there would be any difficulties between Iceland and Denmark. He agreed with Marshal Stalin and the President that all those who declared war by the end of February should be allowed to attend the conference. Denmark would take part in the security organisation when she got the opportunity to speak on her own behalf.

Roosevelt proposed the approval of the report of the Foreign Ministers *in toto*, with an amendment in the sense that United Nations declaring war on the common enemy by March 1 were to be invited to the conference. Roosevelt said that Turkey could be added to the list provided she declared war on the common enemy before the first of March.

Stalin asked about the opinion of the Conference concerning the signing by Byelorussia and the Ukraine of the U.N. Declaration by March 1.

Roosevelt declared that the Conference had already adopted the point of the Foreign Ministers' decision which said that at the U.N. Conference the three Powers would recommend inclusion of the Soviet Republics among the sponsors.

Churchill remarked that it appeared to him to be not entirely logical to invite to the conference all the small countries which had done next to nothing for victory and had declared war only at that last moment, while postponing the invitation of the two Soviet Republics. The sacrifices made by Byelorussia and the Ukraine were well known. He, Churchill, believed that if those two Republics signed the U.N. Declaration they should be invited.

Stalin said that it could happen that when the conference met and heard the recommendation to invite the Soviet Republics someone might get up and say that they had not signed the U.N. Declaration. That is why it would be better for the Soviet Republics to sign the Declaration then. Otherwise how were they to be recommended? He did not want to inconvenience the President but would still ask him to explain what the matter was.

Roosevelt replied that that was a technical matter but an important one none the less. It was a question of agreeing to give the Soviet Union three votes.

Stalin asked if the invitation of the Ukraine and Byelorussia would not be hampered by the fact that they had not signed the U.N. Declaration by March 1.

Roosevelt answered in the negative.

Stalin declared that in that case he withdrew his proposal. He would only like to insert the names of the Republics— the Ukraine and Byelorussia—in the text of the decisions of the Foreign Ministers.

Roosevelt and *Churchill* indicated their consent.

The Dumbarton Oaks question was considered settled, and Roosevelt went on to the Polish question.

Churchill said that with their permission he wanted to say beforehand that he had studied the results of yesterday's conference of the Foreign Ministers and approved of them.

Roosevelt declared that on the question of Polish borders the U.S. delegation had no objections to the first paragraph of the Soviet proposals. The U.S. delegation also agreed that Poland should be given compensation at Germany's expense, namely, East Prussia south of Königsberg and Upper Silesia up to the Oder. However, Roosevelt thought that there was little justification for displacing the Polish border to the Western Neisse.

As for the question of a Polish Government, Roosevelt would like to propose that the Soviet Foreign Minister and the Ambassadors of the United States and Britain to the U.S.S.R. should be authorised to negotiate in Moscow with Bierut, Osóbka-Morawski, Sapieha, Witos, Mikolajczyk and Grabski on the formation of a new Government on the following basis: a Presidential Council should first be set up to consist of three persons, possibly Bierut, Grabski and Sapieha. The Presidential Council would be representative of the power of the President in Poland. That Presidential Council would deal with the formation of a Government consisting of men in the Warsaw Government, democratic elements in Poland and abroad. The Provisional Government thus formed would undertake to stage an election to the Constituent Assembly, which would then elect a permanent Government of Poland. When the Provisional Polish Government of national unity was set up the three Governments would recognise it.

Stalin asked whether in that case the London Government was to be disbanded.

Churchill and *Roosevelt* replied in the affirmative.

Churchill said that when the Provisional Polish Government of national unity was set up, the British Government would withdraw recognition from the Polish Government in London and would accredit its ambassador to the new Government.

Stalin asked whether in that case the national property of Poland which was then at the disposal of the Polish Government in London would remain in Arcyszewski's hands or would be handed over to the new Polish Government.

Roosevelt replied that Poland's property abroad would automatically pass to the new Polish Government.

Churchill remarked that he was not aware of the legal aspect of the matter, but he thought the President was right.

Churchill then declared that the British delegation had drawn up an alternative document on the Polish question which had been handed to the Russian friends. But since the discussion had been started on the President's proposal, Churchill was prepared to continue it in that plane.

Churchill said that he had some amendments to Roosevelt's proposals. He believed that the Conference had reached its crucial point. He was referring to the question whose solution was being awaited by the whole world. If they diverged, continuing to recognise different Polish governments, everyone would take that as a sign of basic contradictions between Great Britain and the United States, on the one hand, and the Soviet Union, on the other. That would have rather deplorable consequences throughout the world, and would lay the stamp of bankruptcy on the Conference. At the same time, it had to be stated that they took differing views of the basic facts or, at any rate, of some of the basic facts. According to the information at the disposal of the British Government, the Lublin, and then the Warsaw, Government was not the kind that could be recognised by the bulk of the Polish people. If they were to renounce the Polish Government in London and back the Lublin Government there was every indication that that would arouse the protest of the world, and of all Poles abroad, without exception.

They had a Polish Army consisting of Poles outside Poland. It had fought gallantly. Churchill did not believe that that Polish Army would be reconciled with the Lublin Government. That Polish Army would regard the British Government's recognition of the Lublin Government and refusal of continued recognition of the Polish Government in London as a betrayal.

The Soviet Government was very well aware that he, Churchill, was not in agreement with the views of the Polish Government in London and considered its actions unwise. However, formal recognition of the new Polish Government set up a year earlier would generate a great deal of criticism of the British Government's actions. People would assert that the British Government had earlier given in to the Soviet Union on the question of Poland's eastern border and had again capitulated to it on the question of the character of the Polish Government. As a result, the British Government would be subjected to accusations in Parliament. The debate that would be started in that connection would be highly regrettable and would have a negative effect on Allied unity.

In Churchill's opinion, the Soviet proposals did not go far enough. Before His Majesty's Government could abandon its position, namely, recognition of the Polish Government in London, and recognise the new Polish Government, it had to be convinced that the new Polish Government was sufficiently representative of the Polish people. Of course, the British Government's difficulties would all disappear once a free election was held in Poland on the basis of universal suffrage. The British Government would welcome any Polish Government that emerged as a result of the election, and would turn its back on the London Government. However, the British Government was highly apprehensive of developments in the interim, before an election was possible.

Roosevelt declared that as a visitor from another hemisphere he stated the existence of a common view shared by the conferees: a general election ought to be held in Poland as soon as possible. What Roosevelt was concerned about, however, was how Poland would be run in the interim, before the staging of a free election.

Stalin said that Churchill complained about the absence of information on Poland and the impossibility of receiving any from there.

Churchill replied that he had some information.

Stalin stated that although Churchill did have some information it did not coincide with that of the Soviet Government.

Churchill replied in the affirmative.

Stalin declared that, in his view, Great Britain and the United States could have informants in Poland. Referring to the leaders of the Warsaw Government, he said that the popularity of Bierut, Osóbka-Morawski and Rola-Zymierski among the Polish people was truly tremendous. What was the basis of their popularity? It was above all that they had not left their country during the occupation. They had remained in German-occupied Warsaw, they had worked in the underground and had emerged from the underground.

This commanded respect among the Polish people, who naturally sympathised with men who had not abandoned them in their hour of need. The Polish people did not like Arcyszewski's men, because they did not see them in their midst in the arduous years of the occupation. The people's mentality had to be taken into account.

The second important fact making for the popularity of the Warsaw Government leaders sprang from the Red Army's victories. The Soviet forces were advancing and liberating Poland. This was creating a great revolution in the Polish people's mind. The Poles were known not to like the Russians, because the Russians had thrice taken part in the division of Poland. However, the Red Army's offensive and its liberation of the Polish people from Hitler occupation had reversed the Polish mood entirely. Their hostility for the Russians had disappeared and had been replaced by a feeling of quite another order: the Poles were happy to see the Russians drive the Germans before them and liberate the Polish population, and this kindled a warm feeling among them for the Russians.

The Poles believed they were celebrating a grand national festival in their history. And the Poles were surprised to see the men from the Polish Government in London refuse to take part in this celebration. The Poles were asking themselves why they saw the members of the Provisional Polish Government at the festivities, but not any of the London Poles? That naturally tended to detract from the prestige of the Polish Government in London.

Those were the two factors which lay at the source of the great popularity enjoyed by the members of the Provisional Polish Government. Could they ignore these facts? Of course, they could not, if they wanted to reckon with the people's will. Such were the considerations he had wanted to express in connection with the question of the prestige of the men from the Warsaw Government.

Concerning Churchill's apprehensions that the conferees could leave without reaching any agreement on the Polish question. What was to be done in that case? They had different information and different conclusions. Perhaps they should summon Poles from the different camps and hear them? Would that increase their information? Churchill was dissatisfied with the fact that the Provisional Polish Government had not been elected. Of course, it was better to have an elected government, but that had been prevented until then by the war. He believed the time was not far off when the election could be held in Poland.

But then, the de Gaulle Government in France had not been elected either, and consisted of diverse elements. Nevertheless, they were willingly dealing with de Gaulle and had concluded agreements with him. Why couldn't the same thing be done with the Provisional Polish Government after it is enlarged? Why was more to be demanded of Poland than of France? He was sure that if the Polish question were approached without bias, it could be solved successfully. The situation was not as tragic as Churchill had depicted it. A way out could be found if they concentrated on the main thing and did not attach too much importance to secondary things. It was easier to reconstruct the existing Provisional Polish Government than to set up an entirely new one. As for the question of the Presidential Council, the matter should be discussed with the Poles themselves.

Roosevelt asked when it would be possible to stage free elections in Poland.

Stalin replied that the elections could be held within a month, unless there was some disaster at the front, unless the Germans beat the Allies, but he hoped that the Germans would not beat the Allies.

Churchill declared that a free election would, of course, set minds at rest in Britain. The British Government would support the new Government and all the other questions would disappear. Of course, they could not ask for anything that would hamper the operations of the Soviet forces. Those operations had priority. But if it proved possible to stage the election within two months, a new situation would be created, and no one could question that.

Roosevelt recommended that the question under discussion should be referred to the Foreign Ministers.

Churchill agreed to that and added that he wanted to raise one small question. It would be highly useful to have an agreement on regular meetings between the three Foreign Ministers for consultations every three or four months, on a rota basis in each of the capitals.

Stalin said that that would be right.

Roosevelt declared that that was a good proposal. However, Stettinius was also busy with South American affairs. That was why Roosevelt believed that the Foreign Ministers' meetings could be held as the need arose, without fixing specified dates.

Churchill proposed that the first meeting should be held in London.

Stalin signified agreement [. . .].

Sixth Sitting at Livadia Palace

Roosevelt proposed that Stettinius should report on the conference of the three Foreign Ministers.

Stettinius declared that on behalf of the Foreign Ministers he wished to make the following brief report on the results of their work. The Foreign Ministers had had a detailed discussion of the Polish question on the basis of the memorandum of the American delegation. The memorandum, in conformity with the proposal of the Soviet delegation, left out the question of the Presidential Council. As for the formula on the creation of a Polish Government, it had been decided to continue discussion of the question and to report that the three Foreign Ministers had not yet reached an agreement. The Ministers' conference had also discussed the question of reparations.

Churchill said that perhaps the Polish question should be discussed first.

Roosevelt agreed.

[Setting forth its view of the memorandum of the U.S. delegation on the question of the Polish Government, the Soviet delegation declared that, being desirous without any further delay to work out a common stand, it was adopting the American proposal as a basis, but was putting forward some amendments to it. The Soviet delegation proposed the following wording for the first clause of the American formula for the creation of a Polish Government: "The present Provisional Polish Government should be reorganised on the basis of a broader democratism through the inclusion of democratic leaders in Poland and abroad. This Government is to be called the National Provisional Government."

At the end of the paragraph, the Soviet delegation proposed the addition of the following words: "non-fascist and anti-fascist parties", with the whole reading thus: "All non-fascist and anti-fascist democratic parties must have the right to participate in these elections and nominate candidates."

The Soviet delegation also considered it necessary to add the following sentence: "When the Polish Government of National Unity is formed in the specified manner, the Three Governments will recognise it." Finally, the Soviet delegation proposed the exclusion of the last clause of the American proposal—concerning the duty of the ambassadors of the Three Powers in Warsaw to observe and report on the fulfilment of the obligation on the staging of free elections—on the ground that the ambassadors of the Three Powers accredited to the Polish Government had full possibility of observing developments in Poland, that being their immediate duty. The Soviet delegation indicated that with these amendments it considered the American proposal acceptable.]

Churchill declared that he was glad that a great step had been made towards agreement on the Polish question. But he wished to make a few general remarks before its discussion was continued. Churchill was of the opinion that it should not be decided in haste. The possibility of agreement was already in the air, but there was a danger of everything being spoiled by undue haste. It was better to give a little more thought to the proposal of the Soviet delegation. It was true that there remained only 48 hours for their meetings. However, Churchill did not wish to ruin the whole thing because of the Conference wanting some 24 hours. If those 24 hours were needed to reach agreement, they had to be found. One thing should not be forgotten: if the participants in the Conference left without reaching agreement on the Polish question, the whole Conference would be regarded as a failure.

Roosevelt proposed that Stettinius should complete his report, after which they would adjourn for half an hour to study the proposals of the Soviet delegation.

Churchill stressed once again that the participants in the Conference had a very valuable prize almost in their grasp. They must not let the prize be broken because of undue haste. They must have a little time for thought. However, Churchill did not object to Roosevelt's proposal.

Stalin also accepted Roosevelt's proposal.

Stettinius, continuing his report, said that he would go on to the question of reparations. The American delegation had submitted its project of the principles of levying reparations on Germany. The delegations were unanimous on Points 1 and 2 of the American draft.[1] On Point 3 they had reached a compromise, namely: the Moscow Reparations Commission would take as a basis for its work the total amount of reparations of $20,000 million, by way of lump withdrawals and annual goods deliveries, of which 50 per cent were earmarked for the Soviet Union.

On this point, Eden had made a reservation to the effect that he had not yet received instructions from London. The Soviet delegation declared that the reparations would be calculated on the basis of 1938 prices, with increases between 10 and 15 per cent, depending on the nature of the object.

Stettinius then dealt with the forthcoming conference of the United Nations. The American delegation, he said, proposed that before the conference the future permanent members of the Council should have consultations with each other through diplomatic channels concerning the trusteeship over colonial and dependent peoples.

Churchill [*in great agitation*] resolutely protested against any discussion of the question. Great Britain had been carrying on a hard struggle for so long to preserve the integrity of the British Commonwealth of Nations and the British Empire. He was sure that the struggle would end in complete success, and while the British flag flew over the territories of the British Crown, he would not allow any piece

---

[1] Points 1 and 2 of the American draft read as follows:

"1. Reparations are to be received in the first place by countries which had borne the main burden of the war, had suffered the greatest losses and had organised the victory over the enemy.

"2. Leaving aside the question of the use of German manpower in the form of reparations, a question to be examined later, reparations in kind must be levied on Germany in the following two forms:

"a) Lump withdrawals at the end of the war from Germany's national wealth, both on the territory of Germany proper and outside (equipment, machine-tools, ships, rolling stock, German investments abroad, shares of industrial, transport, shipping and other enterprises in Germany, etc.), with these withdrawals being aimed chiefly to effect the military and economic disarmament of Germany.

"These withdrawals should be completed within two years after the war.

"b) Annual goods deliveries over a period of 10 years after the end of the war." (Retranslated from the Russian.—*Ed.*)

of British soil to be put up for auction before 40 states. The British Empire would never be placed in the dock of an international court on the question of "trusteeship" over under-age nations.

Stettinius reassured Churchill that it was not a question of the British Empire. The American delegation wanted the world organisation to establish trusteeship, in case of necessity, over territories which would be taken away from the enemy.

Churchill declared that he had no objections if the question was of enemy territories. It might be the appropriate thing to establish trusteeship over these territories.

Stettinius added that the conference of the Three Ministers recognised it as desirable to have a discussion of the trusteeship question at the United Nations Conference.

Churchill insisted on a qualification in the text of the decision that the discussion of the trusteeship question in no sense related to the territory of the British Empire. Turning to Stalin, Churchill asked what his feelings would have been if an international organisation had offered to place the Crimea under international control as an international holiday resort.

Stalin replied that he would willingly make the Crimea available for Three-Power conferences.

Stettinius declared that the sub-commission set up to work out the question of invitations to the United Nations Conference continued its work and would report that day on the results to the Foreign Ministers.

[*It was then decided, on the proposal of Stettinius, that the persons appointed by the British and the Soviet sides, should prepare a report on the Yugoslav question.*]

Churchill remarked that there were no considerable differences on the Yugoslav question.

Stettinius declared that it had been decided to put the Tito-Subasić agreement into effect before the conclusion of the Crimea Conference, in spite of "King Peter's whims".

Churchill declared that the British delegation had two highly valuable amendments to the Tito-Subasić agreement. They had been handed to the Russian friends. If the participants in the Conference decided the amendments to be appropriate, they could be recommended to Subasić and Tito for acceptance.

111

Stalin remarked that the Soviet side could also make its own amendments. The British delegation would then propose something else. The question was being dragged out, while the situation in Yugoslavia remained unstable.

Churchill declared that Tito was a dictator in his country. They could ask him to accept the amendments.

Stalin replied that Tito was not a dictator at all. The situation in Yugoslavia remained indefinite.

Eden declared that there was no question of changing the Tito-Subasić agreement. The question was only of the two assurances which Subasić would ask of Tito in any case.

Stalin said that the amendments tabled by the British boiled down to having the deputies of the Skupština who had not compromised themselves by collaboration with the Germans included in the Anti-Fascist Veće. The second amendment consisted in the proposal that the legislative acts adopted by the Anti-Fascist Veće should be subsequently confirmed by the Constituent Assembly. The Soviet delegation was essentially in agreement with those amendments. They were correct. But he considered that they should in no way delay the formation of a new Government.

Eden declared that the British Government wanted an immediate implementation of the Tito-Subasić agreement. Later, Tito could be asked to accept the amendments in question.

Stalin agreed.

Churchill also expressed agreement.

Eden said that Subasić was to have left London for Yugoslavia on February 7.

Churchill remarked that information on whether he had left or not would be available the next day. At any rate, Subasić would leave as soon as the weather permitted.

Stalin declared that before they left the Crimea, the Three Powers should recommend that the Tito-Subasić agreement be put into effect immediately and a single Yugoslav Government formed on the basis of the agreement, regardless of any of the fantastic ideas Peter might have in his head.

Churchill proposed the insertion of a corresponding clause in the communiqué. In that connection, Churchill asked whether there was agreement that the said amendments should be subsequently recommended to Tito.

Stalin replied that he never made empty statements. He always kept his word.

[After the break.]

Roosevelt declared that he had made a closer study of the proposals of the Soviet delegation on the Polish question and had exchanged opinions with the British side. He felt the whole thing now turned on a certain difference in the wording. The participants in the Conference were close to agreement. Great progress had indeed been achieved in this question. But the phrase, "The present Provisional Polish Government should be reorganised on the basis of a broader democratism", would embarrass the position of those Governments which recognised the Polish Government in London. Roosevelt wanted to have the expresssion "the present Provisional Polish Government" substituted by the words "the Polish Government now functioning in Poland".

Furthermore, said Roosevelt, the Soviet delegation had proposed the deletion of the final phrase concerning the duty of the ambassadors of our three states to observe the free elections in Poland. It was better not to do that. In that connection, Roosevelt wanted to recall that there were six million Poles in the United States. In respect of them, some sort of gesture should be made to reassure them that the elections in Poland would be fair and free. Roosevelt believed that, considering that the participants in the Conference were so close to agreement, it would be advisable for the Foreign Ministers to work a little that night and report the next day on the results of their work to the Conference.

Churchill agreed with the President that great progress had been made that day towards a joint statement by the Allied Powers on the Polish question. Churchill had no objections to have the matter finally elaborated by the three Foreign Ministers. But at the moment he wanted to dwell on two small points which flowed from what Marshal Stalin had said the previous day. Marshal Stalin had told how Poland had been liberated and how the enemy had been expelled from the country by the Red Army. That was a new fact of very great significance. That is why Churchill believed it would be advisable to emphasise the fact before the whole world and to open the declaration on Poland with something like the following words: "The Red Army has liberated Poland. This makes it necessary to set up a fully representative Polish Government, which can now be established on a broader basis than was possible before the liberation of Western Poland."

The second point Churchill wanted to call attention to was the concluding phrase of the American draft. The British Government was at a disadvantage in negotiations on Polish affairs because it had little knowledge of what was going on in Poland herself. At the same time, the British Government had to take important decisions relating to Poland. Churchill was aware that the relations between the various groups of Poles were highly aggravated. Osóbka-Morawski, for instance, had not long before used rather threatening language in respect of the London Government: the Lublin Government intended to institute judicial proceedings against all soldiers of the Polish Army and members of the Polish underground, as traitors. This had caused the British Government serious apprehension.

Of course, it was necessary above all to remove all the obstacles in the way of the Red Army's operations. Nevertheless, Churchill wanted to request Marshal Stalin to take account of the British Government's difficult position. The British Government really had no knowledge of what was going on inside Poland, because the only way it could obtain information was to drop parachutists in Poland from time to time or talk with people, members of the underground movement, who arrived from Poland. That was a highly unsatisfactory situation.

How was it to be altered without at the same time creating difficulties for the Red Army's operations? Churchill reiterated that he placed the interests of the operations of the Soviet forces above all else. Still: couldn't the British be given the corresponding opportunities, which, Churchill believed, would also be readily used by the Americans, to see for themselves how the existing dissensions were being settled in Poland? That was why the British delegation thought the final phrase in the American draft was so important.

When elections were held in Yugoslavia, Marshal Tito, as he had understood it, would not object to the presence of Soviet, American and British observers, so that these observers could assure the whole world that the elections were conducted the right way. As for Greece, the British would welcome the presence of Soviet, American and British observers, when the elections took place there. The same applied to Italy. When Northern Italy was liberated, a sharp change would take place in Italy's internal situation, and elections to a constituent assembly or a parliament would have to be held. The British Government believed that a Soviet, American and British observers must have the possibility of attending the elections in Italy so as to assure the Great Powers of their normal conduct.

The considerations expressed by Churchill had real grounds. In Egypt, for instance, victory always went to the Government staging the election. Nahas Pasha had quarrelled with the King and wanted to stage an election. The King said that so long as Nahas Pasha remained a member of the Government, there would be no election. And naturally when Nahas Pasha was expelled from the Government, the King's men won the election and took his place.

Stalin remarked that no real election could be held in Egypt. Bribery there was still widespread. Stalin asked what the literacy percentage in Egypt was. (None of the British delegation was able to answer the question.) In Poland, literacy was as high as 70-75 per cent. Those were people who read the papers and could voice their opinion. There could be no comparison between Egypt and Poland.

Churchill replied that he had no intention of making a comparison between Poland and Egypt. He merely wanted to say that the elections must be free and just. He was interested, for instance, in whether Mikolajczyk would be allowed to take part in the election.

Stalin replied that the question had to be discussed with the Poles.

Churchill asked whether the ambassadors should discuss the question during their negotiations with the Poles in Moscow.

Stalin replied that this had to be done in accordance with the decision which they were going to adopt.

Churchill replied that he had no desire to continue discussing the matter, but he wished to have the possibility of informing Parliament that the elections would be free, and that justice in their conduct had been guaranteed.

Stalin said that Mikolajczyk was a representative of the peasant party. It was not a fascist party. It would, of course, be allowed to take part in the election. Some of the candidates from the peasant party would enter the Government. But he thought the solution of the question should be left until its discussion with the Poles. They would arrive and could be heard. There were men with different views among the Poles.

Churchill declared that the only thing he wanted was, upon his return to Britain, to get the question of Poland's eastern border through Parliament. Churchill believed that to be possible if the Poles could decide between themselves the question of a Government. He, Churchill, did not have too high an opinion of the Poles.

Stalin remarked that there were very good men among the Poles. The Poles were brave fighters. The Polish people had produced some outstanding scientists and artists.

Churchill said that the only thing he wanted was for all the sides to have equal opportunities.

Stalin remarked that all non-fascist and anti-fascist sides would have equal opportunities.

Churchill said that he did not consider it quite right to have the watershed run between fascist and non-fascist. He preferred the term "democrats".

Stalin said that he had before him the draft Declaration on Liberated Europe proposed by the American delegation. The draft contained the following sentence: "The establishment of order in Europe and the reconstruction of national economic life should be achieved in a way that would allow the liberated peoples to obliterate the last traces of fascism and Nazism, and to create democratic institutions of their own choice." (Retranslated from the Russian.—*Ed.*) Those were good words! There the distinction between fascism and anti-fascism was clearly drawn. Those words showed that there could be no unity between democracy and fascism.

Churchill confirmed that no such unity could or would exist.

Roosevelt said that, in his view, Poland would provide an example of the practical implementation of the principles of the Declaration on Liberated Europe. The sentence read out by Marshal Stalin was of great significance, because it gave them the opportunity to obliterate all traces of fascism. The following paragraph of the Declaration said that the peoples could establish provisional government authorities representing all democratic sections of the population, and subsequently to set up permanent ones through free and just elections. Roosevelt would like the Polish elections to be, like Caesar's wife, above suspicion.

Stalin remarked that Caesar's wife only had that kind of reputation. Actually, she wasn't all that lily-white.

Roosevelt said that the elections in Poland had to be absolutely "pure", so pure that no one could cast any doubt on them, and that the Poles themselves—very hot-headed people—could accept the elections without any reservations. Roosevelt summed up by saying that the Foreign Ministers were well aware of the views of their Heads of Government concerning the Polish elections. They should deal with the question that night and report on the results of their work the following day.

Stalin said that he agreed with Roosevelt's amendment: the substitution of the words "the present Provisional Government" by the words "the Provisional Government now functioning in Poland".

Roosevelt went on to the next question, the Declaration on Liberated Europe.

Churchill said that Eden wanted to make a remark on the draft Declaration. Churchill himself agreed with the Declaration; he considered it necessary to note in the record that Great Britain followed the principles of the Atlantic Charter in the sense which Churchill had given it in Parliament upon his return from Newfoundland. Churchill would present the text of his Parliamentary statement at the next sitting [. . .].

Roosevelt proposed that the sitting be closed.

Churchill said that he wanted to discuss the question of war criminals. What he meant was war criminals whose crimes were not connected with definite geographical places.

Roosevelt declared that the question of war criminals was a complicated one. It was impossible to examine it during the current Conference. Wouldn't it be better to refer the question to the three Foreign Ministers? Let them submit a report within three or four weeks.

Churchill said that he had drawn up a draft declaration on war criminals for the Moscow Conference of 1943. At the time, Churchill had made a proposal, which had been adopted, on the handing over of criminals to the countries where they had committed their crimes. The said declaration also made mention of the chief criminals whose crimes were not connected with any specific geographical place. What was to be done with these chief criminals? Churchill thought the first thing to do was to draw up a list of such persons, with the right of adding to it in the future. That would isolate them from their peoples. Churchill believed that the best thing would be to shoot the chief criminals as soon as they were caught.

Stalin asked: What was to be done with criminals who, like Hess, had been caught already? Would he be included in the list which Churchill proposed to draw up? Could prisoners of war be included in the list of criminals? The old view had been that prisoners of war could not be tried.

Churchill replied that, of course, prisoners of war who had violated the laws could be put on trial. Otherwise war criminals would start surrendering in order to avoid punishment. However, Churchill had understood Marshal Stalin to mean that before the chief criminals were shot they should be tried.

Stalin replied in the affirmative.

Churchill asked what the court procedure was to be: juridical or political?

Roosevelt declared that the procedure should not be too juridical. At all events, correspondents and photographers should not be admitted to the trial.

Churchill said that, in his view, the trial of the chief criminals should be a political and not a juridical act. Churchill would like the Three Powers to be clear on this question. However, nothing should be published on the subject to prevent the chief criminals from revenging themselves on Allied prisoners of war.

Roosevelt proposed that the question of the war criminals should be referred for study to the Foreign Ministers of the Three Powers.

[*That was accepted.*]

Stalin asked whether the offensive on the Western front had started.

Churchill replied that a 100,000-strong British Army had started an offensive in the Nijmegen area at 10 o'clock the previous morning. The troops had advanced 3,000 yards on a five-mile front. They had reached the Siegfried Line. The defences were not particularly strong, with the exception of two villages. Several hundred prisoners had been taken. The second wave of the offensive was due to start the following day. The U.S. Ninth Army was extending the front of its offensive. The offensive would be continuous and would steadily grow.

February 10, 1945

Eden read out the text of the Statement on Poland agreed at the conferences of the Foreign Ministers on the night of February 9 and the morning of February 10.

Roosevelt declared that he agreed with the text of the Statement on Poland read out by Eden.

Churchill said that an agreement had been reached on Poland's eastern border, and there was agreement that the Poles should be given East Prussia and the territory up to the Oder. However, Churchill had some doubts about whether the Poles should have their border run along the Neisse River (Western). Churchill added that he had received a cable from the War Cabinet which set out the apprehensions concerning the difficulties involved in resettling large numbers of people into Germany.

Roosevelt remarked that it would be desirable to have the opinion of the new Polish Government on the western border.

Stalin said that the Statement should say something definite about the border.

Churchill believed it was important to issue a statement on the agreement reached on the question of the eastern border (Curzon Line). But then if nothing were said there and then about the western border, people would at once ask where Poland's border in the west was to run. Churchill believed that the opinion of the Poles themselves on the question of the western border should be taken into account and that this question should be settled at the peace conference.

Roosevelt thought that it would be better to say nothing about Poland's borders, because the question still had to be discussed in the Senate, and he, Roosevelt, was not authorised to take any decisions on it.

Churchill declared that something still had to be said about the western border. He thought a suitable formula could be found, since the Three Governments were agreed that Poland was to receive an accession of territory to the west and the north, and that the opinion of the Polish Government was to be taken into account in deciding the question.

Stalin also considered it necessary to have the decision refer to Poland's borders.

Roosevelt agreed with that in principle and proposed that the three Foreign Ministers should be asked to examine the question and add another paragraph on borders to the text of the Statement on Poland.

[*The Conference adopted the proposal and went on to the Declaration on Liberated Europe.*

The Soviet delegation proposed the following addendum to the third paragraph from the end:

"*They will immediately consult with each other on the necessary measures in exercising the joint responsibility established in the present Declaration.*"

The proposal of the Soviet delegation was adopted.]

Eden declared that there was another addendum concerning the French. The text of the addendum was as follows:

"In issuing the present Declaration, the Three Powers express the hope that the Provisional Government of the French Republic may join them in the proposed procedure."

Roosevelt declared that after some thought he had arrived at the conclusion that de Gaulle could join in the Declaration, if the French took part in the Allied control mechanism in Germany. He, Roosevelt, had previously been against France taking part in the Control Council in Germany, but he now favoured French participation in it.

Stalin declared that he had no objection to the French participating in the Control Council, and that he favoured their joining in the Declaration.

Churchill said that that should be said in the communiqué.

Stalin and *Roosevelt* agreed with Churchill's proposal.

[*The Conference went on to the question of Yugoslavia.*]

Eden proposed the dispatch of a cable to Tito and Subasić.

Stalin proposed that the text of the cable should speak of the immediate entry into force of the Tito-Subasić agreement, the inclusion of the members of the Skupština into the body of the Veće, and the approval by the new parliament of the laws adopted by the Veće. He proposed that Point 3 of the cable—saying that the Government was merely a provisional one until the free expression of the people's will—be dropped and the whole text of the cabled message incorporated in the communiqué.

Roosevelt and *Churchill* agreed with Stalin's proposal.

[*The Conference then adopted a decision to entrust the*

working out of the text of the cable to the three Foreign Ministers.]

Eden reported that everything had been agreed on the question of the international security organisation.

[*The Conference went on to the question of reparations.*]

Churchill said that the amount of reparations should not be specified.

Roosevelt agreed that perhaps nothing should be said at that time about amounts of money. It would be better to authorise the Reparations Commission to make a study of the question and then to determine the amount of reparations.

Stalin declared that it would be wrong to create the impression that they intended to levy reparations in the form of money. It was not a question of money but of goods worth $20,000 million. There were already three agreements—with Hungary, Finland and Rumania—which stated the amount of reparations levied in kind, and until then they had not had any misunderstandings on that score. Or was it the wish of the Conference that the Russians should not receive any reparations at all?

Churchill said: Not at all, on the contrary. He wanted to propose that the Commission should study the question of reparations and draw up a report on the levy of reparations.

Stalin raised the question: Was there agreement that goods should be taken from Germany to cover the losses? They had not yet taken any decision on the question of reparations, and even the principles of levying reparations had not been adopted. He proposed the adoption of the following decision: "The Three Powers are in agreement that Germany must compensate in goods (or in kind) the most substantial damage inflicted by her on the Allied nations in the course of the war. The Reparations Commission is to discuss the question of the amounts of compensation for the losses, taking the Soviet-American formula as a basis, and is to report on the results to the Governments." Stalin further pointed out that the American side had agreed to accept the figure of $20,000 million as a basis for discussion, naturally assuming that the compensation of losses was to be in kind. The Soviet side was not proposing the publication of the decision just then. That could be done when all the Three Powers would deem such a step necessary.

Roosevelt declared that he agreed with Stalin's proposals.

Churchill reiterated that the Conference would not bind itself by any figures until the Reparations Commission had made a study of the question and had arrived at definite conclusions.

Stalin replied that they were not obliging the Conference to adopt any figures, but were merely asking the Commission to take the said figure as material for discussion.

Churchill announced that he had received a cable from the War Cabinet and wanted to read out an extract from it. Churchill then declared that the British considered it absolutely impossible to name any amount of reparations just then. Churchill pointed out that the British attached special importance to the capacity of the Germans to pay for their imports. Otherwise, they would find themselves in the position, said Churchill, when they would have to pay Germany, while others received the reparations.

Stalin asked Churchill to name his figure of reparations. The Soviet side did not consider its figure invariable and merely offered it for discussion. He proposed the adoption of a decision on reparations in the following form:

1) The Heads of the Three Governments agreed that Germany must compensate in kind the damage inflicted by her on the Allied nations in the course of the war.

2) To authorise the Moscow Reparations Commission to discuss the question of the amounts of losses subject to compensation and report its conclusions to the Governments.

Roosevelt and *Churchill* declared that they agreed with Stalin's proposal.

Stalin asked ironically: You will not go back on this tomorrow? [. . .]

[*The Conference went on to the question of Poland's borders.*]

Eden read out the British draft of the addendum to the Statement on Poland concerning her borders.

Roosevelt said that on the question of Poland's borders he had an amendment to the text: instead of the words "the Three Governments" insert "the Heads of the Three Governments". Roosevelt explained that if it said "the Three Governments", he, as President, would have to take the question to Congress, something that it was desirable to avoid. In the second phrase, the words "the Three Governments" should be deleted and the word "recognised" written instead. In the last phrase, the words "they agree" should be substituted by "they consider". Roosevelt accepted the text of the addendum to the Statement on Poland with the said amendments.

[*The text of the addendum on Poland's borders was adopted with Roosevelt's amendments.*]

Eighth Sitting at Livadia Palace

February 11, 1945

Roosevelt opened the sitting and proposed to start a discussion of the draft Communiqué.

Stalin proposed that the American draft Communiqué should be taken as a basis for discussion.

Churchill agreed with that.

[*The Conference adopted the American draft as a basis and went on to discuss Section I of the Communiqué: The Defeat of Germany.*]

Churchill proposed the deletion in the second phrase of the word "jointly".

[*Churchill's proposal was adopted.*]

Stalin remarked that the first section of the Communiqué was well drafted, and proposed that they go on to a discussion of the second section.

[*Stalin's proposal was adopted.*]

Eden proposed that the following words should be added concerning the French zone: "The limits of the French zone will be agreed by the four Governments concerned through their representatives on the E.A.C."

[*Eden's addendum was adopted. The Conference went on to a discussion of Section III on Reparation by Germany.*]

Churchill asked that he be shown the draft of the special protocol on reparations from Germany proposed that morning by the Soviet delegation.

After studying the text of the protocol, Churchill remarked that in English "reparation" sounded better and was more impressive than "reparations".

Churchill agreed to leave, in Section III of the Communiqué, the general reference to Germany's reparation of the damage inflicted by her on the Allied countries.

Roosevelt agreed with the text of Section III and Churchill's remarks on it.

Eden did not object to the text of the Soviet protocol on reparations, but proposed that the final discussion of it should be postponed until the entire text of the Communiqué was reviewed.

[*The Conference went on to discuss Section IV on the United Nations Conference.*]

The Soviet delegation proposed the addition of a new paragraph following the first two with this wording: "It was also decided to recommend to the Conference that it should invite the Ukraine and Byelorussia as original members of the international security organisation."]

Roosevelt declared that the·publication of that decision at that time would create political difficulties for him at home, and proposed that they confine themselves to the agreement reached at the Conference to the effect that the Americans would support the proposal to invite the two Soviet Republics as original members of the organisation.

Churchill also believed that great difficulties and disputes could arise in the event of publication of the decision on the Soviet Republics. The British dominions could lodge protests against one state having more than one vote. Churchill needed to contact the dominions and prepare them on the question of the Ukraine and Byelorussia participating as original members in the international security organisation. That is why he proposed that the agreement on the Ukraine and Byelorussia should be written into the decisions of the Conference.

Stalin said that in that case the Soviet delegation could withdraw its proposal, and proposed that they should go on.

Roosevelt declared that Stalin's agreement to withdraw the Soviet proposal would help Roosevelt to avoid a war with the Irish in the United States.

[*The Conference went on to discuss Section V on the Declaration on Liberated Europe.*]

Churchill declared that he had no remarks or amendments.

Roosevelt and *Stalin* declared that they did not have any amendments either.

[*The text of Section V was adopted. The Conference went on to discuss Section VI on Poland. The Declaration on Poland was adopted without amendments.*]

Churchill remarked, with reference to that section, that he anticipated great criticism of the British Government, especially by the London Poles, and accusations that it had surrendered its positions to the U.S.S.R.

Roosevelt declared that he has ten times as many Poles in the United States as Churchill had in Britain, but he would nevertheless back the Declaration on Poland in every way.

[*The Conference went on to discuss Section VII on Yugoslavia. The text of Section VII was adopted. The Conference went on to discuss Section VIII on the Meetings of the Foreign Secretaries.*]

Stalin proposed the adoption of the British text.

[*All agreed. The Conference went on to discuss the section of the British draft which dealt with prisoners of war.*]

Stalin proposed that the section on prisoners of war should not be included in the Communiqué, but that its text should be adopted as a special decision.

Churchill asked whether they could publish the agreement on prisoners of war which was to be signed that day after the morning sitting.

Stalin replied that the agreement could be published.

[*The Conference went on to discuss Section IX on Unity for Peace as for War. The text of the Anglo-American draft of the section was adopted by all without any objections or remarks. The Conference went on to discuss the last section of the American draft Communiqué: Summary.*]

Stalin tabled the proposal: was it not better to exclude the Summary, because it was weaker than the content of the Communiqué itself?

Roosevelt and *Churchill* agreed with that.

[*Discussion of the Communiqué was ended.*]

Roosevelt said that the Communiqué should be signed by the Heads of Government and he, Roosevelt, proposed that Stalin's signature should be affixed first.

Stalin objected by saying that there was a sharp-tongued press in the United States, which could give the impression that Stalin had had the President and the Prime Minister on a lead. That was why he proposed that the Communiqué should be signed in alphabetical order, that is, with Roosevelt's first, Stalin's second, and Churchill's third.

Churchill declared that according to the English alphabet his signature would be first.

Stalin replied that he was prepared to accept Churchill's proposal.

[*The Heads of Government agreed to sign the Communiqué after luncheon, when the Foreign Ministers had made the amendments in accordance with the results of the discussion of the text of the Communiqué at that day's sitting.*]

Returning to the question of the protocol on reparations from Germany, *Roosevelt* said that the draft protocol proposed by the Soviet delegation was acceptable to him.

Churchill declared that he wanted to read the text of the draft protocol once again, as, he thought, it would require some stylistic editing, without however any changes in the content of the protocol. Having read it, Churchill declared that, apart from some stylistic changes, he agreed with the draft protocol.

Churchill proposed that they discuss the time of publication of the Communiqué.

Early proposed that the Communiqué should be published at 8.00 a.m. Washington time on February 13.

[*As a result of the discussion of the question, the Heads of Government agreed to broadcast the text of the Communiqué simultaneously in Moscow, London and Washington, at 23.30 Moscow time on Monday, February 12.*]

COMMUNIQUÉ

ON THE CRIMEA CONFERENCE OF THE HEADS
OF GOVERNMENT OF THE SOVIET UNION,
THE UNITED STATES AND GREAT BRITAIN

For the past eight days, Winston S. Churchill, Prime Minister of Great Britain, Franklin D. Roosevelt, President of the United States of America, and Marshal J. V. Stalin, Chairman of the Council of People's Commissars of the Union of Soviet Socialist Republics have met with the Foreign Secretaries, Chiefs of Staff, and other advisers in the Crimea.

. . . .
. . . .

The following statement is made by the Prime Minister of Great Britain, the President of the United States of America, and the Chairman of the Council of People's Commissars of the Union of Soviet Socialist Republics on the results of the Crimea Conference:

I

THE DEFEAT OF GERMANY

We have considered and determined the military plans of the Three Allied Powers for the final defeat of the common enemy. The military staffs of the three Allied Nations have met in daily meetings throughout the Conference. These meetings have been most satisfactory from every point of view and have resulted in closer co-ordination of the military effort of the Three Allies than ever before. The fullest information has been interchanged. The timing, scope, and co-ordination of new and even more powerful blows to be launched by our Armies and Air Forces into the heart of Germany from the east, west, north, and south have been fully agreed and planned in detail.

Our combined military plans will be made known only as we execute them, but we believe that the very close working partnership among the three staffs attained at this Conference will result in shortening the war. Meetings of the three staffs will be continued in the future whenever the need arises.

Nazi Germany is doomed. The German people will only make the cost of their defeat heavier to themselves by attempting to continue a hopeless resistance.

II

THE OCCUPATION AND CONTROL OF GERMANY

We have agreed on common policies and plans for enforcing the unconditional surrender terms which we shall impose together on Nazi Germany after German armed resistance has been finally crushed. These terms will not be made known until the final defeat of Germany has been accomplished. Under the agreed plan, the forces of the Three Powers will each occupy a separate zone of Germany. Coordinated administration and control has been provided for under the plan through a Central Control Commission, consisting of the supreme commanders of the Three Powers, with headquarters in Berlin. It has been agreed that France should be invited by the Three Powers, if she should so desire, to take over a zone of occupation, and to participate as a fourth member of the Control Commission. The limits of the French zone will be agreed by the four Governments concerned through their representatives on the European Advisory Commission.

It is our inflexible purpose to destroy German militarism and Nazism and to ensure that Germany will never again be able to disturb the peace of the world. We are determined to disarm and disband all German armed forces; break up for all time the German General Staff that has repeatedly contrived the resurgence of German militarism; remove or destroy all German military equipment; eliminate or control all German industry that could be used for military production; bring all war criminals to just and swift punishment and exact reparation in kind for the destruction wrought by the Germans; wipe out the Nazi Party, Nazi laws, organisations, and institutions, remove all Nazi and militarist influences from public office and from the cultural and economic life of the German people; and take in harmony such other measures in Germany as may be necessary to the future peace and safety of the world. It is not our purpose to destroy the people of Germany, but only when Nazism and militarism have been extirpated will there be hope for a decent life for Germans, and a place for them in the comity of nations.

III

REPARATION BY GERMANY

We have considered the question of the damage caused by Germany to the Allied Nations in this war and recognised it as just that Germany be obliged to make compensation for this damage in kind to the greatest extent possible.

A commission for the compensation of damage will be established. The commission will be instructed to consider the question of the extent and methods for compensating damage caused by Germany to the Allied countries. The commission will work in Moscow.

IV

UNITED NATIONS CONFERENCE

We are resolved upon the earliest possible establishment with our Allies of a general international organisation to maintain peace and security. We believe that this is essential, both to prevent aggression and to remove the political, economic, and social causes of war through the close and continuing collaboration of all peace-loving peoples.

The foundations were laid at Dumbarton Oaks. On the important question of voting procedure, however, agreement was not there reached. The present Conference has been able to resolve this difficulty.

We have agreed that a Conference of United Nations should be called to meet at San Francisco in the United States on April 25, 1945, to prepare the Charter of such an organisation, along the lines proposed in the informal conversations at Dumbarton Oaks.

The Government of China and the Provisional Government of France will be immediately consulted and invited to sponsor invitations to the Conference jointly with the Governments of the United States, Great Britain, and the Union of Soviet Socialist Republics. As soon as the consultation with China and France has been completed, the text of the proposals on voting procedure will be made public.

V

DECLARATION ON LIBERATED EUROPE

We have drawn up and subscribed to a Declaration on Liberated Europe. This Declaration provides for concerting policies of the Three Powers and for joint action by them in meeting the political and economic problems of liberated Europe in accordance with democratic principles. The text of the Declaration is as follows:

"The Premier of the Union of Soviet Socialist Republics, the Prime Minister of the United Kingdom, and the President of the United States of America have consulted with each other in the common interests of the peoples of their countries and those of liberated Europe. They jointly declare their mutual agreement to concert during the temporary period of instability in liberated Europe the policies of their Three Governments in assisting the peoples liberated from the domination of Nazi Germany and the peoples of the former Axis satellite states of Europe to solve by democratic means their pressing political and economic problems.

"The establishment of order in Europe and the rebuilding of national economic life must be achieved by processes which will enable the liberated peoples to destroy the last vestiges of Nazism and fascism and to create democratic institutions of their own choice. This is a principle of the Atlantic Charter—the right of all peoples to choose the form of government under which they will live—the restoration of sovereign rights and self-government to those peoples who have been forcibly deprived of them by the aggressor nations.

"To foster the conditions in which the liberated peoples may exercise these rights, the Three Governments will jointly assist the people in any European liberated state or former Axis satellite state in Europe where in their judgement conditions require (a) to establish conditions of internal peace; (b) to carry out emergency measures for the relief of distressed people; (c) to form interim governmental authorities broadly representative of all democratic elements in the population and pledged to the earliest possible establishment through free elections of governments responsible to the will of the people; and (d) to facilitate where necessary the holding of such elections.

"The Three Governments will consult the other United Nations and provisional authorities or other Governments in Europe when matters of direct interest to them are under consideration.

"When, in the opinion of the Three Governments, conditions in any European liberated state or any former Axis satellite state in Europe make such action necessary, they will immediately consult together on the measures necessary to discharge the joint responsibilities set forth in this declaration.

"By this Declaration we reaffirm our faith in the principles of the Atlantic Charter, our pledge in the Declaration by the United Nations, and our determination to build in co-operation with other peace-loving nations world order under law, dedicated to peace, security, freedom, and general well-being of all mankind.

"In issuing this Declaration, the Three Powers express the hope that the Provisional Government of the French Republic may be associated with them in the procedure suggested."

VI

POLAND

We came to the Crimea Conference resolved to settle our differences about Poland. We discussed fully all aspects of the question. We reaffirm our common desire to see established a strong, free, independent and democratic Poland. As a result of our discussions we have agreed on the conditions in which a new Polish Provisional Government of National Unity may be formed in such a manner as to command recognition by the three major Powers.

The agreement reached is as follows:

"A new situation has been created in Poland as a result of her complete liberation by the Red Army. This calls for the establishment of a Polish Provisional Government which can be more broadly based than was possible before the recent liberation of western Poland. The Provisional Government which is now functioning in Poland should therefore be reorganised on a broader democratic basis with the inclusion of democratic leaders from Poland itself and from Poles abroad. This new Government should then be called the Polish Provisional Government of National Unity.

"Mr. Molotov, Mr. Harriman, and Sir A. Clark Kerr are authorised as a commission to consult in the first instance in Moscow with members of the present Provisional Government and with other Polish democratic leaders from within Poland and from abroad, with a view to the reorganisation of the present Government along the above lines. This Polish Provisional Government of National Unity shall be pledged to the holding of free and unfettered elections as soon as possible, on the basis of universal suffrage and secret ballot. In these elections all democratic and anti-Nazi parties shall have the right to take part and to put forward candidates.

"When a Polish Provisional Government of National Unity has been properly formed in conformity with the above, the Government of the Union of Soviet Socialist Republics, which now maintains diplomatic relations with the present Provisional Government of Poland, and the Government of the United Kingdom, and the Government of the United States of America, will establish diplomatic relations with the new Polish Provisional Government of National Unity, and will exchange ambassadors by whose reports the respective Governments will be kept informed about the situation in Poland.

"The Three Heads of Government consider that the eastern frontier of Poland should follow the Curzon line with digressions from it in some regions of 5 to 8 kilometres in favour of Poland. They recognised that Poland must receive substantial accessions of territory in the north and west. They feel that the opinion of the new Polish Provisional Government of National Unity should be sought in due course on the extent of these accessions and that the final delimitation of the western frontier of Poland should thereafter await the peace conference."

VII

YUGOSLAVIA

We have agreed to recommend to Marshal Tito and Dr. Subasić that the Agreement between them should be put into effect immediately, and that a new Government should be formed on the basis of that Agreement.

We also recommend that as soon as the new Government has been formed it should declare that:

1) the Anti-Fascist Assembly of National Liberation (Avnoj) should be extended to include members of the last Yugoslav Parliament (Skupština) who have not compromised themselves by collaboration with the enemy, thus forming a body to be known as a temporary parliament; and,

2) legislative acts passed by the Anti-Fascist Assembly of National Liberation will be subject to subsequent ratification by a Constituent Assembly.

There was also a general review of other Balkan questions.

VIII

MEETINGS OF FOREIGN SECRETARIES

Throughout the Conference, besides the daily meetings of the Heads of Government and the Foreign Secretaries, separate meetings of the three Foreign Secretaries, and their advisers have also been held daily.

These meetings have proved of the utmost value and the Conference agree that permanent machinery should be set up for regular consultation between the three Foreign Secretaries. They will, therefore, meet as often as may be necessary, probably about every 3 or 4 months. These meetings will be held in rotation in the three capitals, the first meeting being held in London, after the United Nations Conference on World Organisation.

IX

UNITY FOR PEACE AS FOR WAR

Our meeting here in the Crimea has reaffirmed our common determination to maintain and strengthen in the peace to come that unity of purpose and of action which has made victory possible and certain for the United Nations in this war. We believe that this is a sacred obligation which our Governments owe to our peoples and to all the peoples of the world.

Only with the continuing and growing co-operation and understanding among our three countries and among all the peace-loving nations can the highest aspiration of humanity be realised—a secure and lasting peace which will, in the words of the Atlantic Charter, "afford assurance, that all the men in all the lands may live out their lives in freedom from fear and want".

Victory in this war and establishment of the proposed international organisation will provide the greatest opportunity in all history to create in the years to come the essential conditions of such a peace.

February 11, 1945

> *WINSTON S. CHURCHILL*
> *FRANKLIN D. ROOSEVELT*
> *J. V. STALIN*

Protocol of Proceedings of the Crimea Conference

The Crimea Conference of the Heads of Government of the United States of America, the United Kingdom and the Union of Soviet Socialist Republics which took place from February 4th to 11th came to the following conclusions.

WORLD ORGANISATION

It was decided:

(1) that a United Nations Conference on the proposed World Organisation should be summoned for Wednesday, 25th April, 1945, and should be held in the United States of America;

(2) the nations to be invited to this Conference should be:

(a) the United Nations as they existed on the 8th February, 1945 and

(b) such of the Associated Nations as have declared war on the common enemy by 1st March, 1945. (For this purpose by the term "Associated Nations" was meant the eight Associated Nations and Turkey.) When the Conference on

World Organisation is held, the delegates of the United Kingdom and United States of America will support a proposal to admit to original membership two Soviet Socialist Republics, i.e., the Ukraine and White Russia;

(3) that the United States Government on behalf of the Three Powers should consult the Government of China and the French Provisional Government in regard to the decisions taken at the present Conference concerning the proposed World Organisation;

(4) that the text of the invitation to be issued to all the nations which would take part in the United Nations Conference should be as follows:

Invitation

"The Government of the United States of America, on behalf of itself and of the Governments of the United Kingdom, the Union of Soviet Socialist Republics, and the Republic of China and of the Provisional Government of the French Republic, invite the Government of ... to send representatives to a Conference of the United Nations to be held on 25th April, 1945, or soon thereafter, at San Francisco in the United States of America to prepare a Charter for a General International Organisation for the maintenance of international peace and security.

"The above-named Governments suggest that the Conference consider as affording a basis for such a Charter the Proposals for the Establishment of a General International Organisation, which were made public last October as a result of the Dumbarton Oaks Conference, and which have now been supplemented by the following provisions for Section C of Chapter VI:

"C. *Voting*

"1. Each member of the Security Council should have one vote.

"2. Decisions of the Security Council on procedural matters should be made by an affirmative vote of seven members.

"3. Decisions of the Security Council on all other matters should be made by an affirmative vote of seven members, including the concurring votes of the permanent members; provided that, in decisions under Chapter VIII, Section A and under the second sentence of paragraph 1 of Section C, Chapter VIII, a party to a dispute should abstain from voting.

"Further information as to arrangements will be transmitted subsequently.

"In the event that the Government of ... desires in advance of the Conference to present views or comments concerning the proposals, the Government of the United States of America will be pleased to transmit such views and comments to the other participating Governments."

Territorial Trusteeship

It was agreed that the five Nations which will have permanent seats on the Security Council should consult each other prior to the United Nations Conference on the question of territorial trusteeship.

The acceptance of this recommendation is subject to its being made clear that territorial trusteeship will only apply to (a) existing mandates of the League of Nations; (b) territories detached from the enemy as a result of the present war; (c) any other territory which might voluntarily be placed under trusteeship; and (d) no discussion of actual territories is contemplated at the forthcoming United Nations Conference or in the preliminary consultations, and it will be a matter for subsequent agreement which territories within the above categories will be placed under trusteeship.

. . . .

ZONE OF OCCUPATION FOR THE FRENCH AND CONTROL COUNCIL FOR GERMANY

It was agreed that a zone in Germany, to be occupied by the French Forces, should be allocated to France. This zone would be formed out of the British and American zones and its extent would be settled by the British and Americans in consultation with the French Provisional Government.

It was also agreed that the French Provisional Government should be invited to become a member of the Allied Control Council for Germany.

The following protocol has been approved.

Protocol
On the Talks Between
the Heads of Three Governments
at the Crimea Conference
on the German Reparations in Kind

The Heads of the three Governments have agreed as follows:

1. Germany must pay in kind for the losses caused by her to the Allied nations in the course of the war.

Reparations are to be received in the first instance by those countries which have borne the main burden of the war, have suffered the heaviest losses and have organised victory over the enemy.

2. Reparation in kind is to be exacted from Germany in three following forms:

a) Removals within 2 years from the surrender of Germany or the cessation of organised resistance from the national wealth of Germany located on the territory of Germany herself as well as outside her territory (equipment, machine-tools, ships, rolling stock, German investments abroad, shares of industrial, transport and other enterprises in Germany, etc.), these removals to be carried out chiefly for purpose of destroying the war potential of Germany.

b) Annual deliveries of goods from current production for a period to be fixed.

c) Use of German labour.

3. For the working out on the above principles of a detailed plan for exaction of reparation from Germany an Allied Reparation Commission will be set up in Moscow. It will consist of three representatives—one from the Union of Soviet Socialist Republics, one from the United Kingdom and one from the United States of America.

4. With regard to the fixing of the total sum of the reparation as well as the distribution of it among the countries which suffered from the German aggression the Soviet and American delegations agreed as follows:

"The Moscow Reparation Commission should take in its

initial studies as a basis for discussion the suggestion of the Soviet Government that the total sum of the reparation in accordance with the points (a) and (b) of the Paragraph 2 should be 20 billion dollars and that 50 per cent of it should go to the Union of Soviet Socialist Republics."

The British delegation was of the opinion that pending consideration of the reparation question by the Moscow Reparation Commission no figures of reparation should be mentioned.

The above Soviet-American proposal has been passed to the Moscow Reparation Commission as one of the proposals to be considered by the Commission.

MAJOR WAR CRIMINALS

The Conference agreed that the question of the major war criminals should be the subject of enquiry by the three Foreign Secretaries for report in due course after the close of the Conference.

. . . .

AGREEMENT BETWEEN THE ALLIED STATES RELATING TO PRISONERS OF WAR AND CIVILIANS OF THESE STATES

Negotiations have taken place at the Crimea Conference between the British, American and Soviet delegations on the conclusion of a comprehensive agreement concerning measures for the protection, maintenance and repatriation of prisoners of war and civilians of Great Britain, the Soviet Union and the United States of America liberated by the Allied forces now invading Germany. The texts of the Agreements signed on February 11 between the U.S.S.R. and Great Britain and between the U.S.S.R. and the United States of America are identical. The Agreement between the Soviet Union and Great Britain was signed by V. M. Molotov and Mr. Eden. The Agreement between the Soviet Union and the United States of America was signed by Lieut.-Gen. Gryzlov and General Deane.

Under these Agreements, each ally was to provide food, clothing, medical attention, and other needs for the nationals of the others until transport is available for their repatriation. Soviet officers were to assist British and American authorities in their task of caring for Soviet citizens liberated by the British and American forces during such time as they were on the continent of Europe or in the United Kingdom, awaiting transport to take them home.

British and American officers were to assist the Soviet Government in its task of caring for British subjects and American citizens.

With the achievement of agreement, the Three Governments were pledged to give every assistance consistent with operational requirements to help to insure that all these prisoners of war and civilians were speedily repatriated.

AGREEMENT BETWEEN THE THREE GREAT POWERS ON QUESTIONS OF THE FAR EAST

The leaders of the Three Great Powers—the Soviet Union, the United States of America and Great Britain—have agreed that in two or three months after Germany has surrendered and the war in Europe has terminated, the Soviet Union shall enter into the war against Japan on the side of the Allies on condition that:

1. The status quo in Outer-Mongolia (the Mongolian People's Republic) shall be preserved;

2. The former rights of Russia violated by the treacherous attack of Japan in 1904 shall be restored, viz.:

a) the southern part of Sakhalin as well as all the islands adjacent to it shall be returned to the Soviet Union,

b) the commercial port of Dairen shall be internationalised, the pre-eminent interests of the Soviet Union in this port being safeguarded and the lease of Port Arthur as a naval base of the U.S.S.R. restored,

c) the Chinese-Eastern Railroad and the South-Manchurian Railroad which provides an outlet to Dairen shall be jointly operated by the establishment of a joint Soviet-Chinese Company, it being understood that the pre-eminent interests of the Soviet Union shall be safeguarded and that China shall retain full sovereignty in Manchuria;

3. The Kuril Islands shall be handed over to the Soviet Union.

It is understood that the agreement concerning Outer-Mongolia and the ports and railroads referred to above will require concurrence of Generalissimo Chiang Kai-shek. The President will take measures in order to obtain this concurrence on advice from Marshal Stalin.

The Heads of the Three Great Powers have agreed that these claims of the Soviet Union shall be unquestionably fulfilled after Japan has been defeated.

For its part the Soviet Union expressed its readiness to conclude with the National Government of China a pact of friendship and alliance between the U.S.S.R. and China in order to render assistance to China with its armed forces for the purpose of liberating China from the Japanese yoke.

February 11, 1945

> *J. V. STALIN*
> *FRANKLIN D. ROOSEVELT*
> *WINSTON S. CHURCHILL*

THE POTSDAM CONFERENCE

(July 17-August 2, 1945)

First Sitting

July 17, 1945

Churchill: Who is to be chairman at our Conference?

Stalin: I propose President Truman of the United States.

Churchill: The British delegation supports this proposal.

Truman: I accept the chairmanship of this Conference.

Let me put before you some of the questions that have accumulated by the time of our meeting and that require urgent examination. We can then discuss the procedure of the Conference.

Churchill: We shall have the right to add to the agenda.

Truman: One of the most acute problems at present is to set up some kind of mechanism for arranging peace talks. Without it, Europe's economic development will continue to the detriment of the cause of the Allies and the whole world.

The experience of the Versailles Conference after the First World War showed that a peace conference can have very many flaws unless it is prepared beforehand by the victor Powers. A peace conference without preliminary preparations takes place in a tense atmosphere of contending sides, which inevitably delays the working out of its decisions.

That is why I propose, considering the experience of the Versailles Conference, that we should here and now set up a special Council of Foreign Ministers, consisting of the Ministers of Great Britain, the U.S.S.R., the United States, France and China, that is, the permanent members of the Security Council of the United Nations set up at the San Francisco Conference. This Council of Foreign Ministers for preparing a peace conference should meet as soon as possible after our meeting. It is in this spirit and on these lines that I have drawn up a draft for the setting up of a Council of Foreign Ministers for preparing a peace conference which I now put before you.

Churchill: I propose that we refer the matter for consideration to our Foreign Ministers, who will report to us at our next sitting.

Stalin: I agree, but I am not quite clear about the participation of China's Foreign Minister in the Council. After all, this is a question of European problems, isn't it? How appropriate is the participation of China's representative?

Truman: We can discuss this question after the Foreign Ministers report to us.

Stalin: All right.

Truman: About a Control Council for Germany. This Council should start its work as soon as possible, in accordance with the agreement reached. With that end in view I submit for your consideration a draft containing the principles which, in our opinion, should govern the work of this Control Council.

Churchill: I have had no chance to read this document, but I shall read it with full attention and respect, and it then could be discussed. This question is so broad that it should not be referred to the Foreign Ministers, but we should study and discuss it ourselves, and then, if need be, refer it to the Ministers.

Truman: We could discuss this matter tomorrow.

Stalin: Indeed, we could discuss the question tomorrow. The Ministers could acquaint themselves with it beforehand; that would be advisable, because we ourselves will be studying the question at the same time.

Churchill: Our Ministers already have enough to do on the first document. Tomorrow we could refer this second question to them as well, couldn't we?

Stalin: Good, let's do that tomorrow.

Truman reads the content of a memorandum which says that under the decisions of the Yalta Declaration on Liberated Europe the three Powers undertook certain obligations in respect of the liberated peoples of Europe and Germany's former satellites. These decisions provided for an agreed policy of the three Powers and their joint action in the solution of the political and economic problems of liberated Europe in accordance with democratic principles.

Since the Yalta Conference, the obligations undertaken by us in the Declaration on Liberated Europe remain unfulfilled. In the opinion of the U.S. Government, continued failure to fulfil these obligations will be regarded all over the world as indicating lack of unity between the three Great Powers and will undermine confidence in the sincerity and unity of purpose among the United Nations. That is why the U.S. Government proposes that the fulfilment of the obligations of this Declaration should be fully co-ordinated at this Conference.

The three great Allied states must agree to the need for an immediate reorganisation of the present Governments of Rumania and Bulgaria in strict conformity with Paragraph 3, Point "c" of the Declaration on Liberated Europe. Consultations must be held immediately to work out the procedure necessary for the reorganisation of these Governments so that they include representatives of all important democratic groups. After these Governments are reorganised, there may be diplomatic recognition of them on the part of the Allied Powers and conclusion of corresponding treaties.

In conformity with the obligations of the three Powers, set forth in Paragraph 3, Point "d" of the Declaration on Liberated Europe, the Governments of the three Powers must discuss how best to help the work of the provisional Governments in holding free and fair elections. Such help will be required in Rumania, Bulgaria, and, possibly, in other countries too.

One of the most important tasks facing us is to determine our attitude to Italy. In view of the fact that Italy recently declared war on Japan, I hope that the Conference will deem it possible to agree to support Italy's application to become a member of the United Nations. The Foreign Ministers could work out an appropriate statement on this matter on behalf of the United Nations Governments.

Is it necessary to read the whole of this document? Do we have the time?

Churchill: Mr. President, these are very important problems and we must have time to discuss them. The point is that our positions on these issues differ. We were attacked by Italy at the most critical moment, when she stabbed France in the back. We had been fighting Italy in Africa for two years, before America entered the war, and we suffered great losses. We even had to risk the forces of the United Kingdom, and to reduce our defences in the United Kingdom in order to send troops to Africa. We had big naval battles in the Mediterranean. We have the best of intentions in respect of Italy, and we have proved this by letting them keep their ships.

Stalin: That is very good, but today we must confine ourselves to drawing up an agenda with the additional points. When the agenda is drawn up any question can be discussed on its merits.

Truman: I fully agree.

Churchill: I am very grateful to the President for having opened this discussion, thereby making a big contribution to our work, but I think that we must have time to discuss these questions. This is the first time I see them. I am not saying that I cannot agree with these proposals, but there must be time to discuss them. I propose that the President should complete making his proposals, if he has any more, so that afterwards we could draw up the agenda.

Stalin: Good.

Truman: The aim of the three Governments in respect of Italy is to promote her political independence and economic rehabilitation and to ensure the Italian people the right to choose their form of government.

The present position of Italy, as a co-belligerent and as a Power that had surrendered unconditionally, is anomalous and hampers every attempt both of the Allies and of Italy herself to improve her economic and political position. This anomaly can be finally eliminated only through the conclusion of a peace treaty with Italy. The drafting of such a treaty should be one of the first tasks set before the Council of Foreign Ministers.

At the same time, an improvement of Italy's internal situation can be achieved by creating an atmosphere in which Italy's contribution to the defeat of Germany will be recognised. That is why it is recommended that the brief terms of Italy's surrender, and the comprehensive terms of Italy's surrender should be annulled and replaced by the Italian Government's obligations flowing from the new situation in Italy.

These obligations must stipulate that the Italian Government refrains from hostile action against any member of the United Nations; the Italian Government must not have any naval or air forces and equipment, except those that will be established by the Allies, and will observe all the instructions of the Allies; pending the conclusion of a peace treaty, control over Italy should be exercised as the need arises; simultaneously, there must be a decision on how long the Allied armed forces are to remain on the territory of Italy; finally, a fair settlement of territorial disputes must be ensured.

Because I was unexpectedly elected Chairman of this Conference, I was unable to express my feelings at once. I am very glad to meet you, Generalissimo, and you, Mr. Prime Minister. I am well aware that I am now substituting for a man whom it is impossible to substitute, the late President Roosevelt. I am glad to serve, even if partially, the memory which you preserve of President Roosevelt. I want to consolidate the friendship which existed between you.

The matters which I have put before you are, of course, highly important. But this does not exclude the placing of additional questions on the agenda.

Churchill: Do you have anything to say, Generalissimo, in reply to Mr. President, or will you allow me to do so?

Stalin: Please do.

Churchill: On behalf of the British delegation I should like to voice our sincere gratitude to the President of the United States for having accepted the chairmanship of this Conference, and I thank him for having expressed the views of the great republic which he represents and of which he is the head, and wish to tell him: I am sure the Generalissimo will agree with me that we welcome him very sincerely and it is our desire to tell him at this important moment that we shall have the same warm feelings for him that we had for President Roosevelt. He has come at a historic moment, and it is our desire that the present tasks and the aims for which we had fought should be attained now, in peacetime. We have respect not only for the American people but also for their President personally, and I hope this feeling of respect will grow and serve to improve our relations.

Stalin: Let me say on behalf of the Russian delegation that we fully share the sentiments expressed by Mr. Churchill.

Churchill: I think we should now pass on to the ordinary items of the agenda and elaborate some kind of programme for our work to see whether we are able to cope with this agenda ourselves, or whether we should refer a part of the items to the Foreign Ministers. I do not think we should lay down the whole of the agenda at once, but can confine ourselves to an agenda for each day. For instance, we should like to add the Polish question.

Stalin: Still it would be well for all the three delegations to set forth all the questions they consider necessary to put on the agenda. The Russians have questions on the division of the German navy and others. On the question of the navy the President and I had an exchange of letters and had reached an understanding.

The second question is that of reparations.

Then we should discuss the question of trust territories.

Churchill: Do you mean the territories in Europe or all over the world?

Stalin: We shall discuss that. I do not know exactly what these territories are but the Russians would like to take part in the administration of trust territories.

We should like to raise as a separate question the resumption of diplomatic relations with Germany's former satellites.

It is also necessary to examine the question of the regime in Spain. We Russians consider that the present Franco regime in Spain was imposed on the Spanish people by Germany and Italy. It is fraught with grave danger for the freedom-loving United Nations. We think it would be good to create conditions for the Spanish people to establish a regime of their choice.

Churchill: We are still discussing the items to be put on the agenda. I agree that the question of Spain should be put on the agenda.

Stalin: I was merely explaining the idea behind the question.

Then we should also raise the question of Tangiers.

Churchill: Mr. Eden has told me that if we got to the Tangiers question we could reach only a temporary agreement because of the absence of the French.

Stalin: Still it is interesting to know the opinion of the three Great Powers on this matter.

Then there should be a discussion of the question of Syria and the Lebanon. It is also necessary to discuss the Polish question with a view to solving the questions which arise from the fact that the Government of National Unity has been formed in Poland and the consequent necessity to disband the émigré Polish Government.

Churchill: I consider it necessary to discuss the Polish question. The discussion of this question which took place after the Crimea Conference undoubtedly resulted in a satisfactory solution of the Polish question. I quite agree to have the question examined as also the corollary question of the disbandment of the Polish Government in London.

Stalin: That's right, that's right.

Churchill: I hope that the Generalissimo and the President will understand that we have the London Polish Government which had been the basis for the maintenance of the Polish Army which fought against Germany. This produces a number of secondary questions connected with the disbandment of the Polish Government in London. I think that our aims are similar, but we certainly have a more difficult task than the other two Powers. In connection with the disbandment of the Polish Government we cannot fail to provide for the soldiers. But we must solve these questions in the spirit and in the light of the Yalta Conference. In connection with the Polish question we attach very great importance, in Poland's interests, to the matter of elections, which should be an expression of the Polish people's sincere desire.

Stalin: For the time being, the Russian delegation has no more questions for the agenda.

Churchill: We have already presented our agenda to you. If you will allow me, Mr. President, I should like to make a proposal concerning the procedure to be followed at the Conference. I propose that the three Foreign Ministers should meet today or tomorrow morning to select the questions which could best be discussed by us here tomorrow. We could follow the same procedure for the subsequent days of the Conference. The Ministers could draw up a better agenda by selecting three, four or five items. They could meet tomorrow morning and draw up an agenda for us.

Stalin: I have no objections.

Truman: Agreed.

Churchill: I think we have a general outline of our task and an idea of the volume of our work. I think the Foreign Ministers should now make their choice and put it before us, and then we can start working.

Stalin: I agree. What shall we do today? Shall we continue our sitting until the Ministers let us have five or six questions? I think we could discuss the setting up of the Council of Foreign Ministers as a preparatory institution for the coming peace conference.

Truman: All right.

Churchill: All right.

Stalin: We should discuss the question of the participation of China's representative in the Council of Foreign Ministers, if the idea is that the Council will deal with European questions.

Truman: China will be one of the permanent members of the Security Council set up at San Francisco.

Stalin: Is the decision of the Crimea Conference, under which the Foreign Ministers are to meet periodically to examine various questions, to be dropped?

Truman: We propose to set up the Council of Foreign Ministers for a definite purpose: to work out the terms of a peace treaty and to prepare a peace conference.

Stalin: It was established at the Crimea Conference that the Foreign Ministers are to meet every three or four months to discuss separate questions. This seems to be no longer necessary, doesn't it? In that case, the European Advisory Commission seems to be no longer necessary either? That is how I see it, and I should like to know whether or not I am taking the correct view.

Truman: The Council of Foreign Ministers is being set up only for a definite purpose—to work out the terms of the peace treaty.

Stalin: I have no objection to setting up the Council of Foreign Ministers, but then the meetings of Ministers laid down by the decision of the Crimea Conference are apparently called off and one should think that the European Advisory Commission is also no longer necessary. Both these institutions will be replaced by the Council of Foreign Ministers.

Churchill: The three Foreign Ministers, as was laid down at the Crimea Conference, were to meet every three or four months in order to give us advice on a number of important questions relating to Europe. I think if we add the representative of China to the Council of Foreign Ministers of the three Great Powers, this will only complicate matters, because the Council is to discuss questions relating to European countries. When we discuss the peace treaty relating to the whole world, and not only to Europe, the representative of China can be invited. Our three Ministers will be able to do their work more fruitfully and with greater ease. The participation of China's representative in the day-to-day activity of the Council would merely complicate its work. It is very easy to create organisations on paper, but if they produce nothing in reality, I think they are superfluous. In fact, are we not able to solve the question of the future administration of Germany without the participation of China? Let us confine ourselves to the three Ministers in the Council of Foreign Ministers.

Truman: I propose that we should postpone the discussion of the question of terminating the periodic meetings of the Ministers as laid down by the decision of the Yalta Conference. We are now discussing the setting up of a Council of Ministers to draft a peace treaty, and this is quite a different matter. I should like to submit to you the U.S. draft on the Council of Foreign Ministers setting forth the principles of its organisation.

This draft calls for a Council of Foreign Ministers consisting of the Ministers of Foreign Affairs of the U.S.S.R., the United States, Great Britain, China and France. The Council is to meet periodically, and its first meeting is to take place on such and such a date.

Each of the Foreign Ministers is to be accompanied by a high-ranking deputy duly authorised and able to work independently in the absence of the Foreign Minister. He should also be accompanied by a limited staff of technical advisers. A joint secretariat is also to be set up.

The Council is to be empowered to draw up, with the aim of submitting to the Governments of the United Nations, peace treaties with Italy, Rumania, Bulgaria and Hungary. The Council is also to propose ways of settling territorial questions remaining open since the end of the war in Europe. The Council is to prepare comprehensive terms for a peace treaty with Germany which are to be accepted by the future Government of Germany, when a German Government suitable for that purpose is set up.

When the Council of Foreign Ministers deals with matters having a direct bearing on a state not represented on the Council, that state is to be invited to attend the Council meetings to take part in discussing the given question. That does not mean that invariable rules are being laid down for the work of the Council. The Council shall lay down a procedure in conformity with a given problem. In some cases the Council may be convened for preliminary discussion with the participation of other interested states; in other cases it may be desirable to convene the Council before inviting interested sides.

Stalin: Will it be a Council preparing questions for the future international peace conference?

Truman: Yes.

Churchill: The peace conference which will end the war.

Stalin: In Europe the war is over. The Council will determine and suggest the date for the convocation of a peace conference.

Truman: We think the conference should not be called before we are duly prepared for it.

Churchill: It seems to me there is no difficulty in concerting the aim we are striving for. We must set up a Council of Foreign Ministers to draft a peace treaty. But this Council should not substitute the organisations which already exist and deal with day-to-day matters—the regular meetings of the three Ministers and the European Advisory Commission, in which France is also taking part. The Council of Foreign Ministers is a broader organisation. There one can establish to what extent the European Advisory Commission and the regular meetings of the Ministers may deal with the questions of the peace treaty.

Stalin: Who in that case is to be subordinate to whom?

Churchill: The Council of Foreign Ministers is to exist parallel to the Security Council, in which China is also taking part, and parallel to the regular meetings of Foreign Ministers and the European Advisory Commission. Until victory over Japan, China will find it hard to take part in discussing European questions. We cannot benefit in any way from China's taking part in discussing European questions at present. Europe has always been a great volcano, and its problems should be regarded as being highly important. It is possible that at the time when the peace conference will be convened we shall have better news from the Far East and we could then invite China too.

I propose that in principle the peace treaty should be drafted by the five principal Powers, but as for Europe, its problems should be discussed only by the four Powers which have a direct interest in these matters. In this way we shall not disrupt the work of the European Advisory Commission and the regular meetings of Foreign Ministers. Both these organisations will be able to continue their work simultaneously.

Stalin: Perhaps we should refer this question to the Ministers for discussion?

Truman: I agree and do not object to China being excluded from the Council of Foreign Ministers.

Churchill: I think it would be possible to arrange things in such a way that some members would not take part in all the sittings, although they would enjoy full rights, as all the other members, but they would attend the sittings only when there was an examination of questions they were interested in.

Truman: As I see it, this question should be referred to the Foreign Ministers for discussion.

Stalin: Yes, that's right.

Truman: Can we discuss anything more today?

Stalin: Since all the questions are to be discussed by the Foreign Ministers, we have nothing else to do today.

Churchill: I propose that the Foreign Ministers should examine the question of whether there should be four or five members. But that this Council should deal exclusively with preparations for the peace treaty first for Europe and then for the whole world.

Stalin: A peace treaty or a peace conference?

Churchill: The Council will prepare a plan which it will put before the Heads of Government for examination.

Stalin: Let the Foreign Ministers discuss how necessary it is to keep alive the European Advisory Commission in Europe and how necessary it is for the regular meetings of the three Ministers, established in accordance with the Yalta decision, to continue their functions. Let the Ministers also discuss these questions.

Churchill: That depends on the situation in Europe and on what headway these organisations make in their work. I propose that the three Foreign Ministers should continue their regular meetings and that the European Advisory Commission should also continue its work.

Truman: We must specify the concrete questions for discussion at tomorrow's sitting.

Churchill: We should want to have something definite in the bag every night as we return home.

Truman: I should like the Foreign Ministers to give us something definite for discussion every day.

Stalin: I agree.

Truman: I also propose that we should start our sittings at four o'clock instead of five.

Stalin: Four? Well, all right.

Churchill: We submit to the Chairman.

Truman: If that is accepted, let us postpone the examination of questions until 4.00 p.m. tomorrow.

Stalin: Yes, let's do that. There is only one other question: why does Mr. Churchill deny the Russians their share of the German navy?

Churchill: I have no objections. But since you have asked me this question, here is my answer: this navy should be either sunk or divided.

Stalin: Do you want it sunk or divided?

Churchill: All means of war are terrible things.

Stalin: The navy should be divided. If Mr. Churchill prefers to sink the navy, he is free to sink his share of it; I have no intention of sinking mine.

Churchill: At present, nearly the whole of the German navy is in our hands.

Stalin: That's the whole point. That's the whole point. That is why we need to decide the question.

Truman: Tomorrow the sitting is at 4 o'clock.

Second Sitting

July 18, 1945

Truman opens the sitting.

Churchill: I should like to mention one question outside the agenda which is not especially important from the standpoint of international relations and which is of temporary significance. During our meeting at Tehran, members of the press found it very hard to obtain any information on the work of the Conference, and altogether impossible at the Yalta Conference. There are almost 180 correspondents in Berlin who are roaming the environs in a state of fury and indignation.

Stalin: That's a whole company. Who let them in?

Churchill: They are not here, in the zone, of course, but in Berlin. Of course, we can work calmly only if there is secrecy, and we are duty bound to ensure this secrecy. If both my colleagues agree with me, I could, as an old journalist, have a talk with them and explain to them the need for secrecy at our meeting; I could tell them that we sympathise with them, but are unable to tell them what is going on here. I think we should stroke their wings to calm them.

Stalin: What do they want, what are their demands?

Truman: Each of our delegations has special press officers, and it is their duty to protect us from the claims of the correspondents. Let them do their job. We can authorise them to talk to the journalists.

Churchill: Of course, I don't want to be a lamb led to the slaughter. I could talk to them if the Generalissimo guarantees to rescue me with troops in case of need.

Truman: Today our Foreign Ministers have prepared an agenda and recommend it for our consideration. By agreement between the Ministers, Byrnes is to report on the agenda.

Byrnes: Our Foreign Ministers have agreed to propose the following items for inclusion in today's agenda:

1. The question of the procedure and mechanism for peace negotiations and territorial claims.

2. The question of the powers of the Control Council in Germany in the political sphere.

3. The Polish question, specifically, the disbandment of the émigré Polish Government in London.

As for the first item, the procedure and mechanism for peace negotiations and territorial claims (the establishment of a Council of Foreign Ministers), the draft proposed by the U.S. delegation was in principle approved by the Foreign Ministers' conference. The conference adopted a new reading of Clause 3 of the draft on setting up the Council of Foreign Ministers. The first and most important task of the Council of Ministers is to draft peace treaties with Italy, Rumania, Bulgaria, Hungary and Finland, and also to prepare a peace treaty with Germany.

An equally important task of the Council is to prepare and submit to the Governments of the United Nations detailed terms of organisation and holding of the peace conference. The Council must also be used for preparing the question of a peaceful settlement of territorial disputes. For the fulfilment of all these tasks, the Council shall consist of the same members who are permanent members of the Security Council.

When the Council of Foreign Ministers examines questions which have a direct bearing on the interests of states not represented on the Council, these states shall be invited to send their representatives to take part in the discussion of the matter. In some cases, the Council could have a preliminary discussion of the question by itself, before inviting representatives of the interested states.

The Soviet delegation has made the reservation that it retains the right to introduce an amendment and make remarks on Clause 1 of the draft of the U.S. delegation on the establishment of the Council of Foreign Ministers.[1]

The conference agreed that the periodic conferences of the three Ministers established by the decision of the Crimea Conference would not be affected by the work of the Council of Foreign Ministers.

As for the powers of the European Advisory Commission, the conference of Ministers decided to transfer these powers to the Allied Control Councils for Germany and Austria. Thus, the draft proposed by the American delegation for the establishment of the Council of Foreign Ministers was in the main approved, with the exception of the Soviet delegation's reservation on Clause 1.

Stalin: The Soviet delegation withdraws its reservation on Clause 1 of the draft. As for the rest, the Soviet delegation is in agreement and accepts the draft.

Truman: Consequently, the draft on the institution of the Council of Foreign Ministers is adopted without objections.

Stalin: It is possible to accept this text: the three Great Powers represent the interests of all the United Nations and they can take the responsibility upon themselves.

Truman: Let us pass to the second item.

Churchill: Our Foreign Ministers have worked well.

Stalin: To be sure, to be sure.

Truman: The next question is on the political powers of the Control Council in Germany.

---

[1] Clause 1 envisaged that there should be set up a Council consisting of the Foreign Ministers of Great Britain, the Union of Soviet Socialist Republics, China, France and the United States.

Byrnes: The Foreign Ministers discussed the question of the political powers of the Control Council in Germany and of its economic powers. Some of the differences which arose in the discussion of this matter were referred to sub-commissions which were set up. These sub-commissions have not yet completed their work, but the Ministers have agreed that it would be desirable for the Heads of Government to have a preliminary discussion of the political powers of the Control Council in Germany at today's sitting. The Ministers also agreed that the economic questions connected with Germany are so difficult and complicated that they must be referred to a sub-commission of experts. These sub-commissions will report to the Ministers on the matters on which they fail to reach agreement. The Foreign Ministers will then decide which of these questions are to be submitted for the examination by the Heads of Government.

The Foreign Ministers have also agreed that although they would not recommend today a discussion on the question of the German navy and merchant marine, this question would be discussed somewhat later.

Churchill: I want to raise only one question. I note that the word "Germany" is being used here. What is now the meaning of "Germany"? Is it to be understood in the same sense as before the war?

Truman: How is this question understood by the Soviet delegation?

Stalin: Germany is what she has become after the war. There is no other Germany. That is how I understand the question.

Truman: Is it possible to speak of Germany as she had been before the war, in 1937?

Stalin: As she is in 1945.

Truman: She lost everything in 1945; actually, Germany no longer exists.

Stalin: Germany is, as we say, a geographical concept. Let's take it this way for the time being. We cannot abstract ourselves from the results of the war.

Truman: Yes, but there must be some definition of the concept of "Germany". I believe the Germany of 1886 or of 1937 is not the same thing as Germany today, in 1945.

Stalin: She has changed as a result of the war, and that is how we take her.

Truman: I quite agree with this, but some definition of the concept of "Germany" must be given.

Stalin: For example, is there any idea of establishing a German administration in the Sudeten part of Czechoslovakia? That is an area from which the Germans had expelled the Czechs.

Truman: Perhaps we shall speak of Germany as she had been before the war, in 1937?

Stalin: That could be taken formally, but actually that is not so. If a German administration should put in an appearance at Königsberg, we shall expel it, we shall most certainly expel it.

Truman: It was agreed at the Crimea Conference that territorial questions should be settled at a peace conference. How are we then to define the concept of "Germany"?

Stalin: Let us define the western borders of Poland, and we shall then be clearer on the question of Germany. I find it very hard to say what Germany is just now. It is a country without a Government, without any definite borders, because the borders are not ·formalised by our troops. Germany has no troops, including frontier troops, she is broken up into occupation zones. Take this and define what Germany is. It is a broken country.

Truman: Perhaps we could take Germany's 1937 borders as the starting point?

Stalin: We can start anywhere. We have to start somewhere. In that context, we could take 1937 too.

Truman: That was the Germany after the Versailles Treaty.

Stalin: Yes, we could take the Germany of 1937, but only as a point of departure. It is merely a working hypothesis for the convenience of our work.

Churchill: Only as a starting point. That does not mean that we shall confine ourselves to this.

Truman: We agree to take the Germany of 1937 as a starting point.

We have not yet finished with the second question but shall agree on that.

Stalin: Is the political aspect prepared?

Byrnes: The political aspect is prepared and can be discussed.

Stalin: The Russian delegation in the main accepts all the clauses of the political section of this question. There is only one amendment to Clause 5: it would be well to delete the last four lines, for they leave a loophole for the Nazis which they can use.

Truman: I agree that these four lines should be deleted.

Stalin: Very good. We are agreed on all the rest. I should like the drafting commission to edit this text.

Byrnes: A special sub-commission has been appointed for this purpose at the Foreign Ministers' meeting.

Stalin: Good. There are no objections.

Eden: It would be good if the Ministers once again went over this document at their meeting tomorrow morning, after it is submitted by the drafting commission.

Stalin: That will, of course, be better.

Churchill: This draft, Clause 2 (b), speaks of the destruction of armaments and other instruments of war, and of all specialised means for their manufacture. However, there are several highly valuable experimental installations in Germany. It would be undesirable to destroy these installations.

Stalin: The draft says: to seize or destroy.

Churchill: We could use them all together or divide them among ourselves.

Stalin: Yes, we could.

The Soviet delegation has a draft on the Polish question in Russian and in English. I would ask you to study this draft.

Truman: I propose that we should hear out Byrnes's report on the meeting of the Foreign Ministers and then acquaint ourselves with your draft.

Byrnes: The Foreign Ministers agreed to recommend to the Heads of Government that they should discuss the Polish question from two aspects: the disbandment of the émigré Polish Government in London and the fulfilment of the Crimea Conference decisions on Poland in the part relating to the holding of free and unhindered elections in Poland.

[The draft of the Soviet delegation on Poland is then read out:

STATEMENT OF THE HEADS
OF THE THREE GOVERNMENTS
ON THE POLISH QUESTION

"In view of the setting up on the basis of the decisions of the Crimea Conference of the Provisional Polish Government of National Unity and in view of the establishment by the United States of America and by Great Britain of diplomatic relations with Poland, which previously already existed between Poland and the Soviet Union, we agreed that the Governments of Great Britain and the United States of America should sever all relations with the Government of Arciszewski and render to the Provisional Polish Government of National Unity the necessary assistance in the immediate transmission to it of all stock, assets and all other property belonging to Poland, which still is at the disposal of the Government of Arciszewski and of its organs, in whatever form this property may be and no matter where or at whose disposal this property may prove to be at the present moment.

"We also found it necessary that the Polish armed forces, including the navy and merchant marine, now subordinated to the Government of Arciszewski, should be subordinated to the Provisional Polish Government of National Unity, which will determine the further measures to be taken in respect of these armed forces, men of war and merchant ships."]

Churchill: Mr. President, I should like to explain that the burden in this matter falls on the British Government, because when Hitler attacked Poland we welcomed the Poles and gave them sanctuary. The London Polish Government has no assets to speak of, but there is £20 million worth of gold in London which we have blocked. This gold is an asset of the Central Polish Bank. The question of where the gold is to be blocked, and its transfer to some other central bank should be settled in the ordinary way. But this gold does not belong to the London Polish Government.

Stalin: Did you say £20 million sterling?

Churchill: Approximately. I must add that the Polish Embassy in London has now been vacated and the Polish Ambassador no longer lives there. That is why the Embassy is open and can accommodate an Ambassador of the Provisional Polish Government, and the sooner it appoints one, the better.

The question arises, how the Polish Government in London had been financed for five and a half years? It was financed by the British Government. We let them have about £120 million in that period to enable them to maintain their army, maintain diplomatic relations and exercise other functions and also maintain a considerable number of

Poles who had found refuge from the Germans on our shores, the only refuge that was at their disposal.

When the London Polish Government was disavowed, it was decided to pay all employees a three-month salary and then dismiss them. We believed it would be unjust to dismiss them without giving them some compensation.

Mr. President, this is a very important matter, and I ask you to allow me to speak on it. Our position is an exceptional one. We now have to engage in disbanding or transferring the Polish troops who had fought against the Germans by our side. These troops made their appearance from France in 1940. Some of them got to Italy via Switzerland, and continued to trickle in in small parties. We evacuated the Poles who had found themselves in France when she surrendered. They numbered 40,000 or 50,000.

Thus, we set up a Polish Army, consisting of five divisions, which was based in Britain. About 20,000 Poles are now in Germany and are highly alarmed. There is a Polish Corps of three divisions in Italy, which is also in great agitation.

Altogether, the Polish Army consists of 180,000 to 200,000 men.

Our policy is to induce the greatest number of Poles to return to Poland. That is why I was very angry when I read the statement of General Anders, whom the Generalissimo knows. Anders told his troops in Italy that if they returned to Poland they would be sent to Siberia. We have taken disciplinary measures against this general, to prevent him from making such statements in the future.

It will take time to overcome all these difficulties. But it is our policy to induce the greatest possible number of Poles to return to Poland. This also applies to the civilians. Of course, the better the state of things in Poland, the sooner will the Poles return there. I should like to take this opportunity to say that I am glad the situation in Poland has improved in the last two months.

I should like to express my wishes of further success to the new Polish Government which will play its positive part, and although it does not give everything we should like to see, it signifies progress thanks to the patient efforts of the Governments of the three Powers. Mikolajczyk should also be given credit for his part in improving the situation in Poland.

I hope that as the situation in Poland improves, an ever

growing number of Poles will return home. I have promised Parliament that Polish soldiers who do not wish to return to Poland would be given British citizenship and enrolled into the army. It would be desirable that the new Polish Government of National Unity should give assurances that the Poles returning to Poland would have complete freedom and economic security. Such an assurance of the Polish Government would considerably promote the return of the Poles home, to the land liberated by the Red Army.

Stalin: Have you read the draft of the Russian delegation on Poland?

Churchill: Yes, I have. My speech is a reply to the draft of the Russian delegation in proof of the fact that I am fundamentally in agreement, provided what I have just said is taken into account.

Stalin: I realise the difficulty of the British Government's position. I know it gave sanctuary to the Polish émigré Government. I know that in spite of this, the former Polish rulers have caused the Government of Great Britain much trouble. I understand the British Government's difficult position. But I ask you to bear in mind that our draft is not designed to complicate the British Government's position and takes account of the difficulty of its position. Our draft has only one purpose: to put an end to the indefinite situation which still continues to exist in this question, and to dot all the "i"s.

In practice, the Arciszewski Government exists, it has its ministers, and continues its activity, it has its agents and has its base and its press. All this creates an unfavourable impression. Our draft is designed to put an end to this indefinite situation. If Mr. Churchill points out the clauses in this draft which tend to complicate the British Government's position, I am prepared to delete them. Our draft is not aimed at making the British Government's position more difficult.

Churchill: We quite agree with you. We want to eliminate this question, but when a Government is no longer recognised and is not given any grants, it no longer has any possibility for existence. At the same time, you cannot prevent individuals, in Britain at any rate, from living and talking. These people meet with members of Parliament and have their supporters in Parliament. But we, as Government, have no relations with them at all. Mr. Eden and I myself have never met them, and since Mr. Mikolajczyk left, I do not even know what to do with them, and never meet them. I don't know what to do when Arciszewski walks about London and chats with journalists. As for us, we consider them to be non-existent and eliminated in the diplomatic sense, and I hope that they will be completely ineffective soon. But, of course, we must be careful in respect of the army.

The army may mutiny and we may suffer losses as a result. We have a sizable Polish army in Scotland. But our aim is similar to those of the Generalissimo and the President. We merely ask for trust and time and also your help in creating conditions in Poland which would attract these Poles. We would agree to refer the draft of the Soviet delegation for examination by the three Foreign Ministers, with an eye to the discussion that has taken place today, and to the document which had been presented by our Foreign Minister. But I think we have one and the same aim, and the sooner we finish with this question, the better.

Truman: I do not see any essential differences between the Generalissimo and the Prime Minister. Mr. Churchill merely asks for trust and time to eliminate all the difficulties of which he spoke here. That is why I think it will not be too hard to settle this question, especially in view of the fact that Mr. Stalin has said that he is prepared to delete all the controversial points. The Yalta Conference decisions provided that after the establishment of the new Government general elections on the basis of universal suffrage should be held as soon as possible.

Churchill: Perhaps the Foreign Ministers would examine the whole question, including elections?

Stalin: The Government of Poland does not refuse to hold unhindered elections. Let us refer this draft to the Foreign Ministers.

Truman: That is all Mr. Byrnes had to place before the Heads of Government for discussion today. Am I to ask the Foreign Ministers to prepare an agenda for tomorrow?

Stalin: That would be fine.

Churchill: I realise the great importance of the question of political principles to be applied in respect of Germany. I realise that we are unable to discuss this question today, but I hope we shall discuss it tomorrow. The main principle which we should examine is whether we should apply a uniform system of control in all the four zones of occupation of Germany or whether different principles are to be applied to the different zones of occupation.

Stalin: This is the very question that is dealt with in the political part of the draft. It is my impression that we stand for a single policy.

Truman: Quite right.

Churchill: I should like to emphasise this, because it is highly important.

Stalin: That's right.

Truman: Tomorrow we meet at 4 o'clock.

Third Sitting

July 19, 1945

Truman opens the sitting.

Churchill: At the very beginning of yesterday's sitting, the Generalissimo raised the question of the incident on the Greco-Albanian border. We have made due inquiries but have not heard of any fighting there. There may have been small exchanges. There's no love lost between the peoples there.

There is no Greek field division in that area. We know this because our men are there. There are 7,000 men of the National Guards, which are on the border with Albania and Yugoslavia. They are armed and equipped for the purposes of internal protection. On the other side of the border there are 30,000 Albanian troops, 30,000 Yugoslav troops and 24,000 Bulgarian.

I mention this because I believe the Great Power Conference must insist that no such attacks should take place across the borders of any Power. The frontiers will be laid down at a peace conference, and we must let it be known that those who try to determine their frontiers beforehand may find themselves worse off.

Stalin: There is some misunderstanding here. We must not discuss this question here, at this Conference. I did not raise it at the Conference, but spoke of it privately.

Churchill: I agree with the Generalissimo that the question was not raised at a sitting, but if it is placed on the agenda we are prepared to discuss it.

Truman: We are not going to discuss this question but will go on to a discussion of those which will be reported to us on behalf of the Ministers of Foreign Affairs.

[The British delegation then reported that in view of the fact that the American delegation had made an amendment in Article 3 of the draft to set up a Council of Foreign Ministers, the Ministers agreed to refer the article to the drafting committee.

The Foreign Ministers then examined the political section of the agreement on political and economic principles which are to serve as a guide in dealing with Germany in the initial control period. The British delegation recalled that the Heads of Government had examined the draft agreement the previous day and had instructed the Ministers to present their report that day.

The delegation said that the Foreign Ministers had examined the draft, and had made some additions to it, and were now submitting the new draft of the political section of the agreement for the consideration of the Heads of Government. It said the Foreign Ministers believed that when the discussion and co-ordination of the economic section of the draft was over, the Conference would have to consider the publication of the agreement as a whole.

The British delegation then said that the Ministers had gone into the question of Poland; they had a very important and useful discussion of the question, which was then referred to the drafting committee. The Ministers expressed the hope that it would be possible to report to the Conference on the question the next day if the drafting committee was ready.

The Ministers also agreed to submit for the consideration of that day's plenary sitting the questions of the German Navy and merchant fleet, Spain, the fulfilment of the Yalta Declaration on Liberated Europe, Yugoslavia, etc.]

Truman: The first question is that of the German Navy. I think that before tackling this question it is necessary to solve another one, namely, what is to be regarded as the spoils of war and what as reparations. If the merchant marine is an object of reparations, the question should be solved when the question of reparations is considered. We should ask the Reparations Commission to define the range of values that are to be classed as reparations. I show a special interest in Germany's merchant fleet because it might be used in the war against Japan.

Stalin: The Navy, like any other armament, must be taken as spoils of war. Troops laying down their arms must hand in their armaments to those to whom they surrender. The same may be said of the Navy. The proposals of the military representatives of the three Powers make it explicit that the Navy must be disarmed and surrendered. Those are the terms of Germany's surrender. In respect of the merchant fleet it may be asked whether it is to be classed as spoils of war or as reparations; as for the Navy it is part of the spoils of war and is subject to surrender. If you recall the case of Italy you will see that both the Navy and the merchant marine fell into the class of spoils of war.

Churchill: I should not like to take a purely legalistic attitude to this question and use precise terminology. But I want to have a fair and amicable solution of the question, and reach an agreement between the three Great Powers as a part of the general agreement on all questions arising from this Conference. At this point, I should like to consider only the German Navy. In effect, we have all the seaworthy German ships in our hands. I think a general amicable solution of the questions arising from this Conference will be reached—I am sure of this—and that is why we have no objection in principle to a division of the German Navy.

I am not now speaking of the Italian Navy. I think we should discuss this question separately, having in mind our general policy on Italy. Of course, there also arises the question of indemnification. As for Great Britain, she has suffered very heavy losses, she has lost about 10 capital ships, that is, battleships, heavy cruisers and aircraft carriers and besides, at least 20 cruisers and several hundred destroyers, submarines and small craft.

I think submarines should be classed in another category than the rest of the German Navy. These submarines have a special part to play; according to the convention signed also by Germany they were to be used on a limited scale. However, Germany violated the convention and made use of submarines on a rather extensive scale, that is, Germany made illegal use of them, and so during the war we too were forced to abandon the legitimate use of submarines. It is my opinion that these submarines should be either destroyed or scuttled.

I am aware, however, that the latest German submarines, especially the best of them, are of definite scientific and technical interest, and they should be left for study. Information about these submarines must be made available to all three Great Powers. I do not view this matter from the purely naval standpoint and fully recognise the losses suffered by the Red Army during the war. I do not think we should take any final decision here, but after the Conference most of these vessels should be destroyed, while a part may be equally divided between us all.

As for surface ships, they should be divided equally between us provided we reach a general agreement on all other questions and leave here on the best of terms. I have no objection to Russia's receiving one-third of the German Navy, but only with the proviso I have just mentioned. I recognise that such a great and mighty nation as the Russians, who have made such a great contribution to the common cause, must be given a warm reception on the high seas. We shall welcome the appearance of the Russian flag on the seas. I am aware that it is very hard to build a great fleet in a short time. That is why these German ships may be used for study and the creation of a Russian fleet. There is nothing more I can add.

If it is desirable to speak of the merchant marine, I could say a few words here.

Truman: Please.

Churchill: I feel that so long as the war against Japan continues, the German merchant navy could play a considerable part in that war. The possibility of cutting short the war largely depends on the merchant navy. We have all the men we need for the Army, Air Force and the Navy. But we are short of the means of conveyance for these men, and for the transfer of matériel.

Besides, the merchant navy is needed for supplying the British Isles with food, and also for supplying food to the liberated European countries which cannot be fully supplied as it is. Every ton is of great value. America and we have given all our merchant navy to the common effort. I should be very sorry if the 1.2 million tons of Germany's merchant navy did not go into this common effort so as to end the war against Japan as soon as possible.

I should also like to mention the following. Finland has a merchant navy consisting of about 400,000 tons. This navy has passed into the hands of our Russian Ally. The Russian Ally has also taken over some Rumanian ships, including two important transports, which are very necessary for troop transportation. If there is to be a division of the navy into three parts between the Powers, I think the merchant navies of Rumania and Finland should also go into the pool for distribution.

Stalin: We have taken nothing from Finland's merchant navy, and only one vessel from Rumania.

Churchill: I should only like to mention the principles on which we could have a distribution of the merchant navy.

Finally, we should bear in mind that there are other countries besides our three Powers. Norway, for instance, has suffered very heavy losses in her merchant fleet. Norwegian tonnage, especially Norwegian tankers, was a great force. They put their whole navy at our disposal, and it has suffered great damage. Other countries have also lost a great part of their navies. I think it is necessary to raise the question of dividing the merchant navy into four instead of three parts, to set aside the fourth part to satisfy the interests of certain other countries which are not represented here. I merely propose the question for examination and discussion.

Truman: For my part, I want to make a remark on this question. I should be very glad to divide the German Navy into three parts, with the exception of the submarine fleet. But I want the solution of this question to be postponed in the interests of the war against Japan. We would find all these ships very useful, because we shall use them not only for troop transportation but also for the supply of Europe. The present situation is such that we find the available ships altogether inadequate. That is why I very much want to retain all this German surface fleet for the war against Japan. I think it right to say here that when the war against Japan is over, we in the United States will have a great number not only of warships but a great number of merchant ships which could be sold to interested countries. I would be very glad if all the ships of the German merchant navy were made available for the conduct of the war against Japan.

Stalin: What if the Russians fight Japan?

Truman: It goes without saying that the Russians could claim one-third of the fleet, which would then be handed over to them. An agreement could be reached on this.

Stalin: It is the principle we think important.

Churchill: Mr. President, I think we can reach an agreement. I suppose these ships could now be earmarked for each participant, and when the war against Japan is over, these ships could be handed over where they belong.

Stalin: Which ships?

Churchill: I mean the merchantmen. But I think the principle is the most important thing here. It should be borne in mind that the Red Army's offensive along the Baltic coast forced the Germans to abandon their ports, so that the German fleet was expelled from the Baltic Sea. I must admit that I am a supporter of Generalissimo Stalin's proposal concerning the Russian desire to obtain a part of Germany's Navy and merchant fleet, and believe that the only alternative would be to sink the whole navy, but that would be unwise, considering that our Ally wants to have a part of this navy.

Stalin: The Russians should not be depicted as people who are intent on hampering the successful operation of the Allied navy against Japan. But this should not lead to the conclusion that the Russians want to receive a present from the Allies. We want no gifts, but wish to know whether or not the principle is recognised, whether or not the Russian claim to a part of the German navy is considered legitimate.

Churchill: I said nothing of gifts.

Stalin: I did not say you did.

I want a clarification of the question of whether the Russians have a right to one-third of Germany's Navy and merchant marine. I think the Russians have this right and what they will receive they will receive by right. I only want clarity in this matter. If my colleagues think differently I should like to know what they actually think. We shall be satisfied if there is recognition of the principle that the Russians have a right to receive one-third of Germany's Navy and merchant fleet.

As for the use of Germany's merchant fleet, specifically that third which would be recognised as being Russia's by right, we shall of course have no objections to that third being put to the best use by the Allies in their struggle against Japan. I also agree that this question should be settled at the end of the Conference.

I should like to deal with yet another question. Our men have been deprived of access to Germany's Navy and merchant fleet, they were prevented from inspecting the ships. The bulk of the navy is known to be in the hands of our Ally, but our men were deprived of access to these ships and they have no possibility of inspecting the ships of that navy. They should at least be given a chance to study the list of these ships. Is it not possible to lift this ban and give the members of the Russian naval commission an opportunity to inspect the ships of this navy and to find out how many ships there are.

Churchill: We are also in possession of facts when our men were not allowed to inspect some war trophies on the Baltic Sea.

Stalin: Only submarines were seized on the Baltic, but that is an absolutely useless, destroyed submarine fleet. But if there is a desire to inspect it, the opportunity can be given at any time.

Churchill: Our principle is equality and fairness. Therefore I consider your proposal acceptable, but we only ask whether it could be arranged to give our men an opportunity to inspect some highly interesting German property, for instance, on the Baltic Sea, notably some submarines?

Stalin: You are welcome.

Truman: I want to say here on behalf of the United States that you have access to all our zones and you can see anything you want to. But we should like to obtain the same possibility of inspecting what we may find of interest.

Churchill: I spoke here of the difference between submarines and surface ships. Generalissimo Stalin will understand us when we say that as islanders we are highly sensitive on this point. Our island provides us with less than two-thirds of our food. During this war, we have suffered a great deal from submarines. More, in fact, than anyone else. Twice we stood on the brink of disaster. That is why the submarine is not a popular type of warship in Britain. I favour the sinking of the bulk of the submarines.

Stalin: I do too.

Churchill: And I want the rest of the submarines be shared equally between us for scientific and technical purposes, because they are of considerable interest. Twice we stood on the brink of disaster because of the operations of enemy submarines. I agree, therefore, that we should sink the bulk of the submarines and divide the rest among the three Powers. I ask the Generalissimo and the President to excuse me, but in this respect we are in a special position. Our military might has suffered greatly from these submarines. In accepting this principle I merely stipulate that the question of the number of submarines to be sunk and the number to be divided should be settled at the end of the Conference.

Stalin: Good, I agree.

Truman: We have discussed this question sufficiently, and can go on to the next one.

Eden: The next question deals with Spain.

Truman: Does the Generalissimo wish to speak on the question?

Stalin: The proposals have been circulated. I have nothing to add to what is said there.

Churchill: Mr. President, the British Government—the present one and the previous one—have a feeling of hatred for Franco and his Government. I have been misunderstood, and it has been said that I take a friendly attitude to this gentleman. All I said was that there is more to Spanish politics than anti-Franco cartoons. I think that the continued destruction of people thrown into prison for what they did six years ago, and various other circumstances in Spain are, by our British standards, totally undemocratic.

When Franco sent me a letter saying that he, I and certain other Western countries should unite against the threat of the Soviet Union, I sent him, with the permission of my Cabinet, a very cool reply. The Soviet Government may remember this reply, because I sent it a copy of my letter, as I did to the President. So there are no great differences between us concerning the feelings we have for the present regime in Spain.

Where I do see some difficulty in adopting the draft proposed by the Generalissimo is in Point One, which speaks of the rupture of all relations with the Franco Government, which is the Government of Spain. I think that, considering that the Spaniards are proud and rather sensitive, such a step by its very nature could have the effect of uniting the Spaniards around Franco, instead of making them move away from him. That is why I do not think that the rupture of diplomatic relations with the Spanish Government would be a satisfactory way of solving the question.

This may give us some satisfaction but we shall then be

deprived of any contact we may need in hard times. I believe such a step would only strengthen Franco's position, and if his positions are strengthened we shall have to stand his abuse or use our forces against him. I am against the use of force in such cases. I do not think we should interfere in the internal affairs of a state with whom we differ in views, with the exception of cases when this or that state attacks us. Concerning the countries we have defeated, there we should establish our own control. As for the countries that have been liberated in the course of the war, we cannot allow the establishment there of a fascist or a Franco regime. But here we have a country which did not take part in the war and that is why I am against interfering in its domestic affairs. His Majesty's Government will need to have a long discussion of this question before it decides to break off relations with Spain.

I think Franco's power is now jeopardised and I hope that his downfall may be speeded up by diplomatic means. Rupture of relations is, in my opinion, a very dangerous way of tackling the question. Besides, there is always the danger of a possible resumption of the civil war in Spain, which cost her 2 million dead out of a total population of 17 or 18 million. And it would be a pity to interfere actively in this matter at this point, because I believe that there are forces operating there to change the situation for the better. That is my view of the question.

The world organisation set up at San Francisco takes a negative attitude to interference in the affairs of other countries. It would therefore be wrong for us to take an active part in settling this matter. This would run counter to the Charter of the international organisation adopted at San Francisco.

Truman: I have no sympathies for the Franco regime, but I have no desire to take part in a Spanish civil war. I've had enough of the war in Europe. We should be very glad to recognise another government in Spain instead of the Franco Government, but that I think is a question for Spain herself to decide.

Stalin: Is that to say that there will be no change in Spain? I personally think that the Franco regime is being strengthened and it is a regime that fosters semi-fascist regimes in certain other countries of Europe. It should be borne in mind that the Franco regime was imposed on the

Spanish people from outside, and is not a regime that has taken shape in internal conditions.

You are very well aware that the Franco regime was imposed by Hitler and Mussolini, and is their legacy. By destroying the Franco regime we shall be destroying the legacy of Hitler and Mussolini. Nor must we lose sight of the fact that the democratic liberation of Europe implies certain obligations.

I am not proposing any military intervention; I am not proposing that we should unleash a civil war there. I should only like the Spanish people to know that we, the leaders of democratic Europe, take a negative attitude to the Franco regime. Unless we declare this in one form or another, the Spanish people will be justified in thinking that we are not against the Franco regime. They may say that since we have left the Franco regime alone, it means that we support it.

What are the diplomatic means that could show the Spanish people that we are not on the side of Franco but of democracy? Assuming that such a means as the rupture of diplomatic relations is too strong, can't we consider other, more flexible means of a diplomatic order? This must be done to let the Spanish people know that we sympathise with them and not with Franco.

In my opinion it would be dangerous to leave the Franco regime in its present state. The public opinion of the European countries, as the press shows, and also of America, has no sympathy with the Franco regime. If we by-pass this question, people will assume that we have sanctioned, or given our tacit blessing to the Franco regime in Spain. That is a great charge against us. I should not like to be among the accused .

Churchill: You have no diplomatic relations with the Spanish Government, and no one can accuse you of this.

Stalin: But I do have the right and the possibility of raising the question and settling it. How will people know that the Soviet Union sympathises or does not sympathise with the Franco regime? It is the accepted view that the Big Three can solve such questions. I am a member of the Big Three, like the President and the Prime Minister. Do I have the right to say nothing about what is going on in Spain, about the Franco regime and the great danger it presents to the whole of Europe? It would be a great mistake for us to ignore this question and say nothing about it.

Churchill: Every government is quite free to make known its views individually. That is the freedom also enjoyed by the press, as Generalissimo Stalin has mentioned here. The Soviet and a part of the American press have very freely expressed themselves on the state of affairs in Spain. As for the British Government, although we have frequently said this to Franco and his Ambassador, we should not like to discontinue our relations with the Spanish Government.

We have long had trade relations with Spain, they supply us with oranges, wine and certain other products, in exchange for our own goods. If our interference does not bring the desired results, I should not like this trade to be jeopardised. But at the same time I fully understand the view taken by Generalissimo Stalin. Franco had the nerve to send his Blue Division to Russia, and I quite understand the Russian view.

But Spain has not done anything to hinder us, she did not do it even when she could have done so in the Bay of Algeciras. There is no doubt in anyone's mind that Generalissimo Stalin hates Franco, and I think that the majority of Britons share his view, I merely wish to stress that we have not suffered from him in any way.

Stalin: It is not a matter of injury. Incidentally, I think that Britain has also suffered from the Franco regime. For a long time Spain placed her coast at Hitler's disposal for use by his submarines. You can say, therefore, that Britain has suffered from the Franco regime in one way or another.

But I should not want this matter to be viewed from the standpoint of some injury. It is not the Blue Division that matters but the fact that the Franco regime is a grave threat to Europe. That is why I think that something should be done against this regime. If rupture of diplomatic relations is unsuitable, I do not insist on it. Other means can be found. We have only to say that we do not sympathise with the Franco regime and consider the Spanish people's urge for democracy just, we have only to say this and nothing will be left of the Franco regime. I assure you.

I propose: the Foreign Ministers should discuss whether some other, milder and more flexible, form could be found to make it known that the Great Powers do not support the Franco regime.

Truman: That suits me, I agree to refer the matter to the Foreign Ministers.

Churchill: I should oppose this. I think that this is a matter that should be settled in this hall.

Stalin: Of course, we shall settle it here, but let the Ministers examine it beforehand.

Truman: I too have no objection to refer this matter for a preliminary examination by our Foreign Ministers.

Churchill: I consider this to be undesirable because that is a matter of principle, namely, interference in the domestic affairs of other countries.

Stalin: This is not a domestic affair, the Franco regime is an international threat.

Churchill: Anyone can say this of the regime of any other country.

Stalin: No, there is no such regime in any other country as the one in Spain; there is no regime like that left in any country of Europe.

Churchill: Portugal could be condemned for having a dictatorial regime.

Stalin: The Franco regime was set up from outside, by way of Hitler's and Mussolini's intervention. Franco behaves in a most provocative manner, and gives asylum to Nazis. I raise no question about Portugal.

Churchill: I cannot advise Parliament to interfere in Spain's domestic affairs. That is a policy we have been conducting for a long time. At the same time, I should be glad to see a change of regime in Spain, but only in a natural way. I should personally be very happy to see a revolution in Spain, and, say, a constitutional monarchy established there with an amnesty for political prisoners.

But I believe that if I or the British Government were to exert an influence on Spain in that sense, the feelings of the Spaniards would turn against us and in favour of Franco. In my opinion, Franco is now on the way out.

If we here were to take any concerted action, we should only be reinforcing his position. On the other hand, the British Government will in no way support Franco, the present Spanish Government, with the exception of continued trade with Spain, of which I have already spoken here.

Truman: I should be very glad if we agreed to refer the matter for preliminary examination by the Foreign Ministers so that they could find an acceptable formula on this point.

Stalin: I am aware of the difficulties faced by Mr. Churchill in connection with interpellations in Parliament. But this matter can be toned down. What about settling the question like this: no question of the Franco regime is to be raised separately, it being agreed that the question never came up and was never examined separately as a question of the Franco regime.

The three Foreign Ministers are to be asked, considering the exchange of opinion on the question of the Franco regime, to find a suitable formula for the question, including, in particular, Mr. Churchill's formulation that the Franco regime is on the way out and that his regime does not enjoy the sympathies of the democratic Powers, that this regime is not given a high rating by public opinion. Such a formula could be inserted as a point in one of our declarations on Europe. We shall of course have some general declarations, and the formula worked out by the Foreign Ministers could be inserted in there.

This will not put the British Government under any obligation, but the point will contain a brief assessment of the Franco regime, and this will let public opinion know that we are not on the side of the Franco regime. I think we should adopt such a decision. Let the Foreign Ministers give some thought to the form in which it is to be clothed.

Churchill: I have not yet agreed in principle that we should make such a joint declaration on this question.

Stalin: It's not about Spain, but we shall be giving a general evaluation on Europe, and this could be included there as one of the points. Look at what happens: in all our documents we speak of all countries with the exception of Spain.

Churchill: The line I am adhering to is as follows: Spain is a country which had not been involved in the war, and is not a satellite country; nor was she liberated by the Allies; that is why we cannot interfere in her domestic affairs. That is a matter of principle.

Take Yugoslavia, Bulgaria and other countries: there are many issues there which we do not like and which we could criticise. But these countries were involved in the war and were liberated by the Allies.

If you wish we could draw up a declaration on the general principles underlying democratic governments. That is something we could discuss. I have in mind, for instance, the U.S. Constitution. Franco is undoubtedly a very far cry from this Constitution. Countries differ from one another, and that is why if we start interfering, we shall have no end of trouble.

I don't know the mind of the Spaniards, but I think that some are of one mind, others of another; I am sure that many Spaniards would like to be rid of Franco, but without outside pressure. I don't see what the Foreign Ministers could do on the question. I feel that this would give them a lot of hard work, while the discussion of the question would prove to be fruitless.

Truman: I see very little likelihood of an agreement being reached on this question at the present sitting. Wouldn't it be better to return to it later?

Stalin: Maybe, after all, we should refer this matter to the Foreign Ministers so that they should try to find a suitable formula?

Churchill: That's the very point on which we have failed to agree.

Truman: I think we'd better pass on to the next question and return to the question of Spain later.

Churchill: I do not propose a negative solution, I merely propose that we now pass on to a discussion of other matters, and discuss this question later.

Truman: We pass on to the next question.

Eden: The Declaration on Liberated Europe.

Truman: I submitted a document on this question on July 17.

Stalin: I propose that we should now postpone this question, we may table another proposal on this question.

Truman: I have no objection to postponing this question at this time.

Eden: The next question is that of Yugoslavia. We have already submitted a small draft on this question.

Stalin: I think that we are unable to solve this question without hearing representatives from Yugoslavia.

Eden: It should be noted that we reached an agreement in respect of Yugoslavia at the Crimea Conference without the presence of Yugoslav representatives.

Stalin: This is now an Allied country with a legitimate government. The question cannot now be solved without the participation of Yugoslav representatives. At that time, there were two governments, and they could not come to terms. We interfered in that matter. And now there is one legitimate government there. Let us invite representatives from Yugoslavia and hear them, and then adopt a decision.

Churchill: Is it to be Subasić and Tito?

Stalin: Yes.

Churchill: But they don't see eye to eye, there are hard feelings on both sides.

Stalin: I know nothing about this. Let's verify this, let's invite them over here and let them speak their mind.

Truman: Is this matter serious enough for them to be invited over here? I find this inconvenient.

Churchill: We put our signatures to the agreement at the Crimea Conference, but we now find that this Declaration on Yugoslavia is not being fulfilled: there is no election law, the Assembly of the Council has not been enlarged, legal procedure has not been re-established, the Tito administration is under the control of his party police, and the press is also controlled as in some fascist countries.

We find that the situation in Yugoslavia does not justify our hopes as expressed in the Declaration of the Crimea Conference. We supplied Yugoslavia with a considerable quantity of arms at a time when we ourselves were weak, and that is why we are disappointed and regret that events have taken such a turn there. Our proposal is a very modest one, it is that what was said in the Yalta Declaration should be fulfilled.

Stalin: Mr. Churchill has commenced the discussion instead of answering the President's question as to whether the question is serious and important enough for us to discuss at the Conference and invite representatives from Yugoslavia. If the President will allow me I will follow in Mr. Churchill's footsteps and also start discussing this question.

You see, the information which Mr. Churchill has given here concerning the violation of the well-known decisions of the Crimea Conference, this information, according to our sources, is unknown to us. I should think it right to hear the Yugoslavs themselves and give them an opportunity of refuting these charges or admitting that they are correct.

Churchill: I want you to substitute the word "complaint" for the word "charge".

Stalin: It is not a question of words, and I can, of course, substitute "complaint" for "charge". But it is not right to judge a whole state without hearing its representatives.

Churchill: We have now had an opportunity of thinking over this question, and I think it would be advisable for the two sides, namely, Tito and Subasić, to meet here. These difficulties could then be possibly obviated and we could reach an agreed decision. But do you think Marshal Tito will agree to come here?

Stalin: I don't know, we should ask if they can come.

Truman: Before going on to the final stage I should like to make a statement. I have come here as the representative of the United States, and I have come here to discuss world problems with you. But I have not come here to judge each separate country in Europe or examine the disputes which should be settled by the world organisation set up at San Francisco.

If we are going to examine political complaints against anyone, we shall merely be wasting our time. Nothing good will come of it if we start inviting Tito, Franco or other leaders over here. We are not a judicial organ to look into complaints against individual statesmen. We should deal with questions on which we could reach agreement.

Stalin: That is a correct remark.

Truman: We should discuss questions which are of interest to each of us.

Churchill: This, Mr. President, is a question which is also of interest to the United States, because it involves the fulfilment of the decisions which had been adopted at the Crimea Conference. It's a question of principle. Of course, it is quite obvious that the situation in Yugoslavia, the position of Marshal Tito, should be taken into account. Not much time has passed since peace set in in the country. But all we had in mind in our draft was the wish that what was said at the Crimea Conference should be fulfilled.

Stalin: In my opinion, the decisions of the Crimea Conference are being fulfilled by Marshal Tito in their entirety.

Truman: It is true that not all the decisions of the Crimea Conference are being fulfilled by Yugoslavia. We also have complaints to make. This should be pointed out to the Yugoslav Government. But we could postpone this question to the next sitting.

Churchill: I should like to thank Generalissimo Stalin for his patience in discussing this question. If we cannot speak of the differences which sometimes arise between us, if we cannot discuss them here, where can they be discussed?

Stalin: We are discussing them here. But the question cannot be settled without the accused. You have accused the head of the Yugoslav Government, I ask that he be heard and a decision adopted after that. As for discussion we can have any amount of it.

Churchill: I agree with this, but the President is opposed to inviting Tito here.

Stalin: In that case the question will have to be withdrawn.

[...] *Truman*: Today's agenda has run out. Tomorrow's sitting is at 4.00.

Fourth Sitting

July 20, 1945

Truman opens the sitting.

[The Soviet delegation reported that that day's meeting of the three Foreign Ministers dealt with the following questions.

1. Economic principles in respect of Germany.

It was stated that the commission entrusted with the preparation of this question had not yet completed its work and therefore the substance of the question had not been discussed. It was decided to ask the commission to finish its work by July 21.

2. The Polish question.

It was reported that the commission dealing with this question had not yet completed its work, as a result of which the substance of the question had not been discussed. It was decided to ask the commission to finish its work by July 21.

3. On the peaceful settlement.

In view of the fact that the commission entrusted with drafting the text on the question of a peaceful settlement had been unable to fulfil its task because the members of this commission had been busy in other commissions, it was decided that the Foreign Ministers would meet additionally at 15.45 that day to prepare the question for submission at the sitting of the three Heads of Government. At their meeting the Foreign Ministers adopted an amendment to Point 3 of the draft on this question, as a result of which the point would read as follows:

"3. As its immediate important task, the Council would be authorised to draw up, with a view to their submission to the United Nations, treaties of peace with Italy, Rumania, Bulgaria, Hungary and Finland and to propose settlements of territorial questions outstanding on the termination of the war in Europe. The Council shall be utilised for the preparation of a peace settlement for Germany to be accepted by the Government of Germany when a government adequate for the purpose is established.

"For the discharge of each of these tasks the Council will be comprised of the members representing those States which were signatory to the terms of surrender imposed upon the enemy state concerned. For the purposes of the peace settlement for Italy, France shall be regarded as a signatory to the terms of surrender for Italy.

"Other members should be invited to participate when matters directly concerning them are under discussion."

4. The Yalta Declaration on Liberated Europe.

The People's Commissar for Foreign Affairs of the U.S.S.R. handed Soviet draft proposals on the question to the Foreign Minister of Great Britain and the U.S. Secretary of State. In connection with the submitted draft there was a discussion of the question of the situation in Rumania and Bulgaria on the one hand, and in Greece, on the other. As a result of the discussion it transpired that the Foreign Ministers took different views of the situation in these countries.

In particular, the U.S. Secretary of State and the Foreign Minister of Great Britain declared that there were restrictions on the press in Rumania and Bulgaria. The People's Commissar for Foreign Affairs pointed out that there had been some inevitable restrictions on the press in wartime conditions. At present, in view of the war being ended, the possibilities for members of the press to work in these countries could be considerably extended.

The U.S. Secretary of State proposed the conclusion of an agreement between the three Powers on the supervision of elections by the three Powers in Italy, Greece, Rumania,

Bulgaria and Hungary and on free access to these countries for members of the press of the U.S.A., U.S.S.R. and Great Britain, and on the possibility for them to move freely about and freely dispatch their reports. The People's Commissar for Foreign Affairs of the U.S.S.R. declared that he saw no necessity for the dispatch of special observers to Rumania and Bulgaria. As for Greece, the Soviet Government's standpoint was set forth in the document submitted. If the Foreign Ministers of Great Britain and the U.S.A. submitted written proposals on this question, they could be discussed at a meeting of the three Ministers.

5. On Italy.

The U.S. Secretary of State submitted a draft decision of the three Heads of Government saying that they would support Italy's entry into the United Nations, but that they would not support Spain's entry into the United Nations so long as Spain remained under the control of the regime existing in the country. The Foreign Minister of Great Britain declared his support for this proposal and said that if any declaration was drafted on this question he considered it advisable to mention in it that the three Powers would also support the admission to the United Nations of certain neutral countries, such as Sweden, Switzerland and Portugal.

The People's Commissar for Foreign Affairs of the U.S.S.R. raised the question as to whether this proposal could be applied to countries which had ceased to be hostile and had become co-belligerents against Germany. The Foreign Minister of Great Britain declared that the question could be discussed, but that he personally thought that such countries could be admitted to the United Nations after peace treaties had been signed with them. A sub-commission was set up to work out the question.

In this connection it was decided to ask the commission dealing with questions of reparations to study the question of reparations from Italy and Austria.

6. On Poland's western frontier.

The Foreign Ministers of the United States and Great Britain were handed the Soviet Government's proposals concerning the establishment of Poland's western frontiers, together with the relevant map. It was decided to bring up the question at the sitting of the three Heads of Government on July 20.

7. On trust territories.

The Foreign Ministers of the United States and Great Britain were handed the Soviet Government's proposals concerning measures for establishing territorial trusteeship. It was decided to bring this question up at the sitting of the three Heads of Government on July 20.

8. On the agenda of the sitting of the three Heads of Government on July 20.

The Ministers agreed to recommend the following agenda to the three Heads of Government:

1. On the peaceful settlement.

2. The U.S. President's memorandum of July 17 on policy in respect of Italy.

3. The situation in Austria, particularly in Vienna (communication by the Prime Minister of Great Britain).

4. On Poland's western frontier.

5. On trust territories.]

Churchill: Allow me, Mr. President, to raise a small question concerning the procedure of our work for the good of the cause. Our Ministers have been meeting every day to prepare an extensive programme for our afternoon sittings. Today, for instance, they completed their work only by 14.00. This leaves us very little time to go through and discuss the documents they prepare. Wouldn't it be better for us to begin our afternoon sittings at 17.00?

Truman: I have no objection. We now go on to a discussion of the items on the agenda. We discuss the first question.

Churchill: I understand that the Soviet delegation has an amendment to the draft on the establishment of a Council of Foreign Ministers.

Truman: The amendment was read out. I agree with the amendment.

Churchill: (Having read the text of the amendment.) I also agree with this amendment.

Truman: It is necessary to establish the time and place for a meeting of the Council of Foreign Ministers. I am prepared to let the Foreign Ministers decide this matter themselves.

Churchill: I quite agree that the question should be discussed, but it is my opinion that London must be the place; that is where the secretariat should have its permanent seat, but sittings may also take place elsewhere, if that is desirable. In confirmation of my view I should like to recall that London is the capital which was under enemy fire during the war more than the others. As far as I am aware, it is the world's biggest city and one of its most ancient. Besides, it is mid-way between the United States and Russia.

Stalin: That is most important. [*Laughter*.]

Churchill: What is more, it is London's turn.

Stalin: Right.

Churchill: I should only like to add that I flew across the ocean six times to have the honour of conferring with the President of the United States, and twice visited Moscow. However, London is not being used at all as a place for our meetings. There is strong feeling on this point in Britain, and I think Mr. Attlee also has a few words to say about it.

Attlee: I quite agree with what the Prime Minister has said here, and wish to add that our people have a right to see these outstanding personalities visit them. They would be very glad of this. They have gone through a great deal. I think, moreover, that London's geographical situation also has a great part to play. I second the Prime Minister's wish.

Truman: I also agree with the Prime Minister's proposal and agree that geographical location plays a big part.

Stalin: Good, I have no objection.

Truman: But I want to reserve the right to invite the Heads of Government to visit the United States.

Churchill: May I express my gratitude to the President and the Generalissimo for their kind acceptance of our proposal.

Truman: I think that in due time our three Foreign Ministers will be joined by the Foreign Ministers of China and France. I also think that we could let the Foreign Ministers decide on the date the Council is to meet.

[*Stalin and Churchill agree with Truman's proposals.*]

Truman: The second question is on policy in respect of Italy. Our proposals on policy in respect of Italy were submitted at the first sitting. The essence of my proposal is as follows.

I believe that Italy's position would be considerably improved if we recognised her services as a participant in the war against Germany. I propose that the terms of surrender should be replaced by the following obligations on the part of the Italian Government: 1) The Italian Government shall refrain from any hostile action against any of the United

Nations until the conclusion of a peace treaty; 2) The Italian Government shall not maintain any army, naval or air forces or equipment except what it is authorised by the Allies, and shall abide by all the instructions concerning such forces and equipment.

While this agreement is in force, control over Italy should be retained only insofar as is necessary: a) to ensure Allied military requirements so long as the Allied forces remain in Italy or operate from there; and b) to ensure a just settlement of territorial disputes.

Stalin: It would be well for the Ministers to discuss the question of policy in respect of Italy. I have no objections in principle, but some amendments in the drafting may be necessary. It would be well to refer this memorandum to the three Ministers for a final reading and to ask them, at the same time, to discuss, along with the question of Italy, the question of Rumania, Bulgaria and Finland.

There is no reason why we should set apart the question of Italy from those pertaining to other countries. Italy was, of course, the first to surrender, and subsequently helped in the war against Germany. It is true that the force was small, only 3 divisions, but she did help none the less. She is planning to enter the war against Japan. That is also a plus. But there are similar pluses to the credit of such countries as Rumania, Bulgaria and Hungary. They, these countries, moved their troops against Germany on the next day after surrender. Bulgaria had 8-10 divisions against Germany, Rumania had about 9. These countries should also be given some relief.

As for Finland she did not render any serious help in the war, but she is behaving well, honestly fulfilling her obligations. Her position could also be eased.

That is why it would be well, while giving relief to Italy, to give some to these countries as well and to examine all these questions together. If my colleagues agree with my proposal we could ask the three Foreign Ministers to examine these questions as one.

Truman: Italy was the first country to surrender, and, as far as I am aware, the terms of her surrender were somewhat harder than those of the other countries. But I agree that the position of the other satellite states should also be reviewed. I am in full agreement with Generalissimo Stalin on this point.

Churchill: Our stand on the question of Italy is not quite identical with that taken by my two colleagues. Italy attacked us in June 1940. We had serious losses in the Mediterranean and also during the defence of Egypt, which we had to organise at a time when we ourselves were threatened with invasion. We lost many warships and merchantmen in the Mediterranean. We had heavy losses on land, on the coast of North Africa. And these sacrifices increased when Germany moved her troops to Africa. Without support from anyone we had to undertake the campaign in Abyssinia, which ended in the Emperor of Abyssinia being restored to his throne. Special squadrons of Italian air force were dispatched to bomb London.

It should also be mentioned that Italy undertook an absolutely unwarranted attack against Greece, and just before the start of the war she made a similarly unwarranted attack against Albania. All that took place when we were absolutely alone.

I am saying all this because I think that all the losses that we have suffered from Italy should not be forgotten. We cannot justify the Italian people just as we do not justify the German people because it was under Hitler's yoke. In spite of this we have tried to entertain the idea of restoring Italy as one of the major Powers in Europe and the Mediterranean. When I was there a year ago I made a number of proposals to President Roosevelt, and most of these proposals were included in the declaration which was subsequently published.

I don't want it to be thought that I have any feeling of revenge in respect of Italy. I objected to reports appearing in various newspapers saying that we were antagonistic to Italy. I declared on behalf of His Majesty's Government that we viewed the matter with an open heart and wished to obtain the best results. I should like all these considerations to be taken into account.

I want to join the President and the Generalissimo in principle in making a gesture in respect of the Italian people, which suffered a great deal during the war and made efforts to expel the Germans from its territory. That is why the British delegation does not object in principle to concluding peace with Italy. This work will undoubtedly require a few months for the preparation of the peace terms.

I also note that the present Italian Government has no

democratic basis arising from free and independent elections. It merely consists of political figures who call themselves leaders of various political parties. I understand that the Italian Government intends to hold elections before the winter. That is why, although I agree that the Council of Foreign Ministers should start work on drafting the peace treaty, I do not consider it desirable that it should complete this work before the Italian Government is based on democratic principles.

Meanwhile, I must say that I do not quite agree with the U.S. memorandum concerning provisional terms under which the existing armistice terms should be replaced by certain undertakings on the part of the present Italian Government. I think that no Italian Government can give guaranteed assurances unless it rests on the Italian people. If the existing rights stipulated by the surrender are abolished and replaced by obligations on the part of the Italian Government—and it will be a considerable time before the peace treaty is concluded—we shall be deprived of every possibility, except the use of force, to make Italy fulfil our terms. As it is, none of us wants to use force to achieve such aims.

Take Point 1 of the American memorandum: it says nothing about the future of the Italian fleet, Italian colonies, reparations and other important matters. Thus we shall be losing the rights we have under the surrender document.

Finally, I must say that the terms of surrender were signed not only by Great Britain, but also by other states within the British Empire; they were signed by the dominions— Australia, New Zealand and others, who suffered losses during the war. This question will have to be discussed with them. Besides, Greece was the victim of an Italian invasion. I do not want to go further today than to agree in principle that the Council of Foreign Ministers should start to draft the peace terms.

As for the other countries mentioned here, I must say that Bulgaria has no right to make any claims on Great Britain. Bulgaria dealt us a cruel blow and did everything to harm us in the Balkans. Of course, it is not for me to talk of Bulgaria's ingratitude towards Russia. The Russian Army once liberated Bulgaria from the Turkish yoke after many years of savage oppression. In this war, Bulgaria hardly suffered at all, she was Germany's handmaiden, and on her orders attacked Greece and Yugoslavia, doing them a great deal of damage. But nothing is said about disarming Bulgaria. I think she is just as strong as before; she has 15 divisions. Nothing is said about reparations from Bulgaria. I must admit that I am not greatly inclined to an early conclusion of peace with Bulgaria, at any rate less so than to a conclusion of such a peace with Italy.

I am very grateful to my colleagues for having listened to my considerations with such patience. I must say in conclusion that on some points I differ with the President and the Generalissimo.

Stalin: It seems to me that the question of Italy is one of high politics. The task of the Big Three is to dissociate the satellites from Germany, as the main force of aggression. There are two ways of doing this. First, the use of force. This method has been successfully applied by us, and the Allied forces are in Italy, and also on the territory of other countries. But this method alone is inadequate for dissociating Germany's accomplices from her. If we continue to limit ourselves to the use of force towards them, there is the danger that we shall be creating an environment for future German aggression. It is therefore advisable to supplement the force method with that of easing the position of these countries. This, I believe, is the only means, if we view the question in perspective, of rallying these countries round us and dissociating them from Germany for good.

Such are the considerations of high politics. All other considerations, such as those of revenge and injury, no longer arise.

That is the standpoint from which I view the U.S. President's memorandum. I believe it is in line with such a policy, the policy of finally dissociating Germany's satellites from her by easing their position. That is why I have no objections in principle to the proposals put forward in the President's memorandum. They may require some drafting improvements.

Now there is the other side of the question. I have in mind Mr. Churchill's speech. Of course, Italy has also greatly wronged Russia. We had clashes with Italian troops not only in the Ukraine, but also on the Don and the Volga, that is how deeply they had penetrated into our country. But I think it would be wrong to be guided by memories of injury or feelings of retribution and to base one's policy on that. Feelings of revenge or hatred or a sense of compensation received for injury are very poor guides in politics. In politics, I believe, one should be guided by an estimation of forces.

This is how the question should be posed: do we want to have Italy on our side so as to isolate her from the forces which may once again rise against us in Germany? I think we do, and that should be our starting point. We must dissociate Germany's former accomplices from her.

A great many hardships and sufferings were inflicted on us by such countries as Rumania, which put many divisions into the field against the Soviet forces, and Hungary, which had 20 divisions against the Soviet troops in the final stages of the war. Finland inflicted great damage on us. Without Finland's help, Germany could not, of course, have blockaded Leningrad. Finland had 24 divisions against our troops.

Bulgaria has caused us fewer hardships and less injury. She helped Germany to attack and conduct offensive operations against Russia, but she herself did not enter the war against us and sent no troops against the Soviet troops. The armistice agreement provides that Bulgaria is to make her troops available for the war against Germany. This agreement was signed by the representatives of the three Powers —the United States, Great Britain and the U.S.S.R. The agreement says that after the war against Germany ends, Bulgaria's army is to be demobilised and stepped down to peace-time strength. This we shall have to do, and it will be done. Bulgaria cannot resist fulfilment of the agreement, she will have to fulfil it.

Such are the sins of the satellites against the Allies and the Soviet Union in particular.

If we begin to avenge ourselves on them for having caused us great damage, that will be one kind of policy. I am not a supporter of that policy. Now that these countries have been defeated and the control commissions of the three Powers are there to see that they carry out the armistice terms, it is time we went over to another policy, the policy of easing their position. And easing their position means prying them away from Germany.

Now here is a concrete proposal. As far as I have understood, President Truman does not propose the immediate drafting of a treaty with Italy. President Truman merely proposes that the way be paved for the conclusion of such a treaty in the near future; he proposes for the time being the creation of some kind of intermediate state between the surrender terms accepted by Italy and the future peace treaty.

I think it is hard to object to such a proposal. It is quite practicable, and it is timely. As for the other satellites, I believe that we could start by re-establishing diplomatic relations with them. There may be the objection that they do not have freely elected government. But neither is there such a government in Italy. However, diplomatic relations with Italy have been restored. Nor are there such governments in France and Belgium. But there is no doubt in anyone's mind on the question of diplomatic relations with these countries.

Churchill: They were Allies.

Stalin: I understand. But democracy is democracy everywhere, among allies as well as among satellites.

Truman: I understand the situation to be as follows. I have made a concrete proposal concerning Italy. The armistice terms were signed by all three of our states.

Eden: We did not sign on behalf of the dominions.

Truman: The dominions did not sign in respect of the other satellites either. But let us return to the question under discussion. The question of policy in respect of Italy has been placed on the agenda. The Soviet side raised the question of Rumania, Bulgaria, Hungary and Finland. I understand that the Generalissimo has proposed that the question of Italy and of the other satellite countries should be referred to our Foreign Ministers.

It is a matter of working out provisional terms before the conclusion of a peace treaty. I fully agree with the Generalissimo that these treaties must not be based on a feeling of revenge, hatred or injury, but on a sense of justice, so as to create the possibility of peaceful existence for all mankind. And I think that we can fully achieve this here.

I must say a few words on reparations from Italy. Italy's present position is such that we are faced with the question of giving Italy assistance worth from $ 700 million to $ 1,000 million. But I must say that we cannot render similar aid to other countries without getting anything in return. I think that we should here try to prepare the conditions in which these countries could live on their own resources.

I think that both these questions could be referred to the Foreign Ministers, and that they will be able to find the basis of an agreement to enable us to arrive at a common view in respect of all these countries.

Churchill: I think that we are all agreed that the question of Italy should be referred to the Foreign Ministers. I only objected to the rescission of the existing surrender terms, which would deprive us of very substantial rights. I agree with the President that the terms must be eased and that a corresponding gesture should be made in respect of Italy. I have no objection to declaring here that a peace treaty is being prepared for Italy.

I fully agree with everything said by the Generalissimo and the President about it being wrong to determine the future in the spirit of revenge for injuries caused. I heard with great satisfaction this statement by the leaders of the great peoples whom they here represent. I have great sympathy for Italy, and the Government of Great Britain will act in that spirit. I used the word "reparations" in respect of Italy, but we do not of course seek any reparations for ourselves; we had Greece in mind.

Truman: I would propose that the question of Italy and the other countries should be referred to the three Foreign Ministers.

Churchill: I agree that the preparatory work in drafting the peace treaty with Italy should be referred to the Council of Foreign Ministers.

Stalin: Which Council?

Churchill: The future Council of Foreign Ministers. I only made a reservation concerning provisional measures. This could be discussed at the daily conferences of our Foreign Ministers.

Stalin: I would propose that the Foreign Ministers should also discuss the question of Germany's other accomplices. I ask Mr. Churchill not to object to this. [*General laughter*.] I ask that the three Foreign Ministers should discuss, alongside the question of Italy, that of the other countries.

Churchill: I have never objected. [*Laughter*.]

Truman: I also agree.

Let us go on to the next question. It is the communication of the Prime Minister concerning the situation in Austria, particularly in Vienna.

Churchill: I very much regret that during today's discussion I have had to disagree with the opinion of the Soviet delegation a number of times. But I consider that the situation in Austria and in Vienna is unsatisfactory. It was agreed that we were to have different sectors, different zones in Austria. This business has been going on for a long time.

Over two months ago I asked that British officers be allowed into Vienna to inspect the premises we shall need, the airports, and the quarters for our troops. All this had been agreed in principle beforehand. Our officers went to Vienna but the results of their visit turned out to be unsatisfactory; our missions were forced to leave the city and return empty-handed. We have now been prohibited not only entry into Vienna but also the dispatch of our troops into the zone on which agreement had been reached.

Three or four months have already passed since Austria's liberation by the Soviet troops. I don't see why there are such difficulties in this simple matter, and that after an agreement had been concluded on this point. I have been receiving unsatisfactory reports from Field-Marshal Alexander. We still have no place where we could stay. I believe that in view of the signed agreement we should be given such permission.

Yesterday I was asked to find out whether a Russian delegation could visit German ships in British hands. I replied to this question as follows: meet us half-way. If German ships in Britain can be inspected by Russian representatives, I think we should be given access to enemy towns which are under Russian occupation. We have withdrawn our troops from the Russian Zone of Occupation in Northern Germany, and the American troops have also withdrawn from that zone; yet we have no right to send our troops to our zone in Austria.

Stalin: There is an agreement on zones in Austria, but there was no agreement on any zones in Vienna. Some time was naturally required to implement the agreement. This agreement has now been reached, it was reached yesterday. An agreement had to be reached on which airfields were to go to whom. This also takes time. An agreement on this question has also been reached. We received the French reply only yesterday. A day has now been set for the entry of your troops into Vienna, and for the withdrawal of our troops. This could begin today or tomorrow.

Mr. Churchill is highly indignant, but the case is not quite like that. You should not say: they're not letting us into our zone. [*Laughter*.] That is not the expression to use. We were kept out of our zone in Germany for a month. We did not complain, we knew how hard it was to withdraw one's troops and to prepare everything for the entry of the Soviet troops. The Soviet Government has no intention to violate the agreement reached. If that is all there is to the question of the situation in Austria, Vienna in particular, then it has already been settled. The actions in the Berlin area were more reasonable, and there the question was solved sooner.

Field Marshal Alexander is acting less skilfully, and this has also been a factor of delay. He behaves as if the Russian forces were under his command. This has merely served to retard the solution of the question. The British and American military leaders in the zone of Germany did not act that way. There are no obstacles at present to each army entering its own zone, whether it is a question of Vienna or Styria, and that is because an agreement has now been reached.

Churchill: I am very happy that this business has finally been settled and we shall be allowed to enter our zone. As for Field Marshal Alexander, I don't think there is any cause to complain about him.

Stalin: There were no complaints about Eisenhower, no complaints about Montgomery, but there are complaints about Alexander.

Churchill: We beg you to let us have these complaints.

Stalin: I do not want to testify against Alexander, I was not preferring a charge. [*Laughter.*]

Churchill: I feel bound to say that in view of the absence of specific complaints against Alexander, the British Government will continue to have full confidence in him. We shall support all the measures he undertakes.

Stalin: I personally have no complaints, I was merely conveying what the commanders had reported, pointing to this as one of the reasons for delay in the settlement of the question.

Churchill: We are not alone in having an interest in this matter. The American commanders also have an interest in it.

Truman: I consider that complete agreement has been reached on this question.

The next question is that of Poland's western frontier. I understand that the Soviet delegation has considerations on this question.

Stalin: If my colleagues are not ready to discuss this question, perhaps we could pass on to the next one, and discuss this question tomorrow?

Truman: It is better to discuss it tomorrow. This question will be the first one on tomorrow's agenda.

The next question is territorial trusteeship.

Stalin: Perhaps we shall discuss this question tomorrow as well?

Truman: I agree. Our agenda has run out. Tomorrow's sitting is at 17.00.

Fifth Sitting

July 21, 1945

Truman: Mr. Byrnes will report on today's sitting of the Foreign Ministers.

Byrnes: The Foreign Ministers discussed the date of the official establishment of the Council of Foreign Ministers and agreed that the Council should be set up not later than September 1. They also agreed that telegrams should be sent to the Government of China and the Provisional Government of France inviting them to take part in the work of the Council before the public announcement of its establishment. At the request of the British delegation, the drafting commission which is dealing with this question was authorised to make certain small amendments to the text of the proposal submitted.

The next question is that of the economic principles in respect of Germany. Since the sub-commission's report on the question has just been submitted and our delegations have not had the possibility of making a proper study of it, they agreed to postpone discussion of this question until tomorrow.

Next was the Polish question—the dissolution of the London Government and the fulfilment of the Yalta Declaration. A report on behalf of the sub-commission dealing with the question was given by its chairman. In view of the fact that the sub-commission was unable to reach complete agreement, the outstanding questions were thoroughly discussed by the Foreign Ministers. They reached agreement on some of these points, but the following are being referred to the Heads of Government for a final decision. I think that the differences referred to you for decision will be clearer if you have before you the report of the sub-commission's chairman. The questions referred to you for decision are: (a) the point relating to the transfer of assets to the Polish Government and the recognition by the Polish Government of obligations towards the Governments of Great Britain and the United States; (b) the point relating to the holding of elections and freedom of the press.

Concerning the first point of the differences, regarding the transfer of assets to the Polish Government and its recognition of obligations towards the British and American Governments, the chairman of the sub-commission reported the following. The British Government and the Government of the United States have already taken steps to prevent the transfer of Polish property to third persons, property situated on the territory of Great Britain and the United States and under the control of their Governments, whatever the form of that property. They are prepared immediately to take steps to transfer this property to the Polish National Government in accordance with the requirements of the law. For this purpose they are prepared to discuss means and dates for the transfer of this property with the corresponding representatives of the Polish Provisional Government.

The wording of this proposal was the object of differences. The U.S. Government's stand is that the question of the assets must be the subject of discussions between the Government of the Polish State and the Government of the United States. At the same time, they should discuss the question of the Polish Government's obligations. The U.S. Government is sure that the Polish Provisional Government has no doubt that we are prepared to place at its disposal all the property belonging to it, in accordance with our laws.

That is why we proposed the following formulation of the point relating to this question: "The British and United States Governments have taken measures to protect the interests of the Polish Provisional Government as a recognised government of the Polish State in the property belonging to the Polish State located on their territory and under their control, whatever the form of this property may be. They have further taken measures to prevent alienation to third parties of such property. All proper facilities will be given to the Polish Provisional Government for the exercise of the ordinary legal remedies for the recovery of any property of the Polish State which may have been wrongfully alienated."

Shall we discuss these points of differences or shall we go on?

Stalin: Let us first hear the report and then go on to the discussion.

Byrnes: There were no differences on the following point: "The Three Powers are anxious to assist the Polish Provisional Government in facilitating the return to Poland, as soon as practicable, of all Poles abroad who wish to go, including members of the Polish Armed Forces and Merchant Marine. They expect that those Poles who return home shall be accorded personal and property rights on the same basis as all Polish citizens."

There are differences on the following point: "The Three Powers note that the Polish Provisional Government in conformity with the Crimea decisions has agreed to the holding of free and unfettered elections as soon as possible on the basis of universal suffrage and secret ballot in which all democratic and anti-Nazi parties shall have the right to take part and to put forward candidates. It is the confident hope of the Three Powers that the elections will be conducted in such a way as to make it clear to the world that all democratic and anti-Nazi sections of Polish opinion have been able to express their views freely and thus to play their full part in the restoration of the country's political life.

"The Three Powers will further expect that representatives of the Allied press shall enjoy full freedom to report to the world upon the developments in Poland before and during the elections."

The difference is over the Soviet delegation's proposal to delete the last two sentences from the point. Mr. Eden has agreed to this, provided the sentence on the free access of members of the Allied press to Poland is retained.

Thus, the first point at issue is the one concerning the transfer of assets without any mention of liabilities.

Truman: Under our laws it is impossible to speak of assets without saying anything about liabilities. I said as much yesterday. The United States has no intention of shouldering that kind of burden. We cannot undertake the obligation of handing over all the assets to the Polish Government without a discussion of obligations on its part.

Churchill: We agree with the President's proposal concerning the transfer of assets to the Polish Government provided simultaneous mention is made of the obligations undertaken by the Polish Government.

Byrnes: Our wording, which was proposed in the hope of finding a compromise, says nothing either of assets or liabilities. We say that the British Government and the U.S. Government have already taken steps to protect the Polish Government's interests in respect of any property belonging to the Polish State which is located on their territories, whatever the form of that property. The draft also says that both Governments have already taken steps to prevent the transfer of this property to third persons. Besides, it also says that the Polish Government will be given every opportunity to take the usual legal steps to restore any property which may have been unlawfully alienated.

Churchill: Nothing is said here either of assets or of liabilities.

Byrnes: I have already spoken of the points contained in our draft.

Churchill: Nothing is said there of the transfer to the Polish Provisional Government of obligations towards Great Britain, namely, the £120 million which we advanced to the former Polish Government in London. In other words, our position is similar to yours.

Byrnes: If the Soviet Government had any property belonging to the Polish Government this question could also be settled through diplomatic channels. I think there is no need to make public mention of the fact that we are going to transfer to the Polish Government the property belonging to it and which is to be handed over as a result of the U.S. Government's recognition of the Government of Poland.

Churchill: I understand that we now leave aside the idea of assets and liabilities. This question is, of course, more important to us than to the United States owing to our having given bigger advances to the former London Polish Government.

Truman: I don't like the idea being proposed here of making a public announcement of the fulfilment of these obligations.

Churchill: I agree with you.

Stalin: Does the British Government intend to make full recovery from Poland of the advances which it made for the maintenance of the Polish troops?

Churchill: No. That is something we shall discuss with the Poles.

Stalin: We gave the Sikorski Government some funds and also some for organising the army of the Provisional National Government. But we believe that the Polish people have redeemed this debt with their blood. I consider the U.S. Government's compromise proposal acceptable, with the exception of that part of it which says that the Polish Provisional Government will be given every opportunity to take the usual legal steps. I propose that we say instead: The Polish Provisional Government will be given every opportunity in accordance with the requirements of the law. With this amendment, the compromise proposal of the American delegation could be adopted.

Churchill: What's the difference?

Stalin: The difference is that this will obviate the usual red tape which is practised under "the usual legal steps". It will be simpler to say "on the basis of the law". But that is, after all, a small thing, and the proposal of the American delegation can be adopted in its formulation.

Byrnes: The next point on which there were differences regards the following formulation: "The Three Powers note that the Polish Provisional Government in conformity with the Crimea decisions has agreed to the holding..." etc. Mr. Eden has objected to this formulation.

Eden: I proposed a compromise formula, against which the Soviet delegation objected, namely, to delete everything from the words "It is the confident hope of the Three Powers" to the words "their views freely", leaving the last sentence concerning access of members of the Allied press.

Stalin: It is a good thing that Mr. Eden has made a step towards the interests and dignity of Poland. That is to be welcomed. And if he makes another step in that direction, I think we shall all agree with this proposal. [*Laughter.*] The preceding line says that the Polish Government must observe the Crimea Declaration. Why repeat the idea once again? The foreign correspondents will be going to Poland, and not to the Polish Government; they will enjoy complete freedom, and there will be no complaints on their part against the Polish Government. Why need this be repeated again? The Poles will take offence at this, for they will see it as a sign of suspicion that they may refuse to admit any correspondents. Let us end this point on the words: "democratic and anti-Nazi parties shall have the right to take part and put forward candidates", and delete the rest.

Churchill: There's no compromise there. [*Laughter.*]

Stalin: That is a compromise in respect of the Polish Government. [*Laughter.*]

Churchill: I half expected to have the formula strengthened rather than weakened.

Stalin: Why do that?

Truman: We are very much interested in the elections in Poland because we have six million citizens of Polish origin at home. If the elections in Poland are quite free and our correspondents are quite free to send in their reports on the holding and results of the election, this will be very important for me as President. I think that if the Polish Government is aware beforehand that the Three Powers expect it to hold free elections and give free access to members of the Allied press, the Polish Government will, of course, quite painstakingly fulfil the demands contained in the decisions of the Crimea Conference.

Stalin: I think—Mr. Eden, you will note that I am making a compromise—of proposing the following: after the words "put forward candidates" insert a comma, and then go on to say "and representatives of the Allied press shall enjoy full freedom to report to the world on the progress and results of the elections".

Truman: That suits me.

Churchill: The word "note" at the beginning of the paragraph is important in this case. I also agree.

Byrnes: The next question concerns the fulfilment of the Yalta Agreement on Liberated Europe and the satellite countries. The U.S. delegation has submitted two papers on the question, but the Foreign Ministers decided to postpone discussion in order to have the opportunity of studying them. The Foreign Ministers agreed to pass these documents on to the drafting commission. But differences arose on whether the commission should deal with each of these documents separately or as a single document. The Soviet delegation favoured the single-document approach, and the American delegation, the two-document approach. It was agreed that in view of the fact that the question of the policy in respect of Italy and the other satellites had been referred to the Foreign Ministers by the Heads of Government, the Heads of Government would be requested at today's sitting to decide on the instructions for the drafting commission: should it draw up a single document for all these countries or two documents on the basis of the American draft.

Truman: At the first sitting, the American delegation submitted two documents: the first, on the policy in respect of Italy (this question was discussed at length yesterday and the day before), and the second, on the policy in respect of Rumania, Bulgaria, Hungary and Finland. We think that these two questions should be dealt with separately, because Italy was the first country to surrender and then take part in the war against Germany. Besides, there are diplomatic relations between the U.S. Government and Italy, and none between the U.S. Government and the Governments of the above-mentioned countries. But that does not mean that we think the question of Italy should be solved earlier than that of the other countries. I repeat, we believe that these two questions should be examined separately.

Stalin: I have an amendment to the American proposals on the question of the policy in respect of Rumania, Bulgaria, Hungary and Finland. I do not object to these proposals in principle, but I want to make an addition to the second point. It says: "The Three Governments will make a statement" on so and so, and after that I propose to add the following words: "And at the present moment they declare that they consider it possible to re-establish diplomatic relations with them."

Truman: I cannot agree to this.

Stalin: Then the discussion of both drafts—on Italy and on these countries—will have to be postponed.

Truman: We are not prepared to establish diplomatic relations with the Governments of these countries. What is more, we have never been in a state of war with Finland. But, as I have said, when the Governments of these countries are transformed on the basis of free elections, we shall be prepared to establish diplomatic relations with them.

Stalin: I cannot agree without the addendum I have proposed.

Churchill: Time is passing: we have been sitting here

for a week now, and have been putting off a great number of questions.

On this question, the British Government's stand is similar to that of the U.S. Government.

Byrnes: The next question concerns the agenda for today's sitting of the Heads of Government. We have agreed that the Foreign Ministers will recommend to the Heads of Government the inclusion in today's agenda of the two above-mentioned questions which were earlier referred to the Foreign Ministers by the Heads of Government and on which the Foreign Ministers would now like to receive further instructions, and also the three questions carried forward from yesterday's agenda of the Heads of Government sitting. Accordingly the proposed agenda for today's sitting will be the following:

1. The Polish question: dissolution of the London Government and fulfilment of the Yalta Agreement.

2. The question of whether the drafting commission, in working out the question of the policy in respect of Italy and the other satellites, should draw up a separate recommendation for Italy or prepare a single recommendation for all the countries concerned.

3. Poland's western border. The Soviet delegation submitted a document on the question yesterday.

4. Trusteeship. The Soviet delegation also submitted a document on the question yesterday.

5. Turkey. It is considered that the British delegation desires to raise this question orally.

Truman: Allow me to make a statement concerning Poland's western border. The Yalta Agreement established that German territory is to be occupied by the troops of the four Powers—Great Britain, the U.S.S.R., the U.S.A. and France—each of whom is to have its zone of occupation. The question of Poland's borders was touched upon at the conference, but the decision said the final solution of the question was to be made at a peace conference. At one of our first sittings we decided that as the starting point of a discussion of Germany's future borders we take Germany's borders as of December 1937.

We have delineated our zones of occupation and the borders of these zones. We have withdrawn our troops to our zones as had been established. But it now appears that another Government has been given a zone of occupation and that has been done without consulting us. If the intention was to make Poland one of the Powers which is to have a zone of occupation, this should have been agreed upon beforehand. We find it hard to accept such a solution of the question because we had not been consulted about the matter in any way. I take a friendly attitude to Poland and will possibly fully agree to the Soviet Government's proposals concerning her western borders, but I do not want to do this now, because there will be another place for doing this, namely, the peace conference.

Stalin: The decisions of the Crimea Conference said that the Heads of the Three Governments agreed that Poland's eastern border was to run along the Curzon line, which means that Poland's eastern border was established at the conference. As for her western border, the conference decisions said that Poland was to receive substantial accretions to her territory in the north and the west. It was further stated: they, that is, the Three Governments consider that at the appropriate time the new Polish Government of National Unity will be asked for its opinion on the question of the size of those accretions and that the final decision on Poland's western borders would then be put off until the peace conference.

Truman: That is how I understood it myself. But we did not have and do not have any right to give Poland a zone of occupation.

Stalin: The Polish Government of National Unity has expressed its opinion on the western border. Its opinion is now known to all of us.

Truman: No official statement has ever been made on this western border.

Stalin: I am now speaking of the Polish Government's opinion. Now we all know what it is. We can now agree on Poland's western border, and the peace conference is to take the final formal decision on it.

Truman: Mr. Byrnes received the Polish Government's statement only today. We have not yet had any time to study it.

Stalin: Our proposal boils down to expressing our opinion concerning the Polish Government's desire to have a western border running along a certain line. It makes no difference whether we express our opinion today or tomorrow.

As for the question that we have granted the Poles an occupation zone without having the consent of the Allied Powers, it has not been stated correctly. In their notes, the American Government and the British Government have repeatedly suggested that we should not allow the Polish administration to enter the western regions until the question of Poland's western border is finally settled. We could not do this because the German population had gone to the west in the wake of the retreating German troops. The Polish population, for its part, advanced to the west, and our army needed a local administration in its rear, on the territory which it occupied. Our army cannot simultaneously set up an administration in the rear, fight and clear the territory of the enemy. It is not used to doing this. That is why we let the Poles in.

That was the spirit in which we replied to our American and British friends at the time. We were also inclined to do this in the knowledge that Poland was getting an accretion of land to the west of her former border. I don't see what harm there is for our common cause in letting the Poles set up their administration on a territory which is to be Polish anyway. I have finished.

Truman: I have no objections to the opinion expressed concerning Poland's future border. But we did agree that all parts of Germany must be under the control of the four Powers. And it will be very hard to agree to a just decision of the question of reparations if important parts of Germany are under an occupying Power other than one of these four Powers.

Stalin: Is it for reparations that you are apprehensive? In that case, we can waive reparations from these territories.

Truman: We have no intention of receiving them.

Stalin: As for these western territories, there has been no decision on this, and it is a matter of interpreting the Crimea decision. There has been no decision on the western border, the question has remained open. There was only the promise of extending Poland's borders to the west and north.

Churchill: I have quite a lot to say about Poland's western border line but, I understand, the time for it has not yet come.

Truman: It is up to the peace conference   to determine the future borders.

Stalin: It is very hard to restore the German administration in the western strip, everyone has run away.

Truman: If the Soviet Government wants to have help in re-establishing the German administration in these territories, this question could be discussed.

Stalin: Our concept, the Russian concept during a war, in the occupation of enemy territory, is as follows. The army fights, it goes forward and has no worries except winning the fighting. But if the army is to move on it must have a tranquil rear. It cannot fight with the enemy at the front and simultaneously in the rear. The army fights well if the rear is tranquil and if the rear   sympathises with it and helps it. Consider for a moment the situation in which the German population is either on the run behind the retreating troops, or is engaged in shooting our troops in the back. Meanwhile, the Polish population follows in the wake of our troops. In such a situation the army naturally desires to have an administration in its rear which sympathises with it and helps it. That is the whole point.

Truman: I understand this and sympathise.

Stalin: There was no other way out. This does not mean, of course, that I lay down the borders myself. If you do not agree to the line which the Polish Government has proposed, the question will remain open. That is all.

Churchill: But can this question be left without solution?

Stalin: It has to be solved at some time.

Churchill: There is also the question of supplies. The question of food supplies is a highly important one, because these areas are the chief sources of foodstuffs for the German population.

Stalin: Who in that case will work there and raise the grain? There's no one to do this except the Poles.

Truman: We can reach an agreement. I think the substance of the question before us, with which we are concerned, is the kind of administration that will be set up in these areas. We are also interested in whether these areas are to be part of Germany or part of Poland in the period of occupation. Here is the question. We have an occupation zone. France has an occupation zone, the British and the Soviet Union have an occupation zone each. I want to know whether the areas now being dealt with are a part of the

Soviet zone of occupation. I think that at the appropriate time we shall be able to reach agreement concerning Poland's future borders, but now I am interested in the question of these areas during the occupation period.

Stalin: On paper they are still German territory; actually, *de facto*, they are Polish territory.

Truman: What has happened to the local population? There must have been some three million of it.

Stalin: The population has gone.

Churchill: If that is so, it means that they will have to obtain food in the areas to which they have gone, if the areas the Germans have abandoned are not handed over to Germany and are not at Germany's disposal. I understand that according to the Polish Government's plan, which I understand is supported by the Soviet Government, a quarter of all the cultivated land in 1937 Germany is to be taken away from her.

As for the population, it turns out that three or four million Poles are to be moved from the east to the western areas. According to Russian data, Germany's pre-war population in these areas totalled eight and a quarter million. This means that apart from the serious hardships connected with the displacement of such a great number of people, a disproportional burden will be laid on other parts of Germany, and still the food problem will not be solved.

Truman: France will want to have the Saar and the Ruhr, and if we let France have the Saar and the Ruhr, what will be left of Germany?

Stalin: There is no decision on this, but in respect of Poland's western border there is a decision, and it is that the territory of Poland must receive an accretion in the north and the west.

Churchill: There is another remark concerning Generalissimo Stalin's statement that all Germans have left these areas. There is other information to the effect that two or two and a half million Germans have after all stayed behind. Of course, these figures should still be checked.

Stalin: Of course, they should be checked. We have been discussing the border question and have now come to the question of Germany's food supplies. If you want to discuss the question, let's do so, I don't mind.

Churchill: That's true; we were speaking of the border and have now switched to the question of Germany's food supplies. But I only mentioned it because the border question creates some great difficulties for us in the solution of certain other questions.

Stalin: I agree that there are some difficulties with Germany's supply, but the Germans themselves are chiefly to blame for it. The war has brought about a situation in which virtually none of the 8 million Germans have remained there. Take Stettin: It had a population of 500,000, but when we entered Stettin, there were only 8,000 left.

In East Prussia the Germans did the following: the greater part went to the west, into the rear of their troops, and the rest went to the Königsberg area, to the Russians. When we got to the zone earmarked for accretion to Polish territory, there were no Germans there, there were only Poles. That is how things worked out.

In the area between the Oder and the Vistula, the Germans abandoned their fields, and the Poles are cultivating and harvesting them. The Poles will hardly agree to give the Germans what they have cultivated. That is the situation that has arisen in these areas.

Truman: I wish to re-emphasise: in my opinion the zones of occupation should be made available to the Powers on which a decision had been reached. I have no objections to a discussion of Poland's borders, but I believe we cannot solve the question here.

Churchill: We agreed to compensate Poland at Germany's expense for the territory which has been taken from her east of the Curzon line. But the one must balance the other. Poland is now demanding much more than she is giving away in the east. I do not think this is being done for the benefit of Europe, to say nothing of the Allies. If three or four million Poles are moved from east of the Curzon line, three or four million Germans could be moved to the west to make place for the Poles. But the present displacement of 8 million men is something I cannot support. Compensation must be equal to the losses, otherwise it would not be good for Poland herself either. If, as Generalissimo Stalin has said, the Germans have abandoned the lands east and west of the Oder, they should be encouraged to return there.

At any rate, the Poles have no right to create a disastrous situation in the food supply for the German population. I want to re-emphasise this standpoint. I want the

Generalissimo to understand our difficulties just as, I hope, we shall understand his.

We don't want to be saddled with a large German population without any food resources. Take the vast population of the Ruhr basin, in the area of the coal mines. This population is in the British zone of occupation. Unless they are provided with enough foodstuffs, the situation in our own zone will be similar to that in the German concentration camps.

Stalin: Anyhow, Germany cannot do, and has never done, without grain imports.

Churchill: Of course, but she will be even less able to feed herself if the eastern lands are taken away from her.

Stalin: Let them buy grain from Poland.

Churchill: We do not consider this territory to be Polish territory.

Stalin: The Poles live there, and they have cultivated the fields. We can't demand of the Poles that they should work the fields and let the Germans have the grain.

Churchill: Besides, I must point out that the conditions in the areas occupied by the Poles are very strange in general. I have been told, for instance, that the Poles are selling Silesian coal to Sweden. They are doing this when we in Britain have a shortage of coal and are faced with the coldest and harshest winter without fuel. We start from the general principle that the supply of Germany within her 1937 borders with foodstuffs and fuel must be shared proportionally to the size of her population, regardless of the zone in which this food and fuel is located.

Stalin: And who is to mine the coal? The Germans are not doing it, it is the Poles who are, they are working.

Churchill: But they are working in Silesia.

Stalin: The masters have all run away from there.

Churchill: They have gone because they were afraid of military operations, but now that the war is over they could return.

Stalin: They don't want to, and the Poles have not much sympathy with the idea.

Churchill: Yesterday I was deeply touched by the Generalissimo's words when he said that it was undesirable to deal with current and future problems while being guided by a sense of revenge. I believe therefore that what I am saying today will meet with his sympathy because it would be unjust to send such a great number of Germans to us, while Poles had all the advantages.

Stalin: I am speaking of the industrialists who have run away from the coal basin. We ourselves are buying coal from the Poles, like the Swedes, because we are also short of coal in some areas, for instance, the Baltic area.

Truman: It seems to be a *fait accompli* that a considerable part of Germany has been handed over to Poland for occupation. What in that case remains for the exaction of reparations? Even we in the United States are short of coal. However, in spite of this, we are sending 6.5 million tons of coal to Europe this year. I think this part of Germany, namely, the coal basin, should be regarded as remaining with Germany both in respect of reparations and in respect of food supplies. I think the Poles have no right to take over that part of Germany. We are now discussing the question of Poland's future borders. But I believe we are in no position to solve the question here and that it must be settled at a peace conference.

Stalin: Who, in that case, is going to mine the coal there? We, Russians, are short of hands for our own enterprises. All the German workers went into the army, Goebbels's propaganda attained its aim. It remains either to stop all production or to hand it over to the Poles. There is no other way out. As for coal, I must say that within the old borders the Poles had their own coal basin, a very rich one. To this coal basin has been added the Silesia coal basin, which was in German hands. The Poles are working there. We can't take the coal mined by the Poles.

Churchill: The pits in Silesia, I understand, are being worked by Polish workers. There is no objection to the pits being operated as an agency of the Soviet Government in the Soviet zone of occupation, but not of the Polish Government in a zone that has not been granted to Poland for occupation.

Stalin: This would disrupt all relations between two friendly states. I also ask Mr. Churchill to consider the fact that the Germans themselves are short of manpower. The greater part of the enterprises we found in the course of our advance were manned by foreign workers—Italians, Bulgarians, Frenchmen, Russians, Ukrainians, etc. All of these workers had been forcibly driven from their homeland by the Germans. When the Russian troops arrived in these areas, the foreign workers considered themselves free, and went home. Where are the German workers? It turns out that most of them were drafted into the German army and were either killed during the war or taken prisoner.

This produced a situation in which the big German industry was operating with the most insignificant number of German workers, and a great number of foreign workers. When these foreign workers were liberated, they went away, and the enterprises were left without workers. The situation today is such that either these enterprises have to be closed down or the local population, that is, the Poles, must be allowed to work there. You can't drive out the Poles now. This situation has taken shape spontaneously. There is simply no one to blame for this.

Attlee: I want to say a few words concerning the present situation from the standpoint of the Powers occupying Germany. Leaving aside the question of the final border between Poland and Germany, we see before us a country which is beset by chaos but which was once an economic entity. We have before us a country which depended for its food and partly its coal supplies on its eastern areas, partially settled by the Poles. I believe the resources of the whole of 1937 Germany should be used to maintain and supply the whole of the German population, and if a part of Germany is cut off beforehand, this will create great difficulties for the occupying Powers in the western and southern zones.

If there is need of manpower for the eastern areas, it must be found among the population of the rest of Germany, among the part of the German population which has been demobilised or is exempt from work in military industry. This manpower should be sent where it can do the most good to prevent the Allies from being placed in a difficult situation over the next few months.

Stalin: Will Mr. Attlee also take into account the fact that Poland is herself suffering from the aftermath of war and is also an Ally?

Attlee: Yes, but she has found herself in a privileged position.

Stalin: Vis-à-vis Germany. That is how it should be.

Attlee: No, in respect of the other Allies.

Stalin: That is far from being the case.

Truman: I want to say frankly what I think on this question. I cannot agree to the alienation of the eastern part of

1937 Germany in as far as it bears upon settling the reparations question and supplies of food and coal for the whole German population.

Churchill: We have not yet done with this question. Besides, we do have, of course, much more pleasant questions. (*Laughter*.)

Truman: I propose that we now adjourn and perhaps think these questions over. That suits me.

Stalin: All right, that also suits me.

Truman: Tomorrow the sitting is at 5.00 p.m.

Sixth Sitting

July 22, 1945

Truman opens the sitting.

Stalin: I want to inform you that today the Soviet troops in Austria started withdrawing, and in some places they will have to withdraw 100 kilometres. The withdrawal is to be completed by July 24. The advance units of the Allied troops have already entered Vienna.

Churchill: We are very grateful to the Generalissimo for having so swiftly started implementing the agreement.

Truman: The American Government also expresses its gratitude.

Stalin: There is no cause for thanks; it is our duty to do this.

[The British delegation then reported that the Foreign Ministers, at their morning sitting, discussed the following questions.

First question: the Yalta Declaration on Liberated Europe. The Ministers examined a memorandum tabled by the U.S. delegation on July 21. It dealt with three questions: first, supervision of elections in some European countries; second, creation of favourable conditions for members of the world press in the liberated areas and the former satellite countries; and third, procedures governing the work of the control commissions in Rumania, Bulgaria and Hungary.

The British delegation expressed agreement with the U.S. memorandum. The Soviet delegation did not agree with the proposal concerning supervision of the elections.

As for the second and third questions—concerning members of the press and the procedures for the control commissions in Bulgaria, Rumania and Hungary, it was decided to refer these proposals for discussion to a subcommittee composed as follows: Cannon and Russell from the United States; Sobolev, from the U.S.S.R.; and Hayter, from Great Britain.

The Soviet delegation decided to submit a memorandum showing the recent improvements in the status of British and American representatives in the control commissions in Rumania, Bulgaria and Hungary. The Soviet delegation also agreed to draw up a memorandum concerning the changes it considered necessary and desirable in connection with the procedure governing the work of the Allied commission in Italy.

Second question: economic principles in respect of Germany.

A report was submitted by the Economic Subcommittee. The U.S. delegation asked for a postponement of the discussion of the reparations question until the next sitting. The Soviet delegation proposed that there should be discussion of the economic principles which had been agreed in the Subcommittee. Accordingly, the Foreign Ministers decided to discuss only the agreed principles and not to go into the controversial principles or the reparations question. It was decided that the reparations question would be the first item on the agenda of the Foreign Ministers sitting on July 23.

Paragraphs 11, 12, 14, 15 and 17 were adopted, subject to agreement on the rest of the paragraphs which remain in dispute.

As for the other paragraphs, it was agreed that the last sentence in Paragraph 10 should be amended to read as follows:

"Production capacity not needed for permitted production shall be removed in accordance with the reparations plan recommended by the Allied Commission on reparations and approved by the Governments concerned, or if not removed, shall be destroyed."

Paragraphs 13, 16 and 18 were set aside for further discussion.

The Ministers decided to recommend the following agenda for the day's sitting of the Heads of Government:

1. Poland's western frontier—resumption of discussion.

2. Trusteeship—question carried over from the previous day's sitting of the Heads of Government.

3. Turkey—question also carried over from the previous day's sitting.

4. Partial alteration of the western frontier of the U.S.S.R. —proposal of the Soviet delegation.

5. Iran—memorandum submitted by the United Kingdom delegation on July 21.

It was decided to transfer several other questions to the next day's sitting of the Foreign Ministers. These questions were the following:

1. Co-operation in solving urgent European economic problems—proposal of the U.S. delegation.

2. Directive of the Heads of Government concerning control over Germany in accordance with the principles agreed by them—proposal of the U.S. delegation.

3. Tangier—proposal of the Soviet delegation.

4. Syria and the Lebanon—proposal of the Soviet delegation.]

Truman: Do you agree to refer these questions for discussion to the Foreign Ministers at their sitting of tomorrow?

Churchill: I do not know what these proposals concerning Syria and the Lebanon are. This question affects us more than any other state. My colleagues are not affected by this question because only British troops are involved there. Of course, we had difficulties with France on this matter. We are prepared to leave Syria and the Lebanon, we do not seek anything there. But it is impossible to do so now, because a British withdrawal would be followed by the killing of Frenchmen. I should like to know what the matter is before I can take any decision. Perhaps, this may be done here?

Stalin: Certainly. The matter is as follows. The Government of Syria appealed to the Soviet Government to intervene in this affair. It is known that at the time we addressed a note on the question to the French, British and American Governments. We should like to receive the relevant information on this matter, because we are also interested in it. Of course, the question could be examined beforehand at a sitting of the Foreign Ministers.

Churchill: I should prefer to have the first three questions referred for examination to the Foreign Ministers, but to have the question of Syria and the Lebanon discussed here.

Stalin: By all means.

Truman: My proposal is that the first three questions should be referred to the Foreign Ministers and that the question of Syria and the Lebanon should be examined by the Heads of Government after we have discussed the questions on our agenda.

We go on to the first item of the agenda—Poland's western frontier.

As for the U.S. Government's view of this question, it was set forth by me yesterday.

Churchill: I heard you say, Mr. President, that your standpoint was set forth yesterday. I too have nothing to add to the views I have already expressed.

Truman (to Stalin): Have you anything to add?

Stalin: Have you studied the Polish Government's statement?

Truman: Yes, I have read it.

Churchill: Is it Bierut's letter?

Stalin: It is a letter from Bierut and Osóbka-Morawski.

Churchill: Yes, I have read it.

Stalin: Are all the delegations of their old opinion?

Truman: That's obvious.

Stalin: The question remains open.

Truman: Can we go on to the next question?

Churchill: What does it mean: remains open? Does that mean that nothing will be done about it?

Truman: If a question remains open, we can discuss it once again.

Churchill: It is to be hoped that the question will mature for discussion before our departure.

Stalin: Possibly.

Churchill: It would be a pity for us to depart without settling this question, which will surely be discussed in the parliaments of the whole world.

Stalin: In that case let us comply with the Polish Government's request.

Churchill: That proposal is absolutely unacceptable to the British Government. Yesterday, I gave a number of reasons why the proposal is unacceptable. Having such a territory will not benefit Poland. It will tend to undermine Germany's economic position and saddle the occupying Powers with an excessive burden in respect of supplying the western part of Germany with food and fuel. In addition, we have some doubts of a moral order concerning the desirability of such a great displacement of population. We are in principle agreed to a resettlement but in the proportion in which the population is resettled from east of the Curzon Line. But when it comes to resettling 8 or 9 million persons, we consider it incorrect. The information on this question is highly contradictory. According to our date there are 8 or 9 million persons; according to Soviet data, all these people have gone from there. We believe that until this information is verified we can adhere to our figures. So far we have had no possibility of checking what is actually going on there. I could also give other reasons, but should not like to bother the Conference.

Stalin: I do not undertake to object to the reasons given by Mr. Churchill, but I have in mind a number of reasons that are most important.

Concerning fuel. It is said that Germany is left without fuel. But she still has the Rhineland and there is fuel there. Germany will not experience any special difficulties if she is deprived of Silesian coal; Germany's principal fuel base is situated in the west.

The second question, concerning the resettlement of the population. There are no 8, or 6, or 3, or 2 millions of population in these areas. The people there were either drafted into the army and were killed or taken prisoner, or have left these areas. Very few Germans remain on this territory. But this can be verified. Is it possible to arrange to hear the opinion of the Polish representatives concerning Poland's frontier?

Churchill: I am unable to support this proposal at the present time, because of the view expressed by the President concerning the invitation of Yugoslavia's representatives.

Stalin: Let the representatives of Poland be invited to the Foreign Ministers' Council in London and be heard there.

Truman: I have no objections to that.

Churchill: But, Mr. President, the Foreign Ministers' Council will meet only in September.

Stalin: Well, that's when the Council will invite the Polish Government's representatives to London.

Churchill: In order to verify the information?

Stalin: By the time information will have been collected by the three sides.

Churchill: But that will only mean transferring the difficult question from this Conference to the Foreign Ministers'

Council, whereas this Conference is able to settle the question.

Stalin: I, too, think that it is able to do so. On the strength of the decisions of the Crimea Conference it is our duty to hear the Polish Government's opinion on the question of Poland's western frontier.

Truman: That is right. I think the Soviet proposal that the Foreign Ministers' Council invite the Polish Government's representatives to London should be adopted. But that does not, of course, rule out the possibility of the question being discussed at the present Conference.

Stalin: I propose that the Polish Government's representatives should be invited to the Foreign Ministers' Council in London in September and that their opinion should be heard there.

Churchill: That is another question. I thought it was a matter of verifying the data concerning the number of Germans in those areas.

Stalin: It is a matter of Poland's western frontier.

Churchill: But how can the question of the frontier be decided there when the question must be settled at a peace conference?

Truman: I think it will be useful to hear the Poles at the Foreign Ministers' Council in London.

Stalin: That's right.

Churchill: I regret that such an important and urgent question is being referred for solution to a body with less authority than the present Conference.

Stalin: In that case, let us invite the Poles over here and hear what they have to say.

Churchill: I should prefer that because the question is urgent. But it is not hard to foresee just what the Poles will demand. They will, of course, demand much more than we can agree to.

Stalin: But if we invite the Poles they will not accuse us of having settled this question without hearing them. What I want is that no such accusation should be levelled at us by the Poles.

Churchill: But I have not made any accusations against them.

Stalin: It is not you, but the Poles who will say: they have settled the question of the frontier without having heard us.

Churchill: I understand now.

Truman: Is it necessary to settle the question so urgently? I repeat, I think that the final solution of this question should be referred to a peace conference; we ourselves are not able to solve this question. But I think that the discussion of this question here was highly useful and it does not rule out any further discussions. What I do not know is how urgent the question is.

Stalin: If it is not urgent, let us refer the question to the Foreign Ministers' Council. That would not be superfluous.

Truman: But that does not exclude the possibility of further discussing the question here.

Churchill: Mr. President, with all due respect to you, I should like to note that there is a certain urgency about the question. If the settlement of the question is deferred, the *status quo* will be fixed. The Poles will start exploiting this territory, they will settle down there, and if the process continues, it will be very difficult to adopt any other decision later. That is why I still hope that we shall come to some agreement here, so as to know in what state the Polish question is.

I do not imagine how this question can be settled by the Foreign Ministers' Council in London, when we over here have failed to reach agreement. Unless we settle this question, the problem of food and fuel remains open and the burden of supplying the German population with food and fuel will be imposed on us, above all the British, because their zone of occupation has the smallest food resources. If the Foreign Ministers' Council, after hearing the Poles, also fails to reach agreement, the question will be postponed indefinitely. Meanwhile, winter will set in and there will still be no agreement.

I should very much like to meet the Generalissimo Stalin half way in solving the practical difficulties of which he spoke yesterday, the difficulties which arose in the course of events. We should be prepared to submit for your examination a compromise solution which would operate in the intervening period—from the present time until the peace conference. I propose that we draw a provisional line east of which the territory would be occupied by the Poles as a part of Poland until the final settlement of the question at a peace conference; to the west of the line, the Poles, if they find themselves there, could act as representatives of the

Soviet Government in the zone made available to the Soviet Union.

I have had several talks with the Generalissimo since the Tehran Conference and I think we were agreed in general terms that the new Poland should move her borders west to the Oder River. But this is not such a simple question. The difference in views between the Generalissimo and myself is that the British Government, while allowing that Poland should extend her territory, does not wish to go as far as the Soviet Government does. When I speak of the line along the Oder River I have in mind the line of which we spoke two years ago at Tehran, when there was no question of any precise demarcation of the frontier. We are now prepared to propose that the Conference examine a provisional Polish frontier line. If the question is postponed until September, and the Foreign Ministers are made to discuss it with the Poles, this will mean that the question will not be settled before the winter. I shall be sorry if we do not reach an agreement in principle on this question here. In my view, if the question is postponed and referred for discussion by the Foreign Ministers' Council with the participation of the Poles, we shall not benefit in any way from such a settlement.

Our position in respect of the territory and the line is quite clear. Here I should like to find a practical way out of the situation. But if the question is referred to the Foreign Ministers' Council, its solution will be dragged out far too long. I do not regard the question as being quite hopeless of solution here. I am sure that we could find a compromise solution. We could let the Poles have everything that we decide to let them have, and the rest of the territory would be left under the Soviet Government's administration.

I think there is no sense in leaving this question unsolved until September. If we do not settle this question, it will mean a failure for our Conference.

I repeat once again that when we used the expression "the Oder line" we had in mind only an approximate line. The line we propose should be traced on the map; in one place it even goes across the Oder.

I appeal to the Conference to continue its efforts to reach agreement on this question, if not today, then some other day, because if the Foreign Ministers meet in September and have a discussion with the Poles, say, in the course of a fortnight, with the Soviet side again holding one view, and the United States and Great Britain, another, the question may again be left outstanding or we may achieve its settlement far too late. What will be the position of, say, Berlin? Berlin receives some of its coal from Silesia.

Stalin: Berlin does not receive its coal from Silesia but from Torgau (Saxony), as it did in the past.

Churchill: The question of coal for Berlin is very important, because the city is under our common occupation.

Stalin: Let them take it from the Ruhr, from Zwickau.

Churchill: Is that so-called brown coal?

Stalin: No, it is good hard coal. Brown coal is good for use in briquettes, and the Germans have good briquette factories. They have all sorts of possibilities.

Churchill: I merely say that part of the coal for Berlin was received from Silesia.

Stalin: Before the British troops occupied the Zwickau area the Germans got their coal for Berlin from there. Following the departure of the Allied troops from Saxony to the west, Berlin got its coal from Torgau.

Truman: Allow me to restate the U.S. position on this question.

Stalin: By all means.

Truman: I should like to give some extracts here from the Crimea Conference decision.

"The three Heads of Government consider that the eastern frontier of Poland should follow the Curzon Line with some digressions from it in some regions of five to eight kilometres in favour of Poland. They recognise that Poland must receive substantial accessions of territory in the north and west. They feel that the opinion of the new Polish Provisional Government of National Unity should be sought in due course of the extent of these accessions and that the final delimitation of the western frontier of Poland should thereafter await the peace conference."

This agreement was reached by President Roosevelt, Generalissimo Stalin and Prime Minister Churchill. I agree with this decision; I well understand the difficulties of which Generalissimo Stalin spoke yesterday. I also well understand the difficulties in respect of food and fuel supplies of which Prime Minister Churchill spoke yesterday. But I think that these difficulties do not in any way alter the substance of the matter.

Stalin: If you are not bored with this question, I am prepared to speak once again. I, too, start from the decision of the Crimea Conference from which the President has just quoted. It follows from the precise meaning of this decision that with the formation of the Government of National Unity in Poland, we should have obtained the opinion of the new Polish Government on the question of Poland's western frontier. The Polish Government has communicated its opinion. We now have two possibilities: either to endorse the Polish Government's opinion on Poland's western frontier, or, if we are not in agreement with the Polish proposals, to hear the Polish representatives here and only then decide the question.

I consider it expedient to settle the question at our Conference and, since there is no unity of opinion with the Polish Government, to invite its representatives and hear them. But the opinion was expressed here that the Poles should not be invited to this Conference. If that is so, we can refer this question to the Foreign Ministers' Council.

I should like to remind Mr. Churchill and others who were present at the Crimea Conference of the opinion which was then expressed by President Roosevelt and Prime Minister Churchill and with which I did not agree. Mr. Churchill spoke of Poland's western frontier line along the Oder beginning from its mouth, then running along the Oder all the time, until the confluence of the Oder with the River Neisse, east of it. I stood for a line west of the Neisse. According to the scheme of President Roosevelt and Mr. Churchill, Stettin and also Breslau and the area west of the Neisse were to remain with Germany. (Indicates on the map.)

What we are examining here now is the question of frontiers and not of a provisional line. This question cannot be evaded. If you were in agreement with the Poles, it would be possible to adopt a decision without inviting the Polish Government's representatives here. But since you are not in agreement with the Polish Government's opinion and wish to make amendments, it will be well for us to invite the Poles here and hear their opinion. This is a matter of principle.

Churchill: On behalf of the British Government I should

like to withdraw my objection to inviting the Poles here, in order to try to achieve the adoption of some kind of practical decision which would remain in force until the final settlement of the question at the peace conference.

Truman: I have no objection to inviting the Polish Government's representatives here. They could have talks here with our Foreign Ministers.

Stalin: That's right.

Churchill: And then the results of the talks with them could be placed before the Heads of Government.

Stalin: That's right. That's right.

Churchill: Who is to send them an invitation?

Stalin: The Chairman, I think.

Truman: Good. We now pass to the next question. I think that the Soviet delegation has proposals concerning trusteeship.

[Setting forth its proposals on the question of trusteeship, the Soviet delegation declared that what had been formulated in its proposals, submitted in written form, followed from the decisions of the San Francisco Conference. It said furthermore that inasmuch as the main question of trusteeship had been decided by the United Nations Charter, the Conference of the Heads of Government was faced with the concrete question of territories. The Soviet delegation expressed the opinion that the Conference could hardly expect to examine the question in detail but it could, first, discuss the question of Italy's colonial possessions in Africa and the Mediterranean, and second, discuss the question of the League of Nations mandated territories. The Soviet delegation pointed out that its proposals contain two variants of a possible solution of the question of former Italian colonies. It has proposed that the question should be referred for examination to the Foreign Ministers' meeting.]

Churchill: Of course, it is possible to have an exchange of opinion on any question, but if it turns out that the sides differ in their views, the only result will be that we shall have had a pleasant discussion. I think the question of the mandates was decided at San Francisco.

Truman: Allow me to read the article of the United Nations Charter dealing with the question of trusteeship.

"1. The trusteeship system shall apply to such territories in the following categories as may be placed thereunder by means of trusteeship agreements:

"(a) Territories now held under mandate;

"(b) Territories which may be detached from enemy states as a result of the Second World War; and

"(c) Territories voluntarily placed under the system by states responsible for their administration.

"2. It will be a matter for subsequent agreement as to which territories in the foregoing categories will be brought under the trusteeship system and upon what terms."

I believe the Soviet proposals apply to the second paragraph of this article. I agree with the proposal of the Soviet delegation that the question should be referred for discussion to the Foreign Ministers.

Churchill: We agreed with what was adopted at San Francisco but no more than that. Since the question of trusteeship is in the hands of an international organisation, I doubt the desirability of an exchange of opinion on the question here.

Truman: I think it will be quite in order to examine the question here like the question of Poland or any other question.

Churchill: The question of Poland has not been examined by an international organisation.

We expressed our standpoint on the question of trusteeship secretly at Yalta and openly at San Francisco. Our stand is clear and cannot be altered.

Truman: Great Britain's stand is fully ensured by another article of the United Nations Charter, and I see no reason why this question cannot be examined here.

Stalin: We learn from the press, for instance, that Mr. Eden, in a speech in the British Parliament, declared that Italy has lost her colonies for ever. Who has decided that? If Italy has lost them, who has found them? [*Laughter.*] That is a very interesting question.

Churchill: I can answer it. By steady effort, at the cost of great losses and through exceptional victories, the British Army alone conquered these colonies.

Stalin: And the Red Army took Berlin. [*Laughter.*]

Churchill: I want to finish my statement, because Mr. President has questioned the words "the British Army alone conquered". I have in mind the following Italian colonies: Italian Somaliland, Eritrea, Cyrenaica and Tripoli, which we conquered alone and in very difficult conditions.

However, we do not seek territorial gains. We do not want

to derive any advantages from this war, although we have suffered great losses. Of course, as regards human losses they are not as great as those suffered by the Soviet Union and its gallant troops. However, we have emerged from this war in great debt to the United States. We can never expect to have the same strength at sea as the United States. During the war we built only one battleship, and lost ten. But despite all these losses we have no territorial claims. That is why we approach the question of trust territories without any ulterior motives.

Now about the statement made by Eden in Parliament, in which he said that Italy has lost her colonies. This does not mean that Italy has no right to claim these colonies. This does not exclude any discussion, during the preparation of the peace treaty with Italy, of the question of whether a part of her former territories should be returned to Italy. I do not support such a proposal, but we do not object to the question of colonies being discussed either in the Foreign Ministers' Council, when it deals with the preparation of the peace treaty with Italy, or, of course, at a peace conference on the final settlement.

I must say that when I visited Tripoli and Cyrenaica, I saw the work that had been done by the Italians in ploughing and cultivating the land; it was remarkable, in spite of the difficult conditions. What I want to say is that although we do not favour a return of her African colonies to Italy, we do not, at the same time, rule out the possibility of discussing the question. At present, all these colonies are in our hands. Who wants to have them? If there are any claimants to these colonies round this table, it would be well for them to speak out.

Truman: We have no use for them. We have enough poor Italians at home who need to be fed.

Churchill: We examined the question as to whether some of these colonies could be used to settle Jews. But we consider that it would be inconvenient for the Jews to settle there.

Of course, we have great interests in the Mediterranean and any change in the *status quo* in that area would require a long and thorough study on our part.

We do not quite understand what our Russian Allies want.

Stalin: We should like to know whether you consider that Italy has lost her colonies for good. If you consider that she has lost those colonies, which states are we to hand them over to for trusteeship? We should like to know that. If it is too early to speak of this, we can wait, but it will have to be said some time.

Churchill: Of course, we must decide the question of whether we should detach her colonies from Italy, which we have a perfect right to do.

Stalin: That is a question which still has to be decided.

Churchill: And if they are taken away, which we have every right to do, we shall have to decide who is to have trusteeship over them. It is up to the peace conference to decide which colonies are to be taken away from Italy, but the question of the further administration of those territories is within the competence of an international organisation.

Stalin: Are we to understand Mr. Churchill in the sense that the present Conference is not empowered to examine the question?

Churchill: Our Conference cannot settle the question: it must be settled by a peace conference. But, of course, if this *troika* reaches agreement, this will be of great importance.

Stalin: I do not propose to decide, but to examine the question. I think that our Conference is, of course, empowered to examine the question.

Churchill: We are examining the question just now. I have no objection to the Generalissimo saying what he wants and I agree to study the question immediately.

Stalin: It is not a matter of the Generalissimo but of the fact that the question has not been examined and should be.

Churchill: Which question specifically?

Stalin: The question tabled by the Soviet delegation.

Truman: I agree with the proposal of the Soviet delegation to refer the question for discussion by the Foreign Ministers.

Stalin: That's another matter.

Truman: We have no objections to that proposal.

Churchill: We have no objections either, except that we have been referring all the questions to our Ministers.

Truman: That is quite natural.

Churchill: I think there are many more urgent questions which ought to be settled while we are here. We have decided that the question of a peace treaty with Italy will be examined by the Foreign Ministers' Council in September as a matter of first priority, and this will automatically raise the question of what is to be done with these Italian colonies. I am against burdening our Foreign Ministers with this question as well. But the question could be placed on the agenda if the Ministers find they have time to deal with the question.

Stalin: Let's refer it to the Ministers.

Truman: I support that proposal.

Churchill: Let us refer the question to the Foreign Ministers, provided that does not slow down their work on more urgent matters.

Stalin: Now, let's not have such reservations. You can't refer a question with that kind of reservation. Either we refer it, or we do not.

Churchill: If you insist, I give in.

Truman: We refer the question for examination by the Foreign Ministers. [...]

[*The Soviet delegation then handed its proposals concerning the Königsberg region to the delegations of the United States and Britain.*]

Truman: I should like to propose that we refer this question for discussion by the Foreign Ministers.

I have one more question. We have already agreed on inviting the Polish Government's representatives over here. I think the correspondents will want to know why the Polish Government's representatives are being summoned and I think it would be proper to issue a communiqué on the matter.

Stalin: Before the Poles arrive?

Truman: Yes, before their arrival.

Stalin: I suppose we could.

Churchill: That runs counter to the principle we have adhered to until now.

Stalin: It's all the same whether we issue a communiqué or not. I don't mind which way we have it.

Churchill: Shall we state the purpose of their coming here?

Stalin: I don't think we should state the purpose.

Churchill: I request that the purpose of their visit should not be stated.

Truman: Accepted without statement of purpose.

Stalin: Good.

[The Soviet delegation then read a communication on

the Soviet POW camp in Italy. It said that this was Camp No. 5 in the vicinity of the town of Celsinatica, under the control of the British authorities, in which mainly Ukrainians were kept. The Soviet delegation stated that initially the British authorities said that the camp contained 150 men, but when a Soviet representative visited the camp it proved to contain 10,000 Ukrainians, of whom the British command had formed a whole division. Twelve regiments were organised, including a signals regiment and a battalion of engineers. The officer corps was made up chiefly of former Petlyura men, who previously had commands in the German Army. The Soviet delegation stated in conclusion that when the Soviet officer made his appearance at the camp, 625 men at once declared their desire to return to the Soviet Union.]

Churchill: We welcome every manner of observation on your part. I shall demand a special report by telegraph. There may be many Poles there.

Stalin: No, there were only Ukrainians, Soviet citizens.

Churchill: When approximately did all this happen?

Stalin: We got the telegram today, and it happened over the last few months.

Churchill: I've not heard anything of this until now.

[*Truman closes the sitting and sets the next one for 17.00 the next day.*]

Seventh Sitting

July 23, 1945

Truman opens the sitting.

[Reporting on the Foreign Ministers' sitting, the Soviet delegation said the agenda of the day's sitting of the Ministers included the following questions:

1. Reparations from Germany, Austria and Italy.

The People's Commissar for Foreign Affairs of the U.S.S.R. handed to the U.S. Secretary of State and the Foreign Secretary of Great Britain the Soviet delegation's drafts on reparations from Germany and on advance deliveries from Germany on account of reparations.

It was decided to instruct the Economic Commission to make a preliminary examination of both drafts, and then

223

to discuss them at the next meeting of the three Foreign Ministers.

2. Economic principles in respect of Germany.

There was a discussion of Clauses 13, 18 and the new Clause 19, which was proposed by the Soviet delegation. The Soviet delegation announced that it was withdrawing its amendment to Clause 13, and proposed the removal of Clause 18 so that the questions dealt with in the clause would be discussed by the Allied agencies in Germany and then settled by the Control Council, or, in the event of no agreement being reached in the Control Council, by agreement between the Governments. No agreement was reached and it was decided to refer the question of Clause 18 for settlement by the three Heads of Government.

As regards the new Clause 19, proposed by the Soviet delegation, the U.S. Secretary of State declared it to be unacceptable to the United States. The Soviet delegation proposed an alternative draft of Clause 19, according to which priority over all other deliveries was to be given to exports from Germany, as approved by the Control Council, to cover imports. In all other cases, priority was to be given to reparations. No agreement was reached, and it was decided to refer the question for settlement by the three Heads of Government.

3. About the Council of Foreign Ministers.

The draft submitted by the Drafting Commission was adopted without amendments.

4. About Trust Territories.

There was a discussion of the Soviet delegation's draft. The Foreign Secretary of Great Britain declared that the first thing to be settled was whether any Italian colonies were to be taken away from Italy, and which. The question should be settled in drafting the peace treaty with Italy. The question of who was to be given the trusteeship of all the former Italian colonies which it might be decided to take away from Italy should be settled by the international United Nations organisation. The U.S. Secretary of State proposed that the settlement of this question should be postponed until the conclusion of a peace treaty with Italy, when all the territorial questions relating to Italy would be up for solution. The People's Commissar for Foreign Affairs of the U.S.S.R. proposed that the Soviet memorandum should be referred for examination by the first sitting of the

Council of Foreign Ministers in London this September. The British Minister declared that he believed there was no need to refer the Soviet memorandum to the Council of Foreign Ministers, as the question of the Italian colonies would automatically arise during the drafting of the peace treaty with Italy. The People's Commissar for Foreign Affairs of the U.S.S.R. asked that it be noted that the Soviet Government would raise the questions dealt with in the Soviet memorandum at the September sitting of the Council of Foreign Ministers in London.

5. About the directives to the Allied commanders-in-chief in Germany.

It was decided to inform all commanders-in-chief of Allied occupation troops in Germany of the relevant decisions of the Conference, after these decisions had been agreed with the Provisional Government of the French Republic.

For that purpose it was decided to set up a commission consisting of: Murphy and Riddleberger of the United States; Strang and Harrison of Great Britain, and Gusev and Sobolev of the U.S.S.R.

6. About co-operation in settling urgent European economic problems.

To examine the memorandum submitted by the U.S. delegation it was decided to set up a commission consisting of: Clayton and Pawley of the United States; Brand and Cowlson of Great Britain, and Arutyunyan and Gerashchenko of the U.S.S.R.

7. About Tangier.

There was a discussion of the Soviet draft.

It was decided:

(1) To adopt the first paragraph of the Soviet delegation's draft, namely, the following:

"Having examined the question of the Zone of Tangier, the three Governments have agreed that this zone, which includes the City of Tangier and the area adjacent to it, in view of its special strategic importance, shall remain international."

(2) The whole question of Tangier is to be discussed at a meeting of the representatives of the Four Powers—the U.S.S.R., the United States, Great Britain and France—in Paris in the near future.

8. Approval of the text of a message to the Governments of China and France.

It was decided to send a message 48 hours before the publication of the communiqué on the results of the Conference.

9. About the agenda for the sitting of the three Heads of Government on July 23.

It was agreed to recommend to the three Heads of Government the following agenda:

(1) About the Black Sea Straits and other international inland waterways.

(2) About the Königsberg area.

(3) About Syria and the Lebanon.

(4) About Iran.]

[...] *Truman*: Allow me to set forth my views on the Black Sea Straits and international inland waterways in general.

Our position on this question is as follows: We believe that the Montreux Convention should be revised. We believe the Black Sea Straits should become a free waterway open to the whole world, and the right of free passage for all ships through the Straits should be guaranteed by all of us. I have thought a great deal about the question. What has been the cause of all these wars? In the last 200 years, they have all started in the area between the Mediterranean and the Baltic Sea, between France's eastern frontiers and Russia's western frontiers. The last time again peace was broken above all by Germany. I think it is the task of this Conference, and also of the coming peace conference, to prevent a repetition of such events.

Stalin: That's right.

Truman: I believe we shall be largely helping to achieve this aim by establishing and guaranteeing that waterways are free for all nations.

Stalin: Which, for instance?

Truman: I have a proposal on freedom of ways of communication, and I think we should try to bring about a situation in which Russia, Britain, and all other states have free access to all the seas of the world. Here is the proposal. [*Hands in draft proposal.*]

Our draft provides for the establishment of free and unrestricted navigation along all the international inland waterways. The U.S. Government believes that such free and unrestricted navigation should be established for internal waterways running through the territory of two or more states, and that it should be regulated by international agencies on which all the interested states are represented.

We think that such agencies should be set up as soon as possible. The first that should be set up are provisional navigation agencies for the Danube and the Rhine. These provisional agencies should have the functions of restoring and developing the navigation facilities on the said rivers, supervising river shipping to ensure equal opportunities for the citizens of various nationalities and establishing standard rules for the use of these means, and also rules of navigation, and customs and sanitary formalities and other similar matters. Among the members of these agencies should be the United States, the United Kingdom, the Soviet Union, France and the sovereign littoral states recognised by the Governments of these Powers.

I think the same procedure should be applied to the Kiel Canal and that the Montreux Convention should be revised in the same spirit. In that way we shall have free exchange in these areas.

I have tabled these proposals because I do not want in the next 25 years to take part in another war which may break out over the Straits or the Danube.

Our desire is to see a free and economically viable Europe, which would promote the prosperity of the Soviet Union, Britain, France and all other states, and with which the United States could trade on an equal footing and to mutual advantage. I believe our proposal can be a step forward in this direction.

Churchill: I vigorously support the proposal for a revision of the Montreux Convention in order to assure Soviet Russia free and unhindered passage through the Straits for her merchant fleet and Navy both in peace and wartime. I fully agree with the President and with his proposal that the free regime in these Straits should be guaranteed by all of us. The guarantee of the Great Powers and the interested states will undoubtedly be effective.

As for the other waterways mentioned by the President, we in principle agree with the general lines of the President's statement. We also agree with the President's proposal to have the Kiel Canal free and open and guaranteed by all the Great Powers. We also attach great importance to freedom of navigation along the Danube and the Rhine.

Truman: There is no doubt that we take a common view on the question of amending the Montreux Convention.

Churchill: And also on the purposes for which it should be amended.

Stalin: The President's proposals should be given a closer reading; it is hard to catch everything by mere listening. Perhaps we could go on to other questions for the time being?

Truman: The next question on the agenda is the question of transferring the Königsberg area in East Prussia to the Soviet Union. The Soviet document on the question was handed in yesterday.

Stalin: President Roosevelt and Mr. Churchill gave their consent to this at the Tehran Conference, and the question was agreed between us. We should like this agreement to be confirmed at this Conference.

Truman: I agree in principle. I merely ask to be allowed to study the terms, but I am sure that there will be no objections on our side. I agree that Russia should receive certain areas in that territory.

Stalin: Good.

Churchill: The Generalissimo was quite right in noting that the question was raised at the Tehran Conference, and we discussed it again in October 1944.

Stalin: In Moscow.

Churchill: Yes, it was in Moscow, and it was in connection with the talk on the Curzon Line.

Stalin: That's right.

Churchill: I addressed Parliament on this matter on December 15, 1944. I explained that the British Government sympathised with the Soviet standpoint. The only question that arises is the legal side of the transfer of this area. The Soviet draft tabled here seems to demand that we should recognise that East Prussia no longer exists and that the Königsberg area is not under the control of the Allied Control Council in Germany.

As for the British Government, we support the Soviet Government's desire to incorporate this territory into the Soviet Union. I state this in principle. We have not yet, of course, examined the exact line on the map. But I assure the Soviet Government once again of our constant support of the Russian position in that part of the world.

Stalin: We do not propose anything more than that. We

are satisfied if the American Government and the Government of Great Britain approve the proposal in principle.

Churchill: I agree.

Truman: I agree.

Churchill: A slight amendment of the document will be required. If it is to be a part of the communiqué at the end of the Conference, I propose a more general wording of the document.

Stalin: I do not object.

Truman: Thus, we are in principle agreed with the draft proposal of the Soviet delegation.

The next item on the agenda is the question of Syria and the Lebanon.

Churchill: At present the burden of maintaining law and order in Syria and the Lebanon has fallen entirely on us. We have neither the intention nor the desire to obtain any advantages in these countries, with the exception of those enjoyed by other countries. When we entered Syria and the Lebanon to throw out the Germans and the Vichy troops, we reached an agreement with France under which we were to recognise the independence of Syria and the Lebanon. In view of the long historical ties between France and these countries, we declared that we would not object to France having a preferential position there, provided agreement was reached with the new independent Governments of these countries.

We informed de Gaulle that as soon as France concluded with Syria and the Lebanon a treaty satisfactory to these countries, we would withdraw our troops at once. If we were to withdraw our troops now, there would be a massacre of French citizens and the small number of French troops now stationed there. We should not like that to happen, as this would cause great unrest among the Arabs and would probably upset law and order in Saudi Arabia and Iraq. The outbreak of such disorders in that part of the world would lead to disorders in Egypt as well. There could be no worse moment for such disorders among the Arabs than the present one, because the communication line with the Suez Canal would be placed in jeopardy, and the arms and reinforcements for the war in the Far East are moving along that line. The line of communication for conducting the war against Japan is of great importance not only for Great Britain but also for the United States.

General de Gaulle acted very unwisely in that area; contrary to our advice and our requests, he sent a shipload of 500 men to that area, and their appearance caused disorders which have not stopped until now. How stupid that was, for what could these 500 men have done. However, their arrival sparked off disorders.

These disorders aimed against the French at once caused unrest in Iraq, whose Government and people wanted to come to the aid of Syria. The whole Arab world was agitated over the event. However, General de Gaulle has now agreed to transfer the so-called special troops to the Syrian Government.

I hope that we shall reach, if not an agreement, at least a settlement of this question with the French, which would guarantee the independence of Syria and the Lebanon and would assure France of some recognition of her cultural and commercial interests.

Allow me to repeat once again here that Great Britain has no desire to stay there a day longer than is necessary. We shall be very glad to be rid of this thankless task, which we undertook in the interests of the Allies.

In view of the fact that this question concerns France and us only, and also, of course, Syria and the Lebanon, we do not welcome the proposal for a conference which would be attended by the United States and the Soviet Union, besides Great Britain and France, and would adopt a joint decision. The whole burden was on us, we acted on our own, without any assistance, with the exception of some help from France, but we acted in the interests of all. That is why we should not like to have the question discussed at a special conference. Of course if the United States wished to take our place we should only welcome it.

Truman: No, thanks. [*Laughter.*]

When this dispute arose between France and Syria and the Lebanon, the Prime Minister and I had an exchange of letters on the question. When the Prime Minister informed me that Great Britain had enough troops at her disposal to maintain peace in that area, I asked him to do everything he could to maintain peace because we are also interested in the communication line with the Far East running through the Suez Canal. We may have some slight difference with the Prime Minister on this point.

We believe that no state should be given any privileges

in these areas. These areas should be equally accessible to all states. We also believe that France should not have any special privileges vis-à-vis other states.

Stalin: Do I understand that the United States does not recognise any French privileges in Syria and the Lebanon?

Truman: Yes.

Churchill: Our position is such that we should like France to have privileges there because we promised her that when our state was weak and we had to fight the Germans there. But that is our own business, and we do not, of course, have any possibility or right to involve others. Besides, we did not undertake to make any great efforts for France to retain her privileges there. If France manages to obtain any privileges we shall not object, and shall even look kindly on her achievements.

Stalin: From whom can the French secure these privileges?

Churchill: From the republics of Syria and the Lebanon.

Stalin: Only from them?

Churchill: Only from them. The French have their schools, archaeological institutes, etc., there. Many Frenchmen have been living there for a long time, and they even have a song, "Let's Go to Syria". They say that their claims date back to the time of the Crusades. But we do not intend to quarrel with the Great Powers on that account.

Truman: We want all states to have equal rights in these areas.

Churchill: And you, Mr. President, will you prevent Syria from granting any special rights to the French?

Truman: Of course I won't prevent it if the Syrians want to do so. But I doubt that they have such a desire. [*Laughter.*]

Stalin: The Russian delegation thanks Mr. Churchill for his information and withdraws its proposal.

Churchill: I thank the Generalissimo.

Truman: I am also grateful.

We now go on to the next question. It is the question of Iran. Mr. Churchill has a proposal on the question.

Churchill: We have handed the delegations a document on the question and would be glad to know the position of the Great Powers.

Truman: We, for our part, have long been prepared to withdraw our troops from Iran, but we have a great quantity of various materials there which we would like to use for conducting the war in the Pacific.

Stalin: The Russian delegation believes that Tehran, at any rate, could be evacuated.

Churchill: I should also like to deal with the other two points to have done with the draft altogether. About the date specified in the treaty. The treaty says that the troops are to be withdrawn from Iran not later than six months after the end of hostilities. By now only two and a half months have passed since the end of the war. But we promised the Iranians to withdraw the troops as soon as the war against Germany was over.

Here is what I propose: immediate withdrawal of the troops from Tehran, and discussion of further troop withdrawals at the Council of Foreign Ministers in September.

Stalin: I have no objection.

Truman: We shall continue withdrawing our troops from Iran, because there are troops there that we are going to need in the Pacific.

Stalin: That is, of course, your right. We, for our part, promise that our troops will not undertake any action against Iran.

Truman: I have no objection to referring the matter for examination by the Council of Foreign Ministers in London.

Churchill: We also have the question of Vienna. I should like to speak here about the occupation zones, which have been allotted to the British and American troops in Vienna. As regards the British Zone, it turns out that it has a population of 500,000, and because Vienna's sources of food supplies are to the east of the city, we are unable to undertake the feeding of these half million persons. We propose therefore that a provisional agreement be reached for the Russians to supply this population with food pending a permanent agreement. Field Marshal Alexander will make a statement about the actual state of affairs.

Alexander: The situation is such as the Prime Minister has just stated. There are half a million people in our zone. I have no food to send over from Italy. There are small stocks in Klagenfurt, but these would last for three weeks, or a month at the outside. That is why if we undertook to feed this population, the food would have to be brought over from the United States.

Truman: There are about 375,000 people in our zone. Our ships are now engaged in transporting cargos for military operations against Japan, the delivery of food to Europe and certain materials to the U.S.S.R. We are short of transport facilities, so that we should find it hard to keep even our own zone supplied.

Stalin: And what about the French Zone?

Alexander: That is something I don't know.

Stalin: Let me speak to Marshal Konev. I think we could postpone for a month the transfer to our Allies of responsibility for supplying the Vienna population. For how long will this supply need to be organised, till the new harvest, or what?

Churchill: The difficulty is that these 500,000 people in our zone and the 375,000 in the American Zone have always received their foodstuffs from the country's eastern areas.

Stalin: We have an agreement with the Austrian Government under which we allow them some food in return for goods until the new harvest. I think this could be extended until September. But I must still have a preliminary talk with Marshal Konev. Tonight or tomorrow morning I think I shall be able to do that and shall give you my reply.

Churchill: The situation is that Field Marshal Alexander has entered Styria with his troops but hesitates to enter Vienna until the food supply question is settled.

Stalin: Is Vienna's food situation as bad as that now?

Churchill: We don't know, we've not been there.

Stalin: The situation there for the population is not a bad one.

Alexander: If you can help us in this matter we are, of course, prepared to go forward and take over our share of the work.

Stalin: I shall be able to tell you tomorrow.

Churchill: Thank you.

Stalin: It would be a good thing if the British and American authorities agreed to extend the agreement with the Renner Government to their zones as well. That would not signify recognition of the Renner Government or resumption of diplomatic relations, but would put the Renner Government in a position similar to that of the Government of Finland. Its competence would be extended to these zones as well, and that would facilitate the solution of the question.

Truman: We are prepared to discuss this question as soon as our troops enter Vienna.

Churchill: We also agree.

I should like to raise a question of procedure. Mr. President must be aware, like the Generalissimo, that Mr. Attlee and I are interested in visiting London on the Thursday of this week. [*Laughter.*] That is why we shall have to leave here on Wednesday July 25, together with the Minister of Foreign Affairs. But we shall be back by the afternoon sitting on July 27, or at least some of us will. [*Laughter.*] For that reason, could we have our Wednesday sitting in the morning?

Stalin: All right.

Truman: I think so.

Churchill: I propose that the Foreign Ministers should continue to meet as usual, but in the absence of Mr. Eden he would be replaced by Mr. Cadogan.

Stalin: All right.

Truman: Let's agree to have the July 25 sitting at 11.00. Tomorrow's sitting is at 17.00.

Eighth Sitting

July 24, 1945

Truman opens the sitting.

[Reporting on the sitting of the Foreign Ministers of the three Powers, the American delegation said the following:

It was established at the sitting of the three Foreign Ministers that the commission dealing with economic matters and questions of reparations had not yet prepared its report. The Soviet delegation proposed that the question of reparations from Italy and Austria should also be referred to this commission. It handed in two short documents on reparations from these two countries.

It was decided to postpone till tomorrow consideration of the question of economic principles in respect of Germany and reparations from Germany, and also of reparations from Italy and Austria. The Foreign Ministers were informed that the commission on economic questions would meet that night to complete its work.

On July 20, the U.S. delegation handed in a document concerning oil supplies for Europe. It was decided to refer this question also to the commission on economic questions; but in view of the fact that the commission had not dealt with the question, the Foreign Ministers agreed to postpone its discussion.

The next question the Foreign Ministers discussed was that of fulfilling the Yalta Declaration on Liberated Europe and the satellite states. It was admitted that the commission dealing with this question had not yet completed its work, and the discussion of the question was also postponed.

Next came the question of admitting Italy and other countries to the United Nations Organisation. The U.S. delegation suggested that, as the commission dealing with the question had failed to reach agreement, the question should be examined at a sitting of the Foreign Ministers on the basis of the document on which the commission had been working.

The Soviet delegation declared that it would not take part in this discussion because the document did not contain any mention of admitting Rumania, Bulgaria, Hungary and Finland to the United Nations Organisation.

The British delegation suggested to omit the last sentence in Clause 1 of the document.[1] The U.S. delegation agreed with this. The British delegation proposed a new wording for Clause 2 of the document to take into account the interests of other Allied countries concerned with the peace treaty with Italy. The American delegation agreed to include the British proposal in the amended document on the question of admission to the United Nations Organisation.

The U.S. delegation suggested including in the document an additional clause to meet the desires of the Soviet delegation. The clause reads: "The three Governments also hope that the Council of Foreign Ministers may, without undue delay, prepare peace treaties with Rumania, Bulgaria, Hungary, and Finland. It is also their desire, on the conclusion of the peace treaties with responsible democratic governments of these countries, to support their application for membership in the United Nations Organisation."

The Soviet delegation insisted that Bulgaria, Rumania, Hungary and Finland should not be placed in worse condi-

---

[1] The sentence read: "She [Italy] gives promise of becoming a firm supporter of a policy of peace and resistance to aggression."

tions than Italy concerning the question of entering the United Nations Organisation. The American delegation expressed the hope that the additional clause proposed by it would satisfy the Soviet delegation.

As the Foreign Ministers failed to reach complete agreement on this question, it was decided to refer it for solution to the Heads of Government. The question was included in the agenda of the present sitting of the Heads of the three Governments.

It was agreed to recommend to the Heads of Government the following questions for discussion at the present sitting.

1. Admission to the United Nations Organisation. The document submitted by the Foreign Ministers that morning could serve as a basis for a discussion by the three Heads of Government.

2. The Black Sea Straits and free and unrestricted navigation on international inland waterways. The discussion at the previous day's sitting of the Heads of Government was postponed to allow a study of the President's proposals.

The Foreign Ministers also agreed to recommend to the Heads of the three Governments to include the following questions in their agenda for next morning's sitting:

1. The German Navy and merchant marine.
2. Reparations from Germany.

The American delegation then announced that a delegation of representatives of the Polish Provisional Government, led by President Bierut, had arrived at Potsdam in response to an invitation of the U.S. President sent on July 22, in accordance with a decision of the three Heads of Government. At the sitting of the Foreign Ministers the Polish delegation expressed its opinion concerning Poland's western frontier, which can be reduced to the following.

The Polish delegation believes that Poland's western frontier should run from the Baltic Sea through Swinemünde, including Stettin as a part of Poland, and further on along the Oder River to the Western Neisse River and along the Western Neisse to the Czechoslovak border.

Poland's territory in its new form would allow her to discontinue the expatriation of the Polish population to other countries, and would permit full use to be made of the labour of those Poles who had earlier been forced to go to other countries.

From the standpoint of security, great importance attaches to the fact that the frontier line proposed by the Polish delegation is the shortest possible frontier between Poland and Germany and will be easier to defend.

The Germans tried to exterminate the Polish population and destroy Polish culture. From the historical standpoint, it would be fair to set up a powerful Polish state which could defend itself against any German aggression.

These areas were one of the most powerful bases of Germany's arms industry and a base of German imperialism. The proposed solution would deprive Germany of a staging area in the east and a base for the manufacture of armaments.

Poland would become a state without any national minorities.

Before the war, Poland had an excess of rural population, which could not be used for work in industry because industry was not sufficiently developed. Acquisition of these territories would enable Poland to use her rural inhabitants for work in the towns, and those who had emigrated from Poland could return home and find work.

The Polish representatives further said that the Oder River basin should be transferred to Poland *in toto*, for the Oder River itself was not deep enough and drew on waters in the area of the Western Neisse River.

The Polish delegation declared in conclusion that, in its opinion, a decision should be taken and agreement on this question reached as soon as possible to enable the Polish Government to resettle the Poles from abroad as early as possible, to give them an opportunity to take part in the rehabilitation of Poland.]

Truman: The first question on the agenda is that of admitting Italy and other satellite countries, including Finland, to the United Nations Organisation.

Byrnes: The British and American delegations are agreed on this point.

Eden: We fully agree with your initial document, but we have some doubts as regards the second wording. The new wording leaves the impression that we are demanding that the Italian Government should be reconstructed before we start concluding the peace treaty with Italy.

Byrnes: I proposed the new wording in the hope of finding a compromise solution on this question, and also to meet the desire of the Soviet delegation that the other satellites should not be placed in worse conditions as compared with Italy on the matter of admission to the United Nations Organisation. But I should like to draw the attention of the British delegation to the fact that the new wording does not raise any doubts concerning the present Italian Government.

The wording merely provides for the conclusion of peace treaties with responsible democratic governments. That is a matter of the future. The fact alone that the U.S. Government had established diplomatic relations with the present Italian Government is sufficient indication of our attitude to this Government.

Eden: We feel that we have almost agreed with your standpoint, and the question is only one of wording.

Stalin: If it is a matter of making things easier for the satellite states, the present decision should mention that. Things are made easier for Italy, and it is hard to object to this. But at the same time this easing for Italy is not accompanied by a simultaneous easing for the other countries, Germany's former accomplices.

One gets the impression of an artificial division: on the one hand, Italy, whose position is eased, and on the other, Rumania, Bulgaria, Hungary and Finland, whose position is not to be eased. There will be a danger of our decision being discredited: in what way is Italy more deserving than the other countries? Her only "merit" is that she was the first to surrender. In all other respects Italy behaved worse and inflicted greater harm than any other satellite state.

There is no doubt that any of the four states—Rumania, Bulgaria, Hungary and Finland—inflicted far less damage on the Allies than did Italy. As regards the Government in Italy, can it be said that it is more democratic than the Governments in Rumania, Bulgaria or Hungary? Of course not. Has Italy a more responsible Government than Rumania or Bulgaria? No democratic elections have been held either in Italy or any of the other states. In this respect they are equal. That is why I fail to see any reason for this benevolent attitude to Italy and this negative attitude to all the other states, Germany's former accomplices.

Things were first made easier for Italy by the restoration of diplomatic relations with her. A second step is now being proposed, namely, Italy's inclusion in the United Nations

Organisation. Good, let us take this second step in respect of Italy, but then I propose that in respect of the other mentioned countries we should also take the first step that was made in respect of Italy some months ago, namely, that we should restore diplomatic relations with them. This would be just and the gradation would be observed: Italy in the first place, and the rest in the second.

Otherwise, it turns out that in respect of Italy a first step had been made and a second step is being proposed, all because the Italian Government surrendered first, although Italy inflicted more damage on the Allies than all the other states, accomplices of Germany. That is the proposal of the Soviet delegation.

Churchill: In the main lines we are in agreement with the United States' standpoint on this question.

Truman: I should like to say that the difference in our views of the Government of Italy, on the one hand, and the Governments of Rumania, Bulgaria and Hungary, on the other, is due to the fact that our representatives have not had an opportunity to obtain the necessary information in respect of the latter countries. There was no such situation in Italy, where all our Governments—the United States, Great Britain and the Soviet Union—were given an opportunity of freely obtaining information.

We cannot say this about Rumania, Bulgaria and Hungary, where we have not had an opportunity to obtain free information. In addition, the nature of the present Governments of these countries does not allow us to establish diplomatic relations with them at once. But in the document submitted we have tried to meet the Soviet delegation's desire and not to place the other satellites in a worse position than that of Italy.

Stalin: But you have diplomatic relations with Italy and not with the other countries.

Truman: But the other satellites too can obtain our recognition if their Governments satisfy our requirements.

Stalin: Which requirements?

Truman: Concerning freedom of movement and freedom of information.

Stalin: None of these Governments hinders or can hinder free movement and free information for members of the Allied press. There must be some misunderstanding. With the ending of the war the situation there has improved.

Restrictions were also introduced for Soviet representatives in Italy.

Truman: We want these Governments reorganised, and we shall give them our recognition when they become more responsible and democratic.

Stalin: I assure you that the Government of Bulgaria is more democratic than the Government of Italy.

Truman: To meet the Soviet desires we proposed the same formulation in respect of Rumania, Bulgaria and Hungary as in respect of Italy.

Stalin: But this proposal does not include the resumption of diplomatic relations.

Truman: I have said many times already that we cannot resume diplomatic relations with these Governments until they are reorganised as we consider necessary.

Byrnes: The only thing we have proposed for easing Italy's position is support for her application for membership of the United Nations Organisation. I should like to draw your attention to the point of our proposal which speaks in the same words about the other satellites. Thus, the easing of Italy's position will be accompanied by an easing of the position of the other satellites. We have tried here to meet the desires of the Soviet delegation.

Stalin: I propose that the word "responsible", as used in respect of the Italian Government, be deleted wherever it is used. This word tends to belittle the Italian Government's position.

Truman: We are unable to support Governments' application for membership of the United Nations Organisation if they are not responsible and democratic.

Stalin: In Argentina the Government is less democratic than in Italy, but Argentina is nevertheless a member of the United Nations Organisation. If it is a government, it is a democratic government, but if you add "responsible", it turns out that this is some other kind of government. And besides, there should be an addition concerning the resumption of diplomatic relations.

I propose adding to the clause dealing with Rumania, Bulgaria, Hungary and Finland a sentence to the effect that in the near future each of our three Governments will examine the question of resuming diplomatic relations with these countries. That does not mean that they will do this simultaneously and will resume diplomatic relations at one and the same time, but that each of the three Governments will examine the question of resuming diplomatic relations sooner or later. Let me give an example. At present, there are diplomatic representatives in Italy from the United States and the Soviet Union, but no diplomatic representatives either from Great Britain or from France; there are no ambassadors there from these Governments.

Churchill: We consider that our representative in Italy is fully accredited. In virtue of the fact that we are still formally in a state of war with Italy, the status of that representative cannot be fully equated with that of an ambassador; under the British Constitution we cannot, in these conditions, have normal diplomatic relations. But we do call him ambassador.

Stalin: But not of the kind as those of the Soviet Union and the United States.

Churchill: Not quite. About 90 per cent.

Stalin: Not quite, that's true.

Churchill: But the reason is a formal and technical one.

Stalin: That's the kind of ambassador that should be sent to Rumania—such a not-quite ambassador. [*General laughter.*]

Churchill: We have not done that yet.

Truman: We want to do everything we can to achieve a situation in which we could resume diplomatic relations with these Governments. I have already explained the difficulties in solving this problem.

Stalin: The difficulties were there before, but they are no longer there. We find it very hard to adhere to this resolution in its present form. We do not want to adhere to it.

Churchill: We do not want to use words which could cast a shadow on any of us. I only wish to intercede for Italy, and not just because she was the first to drop out of the war. A great deal of time has passed since she dropped out of the war, two years have passed already, if I'm not mistaken. But only a short time—four or five months—has passed since the other countries stopped fighting; Rumania stopped fighting somewhat earlier.

Stalin: First Rumania, and then Finland. But diplomatic relations were resumed with Italy some 7 or 8 months after her surrender.

Churchill: Italy's position is as follows. Two years ago

she dropped out of the war, and has since been fighting on our side to the best of her abilities. Besides, it should be borne in mind that we were in Italy and know everything about the political conditions there. That cannot be said of Bulgaria, Rumania and the other countries. In addition, Italy was not a uniform country: the northern part of Italy was under the yoke of the enemy and was liberated only two months ago. There we fought side by side with Italy, who gave us great support.

But it was always recognised that Italy could not have a fully democratic government until her northern part was liberated. Meanwhile we recognised the Italian Government, we worked with it. I had an understanding with the Soviet Government concerning support for the Government of General Badoglio. At that time I disagreed with our American friends, I wanted to support that Government until the north was liberated, when it would have been possible to form a Government of Italy on a broader base. But the course of events entailed other actions.

We have established friendly relations with Italy. There is no political censorship there. The Italian press frequently attacked me only a few months after Italy's unconditional surrender. There is evidence of a considerable growth of freedom in Italy. Now that the north has been liberated, the Italians are getting ready to stage democratic elections. That is why I see no reason why we should not now discuss the question of a peace treaty with Italy.

I must say that we know nothing concerning Rumania, not to mention Bulgaria. Our mission in Bucharest was placed in conditions of isolation reminiscent of internment.

Stalin: How can you say such things without verifying them?

Churchill: We know this from our own representative there. I am sure the Generalissimo would be surprised to learn of some of the facts which have taken place in respect of our mission in Bucharest.

Stalin: Fiction!

Churchill: Of course, you are free to call our statement fiction, but I have full confidence in our political representative and Air Force Marshal Stevenson. I have known him personally for many years. The conditions for the work of our mission were difficult. There were great delays with planes for our mission. There were complaints from our

Soviet friends about the numerical strength of our mission, which was not so great after all. The Control Commission, which should have consisted of three members, nearly always met as two. The Soviet Commander-in-Chief, who is the chairman of the Control Commission, sometimes met the American representative, and sometimes the British, but rarely the two together. As for Italy, many Soviet representatives have been there.

Stalin: Nothing of the kind, we have no rights in Italy.

Churchill: But at any rate the situation there is such that you are quite free to come to Italy. That is why I don't think the situation in Italy can be compared with the situation in Rumania, Bulgaria and the other countries.

Truman: We must say that our missions in those countries also came up against great difficulties. But we should not like to speak of that here.

Byrnes: In the hope of reaching agreement, I propose that the words "responsible government" should be replaced by the words "recognised government".

Stalin: That is more acceptable. But I think we should also adopt a decision that the three Governments are willing to examine the question of establishing diplomatic relations with these four countries. I propose that at the end of the clause proposed by Mr. Byrnes on the four countries, we should add the following: "The three Governments agree to examine, each separately, in the near future, the establishment of diplomatic relations with Rumania, Bulgaria, Hungary and Finland."

Churchill: But will that not clash with what we have just said here?

Stalin: It will not clash because if we decide to prepare the question of peace treaties with Rumania, Bulgaria and the other countries—and we have not even recognised these countries—it is clear that each Government takes up the question of recognition on its own.

Truman: I have no objections.

Stalin: In that case, we have none either.

Churchill: I think there is a contradiction. I understood the President to say here that he does not now want to recognise the Governments of Rumania, Bulgaria and the other satellite countries.

Truman: It says here that we undertake only to examine the question.

Churchill: This tends to mislead public opinion.

Stalin: Why?

Churchill: Because it follows from the meaning of the statement that we shall soon recognise these Governments; as it is, I am aware that this does not reflect the stand either of the Government of the United States or the Government of the United Kingdom.

Stalin: I agree with the President and want to object to Mr. Churchill. We have already all accepted that we instruct the Council of Foreign Ministers to prepare peace treaties with Rumania, Bulgaria, Hungary and Finland. We all believe that a peace treaty can be concluded only with a recognised government. Consequently, we must mention this recognition in some way, and then there will be no contradiction. If we fail to say that the three Governments intend to raise the question of recognition in the nearest future, we shall have to delete the clause about preparing peace treaties with these countries.

Churchill: I should like to ask the President whether he believes that this autumn the representatives of the present Governments of Rumania, Bulgaria and the others will come to the Council of Foreign Ministers and that we shall discuss the peace treaties with them there?

Truman: The only government that can send its representatives to the Council of Foreign Ministers will be the government which is recognised by us.

Stalin: That's right.

Churchill: The present Governments will not be recognised and that is why it will be impossible to prepare the peace treaties with them.

Stalin: What makes you think so?

Churchill: It follows logically.

Stalin: No, it does not.

Churchill: I may be thinking on wrong lines, but it seems to me that it does.

Stalin: These Governments may be recognised or may not be recognised. No one knows whether they will or will not be recognised. That is just how the wording should be understood: "examine the question of recognition". And there will be a peace treaty with them when they are recognised.

Churchill: Anyone reading this clause will not understand that the U.S. Government does not wish to recognise the present Governments of Rumania and Bulgaria. But if other Governments we can recognise are formed, we shall proceed to draw up peace treaties with them. You must excuse me for insisting on the point in this way, but I ask you to bear in mind that if the document is published, it will have to be explained, especially by me, in Parliament. We say that we shall conclude peace treaties with Governments to which we accord recognition, but we have no intention of recognising these Governments. I find this almost absurd.

Truman: I propose that we refer this question back to the Foreign Ministers for a fresh examination.

Stalin: Mr. Churchill is not right; nothing is said here at all about the conclusion of peace treaties; it says here about preparation. Why cannot a treaty be prepared, even if the government is not recognised?

Churchill: Of course, we can prepare the peace treaty ourselves. In that case, I propose that we replace the preposition "with" by the preposition "for", so that it should read not "peace treaties with Rumania, Bulgaria", etc., but "peace treaties for Rumania, Bulgaria", etc.

Stalin: I have no objection to "for".

Churchill: Thank you.

Stalin: Don't mention it. [*General laughter.*]

Churchill: It would be desirable for the Foreign Ministers to go over the document once again.

Stalin: I have no objection.

Truman: They must take into account the discussion which has taken place here today.

Stalin: Good.

Truman: The next question is the one of the Black Sea Straits and free navigation on international inland waterways. The American delegation has tabled its proposals on the question.

[...] *Stalin*: There are probably more urgent questions than that of the Straits, and this question could be postponed.

Churchill: This question was raised by Great Britain as flowing from the desire to amend the Montreux Convention. I am willing to have it postponed if the Soviet delegation so desires.

Stalin: It would be better to postpone this question. Turkey must be consulted.

Truman: Our proposal on international control means that the Straits will not be in anyone's hands. We shall try to convince the Turks that we are taking a correct stand on this question.

Stalin: All right, let's do that.

Truman: I want to make a suggestion to the Conference. I think it is time we thought about drawing up a communiqué on the work of the Conference. I suggest, therefore, that we appoint a special committee to draw up such a communiqué.

Stalin: All right.

Truman: We must come to an agreement on the membership of the committee.

Stalin: All right.

Truman: We shall ask the Foreign Ministers to submit candidates for the committee.

Stalin: Good. Shall we have a sitting at 11.00 tomorrow?

Truman: Yes.

Stalin: Mr. Churchill expressed doubt on that point.

Eden: At lunch today we expressed the assumption that there may not be enough questions for a sitting tomorrow. But since today's agenda is not exhausted, the undiscussed items will be transferred to tomorrow's sitting.

Truman: As soon as we find that we have no more work we shall go home. [*Laughter.*] But so far we have work.

Churchill: Mr. Attlee and I must be back in London for the opening of Parliament on August 8. At any rate, I am unable to stay here until later than August 6.

Stalin: The question of Poland's western frontier—the last item on today's agenda—has not yet been exhausted.

Churchill: Besides, there is the question raised by the Soviet side concerning the camp in Italy. I should like to give an explanation on this question now.

Stalin: Have we the time and the desire to discuss the question of Poland's western frontier now?

Churchill: We are meeting the Poles and shall have a talk with Mr. Bierut tomorrow morning.

Stalin: Then let's postpone it.

Churchill: In brief, the position in the camp is as follows. In fact, there are 10,000 persons in that camp. But it should be borne in mind that we have just taken 1,000,000 prisoners. A Soviet mission in Rome is now dealing with these 10,000 men, and this mission has free access to the camp. It is reported that the persons in the camp are predominantly Ukrainians but not Soviet citizens. There are also some Poles in the camp, who, as far as we could ascertain, lived in Poland within her 1939 borders. Six hundred and sixty-five persons wish to return to the Soviet Union at once, and steps are being taken to send them. We are also prepared to hand over all others who wish to return.

These 10,000 men surrendered to us almost as an entire military unit, and we have retained it in that form, under the command of its own officers, out of purely administrative considerations. We should be glad if General Golikov would address his complaints to Field Marshal Alexander or his H.Q.

Alexander: I have little to add to what the Prime Minister has said. I should like all those present here to know that I have always given the Russian representatives in Italy complete freedom of movement and also every opportunity to see what they wished. And I think that it is expedient to act in this way because in cases when large numbers of Russian soldiers happen to fall into our hands, the advice of responsible Russian representatives could prove very useful to us. I think, if the Generalissimo agrees, I shall go on acting in the spirit I had acted until now.

Stalin: In such cases we are duty bound by treaty to give each other assistance and not to prevent citizens from returning home, but, on the contrary, to help them return home.

Churchill: If your representative sends a general or goes to the H.Q. himself in connection with this matter, everything necessary will be done.

Stalin: All right. I consider the question settled.

I spoke to Marshal Konev in Vienna today. He has not stopped issuing rations to the population of Vienna, irrespective of zones, and will go on doing so until the Americans and the British find a possibility of undertaking something else.

Truman and *Churchill*: We are very grateful.

Churchill: There was the question of extending the Renner Administration to the British and American zones.

Stalin: It would be good to extend his competence to all the zones.

Churchill: We believe that is one of the first questions we shall have to study when we enter Vienna. We agree in principle that it is desirable to work with a single Austrian administration.

Stalin: Of course, it is better.

Churchill: We have no intention of hampering the local authorities.

Stalin: That will be better.

Truman: Until 11.00 tomorrow.

Ninth Sitting

July 25, 1945

Truman: There was a suggestion yesterday to continue discussion of Poland's western frontiers today.

Stalin: All right.

Truman: I remember that Mr. Churchill had an additional proposal.

Churchill: I have nothing to add. I have had a talk with the Polish delegation, and this morning had the pleasure of meeting Mr. Bierut once again. Mr. Eden had a talk with the Polish delegation yesterday. The Poles agree that there are 1.5 million Germans in the area which they have occupied in the west. I consider that this question is also connected with that of reparations and also with the question of the four Powers' zones of occupation in Germany.

Truman: I consider Mr. Churchill's remark correct. Mr. Byrnes also met the Polish delegation and intends to do so again. Allow me to make a suggestion on a point of procedure. Since these talks of Mr. Byrnes and Mr. Eden will continue, I think it will be better to postpone our discussion on this question until Friday.

Stalin: All right.

Truman: The next question on our agenda is that of the German Navy and merchant marine. I think we have already reached agreement on this question.

Churchill: Of course, concrete proposals on this question must be considered. I think we could tackle these concrete proposals.

Truman: State Secretary Byrnes told me that Assistant Secretary of State Clayton and Admiral Land have dealt with this question, they have been working on concrete proposals. I am prepared to examine the question at any time, but would prefer to hear Mr. Byrnes first and study the documents on this question which I have just received.

[It was decided to postpone discussion of this question.]

Churchill: There is another question which, while not on the agenda, should be discussed, namely, that of transfers of population. There are a great number of Germans who have to be resettled from Czechoslovakia to Germany.

Stalin: The Czechoslovak authorities have evacuated those Germans, and they are now in Dresden, Leipzig and Chemnitz.

Churchill: We think there are 2.5 million Sudeten Germans who must be resettled. In addition, the Czechoslovaks are in a hurry to get rid of 150,000 German citizens, who had earlier been resettled in Czechoslovakia from the Reich. According to our information, only 2,000 of these 150,000 Germans have left Czechoslovakia. This is a great job, moving 2.5 million men. But where are they to be moved to? To the Russian Zone?

Stalin: Most of them are going to the Russian Zone.

Churchill: We don't want them in our zone.

Stalin: But that is not what we suggest. *[Laughter.]*

Churchill: They will bring their mouths with them. I think the real resettlement has not yet started.

Stalin: From Czechoslovakia?

Churchill: Yes, from Czechoslovakia. So far the displacement has been on a small scale.

Stalin: I have information that the Czechs warn the Germans and then evict them. As for the Poles, they have detained 1.5 million Germans to use them on the harvesting. As soon as the harvesting is over in Poland, the Poles will evacuate the Germans from Poland.

Churchill: I don't think this should be done in view of the problems of food supplies, reparations, etc., that is, questions which are still to be settled. We now find ourselves in a situation in which the Poles have the food and the fuel, and we have the population. The supply of this population falls as a heavy burden on us.

Stalin: You must see the Poles' side of it. For five and a half years the Germans made them suffer all sorts of wrongs.

Truman: Yesterday, I listened very attentively to President Bierut's statement on this question. I sympathise with the Poles and the Russians and understand the difficulties facing them. I have already set forth my position with sufficient clarity.

I should like to explain to my colleagues what my powers are in respect of the questions relating to a peaceful settlement. When we discuss here questions which should go into the peace treaty, I am sure everyone will understand that under our constitution the treaty can be concluded only with the consent of the U.S. Senate. There is no doubt that when I support some proposal put forward at the Conference, this means that I shall do everything I can to ensure that the decision is sanctioned by the Senate. But there is of course no guarantee that it will be adopted for sure.

I must tell you that political feelings in America are such that I am unable to support here any proposals unless I obtain support from our public opinion. I am not making this statement in order to change the basis on which the discussion of questions with my colleagues is taking place but merely to explain my possibilities in respect of constitutional power. I want to say that in concluding any peace treaties I have to take into account the fact that they must be approved by the U. S. Senate.

Stalin: Does the President's statement refer only to peace treaties or to all questions discussed here?

Truman: This refers only to agreements and treaties which the Constitution says must be sent for approval by the U.S. Senate.

Stalin: That means all the other questions can be settled?

Truman: We can settle any question here unless it must have the ratification of the Senate.

Stalin: That means that only the question of peace treaties requires ratification by the Senate?

Truman: That's right. I have wide powers but I don't want to abuse them.

Churchill: I propose that we return to the question of the Polish movement westward.

Stalin: We did not prepare for this question, it has been raised by chance. Of course, I agree to have an exchange of opinion, but it is extremely hard to settle it now.

Churchill: I don't want to discuss the question today. I should only like to say that the success of the whole Conference depends on this question. If the Conference ends its work, say, within 10 days, without adopting any decision on Poland, and if the question of an equitable distribution of food over the whole of German territory is not settled, all this will undoubtedly mean failure for the Conference.

We shall then have to return to Mr. Byrnes's proposal that everyone will have to make do with what he has in his zone. I hope that we shall reach agreement on this group of questions which lie at the root of all our work. We must admit that we have not achieved any progress until now.

Truman: I agree with the Prime Minister's opinion that we have not had any progress on these questions.

Stalin: I think that the supply of the whole of Germany with coal and metal is of much greater importance. The Ruhr gives 90 per cent of the metal and 80 per cent of the hard coal.

Churchill: If coal is supplied from the Ruhr to the Russian Zone, it will have to be paid for with food deliveries from that zone.

Stalin: If the Ruhr remains a part of Germany it must supply the whole of Germany.

Churchill: Why then can't we take food from your zone?

Stalin: Because that territory goes to Poland.

Churchill: But how can workers in the Ruhr produce the coal if they have nothing to eat, and where can they obtain the food?

Stalin: It has long been known that Germany has always imported foodstuffs, notably grain. If Germany is short of grain and food she will buy it.

Churchill: Then how will she be able to pay the reparations?

Stalin: She will be able to. Germany still has a lot of some things.

Churchill: It is true that Ruhr coal is in our zone, but I cannot take the responsibility for any settlement which may result in famine in the zone this winter, while the Poles have all the food to keep for themselves.

Stalin: That's not quite right. They recently asked for assistance in grain; they are short of grain, they asked for grain until the new crop.

Churchill: I hope the Generalissimo will recognise some of our difficulties as we recognise his. In Britain, this year, we shall have the most coalless winter because we are short of coal.

Stalin: Why? Britain has always exported coal.

Churchill: That's because the miners have not yet been demobilised, there's a labour shortage in the coal industry.

Stalin: There are enough POWs. We have POWs working on coal, it would be very hard without them. We are rehabilitating our coal basins and are using POWs for that purpose. You have 400,000 German soldiers in Norway, they are not even disarmed, and I don't know what they're waiting for. There you have manpower.

Churchill: I didn't know they had not been disarmed. At any rate, our intention is to disarm them. I am not aware of the exact situation there, but this question was settled by the Supreme Command of the Allied Expeditionary Force. In any case, I shall inquire.

I want to repeat and draw your attention to the fact that we are short of coal because we are exporting it to France, Belgium and Holland. And while we are short of coal for this winter, we fail to understand why the Poles have the possibility to sell coal from a territory which does not yet belong to them.

Stalin: They have sold coal from the Dąbrowa area. It is their area.

I am not in the habit of complaining but must say that our position is even worse. We have lost several million killed, we are short of men. If I began to complain, I am afraid you'd shed tears, because the situation in Russia is so grave. But I do not want to worry you.

Churchill: We are in control of the Ruhr, and we are prepared to exchange Ruhr coal for food.

Stalin: This question needs thinking about.

Churchill: I did not at all expect us to reach any decision today, but I should like the members of the Conference to think during this short break about the great problem they will have to solve.

Truman: If we have nothing else to discuss today, I suggest that we refer the question to the Foreign Ministers.

Churchill: We shall meet again at 5.00 on Friday.

Eden: We have received a notification from Dr. Beneš asking us to discuss here the question of transferring Germans from Czechoslovakia. Can the Foreign Ministers deal with this question?

Stalin: I think the transfer has been made.

Churchill: We don't think that a great number of Germans have already departed from there, and we are still faced with the problem of how to solve this question.

Stalin: Please continue.

Churchill: Let the Foreign Ministers deal with this question and establish the facts.

Stalin: All right.

Truman: I agree.

Before the break, I want to draw your attention once again to the proposal I made concerning international inland waterways. I think the Foreign Ministers could also discuss this proposal of mine.

[*Stalin and Churchill express agreement.*

The Soviet delegation then hands to the U.S. President and the Prime Minister of Britain a memorandum concerning the hindrances being raised to the return home of Soviet citizens from Austria and Germany, and also a memorandum concerning the German troops not yet disarmed in Norway, mention of which was already made at the sitting of the Heads of Government.]

Churchill: But I can assure you that it is our intention to disarm those troops.

Stalin: I have no doubt. [*Laughter.*]

Churchill: We are not keeping them up our sleeve so as later to release them all of a sudden. I shall demand a report on this question at once.

Truman closes the sitting and announces that the next sitting is to take place at 5.00 p.m. on Friday, July 27.

Tenth Sitting

July 28, 1945

Truman opens the sitting.

[Reporting on the sitting of the Foreign Ministers of the U.S.S.R., the U.S.A. and Great Britain on July 25, 1945, the Soviet delegation said the following:

1. The American delegation proposed a discussion at the Ministers' sitting on the question of waterways. It expressed the wish that this question should be discussed in commission beforehand. The British and Soviet delegations agreed to this proposal, and as a result the following commission was set up:

From the U.S.A.: Russel and Riddleberger; from Great Britain: Ward; from the U.S.S.R.: Gerashchenko and Lavrishchev.

2. The American delegation then touched upon the question of resettling the German population from Czechoslovakia.

The British delegation declared that it was not only a matter of resettling the Germans from Czechoslovakia, but also from Western Poland and Hungary. It expressed the opinion that the question of resettling this population would be under the control of the Allied Control Council acting in collaboration with the Governments of Poland, Czechoslovakia and Hungary.

The Soviet delegation proposed that the question should be referred for preliminary examination to a comission so that a meeting of the three Ministers could then examine its draft.

The delegations of the U.S.A. and Britain agreed to this proposal. The following commission was set up:

From the U.S.A.: Cannon; from Great Britain: Harrison; from the U.S.S.R.: Sobolev and Semyonov.

3. The British delegation tabled a proposal to appoint a commission to draw up a draft communiqué on the work of the Conference and a commission to draft a general protocol of the Conference decisions.

The delegations of the U.S.S.R. and the U.S.A. agreed to the proposal. It was decided to set up the following commissions:

a) To draft a communiqué on the work of the Conference:

From the U.S.A.: Walter Brown and Wilder Foot; from the U.S.S.R.: Sobolev and Golunsky.

b) To draft a general protocol on the Conference decisions:

From the U.S.A.: Dunn, Mathews and Cohen; from the U.S.S.R.: Gromyko, Kozyrev and Gribanov; from Great Britain (for both commissions): Bridges, Brooke, Hayter and Dean.

Reporting further on the sitting of the Foreign Ministers on July 27, 1945, the Soviet delegation said that the following items were on the agenda of the sitting of the three Ministers:

I. Outstanding questions.

It was stated that the following questions remain outstanding:

1. The economic principles in respect of Germany.

2. Reparations from Germany.

3. Reparations from Italy and Austria.

4. Oil supplies to Europe.

5. Admission of Italy and other former satellite countries into the United Nations Organisation.

6. Fulfilment of the Yalta Declaration on Liberated Europe.

7. Easing of the armistice terms for Italy and other countries.

8. Poland's western frontier.

9. Co-operation in settling urgent European economic problems.

10. War criminals.

11. Resettlement of Germans from Poland, Czechoslovakia and Hungary.

12. Supplementing the political principles on the treatment of Germany with two points from Point 13 of the draft economic principles.

13. The German Navy.

14. International inland waterways.

II. Admission of Italy and other countries, which have concluded an armistice and have become co-belligerents on the side of the Allies into the United Nations Organisation.

The U.S. delegation declared that if the Soviet and the British delegations were unable to reach agreement on the wording of a document on this question, it was prepared, with the consent of the U.S. President, to withdraw the question from the Conference agenda altogether. The American delegation added that, in its opinion, it was necessary to examine first of all the vital questions, namely, the questions of reparations, the German Navy and Poland's western frontier.

The British delegation proposed that the formulation of the last sentence of the third paragraph, tabled by the Soviet delegation, should be replaced by the following sentence: "The conclusion of peace treaties with the responsible democratic Governments in the states will permit the three Governments to resume normal diplomatic relations with them and to support proposals on their side to become members of the United Nations Organisation."

The Soviet delegation declared the amendment unacceptable.

Insofar as no agreement on this question had been reached at the meeting of the three Ministers, it was decided to submit it for settlement by the Heads of the three Governments.

III. Reparations from Germany.

The Soviet delegation declared that it considered the work of the Reparations Commission unsatisfactory and proposed that the question of reparations from Germany should be examined directly at the meeting of the three Ministers. There were no objections to this proposal. The Soviet delegation then read out Clause 4 of the Crimea Protocol on Reparations and, referring to a statement by the American representative in the Reparations Commission to the effect that he withdrew the U.S. Government's endorsement of the decision set forth in the said clause, asked the American delegation whether the U.S. Government continued to adhere to the Crimea decisions on this question or had altered its position.

The American delegation replied that this was a misunderstanding. In the Crimea the U.S. Government agreed to accept the figure of $20,000 million as a basis for discussion, but since then the Soviet and the Allied armies had wrought great destruction in Germany, some areas had been separated from Germany and it was now impossible for practical purposes to start from the over-all figure which the American delegation had accepted at Yalta as a possible basis for discussion.

The British delegation declared that it abstained from making any proposals.

On the proposal of the American delegation it was recognised advisable to postpone this question until the next conference of the three Ministers, after which they would report to the Heads of the three Governments.

IV. Reparations from Austria and Italy.

The Soviet delegation proposed that its proposals on reparations from Austria and reparations from Italy should be taken as a basis for turther discussion on this question.

The American delegation declared that it did not consider it possible to levy reparations from Austria and Italy in the form of deliveries from current production. In the opinion of the American delegation, it was possible only to make lump withdrawals of war industry equipment which could not be used for peacetime purposes. The British delegation declared that it supported the opinion of the U.S. delegation.

In view of failure to reach agreement it was decided to report the differences that had been revealed to the Heads of the three Governments.

V. Economic principles in respect of Germany.

On the proposal of the U.S. delegation, the discussion of this question was postponed.

VI. Oil supplies to Europe.

The discussion of the question was postponed in view of the fact that the commission had not completed its work.

VII. Economic co-operation in Europe.

It was decided to approve the report of the commission on this question and to report this to the Heads of the three Governments.]

Truman: Which question are we going to discuss now: that of Poland's western frontier or some other?

Stalin: We could discuss this one, or the question of Italy and the other countries. How much time do you have today? Could we work for an hour?

Truman: That suits me. Let's work until 12.00.

Stalin: I want to inform you that we, the Russian delegation, have received a new proposal from Japan. Although we are not duly informed when a document on Japan is compiled, we believe nevertheless that we should inform each other of new proposals. [*Japan's note on mediation is read out in English.*] The document does not contain anything new. There is only one proposal: Japan is offering to co-operate with us. We intend to reply to them in the same spirit as the last time.

Truman: We do not object.

Attlee: We agree.

Stalin: I have nothing more to add.

Truman: There are two questions to which the Soviet delegation wants to draw our attention in the first place. The first question is about Italy and the other satellite countries, and the second, about reparations from Austria and Italy.

Stalin: In addition it would be desirable to raise the question of the German Navy and the question of Poland's western frontier.

Truman: I think that we can discuss any question here

and I am prepared to hear any proposal and then state my opinion on these questions.

Attlee: I want to say that I agree to discuss all these questions. At the same time I should like to express regret that the events which have taken place in Britain have hampered the work of the Conference, but we are prepared to stay here as long as need be and deal with any questions.

Stalin: The question of admitting Italy and the other countries into the United Nations Organisation was discussed at the previous sitting of the Big Three. However, as was stated here, the Foreign Ministers had a different impression of the results of this discussion. The Soviet delegation was under the impression that the question had in the main been agreed between the Heads of the three Governments after the amendments made by the Prime Minister in respect of Bulgaria, Rumania, Hungary and Finland. Wherever there was reference to the peace treaties, it was decided to replace the words "with Bulgaria, Rumania", etc., by the words "for Bulgaria, Rumania", etc. The question was then referred for final drafting by the three Foreign Ministers. But at the Ministers' meeting the British delegation tabled another amendment to the draft, which was not adopted.

At the Conference of the Heads of Government the question was of how the Governments of the said countries were to be called: responsible or recognised. The Russian delegation believes that if we say "responsible" this will be an affront to the Governments because they might think that they are now regarded as being irresponsible. If we say "recognised", as we agreed here at the Conference of the three Heads of Government, there will be no offence. Each of our Governments is free to recognise the Governments of these states when it deems them to be democratic. There will be no offence for the Governments, and the meaning, the content, will remain the same. We here adopted a decision and then the Ministers got together and reversed it. That is wrong. This was agreed in principle.

Truman: I ask Mr. Byrnes to speak on this point.

Byrnes: At the meeting of the three Foreign Ministers the Soviet delegation declared that, as far as it remembered, the U.S. delegation had accepted its proposal. On behalf of the American delegation I said that the President accepted the proposal of the Soviet delegation in principle and added that these proposals should be referred for drafting by the Foreign Ministers: the President had in mind the replacement of only one word, namely, the word "to discuss" by the word "to examine" (which makes a difference in English). That means that there were no differences between the American and the Soviet delegation on this matter.

But I told the Foreign Ministers at the time that, as far as I recalled, Mr. Churchill had objected to the Soviet delegation's proposal concerning the study of the question of recognising the Governments of the satellite countries. At the conclusion of the Conference of the three Heads of Government, Mr. Churchill informed me that he was not in agreement with this proposal. I also told the Foreign Ministers that the American delegation had initially made its proposal on Italy to grant her some relief. The proposal merely said that the three Powers would issue a declaration to the effect that they would support Italy's entry into the United Nations Organisation.

The British delegation proposed that we include certain neutral countries among those whose entry into the United Nations Organisation we would support. We agreed with that. The Soviet delegation proposed the inclusion in the document of a clause on the Franco regime and, to meet the Soviet delegation half-way, we added a clause concerning the negative attitude taken by the three Powers to Spain's becoming a member of the United Nations under the Franco regime.

The Soviet delegation then proposed the inclusion of a clause concerning the Governments of Bulgaria, Rumania, Hungary and Finland. We agreed to that clause with certain amendments. After that there was a proposal to change the wording of the clause on these countries. We agreed to that as well.

Unfortunately, one gets the impression that when we agree with our Soviet friends, the British delegation withholds its agreement, and when we agree with our British friends, we do not obtain the agreement of the Soviet delegation. [*Laughter.*] Once again, if the Soviet and British delegations could reach agreement concerning the Soviet proposal we would be prepared to accept the document, but if they are unable to reach agreement, we are prepared to withdraw our modest proposal on Italy.

259

Attlee: Mr. President, I ask permission for Mr. Cadogan to set forth our position on this question.

Cadogan: The document we are examining relates to the question of admitting Italy and the other satellite countries, and also, possibly, certain neutral countries, into the United Nations Organisation. As far as I am aware, the text of the document could be approved with the exception of two points. Generalissimo Stalin has already spoken about one of these points, namely, the replacement of the words "responsible Governments" by the words "recognised Governments". It seems to me that two days ago, when we discussed this question, we agreed to this substitution.

The other question, which is much more complex, relates to Clause 3, which says that the three Governments agree to examine, in the near future, the question of resuming diplomatic relations with Finland, Bulgaria, Rumania and Hungary. Mr. Churchill explained that although he was willing to examine the question of resuming diplomatic relations with these countries, the inclusion of this clause in the declaration could be misleading, because under the constitution the British cannot establish full diplomatic relations with countries with whom they are technically still in a state of war. A compromise proposal was made to the effect that after the signing of the peace treaties we could resume full diplomatic relations with these countries. But it appears that this proposal of ours met with objections on the part of the Soviet delegation.

Stalin: I understood Mr. Cadogan to say that he agrees to say "recognised Governments" instead of "responsible Governments".

Cadogan: Yes.

Byrnes: We find this acceptable: "recognised" instead of "responsible".

Stalin: There is no distinction here between the situation of the Allies and Italy, on the one hand, and the Allies and other countries, on the other. There is no freely elected Government in Italy, or in Rumania, or in Hungary, or in Bulgaria. There is such a Government only in Finland. In all these countries, as in Italy, the Governments have been formed by agreement between the main parties.

If Italy has been recognised by the U.S.A. and the Soviet Union, and to the extent of 90 per cent by the British Government, why is it not possible to raise the question of examining the problem of establishing diplomatic relations, say, with Rumania, Bulgaria and Hungary? From the standpoint of democracy, the situation there is the same as in Italy. But Italy has been recognised by the three Powers. It does not say here: to establish full diplomatic relations. I must say I fail to understand the meaning of the amendment of which Mr. Cadogan has spoken. Why make such a distinction between Italy, which does not have a freely elected Government, and the other countries, which, with the exception of Finland, have no freely elected Governments either?

Bevin: Does not the difference lie in the fact that in respect of Italy we know what the situation there is, and we know nothing about the situation in the other countries?

Stalin: You are not being asked to commit yourself to a recognition of these Governments. While you discuss the question of recognition you will have the opportunity of studying the situation in these countries.

Bevin: But why should we undertake this obligation before we know what the situation is in these countries?

Stalin: We also knew little about Italy when we established diplomatic relations with her, possibly even less than you now know about these countries. The question is to open for these countries, beginning with Italy and ending with Bulgaria, some ways of easing their position. For Italy there is the prospect of entry into the United Nations Organisation. This is the second step in easing her position, the first having been the fact that diplomatic relations were resumed with her six or eight months after her surrender. The second step towards relief of Italy's position consists in the fact that two years after her surrender we give her an opportunity of joining the United Nations Organisation.

The task now is to make the first step in respect of the other countries: to ensure the discussion of the question of their recognition by the three Powers. It is proposed to do this ten months after their surrender. If we agreed to ease Italy's position, we must do something in this respect for the other countries as well. That is the point.

Attlee: I think it was explained here that we find it impossible to resume full diplomatic relations with these countries until the signing of the peace treaties. The difficulty lies in the fact that the adoption of the Soviet proposal creates the impression that we intend to do something in respect of these countries which it is impossible for us to do. The amendment proposed by the British delegation, consisting in the statement that full diplomatic relations with these countries will be resumed after the conclusion of the peace treaties with them, states what is possible.

Stalin: Why not put it this way: the three states will examine, each separately, the question of establishing full or partial diplomatic relations. Diplomatic relations will have to be resumed with Finland in any case, it is not nice to drag out the solution of this question, since a freely elected Government has been formed there. The question concerns the other countries.

Attlee: It seems to me that this proposal does not correspond with reality.

Stalin: Good, in that case, let us adopt the American formula: instead of "to discuss" say "to examine".

Attlee: It seems to me that a change of words does not alter the substance of the matter. One question put in Parliament will give the whole thing away.

Stalin: But we are not concealing anything. What is there to give away? It is one thing to discuss, and another, to examine. You will have to examine the question in any case. It would be strange if we failed to examine the question of recognising these Governments. What is so terrible or new in this? I think the British could accept the American wording. You do not stand to lose anything, but only to gain from the public opinion in these countries.

Bevin: When we return we shall be asked in Parliament about the meaning of what we have done. I want to give the people an absolutely honest answer. If I recognise a Government, I really recognise that Government. And I have no wish to cover up with words things which could be misconstrued. I would prefer to adopt the very latest American proposal and postpone the settlement of the question.

Stalin: Let's put it off.

Truman: Which question shall we discuss now, that of Poland's western frontier or reparations from Italy and Austria?

[*It was decided to discuss the question of reparations.*]

Truman: In that case, I want to make a statement on reparations from Italy. As I said on the first day of the discussion on the question of Italy, rather, the question of easing the terms of the armistice with Italy, we and the

British Government have had to give Italy about $500 million to restore her economic situation. We expect to give Italy another $500 million for the same purpose. The U.S. Government is prepared to make this money available for a specified purpose, of which I have already spoken, but not to enable Italy to pay reparations to Allied and other countries. If Italy has armaments plants with heavy equipment which the Soviet Union needs, we agree to have the Soviet Union take that equipment. But the money we intend to give Italy must be covered mainly by exports from Italy.

Stalin: It could be accepted that no reparations are to be taken from Austria since Austria was not an independent state. But our Soviet people find it very hard to understand the absence of any reparations from Italy, which was an independent state and whose troops reached the Volga and took part in devastating our country. Austria did not have any armed forces of her own, reparations from her may be waived. Italy had her own armed forces and she must pay reparations.

Truman: If there are objects for reparations in Italy, I absolutely agree to hand them over to the Soviet Union. But we are not prepared and do not agree to give money to Italy for her to use to pay reparations to Allied and other countries.

Stalin: I see the President's point, but I want the President to see mine as well. What gives the Soviet people the moral right to speak of reparations? It is the fact that a sizeable part of the Soviet Union's territory was occupied by the enemy forces. For three and a half years the Soviet people were under the heel of the invader. But for the occupation, perhaps the Russians would not have the moral right to speak of reparations. I say perhaps.

Truman: I fully sympathise with you.

Stalin: The President says that Italy may have equipment which the Russians need and that this equipment might go to meet the reparations. Good, I do not want to ask a great deal, but I should like to set a rough figure for these reparations. Italy is a big country. What amount could be got from Italy, what would be the value of these reparations? If the President is not prepared to answer this question, I am willing to wait, but some figure for reparations must be established.

Truman: I cannot answer that question just now.

Bevin: In establishing the amount of reparations I propose that what America and Great Britain are now giving Italy should not be taken into account; what should be taken into account is what Italy has at the present time.

Stalin: Of course, I have no intention of ignoring the interests of America or Britain.

Attlee: I want to say that I fully agree with what the President has said. At the same time, I have complete sympathy with the Russian people for what they have suffered. But we have also suffered a great deal from the attack by Italy. We also have devastated lands, and the feelings of the British people can be easily imagined if Italy had to pay reparations from the money actually made available to her by America and Great Britain. Of course, if Italy has any equipment which could be withdrawn, that is another matter, but our people will never agree to have reparations paid from the money given by us and America.

Stalin: We agree to take the equipment.

Attlee: Military equipment.

Stalin: Military equipment.

Attlee: These are to be lump withdrawals of military equipment and not reparations withdrawals from current production?

Stalin: These are to be lump withdrawals.

Bevin: I want to ask: is it a question of military equipment for the manufacture of military items?

Stalin: No, why? It is a question of equipment at war plants which will be used to make peace-time goods; we are withdrawing the same kind of equipment from Germany.

Attlee: What I had in mind was equipment that cannot be used for civilian production.

Stalin: Every kind of equipment can be used for civilian production. We are now switching our war plants to civilian production. There is no military equipment that cannot be used to make civilian goods. For example, our tank plants have started to make cars.

Bevin: It will be very hard to determine what you will take.

Stalin: Of course, we cannot now specify the equipment. We only want a decision adopted here in principle, and then we shall formulate our demands.

Truman: As I understand it you want it agreed in principle here that Italy must pay reparations?

Stalin: Yes, that is correct. It is necessary to determine the amount of reparations, and I am willing to receive a small amount.

Truman: I don't think there are great differences of principle between us on this question. The only thing I want is that this should not affect the advances we have given to Italy.

Stalin: I do not have these advances in mind.

Bevin: The following question arises: what is to be taken in the first place? The primary claims in respect of Italy are those of Great Britain and the United States, which have granted her a loan; reparations are secondary.

Stalin: We cannot encourage Italy and other aggressors in letting them emerge from the war scot free, without paying for at least a part of what they have destroyed. To waive this is to pay them a bonus for the war.

Truman: I absolutely agree with you.

Bevin: I can't hear, it's that plane. [*Stalin's statement is repeated to Bevin.*]

Truman: I agree with the Generalissimo's statement that the aggressor must not receive a bonus, but must suffer punishment.

Stalin: The British were especially hard hit by Italy.

Attlee: We are not forgetting it.

Truman: Shall we fix the time for our sitting tomorrow? Let's say five, as usual.

Stalin: All right.

Truman: Perhaps we could start our work at four? With everyone's consent, we shall start our sitting tomorrow at four o'clock.

Eleventh Sitting

July 31, 1945

Truman: Mr. Bevin will report on yesterday's meeting of the Foreign Ministers.

Bevin: I propose that no special report be made, because almost all the items on yesterday's agenda of the Foreign Ministers have been included on today's agenda of the Big Three sitting.

[*Bevin's proposal is adopted.*]

Truman: The first item on our agenda is the U.S. proposals on German reparations, on Poland's western frontier, and on admission to the United Nations Organisation. Mr. Byrnes will now report on these proposals.

Byrnes: Our proposals on reparations were tabled as part of the general proposals relating to three outstanding questions. These questions are: the question of reparations, the question of Poland's western frontier, and the question of admission to the United Nations Organisation. These three questions are interconnected. The U.S. delegation said at the meeting of the Foreign Ministers that it is prepared to make concessions on Poland's western border and admission to the United Nations Organisation, provided agreement is reached on all three questions.

Stalin: They are not connected with each other. They are different questions.

Byrnes: That is true, the questions are different, but they have been before us for a fortnight and we have failed to reach any agreement on them. The U.S. delegation has tabled its proposals on all three questions in the hope of reaching agreement. But we declare here once again that we shall not make any concession in respect of the Polish border, unless agreement is reached on the other two questions.

Our proposals on reparations, which were discussed at yesterday's meeting of the Ministers, provided that 25 per cent of the capital equipment of the Ruhr area which is not required for the maintenance of a peace-time economy would be handed over to the Soviet Union in return for food, coal, zinc, potassium, oil products, timber, etc., from the Soviet zone. In addition, we proposed that 15 per cent of such capital equipment which is considered unnecessary for the maintenance of a peace-time economy should be handed over from the Ruhr to the Soviet Union without any payment or exchange.

During yesterday's discussion, the British delegation declared that it could not agree to have all this handed over from the Ruhr area only, but it could agree to the transfer of equipment to the Soviet Union from all the Western zones. We agreed that the only difference between the British and American proposals consisted in the percentage, and that if the percentage is applied to all three Western zones of occupation, it should be halved as compared with that established for the Ruhr area, namely, 12.5 per cent instead of 25, and 7.5 per cent instead of 15.

The Soviet delegation did not agree with this proposal, but the American and British delegations believed that this would be simpler in administrative terms. We also believed that withdrawals from all three Western zones would be to the greater advantage of the Soviet Union.

Stalin: We also consider it correct that withdrawals should be made not only from the Ruhr, but from all Western zones.

Byrnes: This will give you a wide choice of equipment, since it could come from the American, British and French zones.

There was a proposal at the Foreign Ministers' meeting that the question be solved who is to decide which equipment is not required for the maintenance of a peace-time economy and is available for reparations. The Soviet delegation believed that it should be precisely specified who is to determine the quantity and nature of the industrial equipment not required for a peace-time economy and available for reparations. I proposed that the relevant decision should be made by the Control Council on directions from the Allied Reparations Commission and should be subject to the final approval of the Commander-in-Chief of the zone from which the equipment is to be withdrawn. I proposed that the decision should be taken by the Control Council, because all the four Powers are represented on the Control Council and because it is an administrative organ vested with executive functions, while the Reparations Commission is an organ which elaborates general policy on reparations.

I repeat here the proposal I made yesterday, namely, that the withdrawal of capital equipment should be completed within two years, and that deliveries to the Soviet Union in exchange for deliveries from its zone of occupation should continue for five years. I also proposed that the reparations claims of other countries should be met from the Western zones of occupation.

The two other questions of which I spoke, and which in our proposals are treated as one, are the question of Poland's western border and the question of admission to the United Nations Organisation. We agree to the settlement of these questions provided agreement is reached on the main question, that of reparations.

Under our proposal on Poland's western frontier, the Polish Government is given the right to establish a provisional administration on the whole territory the Poles have demanded.

As for the question of admission to the United Nations Organisation, three days ago we withdrew our proposals. However we now make another proposal on the question whose wording, we hope, should satisfy the Soviet Union.

The wording of the proposal we discussed four days ago was: "The three Governments agree to examine each separately in the near future, in the light of the conditions then prevailing, the establishment of diplomatic relations with Finland, Rumania, Bulgaria and Hungary." The British delegation declared that that was unacceptable to it, since the British Government could not agree to establish full diplomatic relations with countries with which it was in a state of war. The head of the Soviet Government then asked whether the British Government was prepared to accord full or partial recognition to the Governments of these countries. That is why I now table a proposal with the following wording: "The three Governments express the desire to examine each separately in the near future, in the light of the conditions then prevailing, the question of establishing diplomatic relations with Finland, Rumania, Bulgaria and Hungary to the extent possible prior to the conclusion of peace treaties with these countries."

I hope that our Soviet and British friends are prepared to accept our proposal in this wording.

Stalin: I have no objection in principle to this wording.

Byrnes: We also proposed to add another clause, to the effect that the three Governments express the desire that, in view of the change of conditions as a result of the ending of the war in Europe, members of the Allied press should enjoy complete freedom in reporting to the world the events in Bulgaria, Rumania, Hungary and Finland. This is almost the same wording which we agreed upon when discussing Poland.

Stalin: This can be accepted, but there should be a change in the wording to say, instead of "The three Governments express the desire", "The three Governments do not doubt that ...", etc.

Byrnes: As regards the United States, this is acceptable to us. I think we should now adopt the document as it is.

Thus, we have tabled three proposals, and I very much hope that all three will be adopted here.

Stalin: We have proposals on reparations.

[The following proposals of the Soviet delegation on reparations from Germany are then read out:

"1. Reparations shall be levied by each Government in its own zone of occupation. They shall have two forms: lump withdrawals from the national property of Germany (equipment, materials), which shall be made during two years after surrender, and annual commodity deliveries from current production, which are to be made during 10 years after surrender.

"2. The reparations are designed to promote the earliest economic rehabilitation of the countries which have suffered from the German occupation, with an eye to the need for the utmost reduction of Germany's military potential.

"3. Over and above the reparations levied in its own zone, the U.S.S.R. is to receive additionally from the Western zones:

"a) 15 per cent of the basic industrial equipment, in complete sets and good repair—primarily in the field of metallurgy, chemistry and machine-building—which, as specified by the Control Council in Germany on a report of the Reparations Commission, is subject to withdrawal in the Western zones by way of reparations; this equipment shall be handed over to the Soviet Union in exchange for an equivalent quantity of foodstuffs, coal, potassium, timber, ceramic goods and oil products in the course of five years;

"b) 10 per cent of the basic industrial equipment levied in the Western zones by way of reparations, without any payment or exchange of any kind.

"The amount of equipment and materials subject to withdrawal in the Western zones by way of reparations is to be established not later than within three months.

"4. In addition, the U.S.S.R. is to receive by way of reparations:

"a) $500 million worth of shares in industrial and transport enterprises in the Western zones;

"b) 30 per cent of German investments abroad;

"c) 30 per cent of the German gold which the Allies have at their disposal.

"5. The U.S.S.R. undertakes to settle Poland's reparations claims from its share of the reparations. The United States and Great Britain are to do the same thing in respect of France, Yugoslavia, Czechoslovakia, Belgium, Holland and Norway."]

Stalin: Mr. Byrnes proposed here that these three questions should be bound up into a single whole. I understand his standpoint: he proposes the tactics which he considers expedient. It is the right of each delegation to make such proposals, but the Soviet delegation will nevertheless vote separately on each of these questions.

The Russian delegation has put forward its proposals. The question of reparations from Germany is the chief one causing disputes and differences. Our considerations have been set forth here. You may have noticed that the Russian delegation took the standpoint of the American delegation, for it gave up the idea of stating a definite figure and quantity, and went over to percentages.

Digressing somewhat from the main subject, I should like to speak of the withdrawals which the British made from the Russian zone before its occupation by Soviet troops. What I mean is the removal of goods and equipment. In addition, there is a note from the Soviet military command to the effect that the American authorities drove away 11,000 railway cars from the same territory. I do not know what is to be done with this property. Is this property to be returned to the Russians or compensated for in some other manner? In any case, the Americans and the British are taking equipment not only from their zones, but have also taken some from the Russian zone, whereas we did not drive away a single car and did not take any equipment from the plants in your zones. The Americans had promised not to remove anything, but they did.

Now on the substance of the matter. I think we have a possibility of reaching agreement on the question of reparations from Germany. What are the main propositions of the American plan? The first is that each makes withdrawals from his own zone of occupation. We agree to this. Second: equipment is to be removed not only from the Ruhr, but from all the Western zones. We have accepted this second proposal. Third proposal: a part of the reparations taken from the Western zones is to be covered with a corresponding equivalent from the Russian zone over a period of 5 years. Then there is the fourth proposition: it is that the Control Council is to determine the volume of the withdrawals from the Western zones. That is also acceptable.

What in that case are the differences? We are interested in the question of the time limit, the question of the final calculation of the volume of reparations. Nothing is said of this in the American draft. We should like to establish a period of three months.

Byrnes: The question of time should be agreed.

Stalin: It is a question of the time limit for determining the volume of reparations. Some period has to be proposed. We propose three months. Is that enough?

Truman: I think it is.

Attlee: That is a short period. I must think a little.

Stalin: It's worth thinking about, of course. It may be three, four or five months, but some time limit should be laid down.

Attlee: I propose six months.

Stalin: Right, I agree.

Then there is the percentage of withdrawal. Here again agreement can be reached. One per cent either way does not make much difference. I hope that in this matter of establishing the withdrawal percentage, the British and the Americans will meet us half way. We have lost a great deal of equipment in this war, a terrible quantity of it. At least one-twentieth part of it should be restored. And I expect Mr. Attlee to support our proposal.

Attlee: No, I cannot do that.

Stalin: Think a little and support us.

Attlee: I thought of this all day yesterday. [*Laughter.*]

Stalin: What have we got then? I think we must try to reach a general agreement on this question.

Bevin: The Soviet document does not contain the words I used yesterday, namely, "equipment not needed for peacetime economy".

[*The Soviet delegation once again reads out the relevant section of its proposals on the question of reparations.*]

Bevin: I propose that you accept this phrase of mine, which expresses my idea quite precisely.

Stalin: What is the gist of it?

Bevin: The Control Council is first of all to determine the

271

quantity of equipment which is to remain for the maintenance of Germany's peace-time economy.

Stalin: That is the same thing.

Bevin: In that case, you will perhaps accept my phrase?

Stalin: But what's the difference?

Bevin: There is a great deal of difference. I don't want there to be any misunderstandings later. Your text may be interpreted in a different way, namely, as 15 per cent of all equipment.

Stalin: No, we have in mind 15 per cent of the equipment subject to withdrawal, that is, equipment which is not required for the maintenance of Germany's peace-time economy.

Bevin: I would propose that this should be inserted in the document, so that everything would be quite clear.

Stalin: But what is not clear? The Control Council is to determine which equipment is required for the peace-time economy of Germany. What is left is to constitute the total volume for reparations.

Byrnes: Our wording expresses the common view of the British and American delegations.

Stalin: What do you propose?

Byrnes: The quantity of industrial equipment which is recognised as unnecessary for peace-time economy and is therefore available for reparations is determined by the Control Council on the directives of the Allied Reparations Commission and is subject to final approval by the Commander of the zone from which the equipment is removed.

Stalin: I do not object.

Byrnes: Consequently, the only question which remains open is that of percentage. You want 15 per cent and 10 per cent, instead of 12.5 and 7.5 per cent?

Stalin: Yes.

Byrnes: But in addition you want to receive by way of reparations $500 million worth of shares of industrial enterprises in the Western zones, 30 per cent of Germany's investments abroad, and 30 per cent of the German gold which is at the disposal of the Allies. About the gold, as far as I am aware of the opinion of our Staff, I can say that there is some gold which once belonged to other countries. It would be unfair to reject those countries' claims.

Stalin: This applies to German gold.

Byrnes: According to our information, there is no German gold, because all this gold was plundered by the Germans during the war. We must return this gold to the countries to which it once belonged. If the Soviet delegation insists that the Soviet Union should receive in addition to these percentages $500 million worth of shares of industrial enterprises, as the Soviet proposals state, 30 per cent of Germany's investments abroad, and 30 per cent of the gold, this question should be discussed here.

Stalin: We should like to have this if it is possible.

Byrnes: What do you have in mind when you speak of Germany's investments abroad?

Stalin: The investments the Germans had in other countries, including America.

Byrnes: As for the investments in America, we have blocked them, and legislation is required to lay claim to these funds. Congress appears to have done that already. I have no doubt that there will be all sorts of claims to these funds also from refugees who are in America. This question calls for a legal settlement.

Besides, I am sure that if, for instance, there is a certain quantity of German investments in the countries of Latin America, the Governments of those countries will have claims to these resources.

Stalin: That may be.

Bevin: We agreed yesterday that France should be included in the Reparations Commission so as to take part in deciding on the equipment subject to withdrawal by way of reparations. I should like to have France included in this commission.

Stalin: I do not object.

Bevin: Concerning the percentages. I thought that at yesterday's sitting of the Foreign Ministers we met you half way by agreeing to 12.5 per cent.

In addition, I should like to know: will not the reparations question hinder the ordinary exchange of goods over the whole of Germany, considering that we have agreed on the economic principles and normal exchange of goods in Germany?

Stalin: Well, we shall discuss that question when we come to the economic principles.

Bevin: The settlement of the gold question presents great difficulties. As for Germany's assets abroad, would you agree to confine yourself to the assets in neutral territories?

Stalin: I think that could be accepted.

Byrnes: We cannot agree to any addition to our main proposal. I have in mind Clause 4 of the Soviet proposals.

Stalin: In that case the percentage will have to be raised. On Clause 3 let us raise the percentage, considering that you have removed much equipment from our zone. [*Laughter*.] A vast amount of equipment was destroyed in our country, and at least a small part of that equipment should be covered.

Truman: I should like to make the following remark concerning withdrawals from your zone. We learned of this three days ago, when we got a list of this equipment. I wrote to General Eisenhower asking him to look into the matter and report. If such a withdrawal did take place, I assure you that it was not made on the orders of the U.S. Government. I assure you that we shall find possibilities for compensation.

Stalin: I propose that we return to the discussion of the question of percentages.

Truman: If you are prepared to withdraw Clause 4 I am prepared to accept 15 per cent and 10 per cent.

Stalin: Good, I withdraw it.

Bevin: We shall find it hard to satisfy France, Belgium and Holland from the quantity of equipment left. I should propose 12.5 per cent and 10 per cent. In addition, we ask the withdrawal of Clause 4.

Stalin: We have already agreed to that. The United States has shown understanding of our position, how is it that you do not wish to do the same?

Bevin: We are responsible for the zone from which the greatest quantity of equipment is to be withdrawn, and in addition there will be large claims on the part of France, Belgium and Holland.

Byrnes: The final phrase in our proposals says that the reparations claims from other countries entitled to reparations are to be covered from the Western zones of occupation. I request that our wording concerning the claims of other countries be discussed.

Stalin: All right, I agree not to name the countries, and state this in general terms.

Byrnes: I think that would be more expedient, for it has already been mentioned that Greece is not in the list. We also think that it is expedient to state this in general terms.

Stalin: Good.

Bevin: It has occurred to me that if you receive the percentages you demand, then, with what you receive from your own zone, you will have more than 50 per cent of all German reparations.

Stalin: Much less. What is more, we give an equivalent for the 15 per cent, which is actually an exchange of reparations and not fresh reparations. We receive only 10 per cent reparations from the Western zones. Those are the reparations proper; as for the 15 per cent, they are given for a definite equivalent. Our demands are minimal. We receive from you 10 per cent, and on the rest we exchange and pay an equivalent. You have the 90 per cent. If we receive 7.5 per cent instead of 10 per cent reparations, that will be unfair. I agree that it should be 15 per cent and 10 per cent. That is fairer. The Americans agree. What about you, Mr. Bevin?

Bevin: All right, I agree.

Truman: We also agree.

Byrnes: Thus, our draft proposals with the new percentages, plus the establishment of a time limit for determining the amount of reparations, are accepted.

Stalin: We seem to have exhausted all our differences on the question of reparations. Can we refer this draft for final editing?

[*The proposal is accepted, and a commission is set up to edit the adopted decision.*]

Truman: The next question is on Poland's western frontier.

Byrnes: We handed in our proposals yesterday, and they were discussed yesterday. I do not think we should read them out again. If there are any remarks or amendments, I am ready to hear them, but I hope that our Soviet and British friends will accept our proposals.

Bevin: As for the position of the British Government, I have instructions to keep to the frontier along the Eastern Neisse. That is why I should like to know precisely the substance of the new proposal. Does the whole of this zone pass into the hands of the Polish Government and will the Soviet troops all be pulled out of there, as was the case in other zones, where the troops of one side fell back and the other side took over the zone?

I met the Poles and asked them about their intentions concerning the fulfilment of the declaration mentioned in the U.S. document. I asked them about their intentions concerning the staging of free and unhampered elections by secret ballot. They assured me that they intend to carry out these elections as soon as possible and expect to do so in early 1946. But this will, of course, depend on some conditions enabling them to carry out these elections.

They also agreed on freedom of the press in Poland and on access of foreign correspondents to Poland and the possibility of sending their dispatches without censorship. They gave me assurances concerning freedom of religion all over the country.

But there is still one other very important question, namely, that of the repatriation not only of civilians, but of the troops which are under Allied command in various countries. I asked the Poles to make a statement on this question so that we could be sure that these men, upon their return to their homeland, would be placed in the same conditions as all the other citizens.

The next question, which especially concerns the Soviet Government and the British Government, and which the Polish Government is now unable to settle, is the question of a military air line between Warsaw, Berlin and London, to enable the British Government to maintain constant contact with its ambassador in Warsaw. I should like to have an agreement on this point at once. The document tabled by the United States says that this zone is to be under the administration of the Polish Government and will not constitute a part of the Soviet zone. As Mr. Byrnes put it, this zone will be under the responsibility of the Poles. However, I take it that although we have placed this zone under a Polish administration, it remains under the military control of the Allies.

Byrnes: We have found ourselves in a situation in which Poland, with the consent of the Soviet Union, is actually administering the territory. In view of this, the three Powers have agreed to leave the administration of this territory in Poland's hands, to obviate any further disputes concerning the status of this territory. There is, however, no need for Poland to have a representative on the Control Council.

Bevin: I do not insist. If we all understand what it is all about, I do not object. I shall be asked various questions upon my return, and I should like to know what is to happen in this zone. Will the Poles take over the whole zone, and the Soviet troops pull out?

Stalin: The Soviet troops would pull out if this territory did not constitute the Red Army's communications, along which the Red Army's units are kept supplied. There are two roads there: one running to Berlin from the north, and the other, south of Kraków. These two lines are the Soviet Army's supply lines. It is the same thing that you have in Belgium, France and Holland.

Bevin: Is the number of troops limited to these objectives?

Stalin: Yes, indeed. We have already pulled out from over there four-fifths of the troops that were there during the war against Germany. We also intend to reduce the number still there. As for the zone that is going to Poland, according to the proposal that has been made, Poland is actually administering that zone already and has its own administration there; there is no Russian administration there.

Bevin: Could you now help us with this military air line? We tried to reach agreement on this matter with the Polish Government but it cannot agree at present.

Stalin: Why can't it?

Bevin: I take it that this question concerns the Soviet military command because we have to fly over a part of the Russian zone.

Stalin: But you are already flying across the Russian zone to Berlin.

Bevin: Can you agree to us flying to Warsaw?

Stalin: We shall agree to it if an arrangement can be made for us to fly to London over France. [*Laughter*.] Besides, agreement must be reached with the Poles. Here is the way I see it: an air line is to be established between Berlin and Warsaw, and British or Polish planes will fly it, according to a treaty between Britain and Poland. As regards an air line to Moscow along this route, Russian flyers will take over from the point where the border with Russia begins. As regards the satisfaction of the needs of the Russians for flights to Paris and London, British or French planes will apparently fly there. We shall then have a London-Paris-Moscow line. That is how I see it.

Bevin: Of course, this whole question of air communications is much too big to be solved here now, but we shall always be prepared to discuss this question concerning an air line between London and Moscow. What I ask you now is to help us establish a line between London and Warsaw, which we need for our convenience.

Stalin: I understand. I shall do all I can.

Bevin: Thank you.

Truman: Have we finished with the Polish question?

Stalin: Is the British delegation in agreement?

Bevin: It is.

Stalin: As I see it, it is up to the Poles now. All right, we have finished with that matter.

Bevin: We must inform the French about the change in Poland's frontier.

Stalin: Yes, of course.

Byrnes: Our next proposal concerns the entry of Italy and the other satellites into the United Nations Organisation. We have already handed in our document on this question.

Bevin: The British delegation agrees.

Stalin: Our amendment has already been stated. It concerns the new Clause 4, or rather the phrase in it which starts with the words: "The three Governments express the desire that", etc. We propose to say: "The three Governments do not doubt that", etc.

[*Truman* and *Attlee* agree to this amendment of the wording.]

Truman: A decision on economic principles in respect of Germany was deferred until the solution of the reparations question. I think there will now be no difficulty in solving this question.

Byrnes: I have two proposals concerning the document on economic principles which I wish to announce. The first concerns Clause 13, which deals with general policy in respect of the monetary and banking system, centralised taxes and tariffs. (He reads out a drafting amendment which is accepted.) In addition, I propose to add to this clause another sub-clause "g" concerning transport and communications. This should also be centralised.

Stalin: This calls for some kind of centralised German administrative machinery. It is hard to conduct overall policy in respect of Germany without some kind of centralised German machinery.

Byrnes: That is correct.

The second proposal concerns sub-clause "d" of Clause 14. I propose an amendment of the last phrase to read as follows: "Except where determined by the occupying power concerned to be required for necessary imports, no grant or credit to Germany or Germans by any foreign persons or governments can be permitted."

Bevin: Perhaps it is better to leave out this phrase altogether?

Byrnes: I agree. I have another remark. As a result of our agreement on reparations, we consider that Clause 18 is superfluous.

[*Stalin* and *Bevin* express their agreement to drop the clause.]

Bevin: There is also the question of priority payments for imports, something we spoke about at yesterday's sitting of the Foreign Ministers. The British delegation yesterday proposed the inclusion of the following phrase in the economic principles: "Payment for approved imports into Germany shall be a first charge against the proceeds of exports out of current production and out of stocks of goods."

The Soviet delegation proposed the addition of the following phrase: "As regards the rest, priorities should be given to reparations, as compared with the satisfaction of other economic needs." The British and American delegations were unable to accept this Soviet proposal. The British delegation requests that its proposal be adopted.

Stalin: We think this question no longer arises.

Truman: That is how I understand it.

Bevin: I think this contradicts the treatment of Germany as a single whole in respect of export, import, etc. This will divide Germany into three zones, and we shall not be able to deal with Germany as a single entity in matters such as the levying of taxes, etc.

Stalin: This requires a centralised German administrative machinery through which the German population could be influenced. This question will be discussed in the section "Political Principles in Respect of Germany".

Bevin: We agreed in principle to the establishment of such a centralised machinery, but tabled some amendments. Perhaps we could leave this question and go on to the political principles, and we shall then see what can be done on this question as well.

[*Stalin* and *Truman* express their agreement.

The Soviet delegation recalls that in connection with the discussion of the question of economic principles, it tabled a proposal on the question of the Ruhr area which says that the Ruhr industrial area should be regarded as a part of Germany and that four Power control should be established in respect of the Ruhr area, for which purpose an appropriate Control Council should be set up consisting of representatives of the United States, Great Britain, France and the Soviet Union.]

Bevin: As I said yesterday, I am unable to discuss this question in the absence of the French. This is a major question of principle, and the French are closely concerned with it.

Stalin: Perhaps we could put off the question of control over the Ruhr area, but the idea that the Ruhr area remains a part of Germany should be reflected in our document.

Truman: It is undoubtedly a part of Germany.

Stalin: Perhaps we could say this in one of our documents?

Bevin: Why is the question being raised?

Stalin: It is being raised because at one of the conferences—at the Tehran Conference—there was a question of separating the Ruhr from the rest of Germany and making it a separate area under the control of the Council. A few months after the Tehran Conference, when Mr. Churchill came to Moscow, this question was also discussed during an exchange of views between the Russians and the British, and once again the idea was expressed that it would be a good thing to set the Ruhr apart as a separate area. The idea of separating the Ruhr area from Germany arose from the thesis of the dismemberment of Germany. Since then, there has been a change of view on this question. Germany remains a united state. The Soviet delegation asks: do you agree to have the Ruhr area remain a part of Germany? That is why the question was raised here.

Truman: My opinion is that the Ruhr area is a part of Germany and remains a part of Germany.

Stalin: It would be a good thing to say this in one of our documents. Does the British delegation agree that the Ruhr remains a part of Germany?

Bevin: I cannot agree because I do not now have a picture of the foregoing discussion of this question. I know that the internationalisation of the Ruhr had been suggested in order to reduce Germany's war potential. This idea was discussed. I agree that pending a solution of this question the Ruhr remains under the administration of the Control Council. But I should like to have an opportunity to talk this over with my Government and propose to refer the question to the Council of Foreign Ministers so as to have time to study it thoroughly.

[*Stalin and Truman agree to Bevin's proposal.*]

Truman: The next question is that of political principles.

Bevin: The Soviet delegation has tabled a draft on the question of organising a centralised German administration, which is to help the Control Council. We propose the adoption of our draft on this question which is shorter. We propose that no central German Government should be set up for the time being.

I move the adoption of our short draft instead of the draft of the Soviet delegation.

Stalin: It can be adopted.

Truman: I have no objections.

Bevin: As for Clause 19 of the economic principles, I suggest that we refer this clause to the Economic Commission. Let it discuss this question now, while we are here.

Stalin: Let it discuss it.

Truman: The next question is that of resettling the German population from Poland and Czechoslovakia.

Byrnes: The report of the commission dealing with this question was adopted *in toto*, with the exception of the last phrase, which says: "The Czechoslovak Government, the Polish Provisional Government and the Control Council in Hungary are at the same time being informed of the above and are being requested meanwhile to suspend further expulsion, pending an examination by the Governments concerned" of this question. I think this last point is very necessary, then the decision will be effective.

Stalin: But I am afraid such a decision will not yield serious results. The point is not that the Germans are expelled from these countries. Things are not quite so simple. They are placed in a position where it is better for them to leave these areas. The Czechs and the Poles can say that there is no formal ban on Germans living there, but in fact the Germans are placed in such a position that it is impossible for them to live there. I am afraid that if we adopt such a decision it will not yield any serious results.

Byrnes: This clause says that these Governments will be requested to temporarily suspend the eviction of the German population pending the discussion of the question in the Control Council. If these Governments are not expelling the Germans and are not making them leave Poland or Czechoslovakia, then the document will not, of course, yield any results. But if they are doing so, we can request them to stop this for a time. According to our information they are making the Germans leave Poland and Czechoslovakia. The resettlement of Germans in other countries increases our burden. We want these Governments to collaborate with us in this case.

Stalin: The Poles and the Czechs will tell you that they have no orders to evict the Germans. If you insist I can agree to this proposal, but I am afraid it will yield no great result.

Truman: If you agree, we shall be thankful. This proposal may not alter the existing situation, but it will give us an opportunity of addressing these Governments.

Stalin: Good, I do not object.

Bevin: We should like to inform the French of this.

[*Stalin and Truman agree.*]

Stalin: We should like to finish discussing the question of the German Navy.

Truman: This question is not yet ready today.

Stalin: Let us agree to prepare it for tomorrow.

Truman: All right, I agree. I was going to leave tomorrow, but I could stay.

Stalin: In principle a decision on the German Navy was adopted, but it was not finally drawn up. This question has been decided by the three Heads of Government, and the decision should be drawn up.

Truman: The commission could report tomorrow morning.

Stalin: Good. Perhaps we should refer the matter to the Ministers, since the question has been decided in principle.

Bevin: Perhaps an agreement will be reached.

Byrnes: According to our information, the commission hopes to reach agreement today. Their sitting is fixed for tonight.

Stalin: It was decided in principle that the Soviet Union is to receive one-third of the Navy, with the exception of submarines, most of which are to be sunk, and one-third of the merchant fleet. I ask you not to postpone the question, but to settle it tomorrow.

[*Truman and Attlee express agreement.*]

Truman: The delegation of the United States has tabled a document concerning a review of the procedure in the Allied Control Commissions in Bulgaria, Rumania and Hungary.

Byrnes: Our proposals concerning the fulfilment of the Yalta Declaration on Liberated Europe were tabled and examined. We were unable to reach agreement on some sections of the proposal. But agreement was reached on two clauses relating to a review of the procedure in the Allied Control Commissions in the three countries. Clause I says:

"The three Governments have taken note that the Soviet Representatives on the Allied Control Commissions in Rumania, Bulgaria and Hungary have communicated to their United Kingdom and United States colleagues proposals for improving the work of the Control Commissions, now that hostilities in Europe have ceased. These proposals include provisions for regular and frequent meetings of the three representatives, improved facilities for British and American representatives, and prior joint consideration of directives."

Clause 2 reads:

"The three Governments agree that the revision of the procedures of the Allied Control Commissions in these countries will now be undertaken, using as a basis of discussion the above-mentioned proposals, and taking into account the interests and responsibilities of the three Governments which together presented the terms of armistice to the respective countries."

We ask you to examine these clauses and hand you a document entitled "Revised Allied Control Commission Procedure in Rumania, Bulgaria and Hungary", dated July 31, 1945.

Stalin: This question was not on the agenda. Perhaps we shall not object once we have examined the question.

Byrnes: It could be examined tomorrow.

Stalin: Good, let us examine it tomorrow.

Truman: The next question is that of Yugoslavia. There are the British proposals.

Stalin: We have just circulated a draft on the Greek

question. As for Yugoslavia, we handed in a draft on Trieste and Istria yesterday.

Bevin: I think we have presented a rather reasonable proposal on Yugoslavia. The Soviet delegation has tabled two other proposals. I propose that we refrain from examining all three proposals.

Stalin: Good.

Truman: The last question is that of war criminals.

[The Soviet delegation declared that it was prepared to adopt the British delegation's draft as a basis on this question with one small amendment. It proposed that in the last phrase of the draft, which said that the three Governments considered it a matter of great importance to have the trial of the chief criminals begin as soon as possible, there should be an addition after the words "chief criminals" of the words: "such as Göring, Hess, Ribbentrop, Rosenberg, Keitel, and others".]

Attlee: Our difficulty in selecting the war criminals lies in the fact that we have submitted the draft agreement to the prosecutor and he may include a number of other persons. We believe therefore that it would be best to confine ourselves to our earlier proposal, without naming the chief war criminals.

Stalin: Our amendment does not propose that only these men alone should be put on trial, but we propose that men like Ribbentrop and others should be tried. It is no longer possible to avoid mentioning certain persons who are known as the chief war criminals. A great deal has been said of the war criminals, and the peoples expect us to give some names. Our silence on this question harms our prestige. I assure you that is so. That is why we shall gain politically and satisfy European public opinion if we name some persons. I do not think the prosecutor will take offence if we name them as examples. The prosecutor can say that some persons have been wrongly named. But there is no reason for the prosecutor to take offence. We shall only gain politically if we name some of these men.

Byrnes: When we discussed this question yesterday, I considered it unsuitable to name definite men or to try to determine their guilt here. Each country has its own "favourites" among the Nazi criminals, and if we fail to include these criminals in our list, it will be hard for us to explain why.

Stalin: But the proposal says: "such as . . . and others". This does not limit the number, but makes for clarity.

Byrnes: This gives an advantage to those you name. [*Laughter*.]

Attlee: I don't believe a listing of names will enhance our document. For instance, I believe that Hitler is alive, but he is not on our list.

Stalin: But he is not in our hands.

Attlee: But you give the names of the chief criminals as examples.

Stalin: I agree to include Hitler [*General laughter*], even if he is not in our hands. I am making a concession. [*General laughter*.]

Attlee: I think the world is aware who the chief criminals are.

Stalin: But, you see, our silence on this matter is interpreted as an intention on our part to save the chief war criminals, that we are taking it out on the small criminals and allowing the big ones to escape.

Byrnes: Today, I had a telephone conversation with Justice Jackson, the Chairman of our Supreme Court. He is our representative on the War Criminals Commission which is meeting in London. He expressed the hope that today or possibly tomorrow there would be agreement on an International Tribunal. Justice Jackson is going to call me tomorrow morning to inform me on the question of the Tribunal. The report on the establishment of the International Tribunal will be good news for the peoples who are expecting an early trial of the war criminals.

Stalin: That is another question.

Byrnes: But we can include in our statement that an agreement has been reached in London. That will make our statement highly effective.

Stalin: Without naming some persons, especially the odious ones, among the German war criminals, our statement will not be politically effective. I consulted Russian jurists, and they think it would be better to name some persons as a guideline.

Truman: I want to make a proposal. We are expecting news from our representative in London tomorrow morning. Why not put off this question until tomorrow?

Stalin: Good.

19*

Truman: I am very much interested in the question of inland waterways. It would be good to discuss this question and reach some decisions in principle. We discussed the question on July 23, and it was referred to a commission which, as far as I am aware, has not met even once. I very much want some sort of definite decision worked out concerning the use of these means of communication, because freedom of movement along these routes is of great importance. I believe that a common policy on the use of these inland waterways can play an important part. It is quite possible that we may not be able to reach agreement on the details of this question, but I think that this question is so important that it should be discussed.

Attlee: I agree on the whole with the American proposals on the question.

Stalin: This question arose in connection with that of the Black Sea Straits which was before us. The question of the Black Sea Straits was inserted in the agenda by the British and was then postponed. The question of inland waterways was raised here additionally. This is a serious question, and it requires study. The question was brought up unexpectedly for us, and we do not have the relevant material to hand. This question is a new one, it needs men who know about it. Perhaps something could be done before the end of the Conference, but there is little hope for that.

Truman: I move that this question should be referred to the Council of Foreign Ministers in London, and before then all the necessary material can be collected and the question studied.

[*Stalin and Attlee agree.*]

Truman: May I inform the representatives of the Polish Government who are here of our decisions on Poland's western frontier?

Stalin: All right.

Truman: Who can be entrusted with this communication?

Stalin: This could be done by the Ministers or a written communication could be sent. Or the President could be asked to do this, since he heads our Conference.

Truman: Good. I want to inform you that the commission on drafting the communiqué is working well. At what time do we meet tomorrow? At 4.00?

Stalin: I think that we shall have to meet twice: let us fix the first sitting for 3.00, and the second for 8.00 p.m.

That will be the concluding sitting.
[*Truman and Attlee agree.*]

Twelfth Sitting

August 1, 1945

Truman: Mr. Byrnes will report today on the sitting of the Foreign Ministers.

Byrnes: The commission dealing with the question of reparations from Germany has reported that it has failed to reach agreement on all the questions of the draft agreement on reparations. The representatives of the United States and Great Britain believed that, in exchange for the agreed percentages of capital equipment made available to the Soviet Union under Point 4 of the draft agreement, the representatives of the Soviet Union agreed to waive their claims to German assets abroad, the gold seized from the Germans, and the shares of German enterprises in the Western zones of occupation. Accordingly, the representatives of the United States and Britain believed that Germany's assets abroad should be included in Point 3 as a source of reparations for other countries besides the Soviet Union. They declared that unless this is done, the agreed percentages of industrial equipment in Point 4 are unacceptable to the representatives of the United States and Britain.

The Soviet representative held that no agreed decision had been adopted concerning the Soviet Union's waiver of claims to Germany's assets abroad, gold and shares. That is why the Soviet representative did not agree to the inclusion of German assets abroad in Point 3, and recommended that the question should be referred for solution to the Heads of Government.

The representatives of the United States and Britain declared that the draft agreement on reparations would be acceptable to them, provided the Soviet representative agreed to the above-mentioned proposals concerning Germany's assets abroad, gold and shares. The Soviet representative declared that he was unable to agree with this approach on the part of the representatives of the United States and Britain.

The question is whether or not it can be considered that the Big Three yesterday reached agreement on the question of reparations, when the Soviet representative declared that he would not insist on the Soviet Union being given 30 per cent of German gold, shares and assets abroad.

Stalin: How are we to understand your proposals that the Soviet Union makes no claim to industrial shares? Does that relate only to the Western zone?

Truman: I think that when the Foreign Ministers spoke of the Western zone, they had in mind the zones of the United States, Great Britain and France.

Stalin: Can we not agree on the following: the Soviet delegation waives its claim to gold; as for shares of German enterprises in the Western zone, we also waive our claim to them, and will regard the whole of Western Germany as falling within your sphere, and Eastern Germany, within ours.

Truman: We shall have to discuss this proposal.

Stalin: As to the German investments, I should put the question this way: as to the German investments in Eastern Europe, they remain with us, and the rest, with you.

Truman: Does this apply only to German investments in Europe or in other countries as well?

Stalin: Let me put it more specifically: the German investments in Rumania, Bulgaria, Hungary and Finland, go to us, and all the rest, to you.

Bevin: The German investments in other countries go to us?

Stalin: In all the other countries, in South America, in Canada, etc., all this is yours.

Bevin: Consequently, all German assets in other countries lying west of the zones of occupation in Germany will belong to the United States, Great Britain and the other countries? Does this also apply to Greece?

Stalin: Yes.

Byrnes: How does this apply to the question of the shares of German enterprises?

Stalin: In our zone they will be ours, and in your zone, yours. There are the Western and the Eastern zones.

Byrnes: We took your proposal of yesterday to mean that you will have no claims to shares in the western zone.

Stalin: We shall not.

Byrnes: Do you also withdraw your second proposal, on investments abroad?

Stalin: There the matter is somewhat different.

Bevin: Yesterday, when we were dealing with the question of reparations, I understood that the Soviet delegation waived its claims to Germany's investments abroad.

Stalin: I believed that the investments in the Eastern zone were ours. We had in mind the Western zone, when we spoke of waiving claims to investments. We waive claims to investments in Western Europe and in all other countries. It is known that there were many more German investments in Western Europe and in America than in the East. We had hoped to receive 30 per cent of these investments, but subsequently waived this. But you too must waive your claims to Eastern Europe.

Bevin: I must say that when I agreed to the Generalissimo's proposal I took the proposal to mean that the Soviet delegation waived claims to any German investments abroad at all.

Stalin: But not in Rumania, Bulgaria, Hungary and Finland.

Byrnes: That is understandable. I should like to specify the matter of the shares of industrial or transport enterprises in Germany. Say, the head office of such an enterprise is in Berlin, but the enterprise itself and its property is in the Western zone or in the United States, will you make any claim in respect of such enterprises?

Stalin: If the enterprise is in the West, we shall make no claim to it. The head office may be in Berlin, that is immaterial, the point is where the enterprise itself is located.

Byrnes: If an enterprise is not in Eastern Europe but in Western Europe or in other parts of the world, that enterprise remains ours?

Stalin: In the United States, in Norway, in Switzerland, in Sweden, in Argentina [*General laughter*], etc.—all that is yours.

Bevin: I should like to ask the Generalissimo whether he is prepared to waive all claims to German assets abroad outside the zone of Russian occupation troops?

Stalin: Yes, I am.

Byrnes: What about the gold?

Stalin: We have already withdrawn our claims to the gold.

Byrnes: There are German assets in other countries. How is the Soviet proposal to be understood in this context?

Stalin: We keep only what is in the Eastern zone.

Byrnes: I believe it to be very important for us to understand each other. Mr. Bevin's question is whether the Russian claims are confined to the assets in the zone occupied by the Russian army? I should like you to accept Mr. Bevin's standpoint.

Stalin: We agree.

Byrnes: A few minutes ago you spoke of the assets in Bulgaria, Rumania, Hungary and Finland. Now I want to clarify everything so that there should be no misunderstandings in the future. Does your proposal mean that you make no claim to the assets outside your zone of occupation? You have claims only to the assets in the Soviet zone?

Stalin: Yes. Czechoslovakia is not included, Yugoslavia is not included. Eastern Austria will be included.

Bevin: It is clear that the assets belonging to Great Britain and the United States in that zone will not be affected.

Stalin: Of course, not. We're not fighting Great Britain or the United States. [*General laughter.*]

Bevin: But during the war these assets may have been seized by the Germans.

Stalin: That will have to be examined in every case.

Truman: I think that we agreed yesterday to meet the claims of Czechoslovakia and Yugoslavia. But what happens if they do not lay claim to German assets on their territory?

Stalin: We shall make no claim to Germany's assets in Czechoslovakia, Yugoslavia and Western Austria.

Perhaps we shall expound our proposal in the protocol?

Byrnes: I think it would be better to do that in order to avoid any misunderstandings.

Stalin: Good.

Byrnes: Perhaps we should publish it?

Stalin: It's all the same, as you wish.

Byrnes: I want to call your attention to the sentence in Clause 3 of the report of the Reparations Commission which says that the reparations claims of the United States, the United Kingdom and other countries entitled to reparations are to be met from the Western zone and from German assets abroad. In view of the agreement we have just reached, I do not believe that there will be any differences on this wording.

Stalin: I propose that we say "and from the appropriate German assets abroad". This wording can be specified in the protocol.

Byrnes: Let us have the drafting commission put this proposal into shape.

Stalin: I have no objections.

Attlee: I have two questions which I should like to raise here: the first, that the French Government should be invited by the Governments of Great Britain, the U.S.S.R. and the United States to be a member of the Reparations Commission as of today.

Stalin: Let us also invite Poland, she has suffered heavily.

Attlee: I understood that we agreed to invite France.

Stalin: And why can't Poland be invited?

Truman: You agreed yesterday that the Soviet Union would undertake to meet Poland's reparations claims, while we, for our part, undertake to meet the reparations claims of France and other countries. I think the inclusion of France in this commission would cause some confusion.

Stalin: Does Mr. Attlee insist?

Attlee: I should like to.

Stalin: Good, I do not object.

Attlee: My second question is the following: I submitted a memorandum concerning the fact that the British and American commanders have to supply 40,000 tons of foodstuffs a month and 2,400 tons of coal a day to the British and American sectors in Berlin for 30 days, beginning from July 15. The Control Council should be immediately instructed to draw up a programme for the supply of food, coal and other types of fuel to the Greater Berlin area over the next six months. These quantities will be delivered to the Greater Berlin area by the Soviet Government in the form of advance deliveries under Point 4(a) of the reparations agreement. These are practical measures which will provide for current requirements.

Stalin: The question has not been prepared, we are not acquainted with this question, and we know nothing of the opinion of the Control Council on it. Consequently, we find it very hard to settle this question now. I think we should find out beforehand the opinion of the Control Council on how it intends to satisfy the needs of the population, and what its plans are concerning supply.

Attlee: I understood that deliveries of capital equipment from the Ruhr basin are to start now, and I think that the supply of the necessary food and fuel for the Greater Berlin area should also start now. Of course, the quantity can be fixed by the Control Council.

Stalin: Of course, there must be an agreement, but a quantity has to be specified, and that is something we cannot do now, without a report from the Control Council on its plans in this respect. I must say that the Control Council will solve this question better than we could settle it here; it takes a practical approach to solving this question.

Attlee: That is just what I am asking for. I am asking that the Control Council should draw up a programme, but in principle we should agree on that here.

Stalin: I have no information on how things stand. I can decide nothing without authentic materials. I can't take figures out of thin air. The figures must be justified.

Attlee: I'm not asking about figures, in my memorandum I ask that the Control Council should draw up this programme.

Stalin: 40,000 tons of food a month, 2,400 tons of coal a day—where do these figures come from, how are they justified?

Attlee: These figures have been agreed upon, and these quantities are already being supplied.

Stalin: I did not know that.

Bevin: The question is that there is a provisional agreement on monthly deliveries for Berlin.

Stalin: Who has agreed to this?

Bevin: A provisional agreement on deliveries was concluded in the Control Council, under which the British and American authorities undertook to supply these quantities for Berlin during a month, and this is now being done. We propose that the Control Council should draw up the necessary programme in principle, and that the Soviet authorities should start supplying the said quantities when the month expires. When the period runs out, the question arises: who is to go on supplying the food and fuel?

Stalin: We must hear the Control Council and its considerations. Then we can decide something.

Attlee: I understood you to say that you want the deliveries of capital equipment from the Ruhr basin to be started right away. We ask for the same thing in respect of your deliveries of food and fuel.

Stalin: I understand that, but I should like to know what the Control Council thinks, so that we can discuss it and adopt a decision. I think the question should be postponed.

Bevin: We want to work with each other.

Stalin: And what if we are not ready for the question, what are we to do?

Bevin: In that case it will have to be postponed.

Stalin: That is just what we are asking.

Bevin: We merely wanted to reach a mutual agreement to help each other.

Stalin: We are not prepared for this question, I have had no occasion to consult with the Control Council and find out what it thinks.

Truman: It looks as if we have exhausted all our differences on the reparations question?

Attlee: I understood the Generalissimo to say that we shall not be demanding reparations from Austria. Perhaps we should enter this in the protocol?

Stalin: It could be entered in the protocol.

Byrnes: The next question is that of economic principles in respect of Germany. The representatives of the United States and Britain propose the inclusion of a clause on German assets abroad in the document on economic principles. It will be Point 18, reading as follows: "Appropriate steps shall be taken by the Control Council to exercise control and the power of disposition over German-owned external assets not already under the control of United Nations which have taken part in the war against Germany."

Stalin: Is that an amendment or a new proposal?

Byrnes: It is a recommendation to the commission on economic questions. It proposes the inclusion of this point in the document on the economic principles in respect of Germany.

Stalin: Will not an amendment to this point be necessary after adoption of the decision on reparations? We learned of this point after we had agreed on the question.

Byrnes: The Soviet representatives in the commission for economic questions declared that they have little interest in the matter and reserved their position until the question is studied. The question concerned relates to control.

Stalin: I do not object.

Truman: Thank you.

Byrnes: The commission has not had time to reach agreement on Point 19 of the draft on economic principles relating to the question of payment for imports to Germany. Besides, the Soviet representative declared that he is not yet prepared to continue discussing the question of oil deliveries to Western Europe.

Stalin: We do not object to the British formulation of Point 19.

Byrnes: I understand that the British representatives have agreed with the American representatives that if Point 19 is adopted there should be added the words proposed by the American representatives to the effect that the condition stipulated in the point will not be applicable to equipment or foodstuffs specified in Points 4 (a) and 4 (b) of the agreement on German reparations. We believe that the addendum flows from the agreement on reparations we reached yesterday.

Stalin: Good.

Attlee: I agree.

Byrnes: Thus, we have finished with all the differences over the draft on economic principles.

The next question is that of war criminals.

Bevin: Please excuse me, but I think we should inform the French of these economic principles.

Stalin: If you wish.

Byrnes: The next question is that of war criminals. The only question remaining open here is whether the names of some of the major German war criminals should be mentioned. The representatives of the United States and Britain, at today's meeting of the Foreign Ministers, deemed it right not to mention these names, but to leave that to the prosecutor. They also agreed that the British text should be adopted. The Soviet representatives declared that they agree with the British draft, provided some names are added.

Stalin: I think we need names. This must be done for public opinion. The people must know this. Are we to take action against any German industrialists? I think we are. We name Krupp. If Krupp will not do, let's name others.

Truman: I don't like any of them. [*Laughter.*] I think that if we mention some names and leave out others, people may think that we have no intention of putting those others on trial.

Stalin: But these names are given here as examples. It is surprising, for instance, why Hess is still in Britain all provided for and is not being put on trial. These names must be given; this will be important for public opinion, for the peoples.

Bevin: Don't worry about Hess.

Stalin: It's not a question of what I think, but of public opinion, and the opinion of the peoples of all the countries which had been occupied by the Germans.

Bevin: If you have any doubts about Hess I can promise that he will be put on trial.

Stalin: I am not asking for any undertakings on the part of Mr. Bevin, his statement is enough to leave me in no doubt that this will be done. But it is not a question of me, but of the peoples, of public opinion.

Truman: You are aware that we have appointed Justice Jackson as our representative on the London Commission. He is an outstanding judge and a very experienced jurist. He has a good knowledge of legal procedure. Jackson is opposed to any names of war criminals being mentioned, and says that this will hamper their work. He assures us that the trial will be ready within 30 days, and that there should be no doubt concerning our view of these men.

Stalin: Perhaps we could name fewer persons, say, three?

Bevin: Our jurists take the same view as the Americans.

Stalin: And ours take the opposite view. But perhaps we shall agree that the first list of the German war criminals to be brought to trial should be published not later than in one month?

[*Truman* and *Attlee* agree with Stalin's proposal.]

Byrnes: The next question is one concerning the use of Allied property as reparations from satellites or as war booty. I handed in this proposal yesterday. At today's sitting, the Soviet delegation asked to be given the possibility to make a more detailed study of the proposal.

[The Soviet delegation said that in view of the fact that there had actually been no break between the two sittings that day, it had not had time to study the wording of the proposal. It said that the proposal appeared to be correct and acceptable in substance, but its formulation had to be studied.]

Byrnes: I am prepared to postpone it until tonight.

Attlee: I propose that the agenda of tonight's sitting should contain as few items as possible.

Byrnes: The next question is that concerning the supply of oil to Western Europe. The question is now being examined in the economic commission.

The next question is that of the anti-Soviet activity of White Russian émigrés and other persons and organisations hostile to the U.S.S.R. in the American and British zones of occupation in Germany and Austria. The Anglo-American representatives have declared that they would examine the situation and the facts set out in the Soviet document, and would inform the Soviet Union at once of the results of their investigation, after which they would be prepared to discuss measures for stopping this activity.

The Soviet delegation has called attention to the memorandum which it handed to the British and American delegations concerning the repatriation of Soviet citizens. The British representatives declared that they would clarify the situation of which the Soviet document speaks and would deal with the matter immediately upon their return to London.

The Soviet representatives handed in a new document on this question and stressed the great importance they attach to it. The American and British representatives promised to deal with the matter as soon as possible.

The Foreign Ministers discussed the report of the commission drafting the protocol of the Conference. The commission failed to reach agreement on four questions, but the Foreign Ministers managed to reach agreement on these questions. They also agreed that only the key decisions of the Conference would be included in the protocol. They indicated to the protocol commission that the new decisions of the Conference should also be included in the protocol.

The next question is that of reviewing the procedure of the Allied Control Commissions in Bulgaria, Rumania and Hungary. The U.S draft on the question was adopted with the exception of the second sentence. It was decided that the sentence would be replaced by the third, fourth and fifth points of the letter from the Soviet representative handed to the representatives of the United States and Great

Britain in the Allied Control Commission for Hungary. This question was referred to the drafting commission, which, after discussion, recommends to us the following text:

"The Three Governments took note that the Soviet representatives on the Allied Control Commissions in Rumania, Bulgaria and Hungary have communicated to their United Kingdom and United States colleagues proposals for improving the work of the Control Commissions, now that hostilities in Europe have ceased.

"The Three Governments agreed that the revision of the procedures of the Allied Control Commissions in these countries would now be undertaken, taking into account the interests and responsibilities of the Three Governments which together presented the terms of armistice to the respective countries, and accepting as a basis, in respect of all three countries, the Soviet Government's proposals for Hungary."

Can we adopt the proposal of the drafting commission in this form?

Stalin: I have no objections.

Truman: Today, I received the President of Poland and four members of the Provisional Polish Government. I informed them of the decisions on Poland and handed them a copy of these decisions. They will refrain from making any statements on these decisions pending their publication in the press. They asked me on behalf of the Polish Government to convey their gratitude to all three Governments represented at the Conference.

Bevin: I should like to mention that the difficulties concerning the London-Warsaw air line, of which I spoke yesterday, have been removed. We have reached agreement with Poland on this question.

Byrnes: At the meeting of the Foreign Ministers I proposed that the words "and radio representatives" should be added in the documents on Poland and on admission to the United Nations Organisation, where they deal with the facilities which are to be extended to members of the Allied press.

Stalin: I don't think we should do that.

Attlee: I do not consider it expedient either.

Truman: We in America have a different radio situation than in other countries, such as Britain. The British radio is under Government control, but in America the radio is in the same position as the newspapers. We should like the radio representatives to have the same rights as newspaper correspondents.

Stalin: It's not worth while.

Truman: The representatives of the American radio will act in the same way as newspaper correspondents, but they will file their reports for the American radio.

Stalin: I should not advise doing that. Besides, agreement must be reached with Poland.

Bevin: But you will not object, will you, against an agreement with the Governments concerned?

Stalin: No, why should I?

Truman: That is acceptable to us.

Stalin: You are welcome. But let us decide not to write about that here.

Truman: Good, I agree.

Byrnes: The next question is that of the German Navy and merchant fleet.

Truman: I understand that the report of the commission on this question is adopted and we confirm the prepared decision.

Stalin: That's right.

Byrnes: It was also agreed that the text of the decision was to be published later.

Bevin: Mr. President, I have drawn up the text of the point concerning the share of Poland and the other countries, which I think we could accept. It says: "The United Kingdom and the United States will provide out of their shares of the surrendered German merchant ships appropriate amounts for other Allied states whose merchant marines have suffered heavy losses in the common cause against Germany, except that the Soviet Union shall provide out of its share for Poland."

Stalin: I have no objections.

Truman: I agree.

Attlee: Before we adjourn, I should like to ask whether the Heads of Government think it appropriate to send Mr. Churchill and Mr. Eden a telegram expressing thanks for their participation in the first half of the Conference and for their participation in other conferences?

Stalin: That would be appropriate.

Truman: I agree.

[*After the interval*]

Byrnes: Did you have time to study our document concerning the use of Allied property as payment for reparations by satellites or as war booty?

Stalin: I see no difficulties in settling this question as regards the substance, but I must have consultation on its formulation.

Attlee: I think the document requires some study, as not all its propositions appear to be acceptable.

Byrnes: In what respect is the draft unacceptable?

Attlee: Where the property belonging to the Allied countries has been withdrawn from the satellite countries as war booty, it is natural that the satellite countries must compensate the Allied countries to whom the property belonged. But where the property is seized by a third party, there arises the question: must it pay the Allied countries for this property or must we make the satellite countries pay for the property. In addition, I think that Point 3 dealing with currency also requires discussion. It seems to me that all this still needs to be studied.

Truman: Good.

Perhaps we could now acquaint ourselves with the communiqué?

Stalin: The commission has not yet finished drafting it.

Attlee: I propose that the commission on the drafting of the protocol and the commission on the drafting of the communiqué should deal with this question immediately, and that we should adjourn and meet again as soon as the commissions have completed their work. We could agree by telephone on the time of the meeting. The Heads of Government would deal with the question of the communiqué, and the Foreign Ministers with that of the protocol.

Stalin: It would be well to fix the time for the opening of the sitting, say 8.30 or 9.00 o'clock. The time is set to give the commissions a spur, then they will try hard.

Truman: A three-hour break suits me.

Byrnes: There was also the President's proposal on inland waterways. The protocol commission and the communiqué commission have not yet reached agreement on the decision adopted in connection with the President's proposal.

Truman: This question has been referred to the Council of Foreign Ministers in London, but I am interested in having the communiqué say this. I should ask that mention of this be made in the communiqué.

Stalin: We have not discussed it.

Truman: I spoke thrice on the question, and the commission examined it for several days.

Stalin: It was not in the list of questions, we were not prepared for the question, and had no materials; our experts on this question are in Moscow. Why such haste; why should there be such a hurry?

Truman: This question has not been finally settled but referred to the Council of Foreign Ministers in London.

Stalin: No mention of the Black Sea Straits will be made in the communiqué either, although the question was on the agenda. The question of waterways arose as a free supplement to the question of the Straits. And I don't see why such preference should be given to the question of inland waterways over that of Straits.

Truman: The question of the Black Sea Straits will be mentioned both in the communiqué and the protocol.

Stalin: I think there is no need to put it into the communiqué, but only into the protocol.

I propose that no mention be made in the communiqué either of the Straits or the inland waterways, but that both these questions be included in the protocol only.

Truman: Good, there are no objections.

Bevin: I propose that we ask France to subscribe to our decision concerning war criminals. France is a member of the Council of Foreign Ministers in London.

Stalin: Good.

Truman: I do not object.

I still fail to understand why a decision adopted by us here and included in the protocol should not also be included in the communiqué.

Stalin: There is no need of it. As it is, the communiqué is much too long.

Truman: I should like to ask one question: are there any secret agreements at this Conference?

Stalin: No, not secret ones.

Byrnes: I should like to stress that we decided to refer the question of inland waterways to the Council of Foreign Ministers. Thus, we have an agreement on this question. Have we the right to make public the decision on this question? And if it is not included in the communiqué, but only in the protocol, can we officially put this question before the Council of Foreign Ministers?

Stalin: We should take the materials of the Crimea Conference or the Tehran Conference. At the Tehran Conference a number of questions were included in the protocol, but there was another series of decisions which were of interest to all and which determined our policy in respect of key issues. These decisions were included in the communiqué.

Take the work of the Crimea Conference. It too had two series of decisions on record. The first series—the greater one—went into the protocol, and no one insisted on it being transferred into the communiqué. The other series—the much smaller one—went into the communiqué. These were decisions determining our policy. I propose that we keep to this good rule, otherwise we shall have a whole volume instead of a communiqué.

Some of the decisions have no serious significance, some of the questions, like the one of the inland waterways, were not even discussed, and they will go into the protocol, so that no one reproach us with concealing these questions. It is a different matter with the questions of Germany, of Italy, of reparations, etc., which are of great significance, and they go into the communiqué. I think we should not break with this good tradition, and that there is no point in including all these questions in the communiqué. A communiqué is a communiqué, and a protocol is a protocol.

Truman: I do not object to this procedure, if it is adopted for all our decisions. But if I have to make a statement in the Senate to the effect that the question has been referred to the Council of Foreign Ministers, shall I have the right to do so?

Stalin: No one can encroach on your rights.

[*Truman closes the sitting.*]

Thirteenth (Final) Sitting

August 1, 1945

Truman opens the sitting.

Byrnes: The commission for economic questions has prepared a report on reparations. Proposals acceptable to all delegations have been worked out. Paragraph 1 says that the Soviet reparations claims are to be met from the zone of Germany occupied by the Soviet Union and the appropriate German investments abroad.

I call your attention to Paragraphs 8 and 9 of this document. I am very reluctant to propose an amendment right now, but I think this will be in the general interest. Paragraph 8 says: "The Soviet Government renounces all claims to shares of German enterprises", etc. I propose the addition of "in respect of reparations" after the words "all claims". The purpose of this amendment is to avoid creating the impression that the Soviet Union has some other claims to German enterprises apart from reparations. The same amendment should be made in Paragraph 9, which deals with the claims of the United States and the United Kingdom.

Stalin: That is right.

Byrnes: That is my only amendment. Can the reparations document be considered as approved?

Bevin: And how are we to consider, for instance, the case of plants belonging to British subjects which were taken over by the Germans for military purposes before 1939? In that case, owing to this amendment, the British will be deprived of their own property.

Byrnes: In the case cited by Mr. Bevin the amendment does not affect the situation.

Bevin: I do not object.

Byrnes: We can now discuss the question of the use of allied property to pay reparations or as war trophies, if the Soviet delegation has had time to study the proposal.

Stalin: We have not had time to consider the wording of the draft. I propose that we record the following decision: "The Conference decided to accept the American proposal in principle. The wording of the proposal to be agreed through diplomatic channels."

We have not had time to give thought to the wording, but we agree with the proposal in substance.

Truman: I agree with the proposal of the Soviet delegation.

Attlee: So do I.

Byrnes: I have been informed that the commission charged with drawing up the protocol has reached agreement. I do not believe there is any need to read out the protocol in full, but only those points on which there were differences. Of course, we should add to it the Soviet delegation's proposal concerning war trophies which we have just adopted. I have no other amendments.

Stalin: I have an amendment. On the question of Poland's western frontier, the second paragraph says that the boundary line must run from the Baltic Sea through Swinemünde, as if the line passes through the town itself. I propose, therefore, that we say that the boundary line runs from the Baltic Sea immediately west or a little west of Swinemünde. That is what the map shows.

[*Truman and Attlee agree with the wording "immediately west of Swinemünde".*]

Stalin: The second amendment is about the boundary line of the Königsberg Region. The second paragraph says that the boundary line is subject to expert examination. It is proposed to say: "The exact line on the ground should be established by experts of the U.S.S.R. and Poland."

Bevin: We cannot leave this only to the Soviet Union and Poland.

Stalin: But this concerns the boundary line between Poland and Russia.

Bevin: But this must be recognised by the United Nations. We agreed that at the Peace Conference we would support the Soviet desire concerning this frontier, and now you say that it is to be determined by the Soviet Union and Poland and that we have nothing to do with it.

Stalin: This is a misunderstanding. The general boundary line is determined by the Peace Conference, but there is another concept—the line of demarcation on the ground. The general boundary line is given, but the line of demarcation on the ground may deviate from the imaginary line by half a kilometre or less to one side of it or the other. Say, the boundary line runs through a village. Why should the frontier line cut it in half? Only Poland and Russia are interested in laying down the actual line of demarcation on the ground. If you think that this is not entirely guaranteed, whom would you like to include in the commission? Someone from Britain or the United States? Anyone you wish, we do not mind.

Attlee: I think the question is as follows. We agreed to accept the proposal concerning the frontier in principle. As for the final demarcation of the territory, the precise determination of the frontier, that is the business of the Peace Conference. If we now hand this business over to the experts of Poland and Russia we shall be disrupting the technical work of the Peace Conference.

Stalin: What's Mr. Bevin's opinion?

Bevin: We want to have a commission of experts appointed by the Peace Conference.

Stalin: I fail to see the point.

Byrnes: I believe the following wording could be proposed: if there is agreement on the frontier between Poland and the Soviet Union at the Peace Conference, that will be the end of the matter, and no experts will be required. But if there are differences between Poland and Russia during the Peace Conference a commission of experts will have to be appointed, with the composition determined by the Council of Ministers of Foreign Affairs or the Peace Conference itself. But that is only in the event of differences between Poland and the Soviet Union.

Stalin: Let the old wording stand. But it says nothing of which experts are to be on the commission.

[*Truman* and *Attlee* agree to retain the old wording.

The Soviet delegation then tabled an amendment to the section on the conclusion of peace treaties and on admission to the United Nations Organisation. The Soviet delegation pointed out that there was a contradiction between the first and the third paragraph of the document. The first paragraph said that the Three Governments considered it desirable that the present anomalous position of Italy, Bulgaria, Rumania, Hungary and Finland should be terminated after the conclusion of peace treaties, whereas the third paragraph provided for the possibility of establishing diplomatic relations with Finland, Rumania, Bulgaria and Hungary prior to the conclusion of peace treaties with these countries. The Soviet delegation proposed the deletion from the first paragraph of the words "after the conclusion of peace treaties".]

Attlee: In my opinion, that is wrong, because when we drafted the third paragraph we had in mind the establishment of diplomatic relations "to the extent possible". If the words "after the conclusion of peace treaties" are excluded from the first paragraph, it will mean that we shall be going farther than we intended to. These words should be left in.

Stalin: But the first paragraph says that diplomatic relations can be re-established only after the conclusion of peace treaties, and the third paragraph says something different. This leads to a contradiction.

Attlee: That is just why the British want to include these words. The first paragraph provides for mandatory action, namely, the establishment of diplomatic relations after the conclusion of peace treaties, whereas the third paragraph proposes that an effort should be made to do this, insofar as possible, before the conclusion of peace treaties.

Stalin: We cannot agree with that, because the effort which is assumed in the third paragraph to establish diplomatic relations is explicitly denied in the first paragraph. That changes the meaning of the whole decision. How can we agree to that?

Attlee: I do not think there is any contradiction there: in the first instance it is a question of establishing normal relations, that is, full diplomatic relations, and in the second, of an effort to come as close as possible to establishing such relations.

Stalin: I'm afraid I cannot agree with this interpretation. Let us take a concrete example—Finland. There is no reason at all to object any more to restoring diplomatic relations with Finland, but in the first paragraph the words "after the conclusion of peace treaties" explicitly prohibit the establishment of diplomatic relations. That is quite wrong.

Attlee: We are still in a state of war with Finland.

Stalin: The state of war with Italy is not yet over either, but America already has diplomatic relations with Italy, and so do we.

Attlee: I think we are now returning to something we already discussed a few days ago. We fully explained our standpoint, and we met the Soviet Union as far as we could under our constitution. We believe that we have made big concessions, beyond which we cannot go.

Stalin: Nothing will come of this. Finland has much more right than Italy to the establishment of diplomatic relations. Finland has a freely elected government, it has long since ended the war against the Allies and declared war on Germany. Italy has no freely elected government, and her participation in the war against Germany since her surrender has been minimal. On what grounds should we delay establishment of diplomatic relations with Finland? Where is the logic in that?

Bevin: I want to reach agreement and therefore make the following proposal. I propose the following wording for the first paragraph: "The Three Governments consider it desirable that the present anomalous position of Italy, Bulgaria, Finland, Hungary and Rumania should be terminated by the conclusion of peace treaties. They trust that the other interested Allied Governments will share these views."

Stalin: Good. The Soviet delegation has no more amendments.

Bevin: Hurrah! [*General laughter.*]

Byrnes: The next question is that of the communiqué. We have received from the British delegation a new wording of the introductory part. We have no objections to it.

Stalin: Is there any great difference? What is the difference?

Byrnes: On the second page there are changes of a purely drafting nature, the meaning is unchanged.

Stalin: Perhaps we could do this: after the translation into Russian, we shall examine this alteration, and shall now go on to the next section.

[*Truman and Attlee agree.*]

Byrnes: Section II—on the institution of the Council of Foreign Ministers. There are no differences here.

[*Section II is adopted.*]

Byrnes: Section III—on Germany. The words "loudly applauded" in the first paragraph have evoked objections.

Stalin: Let us say: "openly approved".

Bevin: Blindly obeyed, that is obeyed in a stupid manner.

Stalin: I propose that we put it this way: "whom, in the hour of their success, they openly approved and blindly obeyed".

[*The proposal is accepted.*]

Byrnes: Are there any other amendments?

Stalin: No.

Bevin: Paragraph 12 of the economic principles repeats what is already said in Paragraph 9 (IV) of the political principles.

Stalin: I propose that we delete this expression from the economic principles and leave it in the political principles. [*All agree.*] We have no other amendments.

Byrnes: Section IV—on reparations from Germany. There are no amendments.

Section V—on Germany's Navy and Merchant Marine.

Stalin: There is an agreed decision; we have no amendments.

Byrnes: Section VI—on Königsberg and the Adjacent Area.

Stalin: I agree.

Byrnes: Section VII—War Criminals.

Stalin: I think the first introductory paragraph should be excluded and only the second paragraph retained, beginning with the words: "The Three Governments have taken note, etc."

Bevin: We have already done that.

Stalin: Good.

Byrnes: Section VIII—on Austria.

[The Soviet delegation proposes the exclusion· from the section on Austria of the last sentence—concerning reparations, leaving it only in the protocol.]

Truman: We accept the proposal of the Soviet delegation— to exclude the last sentence from the communiqué.

Byrnes: Section IX—on Poland.

Stalin: There are no amendments.

Bevin: I wish to propose a small amendment of the wording. In the second paragraph to say "they defined their attitude in the following statement" instead of the words: "their position was defined in the following statement".

Stalin: All right.

Bevin: On the second page, also concerning Poland, I should substitute the words "Concerning Poland's western boundary they established the following standpoint" for the introductory words "the agreement was reached on the western boundary of Poland".

Truman: I have already informed the representatives of the Polish Government that we agreed on the earlier wording.

Stalin: In that case it is better to leave the old wording.

Bevin: I find Generalissimo Stalin's expression, "immediately west of Swinemünde" very apt.

Stalin: Yes, it will be better to put it that way. Let's go on to the tenth section.

Bevin: Here I wish to make a small amendment, mainly of a psychological nature. I would phrase the introductory part of Section X as follows: "The Conference agreed upon the following statement of common policy for establishing, as soon as possible, the conditions of lasting peace after victory in Europe." This reads better.

Stalin: The wording is essentially the same, there is nothing new in it.

Truman: Both are acceptable.

Bevin: It reads better in English. Maybe it reads worse in American? [*Laughter.*]

Truman: Both are acceptable.

Stalin: The earlier wording contains the same idea which Mr. Bevin has expressed, but it is set out more briefly. Of course, we could accept either.

Bevin: Suppose you prefer our wording this time. [*Laughter.*]

Stalin: If Mr. Bevin insists, I suppose we could accept his wording.

Truman: I agree. Section XII—regarding the revision of Allied Control Commission procedure in Rumania, Bulgaria and Hungary.

Stalin: That has been agreed.

Truman: Section XIII—transferring of German populations.

Stalin: Here the formulation is already better—"orderly transfers".

Truman: The question of military negotiations.

Stalin: It is of general interest. I do not object to its inclusion in the communiqué.

Bevin: The British delegation has one question on Section XII—on revising the procedure in the Allied Control Commissions for Rumania, Bulgaria and Hungary. The last three lines say: "and accepting as a basis, in respect of all three countries, the Soviet Government's proposals for the Allied Control Commission in Hungary". But we do not say what these proposals are. That is why we could say: "and accepting as a basis the agreed proposals".

Stalin: All right. Which signatures are to stand under the communiqué?

Truman: All will sign.

Stalin: Good.

Truman: Let us return to the introductory part of the communiqué.

Stalin: We have no objections.

Bevin: We should like to publish the communiqué in the press on Friday morning.

Stalin: And when can it be broadcast on the radio?

Bevin: At 9.30 p.m. GMT on Thursday.

Stalin: Good.

Byrnes: Concerning the Ruhr area. The Russian text of the protocol says that the Conference examined the Soviet proposals concerning the Ruhr industrial area. It was decided to refer this question for discussion by the Council of Foreign Ministers in London. The English text of the protocol makes no mention of the Ruhr area. I understand that no such decision was taken, but the President says that it was adopted on his proposal. I propose, therefore, that the wording should be made more precise. It says nothing here of the content of the Soviet delegation's proposal which is being referred to the Council of Foreign Ministers in London.

Stalin: I think this question should be deleted.

Truman: Good.

Stalin: [After studying the text of a message of greetings to Churchill and Eden.] I have no objection to the proposed text of the greetings.

Attlee: I propose that the telegram in English should be signed by the President and the Generalissimo.

Stalin: Could the President, as the Chairman of the Conference, sign first?

Attlee: All the three signatures will be there.

[The telegram of greetings is signed by the three Heads of Government.]

Byrnes: I think that we should appoint representatives to verify the text of the protocol.

[Representatives are appointed to a commission to edit the protocol.]

Truman: I declare the Berlin Conference closed. Until our next meeting, which, I hope, will be soon.

Stalin: Let's hope so.

Attlee: Mr. President, before we separate I should like to express our gratitude to the Generalissimo for the excellent measures taken both for our accommodation here and to provide the conditions for work, and to you, Mr. President, for so ably presiding over this Conference.

I should like to express the hope that this Conference will be an important milestone on the road which our three nations are taking together towards a stable peace, and that the friendship between the three of us who have met here will be strong and enduring.

Stalin: That is also our hope.

Truman: On behalf of the American delegation I want to thank the Generalissimo for everything he has done for us, and I wish to join Mr. Attlee in what he has said here.

Stalin: The Russian delegation joins Mr. Attlee in the gratitude he expressed to the President for his able and apt chairmanship.

Truman: I thank you for your kind co-operation in settling all the important questions.

Stalin: I should personally like to thank Mr. Byrnes, who has helped our work very much and has promoted the achievement of our decisions.

Byrnes: I am deeply touched by the Generalissimo's kind words, and I hope that together with my colleagues I have been of use in the work of the Conference.

Stalin: The Conference, I believe, can be considered a success.

Truman: I want to thank the other Foreign Ministers and all those who have helped us so much in our work.

Attlee: I join in the expression of these feelings in respect of our Foreign Ministers.

Truman: I declare the Berlin Conference closed.

[*The Conference ended at 00.30 hours on August 2, 1945.*]

COMMUNIQUÉ ON THE TRIPARTITE CONFERENCE OF BERLIN

I

On July 17, 1945, the President of the United States of America, Harry S. Truman, the Chairman of the Council of People's Commissars of the Union of Soviet Socialist Republics, Generalissimo J. V. Stalin, and the Prime Minister of Great Britain, Winston S. Churchill, together with Mr. Clement R. Attlee, met in the Tripartite Conference of Berlin. They were accompanied by the Foreign Secretaries of the Three Governments, Mr. James F. Byrnes, Mr. V. M. Molotov, and Mr. Anthony Eden, the Chiefs of Staff, and other advisers.

There were nine meetings between July 17 and July 25. The Conference was then interrupted for two days while the results of the British general election were being declared.

On July 28, Mr. Attlee returned to the Conference as Prime Minister, accompanied by the new Secretary of State for Foreign Affairs, Mr. Ernest Bevin. Four more sittings then took place. During the course of the Conference there were regular meetings of the Heads of the Three Governments accompanied by the Foreign Secretaries, and also of the Foreign Secretaries alone. Committees appointed by the Foreign Secretaries for preliminary consideration of questions before the Conference also met daily.

The meetings of the Conference were held at the Cecilienhof near Potsdam. The Conference ended on August 2, 1945.

Important decisions and agreements were reached. Views were exchanged on a number of other questions and consideration of these matters will be continued by the Council of Foreign Ministers established by the Conference.

President Truman, Generalissimo Stalin and Prime Minister Attlee leave Conference, which has strengthened the ties between the Three Governments and extended the scope of their collaboration and understanding, with renewed confidence that their Governments and peoples, together with the other United Nations, will ensure the creation of a just and enduring peace.

II

ESTABLISHMENT OF A COUNCIL
OF FOREIGN MINISTERS

A. The Conference reached an agreement for the establishment of a Council of Foreign Ministers representing the five principal Powers to continue the necessary preparatory work for the peace settlements and to take up other matters which from time to time may be referred to the Council by agreement of the Governments participating in the Council.

The text of the agreement for the establishment of the Council of Foreign Ministers is as follows:

(1) There shall be established a Council composed of the Foreign Ministers of the United Kingdom, the Union of Soviet Socialist Republics, China, France and the United States.

(2) (i) The Council shall normally meet in London, which shall be the permanent seat of the joint Secretariat which the Council will form. Each of the Foreign Ministers will be accompanied by a high-ranking Deputy, duly authorised to carry on the work of the Council in the absence of his Foreign Minister, and by a small staff of technical advisers.

(ii) The first meeting of the Council shall be held in London not later than September 1st, 1945. Meetings may be held by common agreement in other capitals as may be agreed from time to time.

(3) (i) As its immediate important task, the Council shall be authorised to draw up, with a view to their submission to the United Nations, treaties of peace with Italy, Rumania, Bulgaria, Hungary and Finland, and to propose settlements of territorial questions outstanding on the termination of the war in Europe. That Council shall be utilised for the preparation of a peace settlement for Germany to be ac-

cepted by the Government of Germany when a government adequate for the purpose is established.

(ii) For the discharge of each of these tasks the Council will be composed of the Members representing those States which were signatory to the terms of surrender imposed upon the enemy State concerned. For the purposes of the peace settlement for Italy, France shall be regarded as a signatory to the terms of surrender for Italy. Other Members will be invited to participate when matters directly concerning them are under discussion.

(iii) Other matters may from time to time be referred to the Council by agreement between the Member Governments.

(4) (i) Whenever the Council is considering a question of direct interest to a State not represented thereon, such State should be invited to send representatives to participate in the discussion and study of that question.

(ii) The Council may adapt its procedure to the particular problem under consideration. In some cases it may hold its own preliminary discussions prior to the participation of other interested States. In other cases, the Council may convoke a formal conference of the States chiefly interested in seeking a solution of the particular problem.

B. In accordance with the decision of the Conference the Three Governments have each addressed an identical invitation to the Governments of China and France to adopt this text and to join in establishing the Council.

C. The establishment of the Council of Foreign Ministers for the specific purposes named in the text will be without prejudice to the agreement of the Crimea Conference that there should be periodic consultation among the Foreign Secretaries of the United States, the Union of Soviet Socialist Republics and the United Kingdom.

D. The Conference also considered the position of the European Advisory Commission in the light of the agreement to establish the Council of Foreign Ministers. It was noted with satisfaction that the Commission had ably discharged its principal tasks by the recommendations that it had furnished for the terms of Germany's unconditional surrender, for the zones of occupation in Germany and Austria, and for the inter-Allied control machinery in those countries. It was felt that further work of a detailed character for the co-ordination of Allied policy for the control of

Germany and Austria would in future fall within the competence of the Allied Control Council at Berlin and the Allied Commission at Vienna. Accordingly, it was agreed to recommend that the European Advisory Commission be dissolved.

III

GERMANY

The Allied armies are in occupation of the whole of Germany and the German people have begun to atone for the terrible crimes committed under the leadership of those whom, in the hour of their success, they openly approved and blindly obeyed.

Agreement has been reached at this Conference on the political and economic principles of a co-ordinated Allied policy toward defeated Germany during the period of Allied control.

The purpose of this agreement is to carry out the Crimea declaration on Germany. German militarism and Nazism will be extirpated and the Allies will take in agreement together, now and in the future, the other measures necessary to assure that Germany never again will threaten her neighbours or the peace of the world.

It is not the intention of the Allies to destroy or enslave the German people. It is the intention of the Allies that the German people be given the opportunity to prepare for the eventual reconstruction of their life on a democratic and peaceful basis. If their own efforts are steadily directed to this end, it will be possible for them in due course to take their place among the free and peaceful peoples of the world.

The text of the agreement is as follows:

THE POLITICAL AND ECONOMIC PRINCIPLES TO GOVERN THE TREATMENT OF GERMANY IN THE INITIAL CONTROL PERIOD

A. POLITICAL PRINCIPLES

1. In accordance with the Agreement on Control Machinery in Germany, supreme authority in Germany is exercised on instructions from their respective Governments, by

the Commanders-in-Chief of the Armed Forces of the Union of Soviet Socialist Republics, the United States of America, the United Kingdom, and the French Republic, each in his own zone of occupation, and also jointly, in matters affecting Germany as a whole, in their capacity as members of the Control Council.

2. So far as is practicable, there shall be uniformity of treatment of the German population throughout Germany.

3. The purposes of the occupation of Germany by which the Control Council shall be guided are:

(I) The complete disarmament and demilitarisation of Germany and the elimination or control of all German industry that could be used for military production. To these ends:—

(a) All German land, naval and air forces, the S.S., S.A., S.D. and Gestapo, with all their organisations, staffs and institutions, including the General Staff, the Officers' Corps, Reserve Corps, military schools, war veterans' organisations and all other military and quasi-military organisations, together with all clubs and associations which serve to keep alive the military tradition in Germany, shall be completely and finally abolished in such manner as permanently to prevent the revival or reorganisation of German militarism and Nazism;

(b) All arms, ammunition and implements of war and all specialised facilities for their production shall be held at the disposal of the Allies or destroyed. The maintenance and production of all aircraft and all arms, ammunition and implements of war shall be prevented.

(II) To convince the German people that they have suffered a total military defeat and that they cannot escape responsibility for what they have brought upon themselves, since their own ruthless warfare and the fanatical Nazi resistance have destroyed German economy and made chaos and suffering inevitable.

(III) To destroy the National Socialist Party and its affiliated and supervised organisations, to dissolve all Nazi institutions, to ensure that they are not revived in any form, and to prevent all Nazi and militarist activity or propaganda.

(IV) To prepare for the eventual reconstruction of German political life on a democratic basis and for eventual peaceful co-operation in international life by Germany.

4. All Nazi laws which provided the basis of the Hitler regime or established discrimination on grounds of race, creed, or political opinion shall be abolished. No such discriminations, whether legal, administrative or otherwise, shall be tolerated.

5. War criminals and those who have participated in planning or carrying out Nazi enterprises involving or resulting in atrocities or war crimes shall be arrested and brought to judgement. Nazi leaders, influential Nazi supporters and high officials of Nazi organisations and institutions and any other persons dangerous to the occupation or its objectives shall be arrested and interned.

6. All members of the Nazi Party who have been more than nominal participants in its activities and all other persons hostile to Allied purposes shall be removed from public and semi-public office, and from positions of responsibility in important private undertakings. Such persons shall be replaced by persons who, by their political and moral qualities, are deemed capable of assisting in developing genuine democratic institutions in Germany.

7. German education shall be so controlled as completely to eliminate Nazi and militarist doctrines and to make possible the successful development of democratic ideas.

8. The judicial system will be reorganised in accordance with the principles of democracy, of justice under law, and of equal rights for all citizens without distinction of race, nationality or religion.

9. The administration of affairs in Germany should be directed towards the decentralisation of the political structure and the development of local responsibility. To this end:

(I) local self-government shall be restored throughout Germany on democratic principles and in particular through elective councils as rapidly as is consistent with military security and the purposes of military occupation;

(II) all democratic political parties with rights of assembly and of public discussion shall be allowed and encouraged throughout Germany;

(III) representative and elective principles shall be introduced into regional, provincial and state (Land) administration as rapidly as may be justified by the successful application of these principles in local self-government;

(IV) for the time being no central German Government

shall be established. Notwithstanding this, however, certain essential central German administrative departments, headed by State Secretaries, shall be established, particularly in the fields of finance, transport, communications, foreign trade and industry. Such departments will act under the direction of the Control Council.

10. Subject to the necessity for maintaining military security, freedom of speech, press and religion shall be permitted, and religious institutions shall be respected. Subject likewise to the maintenance of military security, the formation of free trade unions shall be permitted.

B. ECONOMIC PRINCIPLES

11. In order to eliminate Germany's war potential, the production of arms, ammunition and implements of war as well as all types of aircraft and sea-going ships shall be prohibited and prevented. Production of metals, chemicals, machinery and other items that are directly necessary to a war economy shall be rigidly controlled and restricted to Germany's approved post-war peace-time needs to meet the objectives stated in Paragraph 15. Productive capacity not needed for permitted production shall be removed in accordance with the reparations plan recommended by the Allied Reparations Commission and approved by the Governments concerned or if not removed shall be destroyed.

12. At the earliest practicable date, the German economy shall be decentralised for the purpose of eliminating the present excessive concentration of economic power as exemplified in particular by cartels, syndicates, trusts and other monopolistic arrangements.

13. In organising the German economy, primary emphasis shall be given to the development of agriculture and peaceful domestic industries.

14. During the period of occupation Germany shall be treated as a single economic unit. To this end common policies shall be established in regard to:

(a) mining and industrial production and allocations;
(b) agriculture, forestry and fishing;
(c) wages, prices and rationing;
(d) import and export programmes for Germany as a whole;

(e) currency and banking, central taxation and customs;

(f) reparation and removal of industrial war potential;

(g) transportation and communications.

In applying these policies account shall be taken, where appropriate, of varying local conditions.

15. Allied controls shall be imposed upon the German economy but only to the extent necessary:

(a) to carry out programmes of industrial disarmament and demilitarisation, of reparations, and of approved exports and imports;

(b) to assure the production and maintenance of goods and services required to meet the needs of the occupying forces and displaced persons in Germany and essential to maintain in Germany average living standards not exceeding the average of the standards of living of European countries (European countries means all European countries excluding the United Kingdom and the Union of Soviet Socialist Republics);

(c) to ensure in the manner determined by the Control Council the equitable distribution of essential commodities between the several zones so as to produce a balanced economy throughout Germany and reduce the need for imports;

(d) to control German industry and all economic and financial international transactions, including exports and imports, with the aim of preventing Germany from developing a war potential and of achieving the other objectives named herein;

(e) to control all German public or private scientific bodies, research and experimental institutions, laboratories, etc., connected with economic activities.

16. In the imposition and maintenance of economic controls established by the Control Council, German administrative machinery shall be created and the German authorities shall be required to the fullest extent practicable to proclaim and assume administration of such controls. Thus it should be brought home to the German people that the responsibility for the administration of such controls and any breakdown in these controls will rest with themselves. Any German controls which may run counter to the objectives of occupation will be prohibited.

17. Measures shall be promptly taken:

(a) to effect essential repair of transport;

(b) to enlarge coal production;

(c) to maximise agricultural output; and

(d) to effect emergency repair of housing and essential utilities.

18. Appropriate steps shall be taken by the Control Council to exercise control and the power of disposition over German-owned external assets not already under the control of United Nations which have taken part in the war against Germany.

19. Payment of reparations should leave enough resources to enable the German people to subsist without external assistance. In working out the economic balance of Germany the necessary means must be provided to pay for imports approved by the Control Council in Germany. The proceeds of exports from current production and stocks shall be available in the first place for payment for such imports.

The above clause will not apply to the equipment and products referred to in paragraphs 4(a) and 4(b) of the Reparations Agreement.

IV

REPARATIONS FROM GERMANY

In accordance with the Crimea decision that Germany be compelled to compensate to the greatest possible extent for the loss and suffering that she has caused to the United Nations and for which the German people cannot escape responsibility, the following agreement on reparations was reached:

1. Reparation claims of the U.S.S.R. shall be met by removals from the zone of Germany occupied by the U.S.S.R. and from appropriate German external assets.

2. The U.S.S.R. undertakes to settle the reparation claims of Poland from its own share of reparations.

3. The reparation claims of the United States, the United Kingdom and other countries entitled to reparations shall be met from the Western zones and from appropriate German external assets.

4. In addition to the reparations to be taken by the U.S.S.R. from its own zone of occupation, the U.S.S.R. shall receive additionally from the Western zones:

(a) 15 per cent of such usable and complete industrial capital equipment, in the first place from the metallurgical, chemical and machine manufacturing industries, as is unnecessary for the German peace economy and should be removed from the Western zones of Germany, in exchange for an equivalent value of food, coal, potash, zinc, timber, clay products, petroleum products, and such other commodities as may be agreed upon.

(b) 10 per cent of such industrial capital equipment as is unnecessary for the German peace economy and should be removed from the Western zones, to be transferred to the Soviet Government on reparations account without payment or exchange of any kind in return.

Removals of equipment as provided in (a) and (b) above shall be made simultaneously.

5. The amount of equipment to be removed from the Western zones on account of reparations must be determined within six months from now at the latest.

6. Removals of industrial capital equipment shall begin as soon as possible and shall be completed within two years from the determination specified in Paragraph 5. The delivery of products covered by 4(a) above shall begin as soon as possible and shall be made by the U.S.S.R. in agreed installments within five years of the date hereof. The determination of the amount and character of the industrial capital equipment unnecessary for the German peace economy and therefore available for reparations shall be made by the Control Council under policies fixed by the Allied Reparations Commission with the participation of France, subject to the final approval of the zone Commander in the zone from which the equipment is to be removed.

7. Prior to the fixing of the total amount of equipment subject to removal, advance deliveries shall be made in respect of such equipment as will be determined to be eligible for delivery in accordance with the procedure set forth in the last sentence of Paragraph 6.

8. The Soviet Government renounces all claims in respect of reparations to shares of German enterprises which are located in the Western zones of occupation in Germany as well as to German foreign assets in all countries except those specified in Paragraph 9 below.

9. The Governments of the U.K. and the U.S.A. renounce their claims in respect of reparations to shares of German

enterprises which are located in the Eastern zone of occupation in Germany, as well as to German foreign assets in Bulgaria, Finland, Hungary, Rumania and Eastern Austria.

10. The Soviet Government makes no claims to gold captured by the Allied troops in Germany.

V

DISPOSAL OF THE GERMAN NAVY AND MERCHANT MARINE

The Conference agreed in principle upon arrangements for the use and disposal of the surrendered German fleet and merchant ships. It was decided that the Three Governments would appoint experts to work out together detailed plans to give effect to the agreed principles. A further joint statement will be published simultaneously by the Three Governments in due course.

VI

CITY OF KÖNIGSBERG AND THE ADJACENT AREA

The Conference examined a proposal by the Soviet Government that pending the final determination of territorial questions at the peace settlement, the section of the western frontier of the Union of Soviet Socialist Republics which is adjacent to the Baltic Sea should pass from a point on the eastern shore of the Bay of Danzig to the east, north of Braunsberg-Goldap, to the meeting point of the frontiers of Lithuania, the Polish Republic and East Prussia.

The Conference has agreed in principle to the proposal of the Soviet Government concerning the transfer to the Soviet Union of the City of Königsberg and the area adjacent to it as described above subject to expert examination of the actual frontier.

The President of the United States and the British Prime Minister have declared that they will support the proposal of the Conference at the forthcoming peace settlement.

VII

WAR CRIMINALS

The Three Governments have taken note of the discussions which have been proceeding in recent weeks in London between British, United States, Soviet and French representatives with a view to reaching agreement on the methods of trial of those major war criminals whose crimes under the Moscow Declaration of October 1943 have no particular geographical localisation. The Three Governments reaffirm their intention to bring those criminals to swift and sure justice. They hope that the negotiations in London will result in speedy agreement being reached for this purpose, and they regard it as a matter of great importance that the trial of those major criminals should begin at the earliest possible date. The first list of defendants will be published before September 1.

VIII

AUSTRIA

The Conference examined a proposal by the Soviet Government on the extension of the authority of the Austrian Provisional Government to all of Austria.

The Three Governments agreed that they were prepared to examine this question after the entry of the British and American forces into the city of Vienna.

IX

POLAND

The Conference considered questions relating to the Polish Provisional Government and the western boundary of Poland.

On the Polish Provisional Government of National Unity they defined their attitude in the following statement:

A. We have taken note with pleasure of the agreement reached among representative Poles from Poland and abroad which has made possible the formation, in accordance with the decisions reached at the Crimea Conference, of a Polish Provisional Government of National Unity recognised by the Three Powers. The establishment by the British and United States Governments of diplomatic relations with the Polish Provisional Government has resulted in the withdrawal of their recognition from the former Polish Government in London, which no longer exists.

The British and United States Governments have taken measures to protect the interest of the Polish Provisional Government as the recognised Government of the Polish State in the property belonging to the Polish State located in their territories and under their control, whatever the form of this property may be.

They have further taken measures to prevent alienation to third parties of such property. All proper facilities will be given to the Polish Provisional Government for the exercise of the ordinary legal remedies for the recovery of any property belonging to the Polish State which may have been wrongfully alienated.

The Three Powers are anxious to assist the Polish Provisional Government in facilitating the return to Poland as soon as practicable of all Poles abroad who wish to go, including members of the Polish Armed Forces and the Merchant Marine. They expect that those Poles who return home shall be accorded personal and property rights on the same basis as all Polish citizens.

The Three Powers note that the Polish Provisional Government in accordance with the decisions of the Crimea Conference has agreed to the holding of free and unfettered elections as soon as possible on the basis of universal suffrage and secret ballot in which all democratic and anti-Nazi parties shall have the right to take part and to put forward candidates, and that representatives of the Allied press shall enjoy full freedom to report to the world upon developments in Poland before and during the elections.

B. The following agreement was reached on the western frontier of Poland:

In conformity with the agreement on Poland reached at the Crimea Conference the three Heads of Government have sought the opinion of the Polish Provisional Government of National Unity in regard to the accession of territory in the north and west which Poland should receive. The President of the National Council of Poland and members of the Polish Provisional Government of National

Unity have been received at the Conference and have fully presented their views. The three Heads of Government reaffirmed their opinion that the final delimitation of the western frontier of Poland should await the peace settlement.

The three Heads of Government agree that, pending the final determination of Poland's western frontier, the former German territories east of a line running from the Baltic Sea immediately west of Swinemünde, and thence along the Oder River to the confluence of the western Neisse River and along the western Neisse to the Czechoslovak frontier, including that portion of East Prussia not placed under the administration of the Union of Soviet Socialist Republics in accordance with the understanding reached at this Conference and including the area of the former free city of Danzig, shall be under the administration of the Polish State and for such purposes should not be considered as part of the Soviet zone of occupation in Germany.

X

CONCLUSION OF PEACE TREATIES AND ADMISSION TO THE UNITED NATIONS ORGANISATION

The Conference agreed upon the following statement of common policy for establishing, as soon as possible, the conditions of lasting peace after victory in Europe:

The Three Governments consider it desirable that the present anomalous position of Italy, Bulgaria, Finland, Hungary and Rumania should be terminated by the conclusion of Peace Treaties. They trust that the other interested Allied Governments will share these views.

For their part the Three Governments have included the preparation of a Peace Treaty for Italy as the first among the immediate important tasks to be undertaken by the new Council of Foreign Ministers. Italy was the first of the Axis Powers to break with Germany, to whose defeat she has made a material contribution, and has now joined with the Allies in the struggle against Japan. Italy has freed herself from the Fascist regime and is making good progress towards the re-establishment of a democratic government and institutions. The conclusion of such a Peace Treaty with a recognised and democratic Italian Government will make it possible for the Three Governments to fulfil their desire to support an application from Italy for membership of the United Nations.

The Three Governments have also charged the Council of Foreign Ministers with the task of preparing Peace Treaties for Bulgaria, Finland, Hungary and Rumania. The conclusion of Peace Treaties with recognised democratic Governments in these States will also enable the Three Governments to support applications from them for membership of the United Nations. The Three Governments agree to examine each separately in the near future, in the light of the conditions then prevailing, the establishment of diplomatic relations with Finland, Rumania, Bulgaria, and Hungary to the extent possible prior to the conclusion of peace treaties with those countries.

The Three Governments have no doubt that in view of the changed conditions resulting from the termination of the war in Europe, representatives of the Allied press will enjoy full freedom to report to the world upon developments in Rumania, Bulgaria, Hungary and Finland.

As regards the admission of other states into the United Nations Organisation, Article 4 of the Charter of the United Nations declares that:

"1. Membership in the United Nations is open to all other peace-loving States who accept the obligations contained in the present Charter and, in the judgement of the organisation, are able and willing to carry out these obligations;

"2. The admission of any such State to membership in the United Nations will be effected by a decision of the General Assembly upon the recommendation of the Security Council."

The Three Governments, so far as they are concerned, will support applications for membership from those States which have remained neutral during the war and which fulfil the qualifications set out above.

The Three Governments feel bound however to make it clear that they for their part would not favour any application for membership put forward by the present Spanish Government, which, having been founded with the support of the Axis Powers, does not, in view of its origins, its nature, its record and its close association with the aggressor States, possess the qualifications necessary to justify such membership.

XI

TERRITORIAL TRUSTEESHIPS

The Conference examined a proposal by the Soviet Government concerning trusteeship territories as defined in the decision of the Crimea Conference and in the Charter of the United Nations Organisation.

After an exchange of views on this question it was decided that the disposition of any former Italian colonial territories was one to be decided in connection with the preparation of a peace treaty for Italy and that the question of Italian colonial territories would be considered by the September Council of Ministers of Foreign Affairs.

XII

REVISED ALLIED CONTROL COMMISSION PROCEDURE IN RUMANIA, BULGARIA AND HUNGARY

The Three Governments took note that the Soviet representatives on the Allied Control Commissions in Rumania, Bulgaria and Hungary, have communicated to their United Kingdom and United States colleagues proposals for improving the work of the Control Commissions, now that hostilities in Europe have ceased.

The Three Governments agreed that the revision of the procedures of the Allied Control Commissions in these countries would now be undertaken, taking into account the interests and responsibilities of the Three Governments which together presented the terms of armistice to the respective countries, and accepting as a basis the agreed proposals.

XIII

ORDERLY TRANSFERS OF GERMAN POPULATIONS

The Conference reached the following agreement on the removal of Germans from Poland, Czechoslovakia and Hungary:

The Three Governments, having considered the question in all its aspects, recognise that the transfer to Germany of

German populations, or elements thereof, remaining in Poland, Czechoslovakia and Hungary, will have to be undertaken. They agree that any transfers that take place should be effected in an orderly and humane manner. Since the influx of a large number of Germans into Germany would increase the burden already resting on the occupying authorities, they consider that the Allied Control Council in Germany should in the first instance examine the problem with special regard to the question of the equitable distribution of these Germans among the several zones of occupation. They are accordingly instructing their respective representatives on the Control Council to report to their Governments as soon as possible the extent to which such persons have already entered Germany from Poland, Czechoslovakia and Hungary, and to submit an estimate of the time and rate at which further transfers could be carried out, having regard to the present situation in Germany.

The Czechoslovak Government, the Polish Provisional Government and the Control Council in Hungary are at the same time being informed of the above, and are being requested meanwhile to suspend further expulsions pending the examination by the Governments concerned of the report from their representatives on the Control Council.

XIV

MILITARY TALKS

During the Conference there were meetings between the Chiefs of Staff of the Three Governments on military matters of common interest.

XV

[*Here a list of the U.S.S.R., the U.S.A. and the United Kingdom delegates to the Conference is given.*]

J. V. STALIN
HARRY S. TRUMAN
C. R. ATTLEE

The Berlin Conference of the Three Heads of Government of the U.S.S.R., U.S.A., and U.K., which took place from July 17 to August 2, 1945, came to the following conclusions:

I

ESTABLISHMENT OF A COUNCIL OF FOREIGN MINISTERS

A. The Conference reached the following agreement for the establishment of a Council of Foreign Ministers to do the necessary preparatory work for the peace settlements:

"(1) There shall be established a Council composed of the Foreign Ministers of the United Kingdom, the Union of Soviet Socialist Republics, China, France and the United States.

"(2) (i) The Council shall normally meet in London, which shall be the permanent seat of the joint Secretariat which the Council will form. Each of the Foreign Ministers will be accompanied by a high-ranking Deputy, duly authorised to carry on the work of the Council in the absence of his Foreign Minister, and by a small staff of technical advisers.

"(ii) The first meeting of the Council shall be held in London not later than September 1st, 1945. Meetings may be held by common agreement in other capitals as may be agreed from time to time.

"(3) (i) As its immediate important task, the Council shall be authorised to draw up, with a view to their submission to the United Nations, treaties of peace with Italy, Rumania, Bulgaria, Hungary and Finland, and to propose settlements of territorial questions outstanding on the termination of the war in Europe. The Council shall be utilised for the preparation of a peace settlement for Germany to be accepted by the Government of Germany when a government adequate for the purpose is established.

"(ii) For the discharge of each of these tasks the Council will be composed of the Members representing those States which were signatory to the terms of surrender imposed upon the enemy State concerned. For the purposes of the peace settlement for Italy, France shall be regarded as a signatory to the terms of surrender for Italy. Other Members will be invited to participate when matters directly concerning them are under discussion.

"(iii) Other matters may from time to time be referred to the Council by agreement between the Member Governments.

"(4) (i) Whenever the Council is considering a question of direct interest to a State not represented thereon, such State should be invited to send representatives to participate in the discussion and study of that qestion.

"(ii) The Council may adapt its procedure to the particular problem under consideration. In some cases it may hold its own preliminary discussions prior to the participation of other interested States. In other cases, the Council may convoke a formal conference of the States chiefly interested in seeking a solution of the particular problem."

B. It was agreed that the Three Governments should each address an identical invitation to the Governments of China and France to adopt this text and to join in establishing the Council. The text of the approved invitation was as follows:

COUNCIL OF FOREIGN MINISTERS

DRAFT FOR IDENTICAL INVITATION TO BE SENT SEPARATELY BY EACH OF THE THREE GOVERNMENTS TO THE GOVERNMENTS OF CHINA AND FRANCE

"The Governments of the United Kingdom, the United States and the U.S.S.R. consider it necessary to begin without delay the essential preparatory work upon the peace settlements in Europe. To this end they are agreed that there should be established a Council of the Foreign Ministers of the Five Great Powers to prepare treaties of peace with the European enemy States, for submission to the United Nations. The Council would also be empowered to propose settlements of outstanding territorial questions in

Europe and to consider such other matters as Member Governments might agree to refer to it.

"The text adopted by the Three Governments is as follows:

"In agreement with the Governments of ... the Government of ... extends a cordial invitation to the Government of China (France) to adopt the text quoted above and to join in setting up the Council.

"The Government of ... attaches much importance to the participation of the Chinese Government (French Government) in the proposed arrangements and it hopes to receive an early and favourable reply to this invitation."

C. It was understood that the establishment of the Council of Foreign Ministers for the specific purposes named in the text would be without prejudice to the agreement of the Crimea Conference that there should be periodical consultation between the Foreign Secretaries of the United States, the Union of Soviet Socialist Republics and the United Kingdom.

D. The Conference also considered the position of the European Advisory Commission in the light of the agreement to establish the Council of Foreign Ministers. It was noted with satisfaction that the Commission had ably discharged its principal tasks by the recommendations that it had furnished for the terms of surrender for Germany, for the zones of occupation in Germany and Austria and for the inter-Allied control machinery in those countries. It was felt that further work of a detailed character for the co-ordination of Allied policy for the control of Germany and Austria would in future fall within the competence of the Allied Control Commission at Berlin and the Allied Commission at Vienna. Accordingly the Conference agreed to recommend to the Member Governments of the European Advisory Commission that the Commission might now be dissolved.

[*The subsequent text is omitted, as it is repeated in the Communiqué on the Tripartite Conference of Berlin.— Editor's Note.*]

DISPOSAL OF THE GERMAN NAVY AND MERCHANT MARINE

A

The following principles for the distribution of the German Navy were agreed:

(1) The total strength of the German surface navy, excluding ships sunk and those taken over from Allied Nations, but including ships under construction or repair, shall be divided equally among the U.S.S.R., U.K., and U.S.

(2) Ships under construction or repair mean those ships whose construction or repair may be completed within three to six months, according to the type of ship. Whether such ships under construction or repair shall be completed or repaired shall be determined by the technical commission appointed by the Three Powers and referred to below, subject to the principle that their completion or repair must be achieved within the time limits above provided, without any increase of skilled employment in the German shipyards and without permitting the reopening of any German ship building or connected industries. Completion date means the date when a ship is able to go out on its first trip, or, under peace-time standards, would refer to the customary date of delivery by shipyard to the Government.

(3) The larger part of the German submarine fleet shall be sunk. Not more than thirty submarines shall be preserved and divided equally between the U.S.S.R., U.K. and the U.S. for experimental and technical purposes.

(4) All stocks of armament, ammunition and supplies of the German Navy appertaining to the vessels transferred pursuant to paragraphs (1) and (3) hereof shall be handed over to the respective Powers receiving such ships.

(5) The Three Governments agree to constitute a tripartite naval commission comprising two representatives for each Government, accompanied by the requisite staff, to submit agreed recommendations to the Three Governments for the allocation of specific German warships and to handle other detailed matters arising out of the agreement between the Three Governments regarding the German

fleet. The Commission will hold its first meeting not later than 15th August, 1945, in Berlin, which shall be its headquarters. Each Delegation on the Commission will have the right on the basis of reciprocity to inspect German warships wherever they may be located.

(6) The Three Governments agreed that transfers, including those of ships under construction and repair, shall be completed as soon as possible, but not later than 15th February, 1946. The Commission will submit fortnightly reports, including proposals for the progressive allocation of the vessels when agreed by the Commission.

B

The following principles for the distribution of the German Merchant Marine were agreed.

(1) The German Merchant Marine, surrendered to the Three Powers and wherever located, shall be divided equally among the U.S.S.R., the U.K., and the U.S. The actual transfers of the ships to the respective countries shall take place as soon as practicable after the end of the war against Japan. The United Kingdom and the United States will provide out of their shares of the surrendered German merchant ships appropriate amounts for other Allied States whose merchant marines have suffered heavy losses in the common cause against Germany, except that the Soviet Union shall provide out of its share for Poland.

(2) The allocation, manning, and operation of these ships during the Japanese War period shall fall under the cognizance and authority of the Combined Shipping Adjustment Board and the United Maritime Authority.

(3) While actual transfer of the ships shall be delayed until after the end of the war with Japan, a Tripartite Shipping Commission shall inventory and value all available ships and recommend a specific distribution in accordance with Paragraph (1).

(4) German inland and coastal ships determined to be necessary to the maintenance of the basic German peace economy by the Allied Control Council of Germany shall not be included in the shipping pool thus divided among the Three Powers.

(5) The Three Governments agree to constitute a tripartite merchant marine commission comprising two represen-

tatives for each Government, accompanied by the requisite staff, to submit agreed recommendations to the Three Governments for the allocation of specific German merchant ships and to handle other detailed matters arising out of the agreement between the Three Governments regarding the German merchant ships. The Commission will hold its first meeting not later than September 1st, 1945, in Berlin, which shall be its headquarters. Each delegation on the Commission will have the right on the basis of reciprocity to inspect the German merchant ships wherever they may be located.

[*The subsequent text is omitted, as it is repeated in the Communiqué on the Tripartite Conference of Berlin.—Editor's Note.*]

XIV

IRAN

It was agreed that Allied troops should be withdrawn immediately from Tehran, and that further stages of the withdrawal of troops from Iran should be considered at the meeting of the Council of Foreign Ministers to be held in London in September 1945.

XV

THE INTERNATIONAL ZONE OF TANGIER

A proposal by the Soviet Government was examined and the following decisions were reached.

Having examined the question of the Zone of Tangier, the Three Governments have agreed that this Zone, which includes the city of Tangier and the area adjacent to it, in view of its special strategic importance shall remain international.

The question of Tangier will be discussed in the near future at a meeting in Paris of representatives of the Governments of the Union of Soviet Socialist Republics, the United States of America, the United Kingdom and France.

XVI

THE BLACK SEA STRAITS

The Three Governments recognised that the Convention concluded at Montreux should be revised, as failing to meet present-day conditions.

It was agreed that as the next step the matter should be the subject of direct conversations between each of the Three Governments and the Turkish Government.

XVII

INTERNATIONAL INLAND WATERWAYS

The Conference considered a proposal of the U.S. Delegation on this subject and agreed to refer it for consideration to the forthcoming meeting of the Council of Foreign Ministers in London.

XVIII

EUROPEAN INLAND TRANSPORT CONFERENCE

The British and U.S. Delegations to the Conference informed the Soviet Delegation of the desire of the British and U.S. Governments to reconvene the European Inland Transport Conference and stated that they would welcome assurance that the Soviet Government would participate in the work of the reconvened Conference. The Soviet Government agreed that it would participate in this Conference.

XIX

DIRECTIVES TO MILITARY COMMANDERS
ON ALLIED CONTROL COUNCIL FOR GERMANY

The Three Governments agreed that each would send a directive to its representative on the Control Council concerning questions coming within the scope of his competence.

XX

USE OF ALLIED PROPERTY FOR SATELLITE
REPARATIONS OR "WAR TROPHIES"

The Conference decided to accept in principle the proposal of the American Delegation. [. . .] The wording of this proposal is to be agreed upon through the diplomatic channel.

[*The subsequent text is omitted, as it is repeated in the Communiqué on the Tripartite Conference of Berlin.— Editor's Note.*]

J. V. STALIN
HARRY S. TRUMAN
C. R. ATTLEE

APPENDICES

I

TEHRAN CONFERENCE OF THE LEADERS OF THE THREE GREAT POWERS. Introduction. *International Affairs,* 1961, No. 7, 133-134

To mark the 20th anniversary of the outbreak of the Great Patriotic War of the Soviet Union the Editors of *International Affairs* intend to publish the important documents and material of the principal Allied conferences of the anti-Hitler coalition.

It is well known that these conferences played an outstanding role in consolidating the anti-Hitler coalition headed by the Soviet Union, the United States and Great Britain. These conferences were also of great importance in creating a foundation for the development of friendly Soviet-Anglo-American relations after the war. Unfortunately, as N. S. Khrushchov pointed out, "Soon after the Second World War ended, the influence of reactionary and militarist groups began to be increasingly evident in the policy of the United States of America, Britain and France. Their desire to enforce their will on other countries by economic and political pressure, threats and military provocation prevailed."

It is an incontestable fact, however, that the Second World War, and in particular the conferences of the leaders of the Three Great Powers, namely Tehran, Crimea and Potsdam, yielded convincing evidence that in spite of the radical distinctions in the political and social systems of the U.S.S.R., on the one hand, and of the United States and Britain on the other, they were able to co-operate with success in the struggle against the common enemy, that they sought and found mutually acceptable solutions of the controversial matters that arose between them, although their approach to these matters was at times quite different.

The military and political co-operation of the Soviet Union, the United States and Great Britain during the Second World War is one of the great lessons of history which must not be forgotten, although, regrettably, certain quarters in the United States and Britain are trying to do so.

Opinion in all countries has always shown great interest in Allied conferences during the war; people have always wanted to know the truth not only about the decisions taken—although they were the most important aspect of the conferences—but also about the views expressed by the conferees on the matters under discussion, the stand of the leaders of the Three Great Powers and their intentions.

Since the war there has been a crop of speculation in the West concerning the content of the talks at the Allied conferences. There were numerous attempts in the guise of "documents", memoires and "eye-witness" accounts to falsify the history of wartime international relations. It should be noted that this was done despite President Roosevelt's assurance at the Tehran Conference that "we do not intend to make public anything that will be said here...."

In the past these unseemly efforts were exposed in the Soviet press and given a fitting rebuff; we do not now think it necessary to dwell on this matter again, for the Soviet transcripts of the talks at the Allied conferences now being made public speak for themselves, and their publication will help to restore the truth of history.

They refute the inventions about the Soviet stand which are contained, in particular, in the collection of "documents" on the Tehran and Cairo conferences published by the State Department on June 17 of this year.

In this issue we give you the Soviet transcripts of the talks and sessions of the Tehran Conference, which was held from November 28 to December 1, 1943. They are published almost in their entirety; the parts left out pertain to secondary questions.

The principal question discussed at the conference was, naturally, the further conduct of the war against Nazi Germany. Accordingly, there was a detailed discussion of the opening of the Second Front in Europe, which the United States and Britain had long since promised to open but had not opened even by the time of the Tehran Conference. As a result, in late 1943, the Soviet Union and its army continued to bear the brunt of the war against Nazi Germany.

The discussion of this question is given in the transcript now published in sufficient detail and, in the opinion of the Editors, does not require any commentary. But the attention of readers should be drawn to Churchill's insistent desire to conduct military operations above all in the south of Europe, which, needless to say, could not ease the positions of the Soviet Army to any appreciable degree but conformed to the selfish interests of certain influential quarters in Great Britain.

Eventually, the Western Powers made a new promise at the Tehran Conference in respect of the Second Front: they said it would be opened only in May 1944. It is worth while to recall that the promise was kept in June 1944, when the war, as a result of the heroic efforts and historic victories of the Soviet Army, was already drawing to a close; actually, the opening of the Second Front did much more to further certain political interests of the United States and Britain than to speed up the defeat of Nazi Germany.

In connection with the discussion of military operations the United States and Britain proposed the inclusion of Turkey in the war on the side of the anti-Hitler coalition.

The concrete decisions adopted by the Tehran Conference on military matters were not made public for reasons of security in wartime, but the Three Power Declaration adopted by the conference on December 1, 1943, said: "as to war—our military staffs have joined in our round-table discussions, and we have concerted our plans for the destruction of the German forces. We have reached complete agreement as to the scope and timing of the operations to be undertaken from the east, west and south.

"The common understanding which we have here reached guarantees that victory will be ours."

At the Tehran Conference the American and British representatives once again put forward their plans of dividing Germany. The Soviet Government had always opposed the idea, and while taking part in the discussion of these plans as a matter of course, it prevented any definite decision from being taken. These plans were referred to the European Advisory Commission, which in the transcript is called the London Conference, and then to a special commission under the chairmanship of Anthony Eden, where they were finally shelved due to the stand of the Soviet representative. Thus, it was the negative attitude of the Soviet Union to the plans of dividing Germany that doomed them to failure.

We draw the reader's attention to the plans put forward by Roosevelt at the Tehran Conference to set up a post-war organization of nations to ensure peace and security in the future. The reader will find these plans interesting in many respects.

Those were the principal questions discussed at the conference.

But the meeting of the leaders of the Three Great Powers at Tehran had other results as well. The Three Power Declaration made public at the close of the conference expressed the "determination that our countries would continue to work together both in time of war as well as in the ensuing time of peace.... As for peacetime we are sure that the accord existing between us will ensure stable peace."

It is now even more evident than before that in the post-war years the ruling circles of the United States and Britain abandoned the policy of co-operation in the interests of peace and took the slippery and dangerous path of the cold war. But that policy is doomed.

The lofty ideas of peace and co-operation of nations maintained by the Soviet Government headed by the tireless champion of peace, N. S. Khrushchov, are winning the support of ever broader strata of world opinion.

II

TRANSCRIPT OF THE TALK BETWEEN J.V. STALIN AND F.D. ROOSEVELT, NOVEMBER 28, 1943. *International Affairs,* 1961, No.7, 134-136

Roosevelt inquires about the situation on the Soviet-German front.

Stalin replies that our troops recently withdrew from Zhitomir, an important railway junction.

R asks about the weather at the front.

S replies that the weather is favourable only in the Ukraine, but that on the other sectors of the front there is mud and the soil is not yet frozen.

R says that he would like to divert some 30 or 40 German divisions from the Soviet-German front.

S says that it would be a good thing, if possible.

R remarks that it is one of the questions on which he intends to give explanations in the next few days. The Americans are faced with maintaining a force numbering two million men at a distance of 3,000 miles from the American continent.

S says that there is need of transport and that he fully understands this.

R declares that in the United States ships are being built at a satisfactory pace.

He says that he would later like to speak with Marshal Stalin about the post-war period and about the distribution of the merchant fleet of Great Britain and the United States in such a way as to give the Soviet Union an opportunity to start developing commercial shipping. After the war the merchant navy of Britain and the United States will be much too big, and he, Roosevelt, expects to hand over a part of that navy to other United Nations.

S replies that that would be good. If the United States wants to do this it can very well do so. He feels bound to say that after the war Russia will be a big market for the United States.

R says that after the war the Americans will need great quantities of raw

338

materials, and that is why he thinks there will be close trade ties between our countries.

S agrees with this and adds that if the Americans will deliver equipment to us, we shall be able to deliver to them raw materials.

R says that he had very interesting talks with Chiang Kai-shek. He, Roosevelt, was very careful, and wished to avoid having the Chinese attend his meetings with Churchill and Marshal Stalin. He, Roosevelt, thinks that the Chinese are satisfied with the decisions adopted.

S remarks that the troops of Chiang Kai-shek are not fighting well.

R agrees with this and adds that the Americans are now equipping 30 Chinese divisions in South China. When these divisions are ready, the Americans will equip another 30 Chinese divisions.

S inquires about what is going on in the Lebanon, and who is to blame for the events.

R replies that the blame lies with the French National Committee. The British and the French guaranteed the independence of the Lebanon. The Lebanese got their Constitution and President. They wished to make some amendments to their Constitution. But the French refused them this, and arrested the President and the Lebanese Cabinet of Ministers. At present everything is in order in the Lebanon.

S asks whether quiet in the Lebanon was restored after the British ultimatum.

R replies in the affirmative and says that if Marshal Stalin had met de Gaulle, he would not have liked him.

S says that he does not know de Gaulle personally.

R replies that in his opinion the French are a good people but that they need absolutely new leaders not over 40 years old, who have not held any posts in the former French Government.

S replies that this would take much time.

R agrees with this. He says that the Americans are now arming 11 French divisions. Giraud is a very good general and very pleasant but he has no knowledge of civilian administration and politics in general.

S says that some leading strata in France want to be cleverer than all the Allies and intend to deceive the Allies. They apparently expect the Allies to present them France ready-made, and do not wish to fight on the side of the Allies but prefer to collaborate with the Germans. They are following a course of collaboration with the Germans. As for the French people, they are not being consulted.

R replies that Churchill thinks that France will be fully reborn and will soon become a great Power. He, Roosevelt, does not share this opinion. He thinks that many years will pass before this takes place. If the French think that the Allies will present them France ready-made on a platter they are mistaken. The French will have to work a great deal before France really becomes a Great Power.

S replies that he cannot imagine the Allies shedding blood for the liberation of Indochina so that afterwards France would be given Indochina in order to restore the colonial regime there. He thinks that after what the Japanese have done to the idea of independence in Burma and Thailand, thought should be given to ways of replacing the old colonial regime by a freer regime. He thinks that the acts in the Lebanon are the first steps towards a replacement of the old colonial regime by a new one. He thinks that Churchill favours a freer regime for the Lebanon. He, Stalin, believes that the same thing should be done with Indochina.

R says that he agrees with this 100 per cent. He was very glad to learn that Chiang Kai-shek does not want to have Indochina. The French bossed Indochina for 100 years, and the welfare of the people there at present is lower than 100 years ago. Chiang Kai-shek said that the people of Indochina were not ready for self-government. He, Roosevelt, then gave the example of the Philippines, which several years ago was not prepared for self-government either. By now, thanks to the help of the Americans, the Filipinos are prepared for self-government, and the Americans have promised to give it to them. He, Roosevelt, thinks that three or four trustees should be appointed for Indochina, and in 30 or 40 years the people of Indochina could be prepared for self-government. He, Roosevelt, thinks that the same is true of the other colonies. Churchill is unwilling to act with resolution in implementing this proposal because he fears that this principle will have to be applied to his colonies as well. When Hull was in Moscow he had a document drawn up by Roosevelt himself, on the establishment of an International Commission for the Colonies. This commission would inspect the colonial countries with the aim of studying the situation in these countries and possible improvement of the situation. All the work of this commission would be widely publicized.

S replies that it would be well to do this. Complaints, requests, etc., could be addressed to this commission.

R says that it is better not to speak with Churchill about India, because he, Roosevelt, knows that Churchill has no ideas concerning India. Churchill intends to leave the solution of this question until after the war.

S says that India is Churchill's sore spot.

R agrees with this. But, he adds, Britain will have to do something in India. He, Roosevelt, intends to talk with Marshal Stalin about India one day. He thought that the parliamentary system of government was unsuitable for India. People not concerned with the question of India could solve it better than people directly concerned with this question.

S says that people not concerned with India can naturally take a more objective view of things.

III

TRANSCRIPT OF THE TALK BETWEEN STALIN AND ROOSEVELT, NOVEMBER 29, 1943. *International Affairs,* 1961, No. 7, 143-145

Roosevelt says that he would like first of all to hand Marshal Stalin certain material. He, Roosevelt, received a report from an American officer who spent six weeks among partisans together with Tito. Roosevelt says that he would like Marshal Stalin to acquaint himself with the report, and asks Stalin to return the material after his perusal. Roosevelt then hands Stalin a memorandum concerning the proposal of the American delegation at the Moscow Conference on making available bases for American bombers which are to conduct through bombing raids of Germany. Roosevelt adds that he would also like to hand Marshal Stalin two proposals concerning preparations for the use of Soviet air bases in the Maritime Territory, and also on preparations for a naval operation in the north-western part of the Pacific.

In handing Stalin the two memoranda on these questions, Roosevelt says that he naturally regards the matter as top secret and promises to take all steps to keep it secret. Roosevelt says that apart from this question there are many other things he, Roosevelt, would like to discuss with Marshal Stalin; in particular, it would be well to discuss the future world settlement. It is desirable to do this if possible before his departure. Roosevelt says that it is necessary to set up an organization that would really ensure lasting peace after the war. It is with that aim in view that he, Roosevelt, proposed at the Moscow Conference the signing of a Four Power Declaration, including China in it, which would also be of great importance for the future of the world. Roosevelt adds that he is in no hurry to discuss the question of such an organization, but he would be happy to do it before his departure.

Stalin remarks that there is nothing to prevent such a discussion and that the question can be discussed.

R says that, as he imagines it, a world organization should be set up after the war on the principles of the United Nations, dealing in non-military questions. It should not resemble the League of Nations. It will comprise 35, possibly 50, United Nations, and will make recommendations. This organization will have no other powers than to make recommendations. Such an organization should meet not in any one place but in various places. That would be highly effective. Roosevelt adduces as an example the fact that the meeting of 21 American republics is never held twice in one and the same place.

S asks whether what is meant is a European or a world organization.

R replies that it should be a world organization.

S asks who is to make up the executive organ of this organization.

R replies that he does not remember the details but he thinks that the Executive Committee is to consist of the U.S.S.R., Great Britain, the United States and China, two European countries, one South American country, one Middle East country, one Asian country (apart from China), one British Dominion. Roosevelt says that Churchill does not agree with this proposal because in that case the British would have only two votes, that of Great Britain and of one of the Dominions. Roosevelt goes on to say that this Executive Committee could meet shortly, but preferably not in Geneva or any other such specific place. This Executive Committee would deal with agricultural, food, economic problems, and also the problems of public health. Apart from this committee there would be, as one might say, a Police Committee, that is a committee of countries that would watch over the preservation of peace, and also to prevent a fresh aggression on the part of Germany and Japan. That would be the third organ.

S asks whether the committee would adopt decisions binding on other countries. What would happen if a country refused to carry out a decision adopted by this committee?

R replies that in that event the country refusing to fulfil the decision would be barred from further participation in the decisions of that committee.

S asks whether the Executive Committee and the Police Committee would be part of the general organization or separate organs?

R answers that they would be three separate organs. The general organization would consist of 35 United Nations. The Executive Committee, as he had said, would consist of 10 or 11 countries. And the Police Committee would consist of only four countries. Roosevelt goes on to say that what he has in mind is that if there arises a danger of aggression or of any other violation of the peace, it is necessary to have an organ that could act swiftly, for there would then be no time to discuss the matter even in such an organ as the Executive Committee.

S remarks that in that case it would be a coercive organ.

R says that he would like to adduce as an example the fact that when in 1935 Italy attacked Abyssinia without warning, he, Roosevelt, asked France and Britain to close the Suez Canal in order to deprive Italy of the possibility of continuing the war. Yet neither Britain nor France did anything but referred the matter to the League of Nations. Thus, Italy was given an opportunity to continue her aggression. The organ now proposed by Roosevelt, comprising only four countries, would be able to act swiftly, and in such cases it could rapidly adopt a decision to close the Suez Canal.

S says that he understands this.

R says that he is very happy to have had the opportunity to acquaint Marshal Stalin with his considerations. They are, naturally, as yet of a general nature and require elaboration. He, Roosevelt, would like to avoid the mistakes of the past and for that reason believes that it would be useful to set up, first, the Police Committee, comprising four countries; second, the Executive Committee, dealing with all problems except military problems; third, a general organ in which every country would be able to speak as much as it wanted, and where the small countries could voice their opinion.

S says that he thinks the small countries of Europe will be dissatisfied with such an organization. It might be expedient to set up a European organization, of which the three countries—the United States, Britain and Russia—and possibly another European country, would be members. In addition, a second organization, for instance, an organization for the Far East. That may be better. Stalin says that he considers the scheme described by the President good, but it may be better to set up not one organization, but two: one for Europe, and a second, for the Far East or for the world. Thus, there could be either a European and a Far Eastern organization, or a European and a world organization. Stalin says that he would like to hear the President's opinion on this matter.

R says that in some respects this proposal coincides with Churchill's proposal. The only difference is that Churchill proposed one European, one Far Eastern and one American organization. But the point is that the United States cannot be a member of a European organization. Roosevelt says that it took such an enormous upheaval as the present war to make the Americans send their troops overseas. If Japan had not attacked the United States in 1941, he, Roosevelt, would never have been able to get Congress to send American troops to Europe.

S asks if in the event the world organization proposed by Roosevelt is set up would the Americans have to send their troops to Europe?

R answers that that is not necessarily so. Should the need to use force against any possible aggression arise, the United States could make available its planes and ships, while Britain and Russia would have to send their troops to Europe. There are two methods of using force against aggression. If there arises the threat of revolution or aggression or any other danger of violation of the peace, the country concerned could be quarantined in order to prevent the fire which had started there from spreading to other territories. The second method is for the four nations comprising the committee to present an ultimatum to the country in question to cease its acts threatening the peace, with the alternative of that country's being subjected to bombardment or even occupation.

S says that at yesterday's dinner, when Roosevelt had already left, he, Stalin, had a talk with Churchill concerning the preservation of peace in the future. It must be said, that Churchill takes a very light view of the matter. He thinks that Germany will be unable to re-emerge soon. Stalin says that he does not agree with this. He believes that Germany will be able to re-emerge soon. For that she will need only 15 or 20 years. If there is nothing to restrain Germany Stalin fears that Germany will be able to re-emerge soon. For this Germany will not need many years. The first big war started by Germany in the year 70 of the last century ended in 71. Only 42 years after that war, i.e., in 1914, Germany started a new war; and 21 years later, i.e., in 1939, Germany started yet another war. It is evident that the period required for Germany's restoration is being reduced. It will apparently continue to be reduced. Regardless of the restrictions we impose on Germany, the Germans will be able to dodge them. For if we ban the manufacture of planes, we cannot close down the furniture factories, and it is well known that furniture factories can be rapidly remodelled to produce planes. If we prohibit Germany from making shells and torpedoes, we cannot close down her watch factories, and every watch factory can be rapidly remodelled to produce the most important components of shells and torpedoes. That is why Germany can again be restored and start aggression. The organs it is planned to set up would be inadequate to avert aggression. It is necessary to have the possibility of occupying the most important strategic points to prevent Germany from seizing them. Such points should be occupied not only in Europe, but also in the Far East, in order to prevent Japan from starting a fresh aggression. This organ that is to be set up must have the right to occupy strategically important points. In the event of a threat of aggression on the part of Germany or Japan these points must be immediately seized so as to surround Germany and Japan and crush them. It would be well to adopt a decision that the organization which is to be set up should have the right to occupy strategically important points. Stalin says that those are his considerations.

R replies that he agrees with Marshal Stalin 100 per cent.

S remarks that in that case everything is ensured.

R says that he can be as firm as Marshal Stalin. As for Germany it appears that the Germans might remodel their plants for military production, but in that case there would be need for swift action, and if resolute measures are taken Germany will not have enough time to arm. This is just what the four-nation commission of which he, Roosevelt, spoke, would watch.

S says that there will now be a ceremonial presentation of a sword from King George VI to the city of Stalingrad.

R says that he is aware of that. Roosevelt remarks that he and Marshal Stalin have made great progress in the talks.

IV

TRANSCRIPT OF THE TALK BETWEEN STALIN AND CHURCHILL, NOVEMBER 30, 1943. *International Affairs,* 1961, No. 8, 115-117

Churchill says that first of all he would like to point out that he is half-American, on the maternal side.

Stalin says that he has heard of this.

C goes on to say that he has great affection for the Americans, and that is why what he is going to say now should not be construed as a desire on his part to belittle the Americans. He, Churchill, is entirely loyal to the Americans, but some things are best *tete-a-tete.* First of all, he, Churchill, wants Marshal Stalin to understand that the numerical strength of the British armed forces in the Mediterranean is considerably greater than the numerical strength of the American forces stationed there. He, Churchill, believes that in the Mediterranean there are three or four times more British troops than American. Churchill says that that is why he very much wants Marshal Stalin to understand why Churchill is so interested in the situation in the Mediterranean and in preventing this great British Army from remaining idle. He, Churchill, wants the British troops to be in action throughout the war. In Italy there are 13 or 14 Anglo-American divisions, and nine or 10 German divisions. In Italy there are two armies: the U.S. Fifth Army, half consisting of British troops, and the Eighth Army, entirely British. Churchill says that he is saying all this only because he wants Marshal Stalin to understand why he attaches such great importance to the Mediterranean theatre. At present the situation is such that a choice has to be made between the date of Operation Overlord and the operations in the Mediterranean. But that is not all. The Americans want the British to carry out a landing operation in the Bay of Bengal in March of next year. He, Churchill, does not take a very positive view of this operation. Of course, it would be another matter if the British had enough landing facilities both for the operations in the Bay of Bengal, and for the operations in the Mediterranean; he, Churchill, would then be able to do what he liked in the Mediterranean, and also carry out Operation Overlord on time. The question is, therefore, not only of a choice between operations in the Mediterranean and Operation Overlord, but also between the operation in the Bay of Bengal and the date of Operation Overlord. Churchill wanted to say all this because Marshal Stalin could naturally not understand all this from the preceding talks in the presence of the Americans. Churchill says he thinks, however, that there is a possibility of solving this problem, and that there will be enough facilities for all operations. The Americans are insisting on the staging of Operation Overlord on the appointed date, despite the fact that in the last two months operations in the Mediterranean have suffered rather seriously. The British Army was especially disappointed by the withdrawal of seven divisions from the Mediterranean. The British have already sent three of their experienced divisions to take part in Operation Overlord. The Americans will also shortly send four of their divisions. That explains why the Anglo-Americans were unable to make full use of Italy's debacle.

Churchill goes on to say that at the same time the British are carrying on preparations for Operation Overlord. Churchill then passes to the question of command. He says that he fully agrees that it is vital to appoint a commander-in-chief. Until August the British thought that a British officer would be in command of Operation Overlord, but at Quebec the President made another proposal, namely, that an American officer should be in command of Operation Overlord, while a British Officer would be in command of operations in the Mediterranean. Churchill says that he agreed to this because even at the very start of Operation Overlord the Americans would have a numerical superiority that will increase with time. At the same time, British troops are more numerous in the Mediterranean theatre and the British are more interested in operations in that area. That is why Churchill accepted Roosevelt's proposal and it now remains to appoint a commander-in-chief.

S asks whether this means that a British commander-in-chief is to be appointed in place of Eisenhower.

C replies in the affirmative and says that as soon as the Americans appoint their commander-in-chief, he too will appoint a British commander-in-chief in the Mediterranean area. The delay in the appointment of the American commander-in-chief is connected with domestic considerations and relates to some high-ranking persons in the United States. Churchill expresses the hope, however, that the commander-in-chief of Operation Overlord may be appointed before the conferees leave. Churchill says also that it will apparently be possible to co-ordinate the date of this operation before departure.

Churchill then says that he would like to deal with the question of landing craft. This is a bottleneck. The Anglo-Americans have many troops in the Mediterranean even after the transfer of the seven divisions. In May, there will be a great British and American army in the United Kingdom. The entire disagreement between the British and the Americans revolves around the question of landing facilities.

Churchill says that he wants to explain to Marshal Stalin the questions which are being debated between the British and the Americans. Churchill says that Marshal Stalin may think that he, Churchill, does not devote enough attention to Operation Overlord. That is not so. The fact is that he, Churchill, realizes that he will receive all the necessary facilities for the Mediterranean while sticking to the date for the start of Operation Overlord. He, Churchill, had hoped to secure this from the Americans in Cairo, but unfortunately Generalissimo Chiang Kai-shek was there and Chinese affairs took up almost all of the time. Nevertheless, Churchill is sure that enough landing facilities can be found for all operations.

Churchill then says that he wants to say a few words about Operation Overlord. The British will be ready for the date that is fixed. By that time the British will have 16 divisions, which together with the corps, troops, the communications troops, and anti-aircraft defence units, etc., total about 500,000 men. These are the best British troops and will include battle-wise divisions transferred from the Mediterranean. In addition, the necessary support from the British Navy will be ensured. Finally, the British Air Force consisting of 4,000 first-line aircraft will be ready. In addition, the transfer of American troops is already under way. Until now the Americans have been mainly transferring their air forces and equipment, but in the next four or five months up to 150,000 men will be transferred every month, which will bring the total up to 600,000 or 800,000 by the month of May. The losses inflicted on the German submarines allow these movements to be carried out.

Churchill then goes on to say that he takes a very favourable view of a landing in Southern France when the time comes for Overlord or somewhat earlier or later. He will have enough troops in Italy to carry out this operation while holding back the Germans. Of the 22 or 23 divisions now in the Mediterranean a sufficient number will be set aside for France, the others holding the front in Italy.

Churchill then says that he would like to speak of the forthcoming battles in Italy. The 15th Army Group, consisting of the Fifth and Eighth Armies under the command of General Alexander, is deployed along the eastern section of the front line which runs south of Rome. At present, there are in Italy a total of 500,000 men, i.e., 13 or 14 Anglo-American divisions, and nine or 10 German divisions, but with the present rains the rivers have burst their banks and many bridges have been swept away. Nevertheless the British intend to start an offensive against the Germans in December. Montgomery's army will land on the western coast of Italy, north of the present front line, and will execute a flanking movement.

S asks whether this will be a movement to by-pass Rome.

C replies in the affirmative.

Churchill then says that at the same time pressure will be exerted on the German positions in the south western part of the front line, and a big landing will be carried out on the west coast of Italy, north of the present front line, roughly in the estuary of the Tiber. All these operations are to culminate in the encirclement of all the German troops operating in that area. It will be a miniature Stalingrad. If the operation succeeds it will mean not only the defeat but the destruction of the German troops. The Germans are already in difficulties for they are unable to deliver enough supplies to their army because the Anglo-Americans are destroying their communications. In that, and not in the capture of Rome, lies the importance of the operation in Italy. The successful completion of this operation will allow the Anglo-Americans to move on to the north and to approach close to the Apennines.

Churchill says that he is against advancing into the broad part of Italy. He wants to establish a front in the narrow part. There the Germans could be held in check with the forces released being transferred for the landing in Southern France.

Churchill asks whether Marshal Stalin has any questions on what he has just said, or any other questions.

S says that he must tell Churchill that the Red Army was expecting a landing in Northern France. He fears that if the operation is not staged in May, it will never be staged because the weather will deteriorate and it will be impossible to deliver enough supplies to the landed forces. If the operation does not take place, he must warn that this will create great disappointment and bad feelings. He fears that the absence of this operation would give rise to a very bad feeling of isolation. That is why he wants to know whether Operation Overlord will take place or not. If it does take place, that is good, but if it does not, he wants to know of this beforehand in order to forestall the feelings that may be aroused by the absence of this operation. That is the most important question.

C replies that, of course, the operation will take place provided the enemy is unable to have more troops than the Anglo-Americans can have by that time. If, for instance, the Germans are able to transfer 30 to 40 divisions to France, he, Churchill, does not think that the landing could be successful. He, Churchill, does not fear the landing itself, what he fears is what is going to happen 30 to 40 days later.

S says that as soon as the landing in Northern France takes place the Red Army will in turn start an offensive. If it were known that the operation will take place in May or June, the Russians could prepare not one, but several blows at the enemy. Stalin says that spring is the most suitable time. There is usually a breathing space at the front in March and April, and the troops could have a rest. Ammunition could be brought up and by the time the landing is started in Northern France blows could be dealt at the Germans that would prevent them from transferring troops to France. Meanwhile, the situation is such that the Germans are transferring their troops to the Eastern Front, and will continue to transfer them. The Germans very much fear our advance to the German borders; they realize that they are not separated from us either by a channel or a sea. In the East there is a possibility of approaching Germany. At the same time the Germans are aware that in the West they are protected by the Channel, and that the territory of France must be crossed in order to approach Germany. The Germans will not dare transfer their troops to the West, especially when the Red Army is on the offensive, and it will be on the offensive if it is given help by the allies in the form of Operation Overlord.

Stalin says that all the same he wants Churchill to tell him the date of Operation Overlord.

C replies that he is unable to do so at present, because that is precisely the subject he thinks will be discussed at the luncheon with the President. Churchill says that he wants to hand Marshal Stalin a map shedding light on the situation in Yugoslavia. Marshal Stalin may want to compare the map with his own data.

Churchill hands Stalin the map of Yugoslavia.

The talk continued for one hour.

V

TALK AT THE LUNCHEON, NOVEMBER 30, 1943. *International Affairs,* 1961, No. 8, 117

Roosevelt says that he intends to communicate to Marshal Stalin a good piece of news. The fact is that today the joint staffs with the participation of Churchill and Roosevelt adopted the following proposal:

Operation Overlord is set for May 1944, and will be carried out with the support of a landing in Southern France. The strength of this auxiliary operation will depend on the availability of landing facilities at the time.

Stalin says that he is satisfied with the decision.

Churchill remarks that the exact date of the operation will depend on the phase of the moon.

S says that, of course, he is not asking to be told the exact date, but that the manoeuvre will naturally require one or two weeks in May.

R says that as far as can be judged at the moment, the most suitable time will be the period from May 15 to 20.

S says that he wants to inform Churchill and Roosevelt that by the start of the landing operations in France, the Russians will prepare a strong blow at the Germans.

R says that that would be very good because it would prevent the Germans from transferring their troops to the West.

C says that the British are carrying on large-scale preparations for Operation Overlord. He, Churchill, would like one day—time permitting—to tell Marshal Stalin about some of the details of this preparation. In particular, a rather big problem is presented by the delivery of fuel to the landed forces. The British have a special hollow cable which can be unwound and laid on the bed of the Channel. Fuel will be piped to the opposite shore along this hollow cable which is like a pipe.

S remarks that this is a very good way of delivering fuel and that it will ease the situation very much...

VI

THE CRIMEA AND POTSDAM CONFERENCE OF THE LEADERS OF THE THREE GREAT POWERS. *International Affairs,* 1965, No. 6, 92

In connection with the 20th anniversary of the Soviet people's victory in the Great Patriotic War of 1941-1945, the editorial board of *International Affairs* is beginning publication of the material of the Crimea (Yalta) and Potsdam Conferences of the leaders of the three Great Powers: the Soviet Union, the United States of America and Great Britain.

Those Conferences were of great importance in consolidating the anti-Hitler coalition led by the U.S.S.R., the United States and Britain, and in strengthening the military and political co-operation of those three Powers. The Conferences played a prominent part not only in the common struggle against German fascism and Japanese imperialism, but also in working out the principles of the post-war settlement. They created the possibilities for the further development of friendly relations between the three Great Powers after the victory over the common enemy. It was not the Soviet Union's fault that those possibilities were deliberately ignored by certain circles in the United States and Britain, whose influence prevailed in those countries after the war.

The editors will not comment on each instalment of the material of the Conferences, but on completing the publication they intend to go into the origins of some of the problems discussed at the Conferences and their subsequent development.

No agreed shorthand records or transcripts were made at those Conferences, each delegation making its own.

The present publication includes the Soviet transcript of the discussion of a number of key issues, which the leaders of the three Great Powers had gone into at the Crimea and Potsdam Conferences.

We start with the material of the first three sittings of the Crimea Conference held on the 4th, 5th and 6th of February, 1945

VII

INTRODUCTION TO THE 1969 SOVIET EDITION

The Tehran (November 28th to December 1st 1943), Crimea (Yalta, February 4th to 11th 1945) and Potsdam Conferences of the leaders of the Soviet Union, the United States of America and Great Britain occupy a special place in the history of the Second World War. At these Conferences the leaders of the three Great Powers debated and adopted concerted decisions on the basic military and political questions connected with waging war against Hitler's Germany and post-war arrangements. These Conferences and their concrete decisions were vital to the formation of an anti-nazi coalition, the co-ordination of military efforts and the mobilization of all peoples, for the defeat of nazi Germany.

The Second World War and the Tehran, Yalta and Potsdam Conferences vividly proved the possiblity of co-operation between countries with different socio-economic systems in the struggle against a common aggressor and the possiblity of a mutually acceptable decision on topical questions. Here we do justice to the leaders of the Western countries which during the war entered into military and political co-operation with the Soviet Union against the common enemy, nazi Germany.

The decisions of the "big three" at these Conferences have topical significance today and are closely related to the problems being wrestled with in modern Europe. Among these decisions particularly important are the Potsdam Agreements aimed at smashing militarism and revanchism in Germany and obviating the threat of a new war for the peoples of Europe and the whole world. The socialist countries and all the peace-loving forces of Europe are pressing for the implementation of the Potsdam decisions, for only scrupulous observance of them can obviate the danger hanging over Europe and the whole world as a result of the rebirth in West Germany, with the support and connivance of the United State of America and other Western powers, of the forces which had already plunged the world into the abyss of the most devastating war in the history of mankind.

We present here the text of Soviet records made during the sittings of the three Conferences (no agreed records were made at the Conferences; each delegation made its own records independently). They bear out the Soviet Union's loyalty to the ideas of peace, democracy and progress and its tireless campaign for a just settlement of post-war problems in the interests of peoples, for achieving European security, creating the conditions rendering impossible the rebirth of militarist forces in Germany and a repetition of aggression and for the development of international cooperation and securing the right of every people to determine its destiny independently.

The documents in the book were published in the journal *International Affairs* over the period 1961-1966.